Iraq

Iraq

The Moral Reckoning: Applying Just War Theory to the 2003 War Decision

Craig M. White

LEXINGTON BOOKS
A division of
ROWMAN & LITTLEFIELD PUBLISHERS, INC.
Lanham • Boulder • New York • Toronto • Plymouth, UK

Published by Lexington Books
A division of Rowman & Littlefield Publishers, Inc.
A wholly owned subsidary of The Rowman & Littlefield Publishing Group, Inc.
4501 Forbes Boulevard, Suite 200, Lanham, Maryland 20706
http://www.lexingtonbooks.com

Estover Road, Plymouth PL6 7PY, United Kingdom

British Library Cataloguing in Publication Information Available

Library of Congress Cataloging-in-Publication Data

White, Craig M., 1956–
    Iraq : the moral reckoning : applying just war theory to the 2003 war decision / Craig
M. White.
        p. cm.
    Includes bibliographical references and index.
    ISBN 978-0-7391-3893-9 (cloth : alk. paper) — ISBN 978-0-7391-3894-6 (pbk. : alk.
paper) — ISBN 978-0-7391-3895-3 (electronic)
    1. Iraq War, 2003—Causes. 2. Iraq War, 2003—Moral and ethical aspects. 3. Just war
doctrine. 4. United States—Foreign relations—2001–2009. I. Title.
    DS79.76 .W4834
    956.7044'31—dc22
                                    2009045052

Printed in the United States of America

I dedicate this book:
To Zelda, RIP, my beloved wife of almost 30 years,
For endless love and friendship, and much patience, especially with this project.
I trust she is pleased.

Also,

To Elijah, Arielle, and Maxwell, for help, encouragement, and advice;
To Ron Paul, for his spirited advocacy for the U.S. Constitution;
To Bob, Buck, and Tom for all the discussions, whether they agree or not;
To the hard-working idealists in the U.S. State Department;
To the fine American soldiers and officers I've been privileged to work with;
To Lew Rockwell and the writers on his website:
always stimulating, and often in the right;
To the tutors and students of Thomas Aquinas College;
To Toby Keith *and* the Dixie Chicks,
To the Flying Zucchinis of Nutley, N.J., 1968,
To Maia for being Maia,
And to Beth, for her friendship, encouragement, painstaking editing, and love.

Contents

Preface

After finishing the manuscript of this book, I read a recent book by Andrew Fiala about "the just war myth." In his introduction, Fiala compares just war theory to "the theory of true love," writing that we mustn't assume that "true love actually exists." He goes on, "The just war ideal works in the same way. The just war theory expresses our best moral thinking about war. But it is false to assume that since we know what a just war would be, just wars actually exist. In fact, there are no just wars. Nor is there any good reason to suppose that it is actually possible for there to be just wars."[1]

While I share many of Fiala's concerns expressed elsewhere in his book, I believe just wars are indeed possible. One of our differences is linked, perhaps, to the varying definitions of the word "just." In this context, I do not believe it means morally perfect. That would set a standard no group of human beings could ever meet. I do think it means a war that meets a real, rigorous, and clear standard for what is morally right to begin. (Of course, the fact that a war is justly entered into does not mean it will be justly fought, a distinction discussed in Chapter 1.)

Just war theory is an alternative both to pacifism and to war-is-hell "realism." Unfortunately, it is often applied in a way that takes away most or all of its value. At times those who use or apply the theory have touched lightly on the factual backdrop of a war, analyzed the cause briefly and pronounced it just, endorsed the stated good intentions of the ruler starting the war, and, briskly running through or simply ignoring the remainder of the six classic just war criteria, announced that the war is just. Others claim to believe in just war theory yet casually condemn a proposed or actual war and the government behind it without much evidence of applying the theory to the facts. In both these cases, the level of analysis is far below what is needed. In addition, partisanship often seems to be at work.

Classic just war theory rightly understood offers real, vital guidance for action in an imperfect world. It offers an objective standard that must be applied with care and thoroughness. It is both rigorous enough to allow unjust wars to be clearly seen to be unjust, when the facts are examined in detail, and realistic enough to allow imperfect people to decide at other times, with great care, that a war is both needed and just. Even if often mentioned by name, the theory seems greatly neglected in practice. My hope is that an in-depth analysis, using the rigor called for by the theory, will demonstrate its benefits and even increase the demand that it be applied in the future.

On another note, the title of this book is not meant to suggest that it provides *the* moral reckoning needed for the war in Iraq, as if no one else has analyzed the decision to go to war in moral terms. My intention instead is to emphasize first that just war theory, rigorously applied, provides the most complete moral reckoning available, and second the absolute necessity of such a reckoning for anyone concerned with morality or justice. It would be easier to forget, or to fall back on the presumed moral stance of one party or another, or to console ourselves with the imperfection of all human efforts, and simply dodge the question.

Disclaimer

The author works for the United States Department of State. However, the following book is entirely a personal effort, written in the author's personal time, and in no way represents the views of that institution. The Department of State does not endorse this book. All views expressed herein are entirely the author's own. In addition, the author in his work for the Department had no official or unofficial influence on the making of policy toward Iraq. The author's diplomatic work for the Department had no connection to the decision to go to war in Iraq, although that decision influenced the climate of opinion in which the author worked, especially in the Middle East. Finally, the facts and views expressed in this book are the result of personal study and the author's general knowledge. They are not the result of access to official intelligence, secrets, or confidential material of any kind.

NOTES

1. Andrew Fiala, *The Just War Myth* (Lanham: Rowman & Littlefield, 2008), 3.

Part I

INTRODUCING JUST WAR THEORY

Gradually it was disclosed to me that the line separating good and evil passes not through states, nor between classes, nor between political parties either—but right through every human heart—and through all human hearts.

—Aleksandr Solzhenitsyn (*The Gulag Archipelago* [New York: Harper and Row, Publishers, 1985], 312.)

Use every man after his desert, and who should 'scape whipping?

—Hamlet (William Shakespeare, *Hamlet* [II.ii.1091-92])

Chapter One

An Old Theory,
Today's and Tomorrow's Wars

Justice is much more valuable than gold, and you must not think we shall slacken our efforts to find it.

—Socrates[1]

The struggle for justice may threaten certain forms of peace.

—U.S. Conference of Catholic Bishops, *The Challenge of Peace*[2]

What Is Just War Theory, and Why Does It Matter?

Can war ever be right? Can any war be reconciled with a theory of morality? Those who start wars launch organized campaigns to take over territory or change governments by force, against the will of another group of human beings likely to oppose them with all the force they in turn can muster. To start an offensive or even a defensive war is to plan the deliberate killing of soldiers at least, with the certainty that other human beings will be killed and wounded and maimed, that order will break down for a time, that theft and rape will take place. Families will be broken or destroyed, and there will be massive destruction of property. It is surely strange if a war can be just, for justice usually requires respect for the lives and property of others. Yet in every culture some at least of those who fight and lead wars are considered heroes, not only for their strength but often for the moral values they are said to exemplify.

The question is approached in many ways. Pacifism is one: all wars are wrong, even those fought in self-defense. For most people, this is impossible to reconcile with a deep conviction that self-defense is natural, and defense of the innocent and helpless is heroic. A second approach is a kind of patriotism run amok: all of my country's wars are right by definition. A third approach, like the second, argues from the character of those leading the war rather than the actions they perform, and considers wars just and right if fought by "my" political party, and wrong and evil if fought by the other party. Those who take these last two approaches almost always deny that they do so, but in practice they find it difficult to explain the difference between just and unjust wars, or they do so by dividing humans into good and evil groups. A fourth, fairly common approach is to say that morality simply does not apply to war, that a nation that decides it needs a war for whatever reason is only bound by the pragmatic consideration "will this work?" It is rare to find this last position held consistently. Most of those who talk and write this way apply it to their own nation's wars, but continue to apply a moral standard to other nations.

Most people believe on some level that there are standards of justice that apply even to war. They believe war always brings evils, but that sometimes not fighting can lead to even greater evils. In that sense, making war can in some cases be the right thing to do. At the same time, most people believe in standards of justice even for their own countries, even if they have only vague or unsystematic views, which they may have rarely thought about, on what those standards might be in the case of war.

Just war theory is for those who sense that justice must apply to war. It is a systematic approach to those vague feelings about when going to war can be called just or unjust. It is a profoundly moral way of looking at the use of force among nations that is also quite practical. This book is a rigorous application of classic just war theory to the Bush administration's decision to go to war in Iraq, based almost entirely on information publicly available in the months before the war began.[3] It is written for those who either supported or opposed the war in Iraq on moral grounds, but were never sure exactly why; or those who may have doubts about their earlier support or opposition, or for those who would simply like greater clarity both about this war and about decisions to use force in the future. It is an application of the full, classic just war theory to a broad range of facts relevant to the war decision.

Many people around the world are convinced that the injustice of that war is utterly self-evident. Others, however, are quite as convinced of its self-evident justice. It often appears that those who argue for the "self-evidence" of their conclusion on either side have not questioned in sufficient depth what justice is in relation to going to war. Careful thinking on such an important subject is sure to lead to better understanding, and, possibly, wisdom for the future.

Just war theory begins with the common human feeling that for a nation or group of people to want to obtain some result by force does not excuse them or their fellows from standards of right and wrong. Many cultures have developed at least loose sets of criteria to clarify the conditions in which it is right or wrong to go to war. Classic just war theory in the Western tradition includes a set of criteria developed by medieval European thinkers, building on ideas in Greek and Roman writings, for deciding whether or not a war is just. The classic list of the criteria is this: (1) sovereign authority, (2) just cause, (3) right intention (including "the aim of peace"), (4) proportionality of ends, (5) last resort, and (6) reasonable chance of success.[4]

To expand on those criteria, the questions that need to be asked about a war (whether past, present, or proposed) are these: (1) Is the decision-maker, backed by whatever other authority is needed to be lawful in the country making war, the competent authority to declare, begin, and lead a war (rather than, for example, a private citizen, or a general, or a head of a local organization)? (2) Is the contemplated war to be fought for a just cause (besides self-defense, this could include stopping or possibly punishing some grave evil)? (3) Is the intention right (not for revenge or monetary gain or an increase in power), and is there truly an aim of establishing a just peace if the territory of another country is to be entered or conquered? (4) Is the good likely to be achieved through war greater than the likely destruction a war will cause? (5) Have all other methods short of war for achieving the (just) aim been carefully evaluated, and tried where practicable? (6) And finally, is there a reasonable chance of achieving the aim, or is this, when carefully evaluated, a hopeless cause? (In fact, these questions can be usefully applied to other uses of force against human beings, e.g., by the police, or by adults in restraining or, possibly, punishing a child.)

The first three of the criteria are sometimes called the "core" criteria, while the latter three are sometimes called "prudential," or "pertaining to prudence." In modern English, "prudential" suggests an insurance company, and the word "prudence" suggests a Victorian young lady who decides not to go into town because she might get her stockings muddy. In this context, however, and for the rest of this book, prudence has its ancient and very different meaning as one of the four "cardinal virtues," in fact, the virtue that guides the use of the others. For Aristotle, prudence is a quality that helps a person achieve right results. He wrote, "Virtue ensures the correctness of the end at which we aim, and prudence that of the means towards it."[5] A recent definition that reflects these ancient meanings is "the virtue that disposes practical reason to discern our true good in every circumstance and to choose the right means of achieving it," or, more simply, "right reason in action."[6] The prudent, then, are those who want to do what is right, see the world as it is, and wisely choose the course of action that will achieve what is right in the real world.

Two Main Branches

There are two main branches of just war theory. They are known in Latin as *"jus ad bellum,"* which is concerned with justice in going to war, and *"jus in bello,"* which is concerned with justice in the conduct of war. The second branch deals with such issues as discrimination, or whether those fighting are making sufficient good faith efforts to avoid killing non-combatants; proportionality, or a use of force that is in proportion to the legitimate war aims; and the non-use of intrinsically evil means, such as rape, torture, and so forth.[7] This book deals only with the first branch, *"jus ad bellum,"* justice in going to war—a wide enough subject in itself, yet often applied quite briefly to specific wars.[8]

A Glance at the History of Just War Theory up to Thomas Aquinas

War has always been an extreme state for those involved. Two groups of human beings enter into a conflict in which one side or both may aim to destroy the other group's existing leadership or freedom and take over some or all of its resources. Only killing and destruction seem able to achieve the aim, or to stop the enemy group from achieving its purpose. The ordinary rules of life, against murder, destruction, theft, and lying seem suspended on all sides. Once launched, wars are hard to control. As students of history know well, wars meant by their planners to be local and quick often spread wider and last far longer than anticipated. Despite this seeming suspension of rules during war, and despite the sharp differences in attitudes from one historical period to the next, we find evidence going back thousands of years of people making moral judgments about starting wars.

As noted, classic just war theory in the western tradition has important roots in the thinking of ancient Greece and Rome. Yet although many Greek and Roman writers commented on war and justice, it would be hard to say that just war theory close to its current form existed at that time. First, some of these comments, even if they come from men who wrote a great deal that was wise, seem quite alien to our thoughts about right and wrong. Second, even when writers addressed a number of the important moral issues, they often did not explain them or gather them into a single coherent whole. Two representative writers may illustrate these observations.

Some of Aristotle's ideas about the morality of war seem normal enough to people today, but others certainly do not. He lists in one place some typical causes that appear just to people of his time: repelling or avenging aggression; fighting on behalf of kinsmen or allies; the need to increase the glory, strength, or resources of our home state.[9] It is not clear that he is endorsing all of these as just causes for war, but in his *Politics*, he writes quite clearly of wars "of acquisition," comparing them to hunting, and says that a war to subjugate men who "ought to be governed" by others is "naturally just."[10]

Aristotle mentions as a good aim of warfare the acquisition of territory for the benefit of the conquering state:

> Neither should men study war with a view to the enslavement of those who do not deserve to be enslaved; but first of all they should provide against their own enslavement and in the second place obtain empire for the good of the governed, and not for the sake of exercising a general despotism, and in the third place they should seek to be masters only over those who deserve to be slaves.[11]

Here, dominion over at least some of one's neighbors seems a perfectly acceptable justification for war; at least, if it is done in moderation.

Lest we think Aristotle glorified war, we should balance remarks like those above with his comparison of war and peace:

> The whole of life is further divided into two parts, business and leisure, war and peace, and of actions some aim at what is necessary and useful, and some at what is honorable. And the preference given to one or the other class of actions must necessarily be like the preference given to one or other part of the soul and its actions over the other; there must be war for the sake of peace, business for

the sake of leisure, things useful and necessary for the sake of things honora-ble.[12]

Aristotle here rejects the idea of war as a good in itself. In fact, it is useful and necessary because it should lead to peace, just as business is good and ne-cessary if it leads to leisure. Peace is honorable, war is merely useful.

Going further, Aristotle harshly rejects war for its own sake, as an end in it-self: "We make war in order that we may live at peace. . . . Nobody chooses to make war or provokes it for the sake of making war; a man would be regarded as a bloodthirsty monster if he made [friendly states] into enemies in order to bring about battles and slaughter."[13]

The Roman writer, orator and statesman Cicero appears to have advanced the discussion on the justice of going to war. Consider first these general obser-vations about warfare as an approach to solving problems:

> Then, too, in the case of a state in its external relations, the rights of war must be strictly observed. For since there are two ways of settling a dispute: first, by discussion; second, by physical force; and since the former is characteristic of man, the latter of the brute, we must resort to force only in case we may not avail ourselves of discussion. The only excuse, therefore, for going to war is that we may live in peace unharmed; and when the victory is won, we should spare those who have not been blood-thirsty and barbarous in their warfare.[14]

While Aristotle, who considered many wars natural, nonetheless thought war less "honorable" than peace, and "monstrous" as an end in itself, Cicero takes this thought a step further, and says if there is a way to settle a dispute without war, that is the only human way to settle it. (This thought is at least the seed of today's just war criterion of "last resort.") He also hints at a right way to fight.

In the same book, Cicero stated that "honor" and "safety" are the only rea-sons that can make a war just. However, the thought comes in a fragment at the end of one of the "books" of the *Commonwealth*, is not developed, and is rather mysterious. Neither honor nor safety is defined, but the idea of just cause seems to be implied here.[15]

However, based on another remark, Cicero is sometimes considered to be the first to have made an explicit list of conditions that must be met for a war to be just. In his *Commonwealth*, Book III, he writes: "All wars, undertaken with-out a proper motive, are unjust. And no war can be reputed just, unless it be duly announced and proclaimed, and if it be not preceded by a rational demand for restitution."[16] The requirements here are: (1) a proper motive, (2) a due an-nouncement and proclamation, and (3) a prior demand for restitution. The first of these is not very clearly defined, although the thought is important. It appears to be a different statement of "right intention." While the second does not sound at first like a fundamental moral factor, it is still vital to a sense of right and wrong for most: consider the American reaction to the "sneak attack" on Pearl Harbor. In addition, the word "duly" in "duly announced" implies consideration by the authorities of a society, and their concurrence in the announcement, a factor that is also important for later just war thinking: it is perhaps the "sovereign authority" criterion in embryonic form. Finally, the prior demand for restitution, while it sounds strange to modern ears, is a requirement that other means of achieving a just outcome besides war have been attempted: a requirement very similar to the later "last resort." Cicero then writes briefly both about what makes a war just at the outset (*jus ad bellum*) and justice in the fighting of a war (*jus in bello*). Despite the fact that his remarks are brief and include minimal explanation, it seems fair to say at least that he planted the seed that became just war theory. Sovereign authority, just cause, right intention, last resort, and the whole idea of "*jus in bello*" all appear in early forms in his writings.

As the western half of the Roman Empire fell apart, the writers who inherited classical thought in Europe were often guided by it, but were also guided by Christian sacred writings and traditions. Two major factors stood out in those writings: first, there were the commands and sayings of Jesus, which sometimes appear at first glance to rule out the use of force even for self-defense. There is a passionate commitment to justice in those words, in which "love your neighbor as yourself" is pushed to new heights, and "my neighbor" is defined illustratively as "a Samaritan," a member of a group with whom Jesus' listeners attempted to avoid all dealings. From these sayings alone, one might have guessed that war would be out of the question for Christians, at least in theory.

However, a second factor to consider was the actions of Jesus and Peter and Paul in a number of dealings with Roman soldiers and officers. Neither Jesus nor his immediate followers made any recorded attempts to persuade these warriors to find new jobs, nor recorded statements condemning soldiering as such, and Paul commended the official Roman use of "the sword" in the service of justice. Somehow, despite Jesus' commandment to love one's enemies, and despite the cruelties of the Roman Empire (toward Christians as well as others), it seemed that the Roman use of armed force against its enemies might be just—at least some of the time.

Augustine, who lived through the sack of Rome in 410 AD and the collapse of the western half of the Empire, is almost always cited as the first Christian writer to address in a significant way the subject of when a war may be just. Augustine did not write a treatise on the subject, nor apparently even one complete chapter of a book that systematically addressed it. Rather like Aristotle, he dropped important hints here and there—often quoting and building on Cicero and other classical writers. These scattered hints were later gathered, and became the foundation of the classic theory.

Augustine argues that the proper aim of government is to maintain peace, and this requires the ability to wage war when necessary. He insists that "lawful authority" must authorize going to war. Where Jesus states in the gospel, "all they that take the sword shall perish with the sword" (Matthew 26:52), Augustine interprets the verse to state that with lawful authority, the use of the sword is allowed: "To take the sword is to arm oneself in order to take the life of anyone, without the command or permission of superior or lawful authority."[17] More specifically with regard to war, he writes: "The natural order conducive to peace among mortals demands that the power to declare and counsel war should be in the hands of those who hold the supreme authority."

Augustine describes the kind of cause for which a war may justly be fought, writing, "A just war is wont to be described as one that avenges wrongs, when a nation or state has to be punished, for refusing to make amends for the wrongs inflicted by its subjects, or to restore what it has seized unjustly." He insists on the importance of the right intention of the ruler initiating a war, condemning "the passion for inflicting harm, the cruel thirst for vengeance, an unpacific and restless spirit, the fever of revolt, the lust of power, and such things." He writes with a rhetorical flourish (and perhaps in an echo of Aristotle's comments above), "We do not seek peace in order to be at war, but we go to war that we may have peace." He even urges, "be peaceful . . . in warring, so that you may vanquish those whom you war against, and bring them to the prosperity of peace." However, he speaks of wars that are unjust as well as those that are just (and even concerning just wars he wrote of the "misery" they entailed).[18] Thus he in no way sees war as an unconditional right of the state.

The great medieval philosopher and theologian Thomas Aquinas gathered and synthesized Augustine's wide-ranging comments on war, added his own, and produced a systematic approach to the subject. In the section of his immense *Summa Theologica* dealing with charity, or love, and specifically with sins opposed to the peace that love produces (the list is discord, contention, schism, war, strife and sedition), Aquinas briefly discusses war—not conduct in a war, but whether and when it is just to go to war. Noted just war historian James Turner Johnson believes Aquinas is not even addressing the issue of a purely defensive war, as that would be self-evidently just to Aquinas—on the analogy of self-defense by a man who is attacked (which Aquinas states is justified, within limits). Johnson's analysis of this point seems indisputable.[19]

Significantly, Aquinas' title is "Whether it is always sinful to wage war?" He denies that it is always or "altogether" sinful. In his characteristically organized and compact way, Aquinas then lays out three conditions that must all be met for a war to be just: (1) sovereign authority, (2) just cause, and (3) right intention. Going further than Cicero, he offers wide-ranging explanations of his terms, incorporating all the quotations from Augustine in the preceding paragraphs in his explanations of the three criteria. He also writes that "those who make war justly aim at peace." Following Aquinas, "the aim of peace" is now usually seen as one facet of "right intention."

The case for these criteria is not built on appeals to sacred scripture, although it includes those, but on "natural reason." Because of this, it has appealed through the centuries to people interested in a moral approach to war, regardless of religious affiliation or lack thereof. For example, concerning sovereign authority, he writes:

> For it is not the business of a private individual to declare war, because he can seek for redress of his rights from the tribunal of his superior. Moreover it is not the business of a private individual to summon together the people, which has to be done in wartime. And as the care of the common weal is committed to those who are in authority, it is their business to watch over the common weal

of the city, kingdom or province subject to them.[20]

Aquinas' article is a breath of fresh air after Aristotle's remarks on war (nor is there a hint of Machiavelli or Nietzsche's later thoughts). Aristotle accepts that some people are natural slaves, and thus have no inherent right to be free, and that some groups of people have the right to take the goods and even the freedom of other groups. Aquinas' brief statement of the exceptional cases when war is justified assumes that all groups of human beings have a right not to be attacked, unless they have committed some clearly evil deed—and even then they may only be lawfully attacked with an aim of righting the wrong and bringing peace to those attacked, a startling requirement. There is no justification offered at all for a country taking anything that belongs to another due to its greater power, or wiping out those who have offended it. No religious, racial, or cultural superiority is put forward as justification for war. The image he uses to explain his case for sovereign authority is not a jungle where different creatures prey on each other, but a society with courts, so that the only justification for war is the lack of a higher court. Aristotle's understandable assumption that war is natural, and therefore lawful, is here turned on its head. Instead, Aquinas begins with the question "whether war is always sinful." Placing it in a long list of sins implies strongly (along with his qualified answer and other remarks) that he considers it at least often sinful. On the other hand, it is not sinful or unlawful if and only if it meets all three of the enumerated criteria. While it allows war in limited cases, this is a high moral standard, and moreover one that resonates today with religious and non-religious people alike.

While Aquinas' brief discussion on war does not include the "prudential" criteria, there is strong evidence available that these criteria are very much a part of Aquinas' approach to ethics and human action (see Chapter 11). Here, it is enough to point out that the article on war does not stand alone, but is embedded in Aquinas' vast *Summa*. In that work, both before and after the article on war, Aquinas wrote extensively about what was necessary for any action to be right or just, and made it very clear that prudential considerations were, to his way of thinking, an integral part of the reckoning. Thus those who made the prudential criteria explicit requirements were very much in the spirit of Aquinas, something that can be proven with quotations from other parts of the *Summa*.

Why does Aquinas' list, especially when the implied prudential criteria are included, feel substantially complete? First, it incorporates Cicero's idea about a due declaration, but changes the emphasis to the due authority of the leadership of the group that is to be engaged in such a serious enterprise as war. No private citizens should need their government's authorization to take goods and trade or go into neighboring territory as visitors, or on a mission of good will. War is different—it may involve many or all members of a society in physical or fiscal suffering, as well as moral responsibility, so it must be decided by the representative or representatives of all of the society that begins it. An aggrieved party or a private group seeking justice in some way must not involve its whole society in war on its own authority—the process must go through the leadership. Next, Aquinas makes explicit Cicero's point that a just cause is required, and this involves righting some (serious) wrong. A significant number of possible reasons for war are excluded by this simple statement. Finally, Aquinas, again working from cryptic statements in Cicero, says it is not enough to have a correct outer statement of justice, as it were: the inner motivation, the true aim, of the authority deciding on war must be right. This requirement strikes at the hypocrisy that so easily besets all human beings, especially if we decide that we must force others to do something. Aquinas asserts that if a cause is to be thought right, it must be right to the core.

The three prudential requirements now added to the list may be seen as amplifications of "right intention." If a group of political leaders truly means to create peace, and actually has good will towards the people being attacked, they will certainly apply the last three criteria, consciously or unconsciously. Such a group will have a realistic plan to end the war, and a detailed vision of how to create a peaceful post-conflict situation in the country attacked. They will consider seriously, taking counsel with experts, whether their plan can actually achieve its aim (reasonable chance of success), whether it will cause less damage than the wrong that is its cause (proportionality of ends), and whether there is another way to achieve the aim short of the violence of war (last resort).

(In addition, the whole of the *jus in bello* branch of just war theory can be seen as closely connected to the right intention criterion. An attacker with a right intention will work hard from the beginning to ensure that civilians are not massacred, that rapes are not committed by his soldiers, and so on. Any attacker with no such concerns would not have a right intention.)

The core criteria of contemporary just war theory, then, were first laid down by Aquinas, and even the prudential criteria, explicitly added later by other thinkers, are fully consistent with Aquinas' overall approach to ethics. Aquinas' brief article was greatly developed and elaborated over the following centuries, leading eventually to Protestant and then non-religious versions of the theory, yet his three criteria are still considered, in mainstream versions of just war theory, the core moral conditions for going to war justly.

A few of the later thinkers who clarified or added to the theory are Francisco de Vitoria in the sixteenth century and Francisco Suarez and Hugo Grotius in the sixteenth and seventeenth centuries. Moving to the twentieth and twenty-first centuries, writers often cited on just war theory include Paul Ramsey, Michael Walzer, James Turner Johnson, and Brian Orend, although many others could be named. Scholars have addressed in detail the various contributions of these writers, but in a sense all are developing and elucidating the six criteria laid out here.

The Uses of Just War Theory

War is perhaps the weightiest human endeavor, so none of the six questions implied by the just war criteria is meant to be answered in a few seconds or minutes, nor will anyone apply the theory well without a solid knowledge of the facts related to the particular war in question. The heart of this book will be a discussion, one by one, of these six criteria in relation to the decision to begin the war in Iraq, in light of then-available knowledge. The great advantage of just war theory for anyone thinking about the fairness or justice of a planned war is that the questions are already in place, and the thinker or voting citizen or decision-maker need only go through them one by one, honestly and sincerely, in as much depth as necessary. Generally, the failure to say "yes" to any of the criteria, should lead to the evaluation "unjust" for the entire war. That is indeed a high standard, but it should be clear after careful thought that any planned war that failed to meet even one of the criteria would, in fact, be seriously unjust in some way. For the result, "this is a just war," each question should be substantially answerable: "yes." Ideally, the theory should be used as a framework for a public debate or discussion before entering into war.

Some may ask how useful it is to look closely at a decision that was taken years ago. The first reason this book addresses the justice of going to war in Iraq is that the question is gravely important in itself. Because of this, the justice of what was done should be of great concern to all persons who take morality and the responsibilities of citizenship seriously. While starting a just war is the right thing to do, launching an unjust war is one of the worst crimes a government and a nation can commit. At the Nuremberg trials after World War II, the first charge against many of the surviving German authorities was planning and carrying out an aggressive and therefore unjust war.

Second, the question of the justice of starting a war in the past has practical value for the ongoing situation. Even looking back, achieving clarity on whether a war was begun justly sheds light on the question of what to do next. Analogously, if there is any question whether a business, a relationship, or a situation we are in was entered into wrongly, it makes a great deal of difference to know that. We can hardly even hope to do the right thing in a given situation if we don't know if, and why, we were right or wrong to get into it. As C. S. Lewis wrote, "Evil can be undone, but it cannot 'develop' into good. Time does not heal it. The spell must be unwound, bit by bit, 'with backward mutterings of dissevering power'—or else not."[21] Perhaps we come to realize that our business partner is a criminal whose share of the startup costs was stolen, and it bothers us, or we wake up to the fact that our love affair is hurting the innocent. Conversely, we may come to realize that although we now detest our business partner or spouse, our earlier commitments were made rightly and prudently, and need to be followed through with integrity. What was right to begin is probably right to continue, even if course adjustments are called for and mistakes need to be corrected. What was unjust from the beginning is a very different matter. There we may find ourselves called, first and foremost, to begin undoing the evil we have done.

Third, the question is also practical for the near future. War was a continuous feature of the twentieth century for many countries, and that has not changed with the new century. The United States, which began the Iraq war, has entered into new wars, even if many of them have been small or occasionally almost accidental, throughout its history. Since 1980, for example, a quick list would include Grenada, Panama, Somalia, Kosovo, Afghanistan, and Iraq (twice now), and these are only wars in which U.S. soldiers fought openly, as opposed to those in which the U.S. government supplied, equipped, or trained one side, secretly or otherwise. Influential Americans have in recent months called for the United States to go to war in the near future with Iran or Syria or North Korea. A detailed look at a recent decision to go to war should offer guidance, to those who wish for it, in how to ensure their countries fight only just wars in coming years.

An Appeal for Just Thinking

The justice of going to war is too serious a subject for sarcasm and personal attacks. This book focuses on facts, actions, and principles, not personalities or parties. War is also too serious for restricting sources of news. A wide range of evidence is covered here, from many sources. It is human to tend to trust some sources more than others. However, when verifiable, relevant facts are found in any source, they need to be considered.[22]

During a discussion of some of the issues in this book with a friend, he admitted after some time, "I guess I'm going back and forth between Christ and Machiavelli." He could see that sometimes he wanted the comfort of claiming to be part of a moral nation that acts justly, and at other times he wanted the luxury of saying, "it maintained or increased my country's power, what do I care whether it's right or wrong?" On the one hand, Machiavellians will have little real interest in just war theory, which assumes that there are moral rules governing war. On the other hand, those who hold to some form of morality need to apply it consistently, even if it appears to hurt their cause. Moral standards that are only applied to the other side are no moral standards at all.

NOTES

1. Plato, *The Republic* (London: Penguin Books Ltd, 1987) 75.
2. U.S. Conference of Catholic Bishops, *The Challenge of Peace*, 1983, http://www.usccb.org/sdwp/international/TheChallengeofPeace.pdf (accessed February 15, 2008), paragraph 60.
3. The only exception will be part of Chapter 7, for reasons explained there.
4. James Turner Johnson, *The War to Oust Saddam Hussein* (Maryland: Rowman & Littlefield, Inc., 2002), 38. Johnson separates "right intention" and "the aim of peace," but states that they are closely related. George Weigel, who acknowledges Johnson as a mentor in this field, has almost the same list in a slightly different order, but cites "competent" rather than "sovereign" authority, see Weigel, *Against the Grain: Christianity and Democracy, War and Peace* (New York: The Crossroad Publishing Company, 2008) 210. Chapter 9 of that book, from which the list is quoted, first appeared as the article "Moral Clarity in a Time of War" in the January 2003 issue of the magazine *First Things* (see below in this note). Fiala, in *Just War Myth*, 38, with its sharply different approach from those of Johnson and Weigel, uses the same list, but writes of "proper or legitimate authority." In all three lists, the first three criteria (including "the aim of peace") were first assembled as a complete list by Thomas Aquinas, who quoted Augustine in support of each of them. (Thomas Aquinas, *Summa Theologica*, II-II, 40.) See Appendix A for the full text of this short, readable, oft-mentioned but rarely read article on war. For an online version of the entire *Summa*, see *NewAdvent.org*, http://www.newadvent.org/summa/index.html (accessed December 6, 2007). The other criteria were added by later thinkers,

although, as I argue below, they are implied by Aquinas. Note: there are extensive quotations in this book from three of Weigel's essays, which originally appeared in *First Things* under the titles "Moral Clarity in a Time of War" (published January 2003), "Iraq: Then & Now" (published April 2006), and "Just War and Iraq Wars" (published April 2007). All are readily available on the *First Things* website through the internal search engine, but in accordance with Weigel's request, I am quoting herein from the lightly revised versions of each that appeared in his 2008 book "Against the Grain" as chapters 9, 10, and 11. In some cases, I have indicated the original wording of a short phrase (still available on the internet) as well.

5. Aristotle, *The Nichomachean Ethics* (New York: Penguin Classics, 2003), 163.

6. *Catechism of the Catholic Church*, Second Edition (Washington, D.C.: United States Catholic Conference, Inc.—Libreria Editrice Vaticana, 1997), Section 1806. For an on-line version of the *Catechism*, see http://www.usccb.org/catechism/text/ (accessed January 23, 2008).

7. Fiala, *Just War Myth*, 39.

8. Recently there has been some discussion of the need for a third branch, "*jus post bellum*," or "justice in ending a war." While I sympathize with this interest, I suspect that "right intention," taken seriously, would accomplish much if not all of what is to be considered under this new branch. Right intention already requires the initiator of a war to consider and plan carefully to achieve an end state of stability and peace. Weigel agrees: see Weigel, *Against the Grain*, 253.

9. Aristotle, *Rhetorica ad Alexandrum*, quoted in Mohammad Taghi Karoubi, *Just or Unjust War?* (Aldershot: Ashgate Publishing, 2004), 59.

10. Aristotle, *Politics*, Bk I, Part VIII, in "The Internet Classics Archive," http://classics.mit.edu/Aristotle/politics.html (accessed November 18, 2008). "Now if nature makes nothing incomplete, and nothing in vain, the inference must be that she has made all animals for the sake of man. And so, in one point of view, the art of war is a natural art of acquisition, for the art of acquisition includes hunting, an art which we ought to practice against wild beasts, and against men who, though intended by nature to be governed, will not submit; for war of such a kind is naturally just."

11. Aristotle, *Politics*, Book VII, Part XIV.

12. Aristotle, *Politics*, Bk VII, Part XIV.

13. Aristotle, *Nichomachean Ethics*, 271.

14. Marcus Tullius Cicero, *De Officiis*, Book I, xi, 34, http://www.stoics.com/cicero _book.html (accessed November 18, 2008).

15. Cicero, *Treatise on the Commonwealth*, Bk III, quoted in Karoubi, *Just or Unjust War?*, 60.

16. Cicero, *Commonwealth*, Introduction to the Third Book, in The Online Library of Liberty, http://oll.libertyfund.org/?option=com_staticxt&staticfile=show.php%3Ftitle= 546&chapter=83302&layout=html&Itemid=27 (accessed November 16, 2008).

17. All the quotations from Augustine in this and the following paragraph are cited by Aquinas in his article on war (Appendix A).

18. Augustine, *The City of God*, Book 19, Chapter 5, in "Christian Classics Ethereal Library," http://www.ccel.org/ccel/schaff/npnf102.iv.XIX.5.html (accessed December 4, 2007). This passage is discussed in Chapter 11.

19. Johnson, "Just War, as It Was and Is," *First Things*, no. 149 (January 2005): 17. Johnson's point is supported by Aquinas' actual words, in his first sentence on just cause: "Secondly, a just cause is required, namely that those who are *attacked* [emphasis added], should be attacked because they deserve it on account of some fault." This would be odd language for a war of self-defense.

20. Aquinas, *Summa*, II-II, 40, 1.

21. C. S. Lewis, *The Great Divorce* (New York: MacMillan Publishing Co., Inc., 1946), vi. The quotation within the quotation is from Milton's "Comus," line 817 (see http://www.gutenberg.org/files/19819/19819-8.txt (accessed January 14, 2008)).

22. As an example, the most moving tribute to Pope John Paul II that I have ever read was written by Roger Cohen (see Roger Cohen, "The Polish Seminary Student and the Jewish Girl He Saved," *The New York Times*, April 6, 2005 http://www.ny times.com/2005/04/06/international/worldspecial2/06krakow.html?_r=1&oref=slogin (accessed October 10, 2007). It may not have been easy for a Jewish writer who lost family members in the Holocaust to enter into the mind of a Polish Catholic and find good there, but Cohen managed it. If he had ruled out Polish Catholics as a source of truth beforehand, he would not have succeeded.

Chapter Two

How to Apply the Criteria, and Who Should Do It

When in the Course of human Events, it becomes necessary for one People to dissolve the Political Bands which have connected them with another . . . a decent Respect to the Opinions of Mankind requires that they should declare the causes which impel them to the Separation. . . . Prudence, indeed, will dictate that Governments long established should not be changed for light and transient Causes . . . To prove this, let Facts be submitted to a candid World.

—*The Declaration of Independence* of the United States of America

The strict conditions for legitimate defense [of "the nation or community of nations"] by military force require rigorous consideration. The gravity of such a decision makes it subject to rigorous conditions of moral legitimacy.

—*Catechism of the Catholic Church*[1]

The following are six "Implicit Just War Principles," or IJWPs. In fact, they are simply general rules of moral reasoning, the kind of rules that are necessary in any situation where the facts are less than crystal clear and the consequences serious, applied here to the specific case of war. While they are not always discussed within the framework of just war theory, they appear to be both implied by aspects of the theory and critical for its correct application.

IJWP 1: The Same Neutral Standards Apply to All

This principle is derived from the simple idea of fairness we learned on the playground, or perhaps brought to it. Justice must be understood as meaning applying the same standard to all, in this case all countries or all leaders. There are certainly tremendous differences in the characters of governments and leaders; however, any reasoning about justice must begin with applying the same moral standards, the same universal principles. As an analogy, a person of known bad character, perhaps a local gangster with multiple drug and illegal possession of firearms convictions, is accused of murder. He is not charged as "evil John Smith," but as "John Smith, accused of murder." And if the trail of evidence leads instead to the beloved town doctor, we expect him to be charged with the crime regardless. Just war theory is not the same as a court of law, but if it is to be applied in a legitimate manner, there must be no special pleading. Real analysis must take the place of labeling. A general rule for ensuring that this elementary standard of fair treatment is met is the following: Any principle applied to the country against which war is proposed must be able to be rephrased using any other country, or "x."

A well-known theologian provided an example of ignoring this principle in an essay published in May 2003, writing, "The cause must be just, and the just cause in this case is the disarmament of Iraq."[2] Now presumably this theologian had in mind a cogent argument to show that disarming Saddam Hussein was a just cause, and apparently he attempted to lay out the argument in some more detail later in the essay, but this bare statement fails to appeal to any universal principle. Applying the general principle above, it is only as useful to say "it is a just cause to disarm Iraq" as it is to say "it is a just cause to disarm Country X" (substituting Denmark, Mongolia, Argentina, etc.), especially since it is a generally accepted principle that nations have the right to be armed. The theologian's remark is a bit like a prosecutor summarizing his case for the jury as "the just cause before you is the imprisonment of John Smith."

Some critics might object that this principle calls for "moral equivalence," whereas the "good" and "bad" governments of the earth must not be treated "as if they are the same." Yet although a moral judgment must take into account circumstances, including the character of the actor (as far as that is determinable), moral principles generally apply to actions. Objective criteria that apply to the actions of all must be available for discussing particular actions.

IJWP 2: Critical Terms Must Be Carefully Defined

Using undefined labels for persons and states is not helpful in demonstrating the justice of a cause. Such terms as "rogue state," "terrorist state," "outlaw regime" and so forth need to be defined, as well as "international community" if the user means something other than the nations of the world. Without objective definitions, use of such terms leads to the appearance of a logical argument without its essence. Every government is in fact a mix of good and evil, and the world often does not agree on when a government is beyond the pale.

An argument that uses negative terms in enunciating a principle concerning war needs to define, at least roughly, the threshold at which evil in a regime reaches the point of justifying war. For the sake of reasonable completeness, it should specifically address other nations that have committed similar or worse acts, and not just one administration's or even one country's enemies list. To apply a tough standard only to one's enemies, and not to one's self and one's friends, is clearly hypocritical. (In light of this universal danger of hypocrisy, Jesus warned, "take the log out of your own eye, and then you will see clearly to take the mote out of your brother's.") While many or perhaps most governments have committed at least some human rights abuses, even those guilty of rather egregious abuses are often accepted in organizations such as the United Nations as respectable states (the case of Iraq when it was receiving help from the U.S.

government during its war with Iran, for example). Simple fairness demands objective definitions.

Clear definitions are needed for other categories as well. In public discourse, the words "terror" and "terrorism" are used a hundred times or more for each time a definition is offered. This is not conducive to clear thinking. "The war on terror" is a term less in favor in 2009 than it was earlier, but in its time it needed definition. Was it, for example, a war against every organization that has ever used terror tactics (which need to be defined)? Would that include states that have used such tactics, or are states excused when they use them? Does an act that is labeled terrorism when a non-state actor commits it become something else if committed by a state? Without such definitions, clear thinking is impossible.[3]

IJWP 3: The Burden of Proof Lies on Those Proposing War

This may appear controversial, but the "burden of proof" lies on those proposing war, rather than on those opposing it (with one obvious exception: in a country which is under attack, the burden of proof would be on those opposing defense of the nation against its attackers). This principle is analogous to the legal principle "innocent until proven guilty." It rests on the fact that not being attacked is the presumed right of every nation, just as not being imprisoned is the presumed right of every citizen. Therefore, before attacking another nation or imprisoning a citizen, a case must be convincingly made to show why the presumed right to be left in peace (or in case of a citizen the presumed right to freedom) does not apply in this circumstance.

This principle applies not only in the private deliberations of the governing body (if it is truly seeking to discover whether a proposed cause is just), but also to the public case that governments are obliged to make, out of common decency if nothing else. The American Declaration of Independence begins with the words, "When in the course of human events it becomes necessary . . . to dissolve the political bands . . . a decent respect to the opinions of mankind *requires* [emphasis added] that they should declare the causes which impel them" to a decision as grave as declaring independence from a government with no intention of granting it, an act considered by the British government and the world to be an act of war. After a summary of the case against King George III, the Declaration continues, "To prove this, let Facts be submitted to a candid world," followed by a long and detailed list of accusations. In a similar vein, until the Korean War, the major U.S. foreign wars each began with a declaration of war, an opportunity to "declare the causes." The U.S. Constitution appears to assume that each war that is not purely defensive will begin with a declaration, which by tradition was the place for the government initiating a state of war against another country to make its case to the rest of the world.

More support is found for this principle in the classic tradition from which just war theory grew. In his section on justice, Aquinas considers the question "whether it is lawful to form a judgment from suspicions." In his thesis statement is the following: "Now there are three degrees of suspicion. . . . The third degree is when a judge goes so far as to condemn a man on suspicion: this pertains directly to injustice, and consequently is a mortal sin."[4] This is a repetition of what is stated in a nearby section, which asks "whether it is lawful to judge?" In that section, Aquinas notes that one of the requisites for a legal judgment to be just is that it "be pronounced according to the right ruling of prudence." If this connection is lacking, states Aquinas, "the reason lacks certainty, as when a man, without any solid motive, forms a judgment on some doubtful or hidden matter, and then it is called judgment by 'suspicion' or 'rash' judgment."[5]

If the burden of proof lies on those proposing war, then it follows logically that just as in a courtroom the accused is not obliged to prove his innocence, so in the court of public opinion, those who oppose a planned war do not need to prove that it would be unjust. Instead, in order to win the argument, they should only have to show that the evidence for a just war is doubtful or insufficient. If the evidence is doubtful or insufficient, no justice system should order a person's imprisonment or execution, and by analogy, no country should go to war.[6]

IJWP 4: The Required Standard: Beyond Reasonable Doubt

This principle rests on the fact that war is an extreme remedy for any problem. It always costs human lives, which are precious, and damages property, which is valuable. Often war costs enormous numbers of lives and destroys huge amounts of property of great value. In addition, wars have a way of going far beyond the original intentions of those beginning them, developing lives of their own. They are difficult to end. Anything with such inherent costs and risks must be shown convincingly, not just probably or possibly, to be the right thing to do. As an example of the kind of thinking that takes these costs and risks seriously, the Catholic Catechism states, "The strict conditions for *legitimate defense by military force* require rigorous consideration. The gravity of such a decision makes it subject to rigorous conditions of moral legitimacy."[7] Alphonsus de Liguori, a noted moral theologian of the Catholic Church, wrote: "There is no doubt that since war generally brings in its train so many evils and so much harm to religion, to innocent people, to the honor of women, etc., in practice it is hardly ever just if declared on probable reasons of justice alone and not certain reasons."[8] (Absolute certainty is not a part of human affairs, and the phrase "certain reasons" should be understood in that context.) While these examples may carry more weight for Catholics than for others, in light of the long tradition of just war scholarship in the Catholic Church, they deserve a respectful hearing from all. In addition, the point that war is an extreme remedy is a common one in other branches of the theory. Michael Walzer notes that "it is . . . awful . . . [to start a war]: the aggressor is responsible for all the consequences of the fighting he begins. . . . they are always potentially terrible."[9] From this point, it follows naturally that there must be strong, convincing evidence before beginning a war.

Returning to the analogy of a trial, in the American legal tradition inherited from the English, the standard of proof is: "beyond reasonable doubt." A war is much more serious than the punishment of a convicted criminal. Those advocating war will not have a perfect case, but it should at least meet this standard.

IJWP 5: All the Criteria Must Be Substantially Met

It is not enough to meet some, or even a majority, of the conditions of just war theory. Careful consideration shows that any failure to meet one of the listed criteria would render a war unjust in some serious way.

The paragraph of the Catholic Catechism cited above goes on to note that the conditions of just war must be met "at one and the same time." This is simply a repetition of the statement by Aquinas in his oft-cited article "Of War"[10] that "In order for a war to be just, three things are necessary." All three "necessary" things must be present, or the war is not just. (Lest there be any doubt on this point, a few sentences later, in the section on right intention, Aquinas writes, "For it may happen that a war is declared by the legitimate authority, and for a just cause, and yet be rendered unlawful through a wicked intention.") This may seem a high threshold, but it is certainly the classic one—and again, careful thought will show that failure to meet any one of the criteria would make a war unjust in a serious way. The criteria are connected by an inner logic, and each one is necessary for justice—they are not a random list.

Johnson considers the last three criteria "prudential," "supportive,"[11] and not part of the "deontological core of the [just war] tradition."[12] They are, regardless, critical to the question of the justice of a war, as some thinking will show. Imagine a war that failed only the "proportionality of ends" criterion. How could a war be just if the planners made no calculations about the likely harm a war would cause, or, worse, calculated beforehand that it was likely to cause more harm than it solved? Consider a war that, due to failure to seriously consider other ways to achieve the desired end, failed only "last resort." Could it be moral to launch such a war, in light of the death and destruction that war entails? What right intention could possibly motivate such an act? Or think of a war that failed only "reasonable chance of success." How could it be right to start a non-defensive war that was seen beforehand to be unlikely to achieve the desired end? How could the certain damage such a war entailed be justified? It is clear that these criteria too must be met, or a just war is impossible.

IJWP 6: Secret Justifications for War Are Unacceptable

Finally, secret justifications for war are unacceptable. This principle flows from the imperfection of all governments and the tendency of governments to seek to increase their power. As Lord Acton wrote, power tends to corrupt. The temptation to lie in order to get a desired result, or at the very least to present truth in a misleading way, is powerful, and no human being, much less political party, is immune to it. If there is no check on that temptation (in the form of a demand for a presentation of evidence) before something as serious as a war is launched, then there are no practical limits to wars that can be justified. "We have secret evidence" would trump every objection—and that would render just war theory useless, and therefore meaningless.

U.S. history back to its beginnings suggests that if a government finds clear-cut reasons for war, it owes its citizens and the world a candid look at the evidence. Jefferson's detailed listing of the reasons in the Declaration of Independence sets the standard.

Secret sources and methods exist. Governments can and will assemble evidence built from secret sources. However, such evidence cannot be the decisive evidence on which citizens are called to rely. For the citizens of a country to allow presumed or claimed secret evidence to weigh in their calculations, to express blind trust in any government, however trusted, is in practice a decision to give up on just war theory, just as much as allowing a government to execute prisoners based on secret evidence would be to give up on a theory of criminal justice—or limited government, for that matter. A war is similar in a way to an execution (but more serious because more lives are at risk, and some of the lives lost are certain to be innocent even in a just war). Any punishment of a citizen, but especially an execution, demands a trial, and the sharing of sufficient evidence with an unbiased jury. In a similar way, governments owe their citizens and the world a presentation of the case for war.

If there are witnesses on whose testimony the case for war depends, they should be available—precisely so they may be cross-examined. People walk into embassies and government offices every week and claim to be defectors with first-hand knowledge of some other government's secret programs and plans. While a few such people have real secrets to share, many others are fools, and some are knaves who wish to manipulate other countries. Therefore, such people have to be cross-examined. If the time has truly come for war, such people's testimony has to stand up to sustained examination by doubters, not just by administration officials who answer to the very people who are pushing for war. This is surely a part of the reason for which, in the American Constitution, the Founders put the right of declaring war in the legislative branch, the part of government most open to debate. For similar reasons, the Catholic Church for centuries had a "devil's advocate" whose job was to argue against the saintliness of a candidate for sainthood.

Congress is the place, in the U.S. system, for that thorough examination of the evidence, including cross-examination of witnesses (although even such an examination can be less than critical, which is always to be regretted).[13] When the issue is deadly serious, thoughtful people do not object to having to prove their case. The questioning of any administration's case for war should not be seen as partisanship, but as a required step. If evidence of defectors does not stand up under such hostile cross-examination, then a war should not be based on it. Self-government, as much as just war theory, demands that a government give a sufficient, public, well-examined set of reasons for going to war, regardless of whether there is also additional, secret supporting evidence that cannot be revealed.

An objection is likely to be raised: this will compromise the safety of defectors, and possibly of others who are still in the country to be attacked and who have provided evidence. First, there are ways to safeguard defectors. They can testify before Congress but with some kind of masking of faces and voices. We already have witness protection programs for witnesses against mobsters, and those could be used to protect defectors after their testimony. Second, the risk to the witnesses of leaving their country to testify cannot possibly be as great as the risk to the people of the country being invaded. Wars spread, and modern wars are tremendously destructive. War cannot be justly begun in an unexamined fashion simply to save the lives of a few friendly witnesses.

Another objection might be that certain information is so closely guarded in the alleged enemy country that to reveal it will demonstrate the technical weaknesses of their counter-intelligence systems, allowing them and other enemies to guard against such penetration in the future. In fact, most groups and nations are aware through multiple sources that advanced countries can tap telephone conversations and radio communications, take photographs from satellites, and so forth. The news stories out of each war reveal more such methods. In addition, as a practical matter, it is clear from recent decades that U.S. authorities in favor of war are willing to reveal a certain amount of evidence from technical sources if it is believed that it will earn approval of the war (e.g., Colin Powell's UN presentation in February 2003). Revelation of some quantity of secret evidence appears not to make an initial military victory overly difficult, at least in some cases.

A final objection might be that this is a requirement for perfect information before going to war, whereas in the real world, decisions are always made on imperfect, incomplete information. Not so. This is an argument for something analogous to the standard in a court of law: in a criminal case, the standard of proof is "beyond reasonable doubt." Not perfection, not complete information, but sufficient information—and to ensure that is so, what is offered must be examined.

Who Should "Apply" Just War Theory?

There are two basic answers to this question.[14] First, we make moral judgments about justice, continually. "That's not fair," and "I have a right to . . ." are some of the most common phrases in many human languages. Citizens of countries with representative forms of government commonly make moral and prudential judgments on the actions of their representatives (in all three branches of our government), both before elections based on the promises of politicians, and after, based on their actions. Citizens judge whether what the politicians promised or did was right or wrong, wise or foolish. This is the heart of representative government. If just war theory is the best moral and prudential framework for looking at war, then the more it guides the judgments of millions of citizens as they think about their country's past, current, and proposed wars, the better. Each one of us has some responsibility for the common good. Those who are better educated, and especially those who are in the habit of speaking and writing about issues of concern in national politics, have a greater responsibility to know and apply the theory. All of us as citizens should expect to be presented with clear and compelling reasons for war, satisfying all the criteria. If such reasons are presented, and stand up to questioning, we should support the war; if not, we should oppose it. Therefore, governments should present their just war cases for proposed wars to their citizens and the world. Who should apply just war theory? All thoughtful citizens.

There is a second, more limited answer implied in the first. Duly elected representatives in any system have powers under their implied or written constitutions, including the powers to declare and conduct wars in the nation's interest. While these representatives are human beings like us, with the same decent impulses and the same temptations we all face to abuse power for selfish ends, they are also those authorized, within the limits of the law and each country's constitution, to make decisions about war. As citizens we can hope that they apply just war theory to the decision whether or not to begin or continue wars, as well as to the conduct of wars that are waged, and we can register our opinions on the issue, but we cannot force them to do so according to our lights, nor can we make the decisions for them. Therefore, our elected representatives, too, should apply just war theory.

Despite the consistent use of a courtroom analogy for just war theory, there are a number of important differences. One is that in the case of just war theory and countries with representative governments, there is no body corresponding to a jury that renders a legal verdict. Perhaps in the United States that body is the Congress, yet Congress often appears to have shown too little interest in rendering a verdict according to the theory (see Chapter 3). Yet the difference between the "trial" before a war and a trial in a courtroom is in some senses more favorable to the power of citizens in the case of a war. Juries can be sequestered from "prejudicial" sources, and facts concealed from them. Citizens cannot be locked up, but can dig for information for themselves, if they choose. When juries render verdicts that the mass of citizens see as clearly flawed, those citizens often can do nothing about it, even after the fact. But in a democracy, not only can we make our wishes known before a proposed war, we can "throw the bums out" if we believe political leaders have lied to us, misled us, or ignored our wishes as citizens. We can even call for their impeachment if we believe they deserve that. As Johnson points out, "all citizens of a democracy . . . may rightly hold to account those who . . . bear the office of political responsibility to act according to that responsibility."[15] Again, war decisions are the most morally grave decisions those in government make about the outside world and often the most grave of all their decisions. If just war theory is the best way to look at whether wars are right or wrong, the only reasonable way for citizens to hold officials to account is to demand that war proposals are framed in terms of just war theory, to form judgments as to whether the case presented meets the criteria, and then to act on those judgments, in words and actions, including at the polls.

NOTES

1. *Catechism*, paragraph 2309. Like other quotations at the heads of chapters, this one is meant to stimulate thought. See IJWP 4 for more on the relevance of the Catechism.

2. Richard John Neuhaus, "The Sounds of Religion in a Time of War," *First Things*, no. 133 (May 2003): 76. Father Neuhaus, RIP, passed away January 8, 2009.

3. The FBI has a definition, according to James Bovard, "The Farcical Definition at the Heart of the War on Terrorism," LewRockwell.com, January 31, 2006 http://www.lewrockwell.com/bovard/bovard20.html (accessed October 10, 2007). The definition is: "the unlawful use of force or violence against persons or property to intimidate or coerce a government, the civilian population, or any segment thereof, in furtherance of political or social objectives." The problem there, as Bovard points out, is the word "unlawful," which makes it impossible for a government to commit terrorism. Yet, if a government had planned and committed the 9/11 attacks, would they have been essentially different for that reason? Finally, it is hard to see how the American Revolution would not have fallen under this definition of terrorism. Bovard goes on to suggest that a "far sounder definition was offered by Israeli National Security Council chairman Major General Uzi Dayan, who defined as terrorist in a December 2001 speech 'any organization that systematically harms civilians, irrespective of its motives.' This definition catches all types of terrorism – not just actions that lack political blessings or official sanctions." In an article defending the decision to go to war in Iraq, law professor at the London School of Economics Christopher Greenwood wrote (see Appendix E) "There is . . . no doubt that had those attacks (of September 11) been the work of a state, rather than a terrorist organization like Al-Qaida, they would have been classified as an armed attack for the purposes of Article 51 and the right of self-defense. It would be a strange formalism that regarded the right to take military action against those who caused or threatened such actions as dependent upon whether or not their acts could be imputed to a state." And it *is* a strange formalism to consider some actions "terrorism" only when perpetrated by non-state actors.

An article on terrorism hosted at the U.S. Navy Department Library, entitled "Terrorism: A Navy Department Library Research Guide," http://www.history.navy.mil/library/guides/terrorism.htm (accessed December 4, 2007), notes:

> No one definition of terrorism has gained universal acceptance. For the purposes of this report, however, we have chosen the definition of terrorism contained in Title 22 of the United States Code, Section 2656f(d). That statute contains the following definitions:

> The term "terrorism" means premeditated, politically motivated violence perpetrated against noncombatant (1) targets by subnational groups or clandestine agents, usually intended to influence an audience.

> The term "international terrorism" means terrorism involving citizens or the territory of more than one country.

> The term "terrorist group" means any group practicing, or that has significant subgroups that practice, international terrorism.

> The U.S. Government has employed this definition of terrorism for statistical and analytical purposes since 1983. . . .

> (1) For purposes of this definition, the term "noncombatant" is interpreted to include, in addition to civilians, military personnel who at the time of the incident are unarmed and/or not on duty. For example, in past reports we have listed as terrorist incidents the murders of the following U.S. military personnel: Col. James Rowe, killed in Manila in April 1989; Capt. William Nordeen, U.S. defense attaché killed in Athens in June 1988; the two servicemen killed in the La Belle disco bombing in West Berlin in April 1986; and the four off-duty U.S. Embassy Marine guards killed in a cafe in El Salvador in June 1985. We

also consider as acts of terrorism attacks on military installations or on armed military personnel when a state of military hostilities does not exist at the site, such as bombings against U.S. bases in Europe, the Philippines, or elsewhere.

This second, military definition restricts terrorism to acts committed by "subnational groups." In addition, for most of the attacks against U.S. troops in Iraq since the U.S. presence there began, it would be difficult to argue that "a state of military hostilities did not exist at the site," since various insurgent groups publicly announced their intentions to remove the U.S. presence by force from the entire country, and U.S. forces apparently considered such insurgents fair game for military strikes at any time. "Iraq theater of operations" has its own acronym, ITO, and the British Ministry of Defense site has a "Defense News" section at http://www.mod.uk/DefenceInternet/DefenceNews/InDepth/Uk MilitaryOperationsInIraq.htm (accessed December 4, 2007) that offers "Briefing Maps: Official maps of the theatre of operations." The Iraqi theater covers all of Iraq.

This would mean that attacks on U.S. forces in Iraq have *not* been terrorist attacks according to this official U.S. definition.

The essence of terrorism, I believe, is the use of attacks on civilians for political purposes. Governments as well as other groups that do this should be accused of committing acts of terrorism, for that is what they are. Yet this is certainly not one of the official U.S. definitions.

4. Aquinas, *Summa*, II-II, 60, 3.

5. Aquinas, *Summa*, II-II, 60, 2.

6. Weigel and Johnson would disagree with this principle, I believe, claiming that a "presumption against war" warps classic just war theory. See Chapter 11 for a detailed consideration of their arguments.

7. *Catechism*, paragraph 2309.

8. Alphonsus de Liguori, *De Quinto Praecepto Decalogi*, quoted in *Neo-Conned!: Just War Principles: A Condemnation of War in Iraq*, ed. D. Liam O'Huallachain and J. Forrest Sharpe (Norfolk, VA: IHS Press, 2006), 226.

9. Michael Walzer, *Just and Unjust Wars: A Moral Argument with Historical Illustrations* (New York: Basic Books, 1977), 23.

10. Aquinas, *Summa*, II-II, 40.

11. Johnson, *War to Oust*, 38.

12. Johnson, *War to Oust*, 59.

13. Consider "the 15-year old Kuwaiti girl who shocked the Congressional Human Rights Caucus on October 10, 1990, when she tearfully asserted that she had watched 15 infants being taken from incubators in Al-Adan Hospital in Kuwait City by Iraqi soldiers who 'left the babies on the cold floor to die.'" The girl was later revealed to be the daughter of the Kuwaiti Ambassador to the United States at the time. The whole story was later shown to be almost certainly false. See John R. MacArthur, "Remember Nayirah, Witness for Kuwait?" in *The Iraq War Reader*, ed. Micah L. Sifry and Christopher Cerf (New York: Touchstone, 2003), 135-7.

14. Chapter 11 includes further discussion of this question, in response to statements by neoconservative writers seeking to restrict the field of those who should apply the theory.

15. Johnson, *War to Oust*, 67. The context of this quotation, a discussion of the different roles of citizens, elected officials, and moralists, is analyzed in Chapter 11.

Part II

APPLYING THE CRITERIA

The constant whetting of the knife is tedious, if it is not proposed to cut anything with it.

—George Santayana (Neuhaus, "Santayana Lately Revisited," *First Things*, no. 150 [February 2005]: 29.)

Chapter Three

Sovereign Authority

Ai regi, che son molti, e i buon son rari

—Dante Alighieri, *Paradiso*[1]

Why, indeed, does the human person possess the right to realize his happiness, of which no state can deprive him? Metaphysics replies: because human personality alone is a genuine substantial reality. On the other hand, any group whatever, the state included, is not a real being; it is simply a group of human persons.

Maurice de Wulf, *Philosophy and Civilization in the Middle Ages*[2]

Introduction

Sovereign authority is the first of what Johnson calls the deontological or "primary" just war criteria. Johnson writes, "the person or body authorizing the use of force must be the duly authorized representative of a sovereign political entity."[3] In historical terms, a duke or a general did not have the right to begin a war that would involve the entire nation. Only the national leader could do so. Implied in this criterion is respect for the laws of the nation, which have generally involved some kind of consultation at least.

There is some debate about whether since its creation the United Nations either can or should be the "sovereign authority" envisaged in the theory. Several facts must be considered in response to this question. First, each member state, including the United States, signed the UN Charter[4] and accepted obligations under it voluntarily. Therefore, the Charter functions as a validly ratified treaty, committing each signatory state to take part in the institutions created by it and to act in accordance with what it agreed to do in the Charter. The Charter also indicates that in the event of conflict between obligations under the Charter and obligations under any other international agreement, "obligations under the present Charter shall prevail."[5] From the perspective of the United States Constitution, a validly ratified treaty becomes, along with the Constitution, the "supreme law of the land."[6] Within the United States at least, those who profess to respect the Constitution must take the Charter seriously.

Second, there is one feature of the Charter that might have led to widespread concurrence in the view that the UN Security Council could function as a sovereign authority for just war purposes. That is the provision in Chapter 7, Article 43, that:

> 1. All Members of the United Nations, in order to contribute to the maintenance of international peace and security, undertake to make available to the Security Council, on its call and in accordance with a special agreement or agreements, armed forces . . . necessary for the purpose of maintaining international peace and security.
> 2. Such agreement or agreements shall govern the numbers and types of forces, their degree of readiness and general location, and the nature of the facilities and assistance to be provided.
> 3. The agreement or agreements shall be negotiated as soon as possible on the initiative of the Security Council.[7]

The agreements mentioned in this text were never negotiated. In the absence of UN forces, Security Council resolutions have on occasion authorized Member States to use force, with the understanding that this meant their own armed forces. In light of this lack of its own armed forces, among other missing characteristics, it is difficult to see the UN as any kind of supra-national federal government for the world. The world's peoples and governments could conceivably still push for the UN to evolve in that direction, but for now it has not happened.

THE SOVEREIGN AUTHORITY CLAIM

President Bush explicitly claimed, in his television address immediately before the war began, that the war in Iraq would meet the sovereign authority criterion: "The United States of America has the sovereign authority to use force in assuring its own national security."[8]

DETAILED CLAIM
OF SOVEREIGN AUTHORITY

In the President's March 17, 2003, speech, he exercised the power devolved on him by the U.S. Congress in its October 10, 2002, resolution authorizing the use of force against Iraq. What was in effect a declaration of war by the President was based explicitly on the U.S. right of self-defense, and the UN's resolutions played only a supporting role in justifying the war. The UN had not granted any explicit authority in this case for the U.S. government to enforce UN resolutions through making war on Iraq, and in fact refused to do so when asked, as Bush noted in his address. President Bush claimed that earlier resolutions authorized him to use force: "Under resolutions 678 and 687, both still in effect, the United

States and our allies are authorized to use force in ridding Iraq of weapons of mass destruction."[9] However, his statement about the sovereign authority of the United States makes that the ultimate authority to which he, and therefore his administration, appealed.

THE BUSH ADMINISTRATION MET THE SOVEREIGN AUTHORITY CRITERION

The Bush Administration met the "sovereign authority" criterion. The government of the United States, by all normal measures, possesses sovereign authority. While the United States has, in writing, undertaken to accept certain limitations of its right to make war (including by signing certain treaties and the United Nations Charter), it has not transferred the power of deciding whether those limitations apply in a given case to any other body, including the United Nations. It has retained its sovereignty. Under the existing, accepted system of the United States, the President exercised the inherent authority of a nation-state to declare war in its perceived interest.

EVIDENCE THE CRITERION WAS MET

In a short summary of the sovereign authority criterion, Johnson writes: "The person or body authorizing the use of force must be the duly authorized representative of a sovereign political entity. The authorization to use force implies the ability to control and cease that use, that is, a well-constituted and efficient chain of command."[10]

While this statement reflects a development of historical statements by Aquinas and Cicero before him, it is very much in line with those ideas. Cicero's seminal thought in this area is merely that a war must be "duly announced and proclaimed" (Chapter 1), implying that the established norms in a given society for deciding and announcing war must be followed. Aquinas, in his discussion of this criterion, stresses that private individuals can seek justice through other means, and that it is not their business to "summon the people" to war. He then stresses the right and responsibility of government to seek the common good of the people, including through the use of force against external enemies. The stress in this criterion falls on the responsibilities and capabilities of government. It is largely a procedural criterion.

As Johnson states elsewhere in the same work, in response to a Jimmy Carter editorial, "in just war terms, sovereign authority to use force is a property of a given political community, and that imposes various conditions on it." Johnson goes on to state:

> The United Nations itself lacks several important attributes of sovereign authority: it is not in fact sovereign but takes its power from the agreement of its con-

stituent states; it is not responsible to the people of the world but only to these states; it lacks command-and-control capabilities, thus cannot direct the use of force responsibly; and in the end, it cannot be held accountable for its actions the way an individual state or its government can be. Security Council approval is important as a statement of consensus, but the lack of that consensus does not take away the right of individual states to act according to their reading of their responsibilities.[11]

According to the currently almost universally accepted understanding of authority in the United States system of government, the action followed the approved forms. Thus, whether wise or foolish, right or wrong, it was a legitimate decision of the U.S. government. It was, therefore, an exercise of the sovereign authority of the United States.

OBJECTIONS

Objection One: No Declaration of War

Objection: As Johnson states, "the person or body authorizing the use of force must be the duly authorized representative of a sovereign political entity."[12] But the duly authorized representative of the United States with the authority under the Constitution to authorize the use of force is the Congress. Yet the same Constitution requires a declaration of war, and this did not take place. Therefore, since the duly authorized representative of the sovereign body, the U.S. Congress, did not begin the war according to its fundamental law, this criterion was not met.

Reply: There is indeed a major and obvious problem with the claim that the Bush administration met the sovereign authority criterion: the lack of an official declaration of war by the government of the United States in accordance with its written Constitution. The Constitution of the United States, Article 1, Section 8, is quite clear: "The Congress shall have power . . . to declare war." The Constitution grants this power to no other branch of the United States government. Some may say that this Constitutional stipulation was fulfilled by the Joint Resolution of Congress "Authorization for Use of Military Force against Iraq Resolution of 2002 (H.J.Res.114)," passed on October 16, 2002.[13] But that joint resolution is, clearly not itself a declaration of war. The resolution takes the responsibility of determining or declaring that a state of war exists between the United States and Iraq, and transfers it to the President for his exercise in the (unlimited) future. On October 10, the resolution did not itself declare that a state of war existed between the two countries. If it had, that would have created an awkward situation: for example, it would have justified, presumably, Iraqi attacks on U.S. military assets anywhere. And would it not have led any fair-minded person to expect the United States, as a nation that had formally declared war on Iraq, to recuse itself from questions in the Security Council concerning whether or not Iraq was in compliance with Security Council resolutions?

Yet the Constitution gives the responsibility of making such declarations to the Congress, and not to the President. The Constitution has not been amended, therefore this responsibility stands. What would we think of a ruling by the Supreme Court that in a particular case before it, the Court was authorizing the President, or Congress, to make a determination? Yet this is a valid analogy for what the resolution does: it hands over the intrinsic authority of one branch of government, the Congress, to another branch of government.

It is Congress that is "duly authorized," in Johnson's words, to declare war, which is equivalent to both announcing and authorizing the use of force. If the United States claims to live under the rule of law, how can its Congress get rid of a core responsibility, one laid down in the Constitution that established it? Congress did not even delegate the power to a subordinate body, but handed it off to a different branch altogether. It is hard to see how the intended Constitutional balance is not severely undermined by one branch of the three formally handing over its responsibilities to another. And, obviously, there were no circumstances (such as an enemy occupation of Washington, D.C., for example) that made it impossible for the Congress to fulfill its duty in this sphere.[14]

The Founders, in granting this power to Congress rather than the President, were following a pattern that runs throughout their work: granting authority over various aspects of a single process to different branches of government. In this case, Congress decides whether a war is warranted or justified, and declares war; the President then executes the policy. (As was the case in World War II, the President may initiate the process, coming to Congress and asking for a declaration of war.) Like all such separations of power, it makes government action, by design, more difficult. The idea is that only those acts that truly represent the considered, united will of the people will then be undertaken. In addition, there is the classic concern that the executive may be motivated by pride or vanity to indulge in foreign adventures that will be expensive, in money but also in prestige and blood, for the entire country. The British parliament struggled for hundreds of years to gain control of the king's ability to start wars, largely by refusing him the power to raise war funds through taxation without its consent, hence the United States Revolutionary War slogan "no taxation without representation." This fact was certainly both well known to and on the minds of the Framers as they drew up the Constitution. To address the feared weakness of having one man make such a momentous decision, the Founders placed the power instead in a large body, where debate could be expected, opposing views could be aired, assumptions could be examined, and hesitation could be expected in even seeking any declaration that was not close to unanimous, for fear of telling the world that the nation was embarking on a war while divided. A formal declaration (the necessity of which the Founders apparently assumed), forces the declaring power to take a full, careful reckoning of the facts before it and set them in detail before the world. Such a declaration would encourage the nation making it to set out its war aims in detail—an act indispensable to meeting the requirements of just war theory.

All these advantages were forfeited by the action of Congress in transferring its authority to the President. But the Congress is not alone in deserving blame here. One would expect a President who truly respected the Constitution he had sworn to uphold to submit a declaration of war to the Congress for its approval and to welcome the ensuing debate, even after such an act of Congress. Certainly the Republican Party, which controlled both houses of Congress at the time and proclaims that it believes in the original intent of the Constitution, should have insisted on a declaration of war in order to act consistently with its professed belief. Congressman Ron Paul, standing on Constitutional principle, introduced a formal congressional declaration of war with Iraq on the floor of the House of Representatives (stating plainly that he would vote against it), but his party did not support him.[15] Many Democrats have expressed concern or disagreement with the idea that the original intent of statements in the Constitution should guide present-day officials. However, De mocratic S enator Robert Byrd said what every defender of the Constitution should have immediately seconded, on the floor of the Senate on October 4, 2002:

> This branch of the government [i.e. the Congress], under the Constitution, is the branch consisting of the immediately elected representatives of the people, and under the Constitution it is to declare war. The framers were very wise when they determined that these two matters—the decision to go to war and the making of war—should be in two different places. The decision, the determination to declare war, should flow from this branch, the people's branch, and the matter of making war should be in the hands of a unified commander, the commander in chief.[16]

He went on to warn in vivid language of the Constitutional dangers of Congress giving up its intrinsic powers: "We are giving the President of the United States a blank check, and Congress cannot do that. Congress should not do that. Where is the termination? Where is the deadline? Where is the sunset language that says after this happens this resolution shall no longer exist? There is nothing."

This constitutional revolution goes back to the Korean War (no war since the Second World War has been declared by Congress), but long acceptance does not make it right. As appalling as the revolution is, however, and without withdrawing one word of criticism of it, it is clear that the revolution has taken place. It is reversible: at any time, Congress could warn the President that it would henceforth insist on its Constitutional prerogatives and enforce that warning by defunding any war the President engaged in without its authorization. Such a reversal might not be politically possible—or desired by Americans.

Whether or not there is ever such a return to the Constitutional arrangement, for now the United States as a nation lives in the post-revolution situation. Many Americans appear to assume that the President has always and rightly decided, in lonely majesty, where and when to exert American force. Unless and until this situation is reversed, it must at least be admitted that Congress gave up its authority without any coercion or explicit bribery. Rather than a "power grab," in which one institution seizes what rightly belongs to another, we might call this a "power dump," in which the institution with the authority unwisely but without compulsion hands it to another. A widely accepted custom has replaced the Constitutional arrangement, and, to be realistic, that is legitimate even if questionable in the American system as it presently exists.

Objection Two: The UN Had Sovereign Authority

Objection: the UN had sovereign authority in this case, not the U.S. government.

Reply: One of those who disputed, in the name of just war theory, the President's claim that the United States possesses sovereign authority to act where it perceives its security to be at risk was ex-President Jimmy Carter, in an editorial published in the New York Times in March 2003. Carter claimed that according to just war theory, "the attackers must have legitimate authority sanctioned by the society they profess to represent." He went on:

> The unanimous vote of approval in the Security Council to eliminate Iraq's weapons of mass destruction can still be honored, but our announced goals are now to achieve regime change and to establish a Pax Americana in the region, perhaps occupying the ethnically divided country for as long as a decade. For these objectives, we do not have international authority.[17]

Former President Carter's language here is unclear. Exactly what does: "unanimous vote of approval . . . to eliminate Iraq's weapons of mass destruction" mean? It is true that the Security Council in Resolution 687 (1991) had required the "destruction, removal, or rendering harmless, under international supervision," of such weapons, but Carter appears to be referring to the more recent Security Council vote of November 2002. That, however, had not been to "eliminate Iraq's weapons of mass destruction" (WMD). Resolution 1441 (2002) did not even assume that such weapons existed. Instead, it implicitly threatened to authorize the use of force (it warned of "serious consequences," but made clear that it would itself determine those consequences), unless Iraq complied with the Security Council's wishes in documenting its programs and cooperating with inspectors in order to demonstrate its disarmament of WMD. Nor did the Security Council, in passing the resolution, designate any other body to make the determination of Iraq's compliance or non-compliance for it.

Carter's statement on the necessity for "legitimate authority sanctioned by the society [the attackers] profess to represent" is not very clear. The entire world is usually not called a society. The subsequent invasion by the Bush administration was sanctioned by the legitimate authority of the United States. Bush's claim of UN authority was a secondary claim (which will be dealt with in Chapters 4, 5, and 6). Carter was clearly correct that UN resolutions did not explicitly authorize action to overthrow Saddam, but he appears to mingle the concept of "sovereign authority" with UN authorization. It is true that the United

States made certain commitments in signing the UN charter, but it had made solemn commitments before, in other treaties, as well, without transferring or ceding its sovereignty. It seems to offer more clarity to consider two questions separately: one, whether the United States possesses sovereign authority to start a war, and whether such a decision follows the established internal norms of the United States, and two, whether such an act violates commitments such as those made under the UN Charter.

Carter pointed out that while the UN had clearly ordered Iraq to rid itself of WMD, it had not clearly authorized any particular enforcement mechanism, an important point for future chapters. He pointed out another problem for the Bush administration: the lack of an official, clearly stated war aim, such as a declaration of war might have provided, and the profusion of statements by the president and other officials, encouraged the impression of extremely wide-ranging U.S. government aims that Carter noted.

The UN and Its Limitations

There are some problems with Johnson's brief statement about the UN and its limitations as a candidate for sovereign authority. For instance, it might be read as supporting the claim that a nation with command-and-control capabilities less than those of say, NATO, could not be just, when such capabilities are first new, and second, evolving still. Proponents of just war theory believe it was a useful and accurate theory in Augustine's day (the fifth century AD), when no power on earth had command-and-control capabilities approaching those of the United Kingdom at the time of the Crimean War. Another concern is that Johnson elsewhere is open to the idea of the evolution of just war theory, as in his discussion of preemption, where he appears ready for the theory to evolve in the direction of allowing preemptive action against possessors of WMD.[18] (In the case of preemption, Johnson's sensible conclusion is that "there is no moral consensus" on his suggestion that "there is a serious case for preemption when an avowed enemy has WMD, and all other means of dealing with this threat offer no hope of removing it."[19]) Given the possibility of the evolution of just war theory, it could be argued that there is a broad consensus in the world that the UN should be considered to be the best available version of an "international sovereign authority," despite the limitations noted by Johnson. His argument that the UN "is not responsible to the people of the world but only to [its constituent states]" would have applied to the federal government of the United States in relation to its people before the Civil War, and much more so to Washington, Jefferson, and the other American Revolutionaries fighting the British.

Despite these concerns, Johnson's critique in this context of the UN and his description of the authority (and related responsibilities) of duly constituted governments when it comes to initiating and waging wars is a useful one. While the UN has never "declared war," perhaps its member states should be more cautious in passing resolutions that will be read to create an open-ended authorization for war by others, precisely because, as Johnson notes, the UN cannot truly "direct the use of force responsibly." Perhaps at the least such resolutions should contain crystal clear "sunset language," causing their authorization to expire after perhaps one year, without explicit renewal. Is it responsible to begin what cannot be directed responsibly, or what cannot, in practice, be ended by the body that begins it? (The same argument would call for sunset language for all UN sanctions as well.)

The U.S. government, then, declared war based on its sovereign authority as the government of a nation state. Whether that declaration was supported by a just cause, and whether it was in violation of the solemn agreement by the United States to abide by the UN Charter, as well as whether it met the rest of the just war criteria, must now be examined.

NOTES

1. Dante Alighieri, *Paradiso* (XIII 108).
2. Maurice de Wulf, *Philosophy and Civilization in the Middle Ages* (New York: Dover, 1932), 223. (Quoted in James V. Schall, *Another Sort of Learning: Selected Contrary Essays on How Finally to Acquire an Education While Still in College or Anywhere Else: Containing Some Belated Advice about How to Employ Your Leisure Time When Ultimate Questions Remain Perplexing in Spite of Your Highest Earned Academic Degree, Together with Sundry Book Lists Nowhere Else in Captivity to Be Found* (San Francisco: Ignatius, 1988), 183.)
3. Johnson, *War to Oust*, 38. Aquinas does not mention the "sovereign entity" of Johnson's formula. However, Aquinas' discussion of the "authority of the sovereign" strongly implies that there is no superior entity to which the sovereign could resort in order to right the wrong in question.
4. *Charter of the United Nations*, http://www.un.org/aboutun/charter/ (accessed November 22, 2008).
5. *UN Charter*, art. 103.
6. *The Constitution of the United States*, Article VI, "United States Constitution," Legal Information Institute, Cornell University Law School, http://www.law.cornell.edu/constitution/constitution.articlevi.html (accessed November 22, 2008).
7. *UN Charter*, art. 43.
8. Bush, "The War Begins: 'The Tyrant Will Soon Be Gone'" (television address), in *Iraq War Reader*, 503-4. It strongly appears that President Bush was referring to just war theory in this statement. "Sovereign authority" is not a typical phrase in American politics.
9. Bush, "The War Begins," in *Iraq War Reader*, 504.
10. Johnson, *War to Oust*, 38.
11. Johnson, *War to Oust*, 61.
12. Johnson, *War to Oust*, 38.
13. "Authorization for Use of Military Force against Iraq Resolution of 2002 (H.J.Res.114)" (Joint Resolution of Congress, October 16, 2002), in *Iraq War Reader*, 378-83.
14. For a look at how the generation of the Founders might have seen such an act, note the following clause from the Massachusetts Constitution of 1780: "In the government of this commonwealth, the legislative department shall never exercise the executive and judicial powers, or either of them; the executive shall never exercise the legislative and judicial powers, or either of them; the judicial shall never exercise the legislative and

executive powers, or either of them; to the end it may be a government of laws, and not of men." "CRS Annotated Constitution," Legal Information Institute, Cornell University Law School http://www.law.cornell.edu/anncon/html/art1frag1_user .html (accessed December 4, 2007). The Constitution of Virginia of 1776 had a similar clause, which is quoted on the same website.

15. While the blogosphere carried a great deal of debate on Paul's call for a formal declaration of war, the press largely ignored it. Paul's own October 4, 2002 press release is at http://www.house.gov/paul/press/press2002/pr100402.htm (accessed May 7, 2008).

16. Robert Byrd, "No Place for Kings in America" (Senate speech), in *Iraq War Reader*, 375-77.

17. Jimmy Carter, "Just War – or a Just War? Op-ed by Jimmy Carter 9 Mar 2003" *The Carter Center*, http://www.cartercenter.org/news/documents/doc1249.html (accessed October 10, 2007).

18. Johnson, *War to Oust*, 53.

19. Johnson, *War to Oust*, 53.

Chapter Four

Just Cause I:
An Armed, Reckless Regime
that Harbored Terrorists

The judges will decide the case,
acquitting the innocent and condemning the guilty.

—Deuteronomy 25:1

Judgment is lawful in so far as it is an act of justice. Now it follows from what
has been stated above . . . that three conditions are requisite for a judgment to
be an act of justice: first, that it proceed from the inclination of justice; secondly, that it come from one who is in authority; thirdly, that it be pronounced according to the right ruling of prudence. If any one of these be lacking, the
judgment will be faulty and unlawful.

—Aquinas, *Summa*[1]

Introduction:

While "sovereign authority" tells who may begin a war justly, the "just
cause" and "right intention/aim of peace" criteria form the moral core of a case
for a just war. "Just cause" is the most visible part of that core. When people
who have not studied just war theory are asked what would make a war just,
they tend to turn to questions involving "just cause." In the case of the Iraq war,
a rather complex case was made for a just cause by the Bush administration, and
debate over the parts of that case and how they fit together has been heavier both
before and since the war than for the other just war criteria. Because of all these
factors, there are three chapters for "just cause," covering more material than the
other five criteria. This first chapter lists the entire Bush administration case for
a just cause, but the second half of that case is analyzed in the following chapter.
The third "just cause" chapter covers the case made for the legality of the war by
a number of legal experts.

39

THE JUST CAUSE CLAIM

"The United States and other nations did nothing to deserve or invite this threat, but we will do everything to defeat it. . . . Should we take the risk that he will not some day use these weapons at a time and the place and in a manner of his choosing at a time when the world is in a much weaker position to respond? The United States will not and cannot accept that risk to the American people."[2]

DETAILED CLAIM OF A JUST CAUSE

The President's March 17 Speech

On March 17, 2003, President Bush gave a speech, televised from the White House, in which he announced the end of administration efforts to gain a second UN resolution, and gave Saddam Hussein and family forty-eight hours to leave Iraq or face war. That speech, quoted above, which functioned as a declaration of war (see Chapter 3), appeared to be consciously framed in part around many of the just war criteria, including just cause, sovereign authority, right intention, and last resort. The speech will be referred to again under each of these criteria. Under the "just cause" criterion, the main causes announced in the speech are numbered in the following excerpt:

> (1) [Saddam's regime] "pledged to reveal and destroy all its weapons of mass destruction as a condition for ending the Persian Gulf War in 1991. Since then the world has engaged in twelve years of diplomacy. We have passed more than a dozen resolutions in the United Nations Security Council. . . . Peaceful efforts to disarm the Iraqi regime have failed . . . Intelligence gathered by this and other governments leaves no doubt that the Iraqi regime continues to possess and conceal some of the most lethal weapons ever devised. (2) This regime has already used weapons of mass destruction against Iraq's neighbors and against Iraq's people. The regime has a history of reckless aggression in the Middle East. It has a deep hatred of America and our friends. (3) And it has aided, trained, and harbored terrorists, including operatives of Al Qaeda.
> (4) The danger is clear. Using chemical, biological or, one day, nuclear weapons, obtained with the help of Iraq, the terrorists could fulfill their stated ambitions and kill thousands or hundreds of thousands of innocent people in our country or any other.

> [Numbers (5) through (7) are listed here, but considered in the following chapter.]

> (5) The United States and other nations did nothing to deserve or invite this threat, but we will do everything to defeat it. Instead of drifting along toward tragedy, we will set a course toward safety. Before the day of horror can come, before it is too late to act, this danger will be removed. . . . (6) Under resolutions 678 and 687, both still in effect, the United States and our allies are autho-

rized to use force in ridding Iraq of weapons of mass destruction. This is not a question of authority, it is a question of will. . . . Many nations, however, do have the resolve and fortitude to act against this threat to peace, and a broad coalition is now gathering to enforce the just demands of the world. The United Nations Security Council has not lived up to its responsibilities, so we will rise to ours. . . . Saddam Hussein and his sons must leave Iraq within 48 hours. . . .
(7) If we must begin a military campaign . . . As our coalition takes away [the regime's] power we will deliver the food and medicine you need. We will tear down the apparatus of terror. And we will help you to build a new Iraq that is prosperous and free. In a free Iraq there will be no more wars of aggression against your neighbors, no more poison factories, no more executions of dissidents, no more torture chambers and rape rooms. The tyrant will soon be gone. The day of your liberation is near."[3]

Summarizing these statements gives the following:

1. WMD: Saddam's regime possesses WMD (the term is not defined, but it conventionally includes anything from nuclear weapons mounted on ballistic missiles, to chemical warheads on artillery shells, containing nerve gas, for example, to biological weapons such as anthrax).

2. Evil: Saddam's regime is evil. This is demonstrated by (a) Prior use of WMD, (b) a history of reckless Middle East aggression, and (c) its hatred of America and our friends.

3. The Terrorism Connection: The regime has "aided, trained, and harbored" (past tense) terrorists, "including operatives of Al Qaeda."

4. Danger: The regime constitutes a danger by reason of the deadly combination of all of the above. An evil, reckless regime, hating the United States, possessing "some of the most lethal weapons ever devised," and which traffics with terrorists, *could* kill "thousands or hundreds of thousands" of civilians in the United States or elsewhere by supplying terrorists with WMD.

5. The Right of Preemption: The United States, possessing "sovereign authority to use force in assuring its own national security," and faced with a clear future danger either to itself or some other country may (and will) strike "before the day of horror," and in fact before any concrete evidence of Iraqi plans to act, i.e., preemptively.

6. The UN: The United States is also justified in acting in that it is enforcing earlier UN resolutions: United Nations authority continues to exist for the United States to forcibly rid Iraq of WMD. (Note: this summary ignores "other nations," which seems to have little to do with the justice or lack of justice of the cause. If a cause is legal and just, it is so for a single enforcing nation; if it is unjust, adding a hundred nations would not change that fact.)

7. Liberation: *If* the United States and others act (which they will unless Saddam and his sons leave), the coalition will also provide humanitarian relief, liberate Iraq from a tyrant, help rebuild the country, and so forth. (This point is clearly not part of the main justification of the action, since it will not happen if "Saddam and his sons . . . leave Iraq in 48 hours." If Saddam's failure to leave had been followed by an actual declaration of war, this ambiguity would have been avoided.)

The heart of the case presented by the President, then, is that because of who Saddam was (a reckless, aggressive, mass-murdering tyrant), what he had (WMD), and what he had done in the past (sheltered terrorists, and used WMD on citizens of his own and other countries), the United States was justified in removing him in order to avoid future danger to itself and possibly other countries. As an additional reason, the President added that UN resolutions were still in force, and other countries would help enforce them. Finally, as a kind of addendum, the President added that if military action were to take place, the coalition would end tyranny in Iraq and help Iraqis build a better country. (He could have said, but did not say: "We must liberate Iraq: tyranny such as Saddam's must not stand.")

The Secretary of State's United Nations Speech

Although the President's speech made a number of strong allegations, it did not fulfill in any real detail the function in our Declaration of Independence of "submitting" "Facts . . . to a candid world." The fulfillment of that duty had, it seems, been left to Secretary of State Colin Powell. In a presentation on February 6, 2003, to the United Nations Security Council that lasted about an hour and a half, the Secretary had made stern, powerfully worded assertions, claiming to be sharing "what the United States *knows* [emphasis added] about Iraq's weapons of mass destruction as well as Iraq's involvement in terrorism." Powell explained that his information came from U.S. government intelligence sources and those of other countries. "Some . . . are technical, such as intercepted telephone conversations and photographs taken by satellites. Other sources are people who have risked their lives to let the world know what Saddam Hussein is really up to."[4] At the end of the presentation, after laying out his case, he linked these elements with the others in the President's later speech:

> We know that Saddam Hussein is determined to keep his weapons of mass destruction . . . Given [his] history of aggression, given what we know of his grandiose plans, given what we know of his terrorist associations and given his determination to exact revenge on those who oppose him, should we take the risk that he will not some day use these weapons at a time and the place and in a manner of his choosing at a time when the world is in a much weaker position to respond? The United States will not and cannot accept that risk to the American people. Leaving Saddam Hussein in possession of [WMD] for a few more months or years is not an option, not in a post-September 11 world.[5]

In other words, Powell's case to the United States and the world had the same outline as the President's: it rested on the danger arising from a combination of Saddam's alleged possession of WMD, his reckless and evil character, his involvement in terrorism, and the right of the United States to remove him from power in order to avoid the unacceptable risk he represented.

THE BUSH ADMINISTRATION FAILED TO MEET THE JUST CAUSE CRITERION

This complex case for war failed, on the basis of knowledge available at the time, to meet "the strict conditions" of the "just cause" criterion, when subject to the "rigorous consideration" the theory requires. (1) The proposed evidence for Saddam's possession of WMD and a WMD production program was manifestly inadequate, and countervailing evidence was not considered. (2) Saddam's admittedly reckless, evil, and aggressive character did not constitute the risk alleged, when considered in context (including U.S. government actions over the years). (3) The statement of Saddam's support for terrorism (a grave evil) was vague and misleading, of doubtful validity, and inflated. (4) The danger of an attack on the United States in the near to medium term was quite low (and far-off, possible dangers cannot provide a just cause to attack other nations). (5) Preemptive attack of the kind proposed is not warranted under just war theory (which, however, implies deterrence). (6) The attempt to justify the attack under United Nations resolutions was, when examined in detail, seriously flawed. (7) The belief that the United States would be in a position to help Iraqis "build a new Iraq" after removing its government by force rested on culpable ignorance of well-known facts concerning Iraq's people, history, and culture. (As noted, numbers 5 through 7 are analyzed in the following chapter.)

EVIDENCE THE JUST CAUSE CRITERION WAS NOT MET

Poor Evidence for Weapons of Mass Destruction (WMD)

The proposed evidence for Saddam's possession of Weapons of Mass Destruction (WMD) and a WMD production program was manifestly inadequate, and countervailing evidence was not adequately considered.

This section begins with some definitions of WMD, and the issues of their utility, confusion encouraged by use of the term, and considerations of hypocrisy and justice. Considered next will be the legal case concerning WMD, based on United Nations resolutions. Then the quality of the evidence presented by the U.S. government will be considered, along with reasons that it should have been

seen, by government officials and informed observers, to be inadequate at the
time.

WMD Definitions: Utility, Confusion, Hypocrisy, and Justice

Before looking at the quality of the evidence concerning WMD, it is useful
to consider briefly some more fundamental questions, apart from the legal requirements concerning them. In order to do this, the distinctions among chemical, biological, and nuclear weapons must first be made clear.

The Utility of Chemical and Biological Weapons

The current Chemical Weapons Convention (CWC) was first signed in Paris
in January 1993 by representatives of 129 nations (including the United States).
As of January 19, 2009, there were 185 "States Parties" to the CWC. The convention entered into force for the United States in April, 1997.[6] This Chemical
Weapons Convention, of which the United States is an original signatory, was
preceded by the "Protocol for the Prohibition of the Use in War of Asphyxiation,
Poisonous or Other Gases, and of Bacteriological Methods of Warfare, signed at
Geneva on 17 June 1925" (the Geneva Protocol of 1925), and the "Convention
on the Prohibition of the Development, Production and Stockpiling of Bacteriological (Biological) and Toxin Weapons and on their Destruction signed at London, Moscow and Washington on 10 April 1972." The first and second articles
of the CWC read as follows:

> 1. Each State Party to this Convention undertakes never under any cir-
> cumstances:
> (a) To develop, produce, otherwise acquire, stockpile or retain chemical
> weapons, or transfer, directly or indirectly, chemical weapons to anyone;
> (b) To use chemical weapons;
> (c) To engage in any military preparations to use chemical weapons;
> (d) To assist, encourage or induce, in any way, anyone to engage in any
> activity prohibited to a State Party under this Convention.
> 2. Each State Party undertakes to destroy chemical weapons it owns or
> possesses, or that are located in any place under its jurisdiction or control,
> in accordance with the provisions of this Convention.[7]

The Geneva Protocol of 1925 reaffirmed an earlier prohibition on the use of
poisonous gases in warfare and added a new prohibition on the use of bacteriological weapons. According to the Federation of American Scientists:

> Before World War II the protocol was ratified by many countries, including all
> the great powers except the United States and Japan. When they ratified or ac-
> ceded to the protocol, some nations—including the United Kingdom, France,
> and the USSR—declared that it would cease to be binding on them if their
> enemies, or the allies of their enemies, failed to respect the prohibitions of the
> protocol. Although Italy was a party to the protocol, it used poison gas in the
> Ethiopian war. Nevertheless, the protocol was generally observed in World War

11. Referring to reports that the Axis powers were considering the use of gas, President Roosevelt said on June 8, 1943:

> Use of such weapons has been outlawed by the general opinion of civilized mankind.

> This country has not used them, and I hope that we never will be compelled to use them. I state categorically that we shall under no circumstances resort to the use of such weapons unless they are first used by our enemies.

Although the Senate Foreign Relations Committee favorably reported the protocol in 1926, there was strong lobbying against it, and the Senate never voted on it [which meant it did not enter into force for the United States]. . . . In the latter part of 1974, the Ford Administration launched a new initiative to obtain Senate consent to ratification of the protocol (and simultaneously of the Biological Weapons Convention). . . . The protocol and the convention were ratified by President Ford on January 22, 1975. The U.S. instrument of ratification of the convention was deposited on March 26, 1975, and of the protocol on April 10, 1975.[8]

Looking at these two types of WMD together, in the first half of the twentieth century it was often major powers that used chemical and biological weapons. For example, the United Kingdom, France, Germany, and the United States all used chemical weapons during World War I, and the Germans used anthrax as well. Spain, a European but not a major power, used chemical weapons in the 1920s against rebels in its colony of Spanish Morocco. Italy used mustard gas against Abyssinia (present-day Ethiopia) during its invasion of that independent country in 1936. Japan used biological weapons several times in the late 1930s, and Nazi Germany used both biological and chemical weapons on human beings during World War II.

In the second half of the century, it was often more minor powers using these weapons. In the 1960s, Egypt used chemical weapons in Yemen, and the United States used defoliants in Vietnam that it later designated as banned substances (although their use was not against U.S. treaty obligations at the time). In the 1970s, South Africa used chemical and biological weapons against revolutionaries there. Finally, in the 1980s Iraq used several chemical weapons against Iran.[9]

It is important to note that these weapons, while they kill large numbers of people in ghastly ways, are hardly more horrible in their results than high explosives, for the most part. In both cases, the victims are dead, maimed, blinded, crippled, etc. It is easy in most situations, especially for an advanced military power, to produce as many victims with explosives, napalm, cluster bombs, and other "conventional" weaponry, as it would be with chemical or biological weapons, and the wounded suffer just as much. Chemical and biological weapons are often less deadly than conventional, as they are difficult to apply and spread effectively, even for the military. CIA analyst and author Kenneth Pollack states that in every case when terrorists have used such weapons, they would have killed more persons by using explosives.[10]

The Utility of Nuclear Weapons

Nuclear weapons do kill huge numbers of people per effective bomb. Here is a statement on the Nuclear Non-Proliferation Treaty from the Federation of American Scientists (FAS):

> The Treaty on the Non-Proliferation of Nuclear Weapons, also referred to as the Nuclear Non-Proliferation Treaty (NPT), obligates the five acknowledged nuclear-weapon states (the United States, Russian Federation, United Kingdom, France, and China) not to transfer nuclear weapons, other nuclear explosive devices, or their technology to any non-nuclear-weapon state. Non-nuclear-weapon States Parties undertake not to acquire or produce nuclear weapons or nuclear explosive devices. They are required also to accept safeguards to detect diversions of nuclear materials from peaceful activities, such as power generation, to the production of nuclear weapons or other nuclear explosive devices. . . The Treaty was opened for signature on 01 July 1968, and signed on that date by the United States, the United Kingdom, the Soviet Union, and 59 other countries. The Treaty entered into force with the deposit of U.S. ratification on 05 March 1970. China acceded to the NPT on 09 March 1992, and France acceded on 03 August 1992. In 1996, Belarus joined Ukraine and Kazakhstan in removing and transferring to the Russian Federation the last of the remaining former Soviet nuclear weapons located within their territories, and each of these nations has become a State Party to the NPT, as a non-nuclear-weapon state. In June 1997 Brazil became a State Party to the NPT.
>
> The NPT is the most widely accepted arms control agreement. As of early 2000 a total of 187 states were Parties to the NPT. Cuba, Israel, India, and Pakistan were the only states that were not members of the NPT. [Note that the last three, all of whom have close relations with the U.S., have developed nuclear weapons.][11]

Here is a list of countries known or believed to possess nuclear weapons, with numbers compiled (in some cases estimated) by the Federation of American Scientists (as of March 2008). The first five countries listed are members of the NPT, the second three are non-members who have declared possession of nuclear weapons, and the last, Israel, is "undeclared" (but there is considerable evidence of its possession of these weapons).

Country	Total Weapons	Deliverable
United States	5,400	4,075
Russia	14,000	5,569
United Kingdom	~185	<160
France	348+	348
China	~240	~193
India	~60-70	~60

Pakistan	~60	~60
North Korea	<10	?
Israel	~100	~80[12]

One nation has used nuclear weapons in warfare: the United States. The "Atomic Archive," a project funded by the National Science Foundation (a U.S. federal agency funded by Congress) includes an article entitled "The Atomic Bombings of Hiroshima and Nagasaki," with the following statement about the casualties from those two bombs:

> There has been great difficulty in estimating the total casualties in the Japanese cities as a result of the atomic bombing. The extensive destruction of civil installations (hospitals, fire and police department, and government agencies) the state of utter confusion immediately following the explosion, as well as the uncertainty regarding the actual population before the bombing, contribute to the difficulty of making estimates of casualties. The Japanese periodic censuses are not complete. Finally, the great fires that raged in each city totally consumed many bodies.
>
> The number of total casualties has been estimated at various times since the bombings with wide discrepancies. The Manhattan Engineer District's best available figures are:

Estimates of Casualties

	Hiroshima	Nagasaki
Pre-raid population	255,000	195,000
Dead	66,000	39,000
Injured	69,000	25,000
Total Casualties	135,000	64,000[13]

It may be that nuclear weapons acquired by some of the more recent nuclear powers would not kill many more persons than the two bombs dropped on Japan August 6 and 9, 1945. Even that, however, is destruction hard to imagine. Many of the more modern weapons are vastly more powerful. However, it should not be forgotten that given time, conventional weapons can end lives on a nuclear scale. By many estimates, for example, the total number of persons who have died in the current conflict in Iraq exceeds the death toll of Hiroshima. By some estimates, the toll exceeds the Hiroshima toll by a great deal.[14] (Although it would have been possible to lift the sanctions but continue inspections, it seems possible that, if left alone, Iraq could have acquired nuclear weapons within five to ten years. The question of whether a nuclear-armed Iraq could have been deterred will be considered later in this chapter.)

Confusion and WMD

Non-nuclear WMD, while gruesome weapons, are not in any objective way more gruesome or more lethal than other tools of warfare, certainly not in numbers of victims. If the President was describing chemical and biological weapons when he said there was "no doubt that the Iraqi regime continues to possess and conceal some of the most lethal weapons ever devised," it is hard to see that statement as anything but misleading. A complete literalist could insist that they are "*some* of the most lethal," but then high explosives and napalm are also, in a literal sense, "some of the most lethal weapons ever devised." It would hardly have won rhetorical points to state truthfully that if Saddam had chemical and biological weapons, they were just as lethal as those weapons the U.S. military uses regularly in every war. Nuclear weapons would fit the "most lethal" bill, but administration officials generally appeared to avoid making explicit claims that Iraq possessed nuclear weapons (something very clear in Secretary Powell's statement at the UN). Reading the above statement and the numerous, statements of the President and other high U.S. government officials before the war (and all administrations should be presumed to coordinate such statements carefully), it is appears likely that continual use of the phrase "WMD," which lumps nuclear weapons together with chemical and biological weapons, was chosen at least in part from a rhetorical rather than a substantive point of view: it allowed vague statements of maximum threat to be made, while preserving the sort of literal but misleading truthfulness President Clinton made famous in his sentence "I did not have sexual relations with that woman." Hearing that Iraq "possesses WMD," and knowing that "WMD" includes nuclear weapons, the average listener was likely to conclude this was an assertion that intelligence showed Iraq possessed nuclear weapons, and respond accordingly. Since political figures have a habit of calculating how listeners will respond to quite specific messages, it is hard to believe this was not a part of the Bush administration's political calculations.

Hypocrisy and WMD

Numerous authors have pointed out that Iraq under Saddam used chemical weapons against Iran and against Iraqi Kurds in the 1980s. However, not only did the U.S. government not condemn Saddam officially for these acts at the time, until far into the decade, the United States cultivated close relations with him, trading, sharing intelligence (and even, according to informed accounts, supplying weapons and chemical and biological weapons precursors),[15] helping Iraq by allowing Iraqi oil to be shipped on "neutral" tankers and then insisting that Iran not attack them.[16] (The aggression against neutral shipping appears to have been begun by Iraq. In the total context of pre-war Iranian-backed aggression against Iraq, and Iraq's inability to export much of its oil through an oil pipeline through Syria, an ally of Iran at the time, it can be argued that Iraq's attacks on tankers were acts of desperation, although they would obviously fail just war criteria. U.S. government backing of Iraq in this situation, regardless of the fact that we then saw Iraq as a bulwark against Iran, is hardly compatible with arguing for unbridled Iraqi aggressiveness.) Donald Rumsfeld, as a special envoy of President Ronald Reagan for the Middle East, visited Saddam in December 1983. During this period, Iraqi forces had begun to use chemical weapons "on an almost daily basis" against Iranian "human wave" assaults, something the "known in Washington at least as early as 1983."[17] (There is a picture, widely available on the internet, of Rumsfeld shaking hands with Saddam at this time.) In declassified State Department documents, there is no indication that Rumsfeld raised these concerns directly with Saddam. He did raise the issue once with Saddam's Foreign Minister, Tariq Aziz, but apparently without any indication that further use of these weapons would harm relations with the United States. Subsequent to the meeting, Iraqi use of chemical weapons escalated, which did not prevent the U.S. government from re-establishing diplomatic relations with Iraq in November 1984.[18]

It appears to be a case of national hypocrisy to establish and maintain cozy relations with a dictator while fully aware that he is using chemical weapons against soldiers of a neighboring country, and then against his own citizens (at Halabja in 1988), and then to condemn him later for possessing and using those weapons. (The same goes for supporting him during a war he started and then condemning him for aggression.) At the least, such an about-face demands, in order to escape the charge of hypocrisy, an official admission, at least as widely publicized as the accusations, that the accusing nation was wrong in the past. It seems such an official admission from the U.S. government has not been made.

Abstract Justice

Given that the United States and many of its allies possess significant stores of WMD, (the United States has destroyed most of its chemical weapons stocks, and has committed to destroying the rest by 2012, but still possesses huge quantities[19]) and given the warm official U.S. relations with Iraq while it used the chemical variety, it does not appear that simple possession of such weapons, in and of itself, could be cited as a just reason to go to war against the possessor. Violations of agreed-upon UN resolutions forbidding Iraq to have them are of course a different story.

The Legal Case: the UN Resolutions and Ensuing History

In March 2003, there were UN Security Council resolutions on the books (in place since 1991) that insisted that Iraq accept the internationally-supervised destruction of its chemical, biological, and nuclear weapons, and the dismantling of any programs related to producing these weapons. UN Security Council Resolution (UNSCR) 687 of April 3, 1991, states (paragraph 8) "Iraq shall unconditionally accept the destruction, removal, or rendering harmless, under international supervision, of: (a) All chemical and biological weapons and all stocks of agents and all related subsystems and components and all research, development, support and manufacturing facilities related thereto." Concerning nuclear weapons, in paragraph 12 the resolution states: "Iraq shall unconditionally agree not to acquire or develop nuclear weapons or nuclear-weapon-usable material or any subsystems or components or any research, development, support or manufacturing facilities related to the above." (Interestingly, the resolution also states in paragraph 14 "the actions to be taken by Iraq in paragraphs 8 to 13 represent steps towards the goal of establishing in the Middle East a zone free from weapons of mass destruction and all missiles for their delivery and the objective of a global ban on chemical weapons.")[20]

Under pressure from an unexpectedly aggressive UN inspection regime, Iraq in March 1992 admitted that its first WMD declaration had been incomplete and submitted a revised declaration. It then stated that it had destroyed all the weapons discussed in its revised declaration (which did not include biological weapons, which, at that point, it denied ever having) and dismantled the programs that produced them. However, it said it had destroyed the weapons and material without international supervision and with very little documentation,[21] a method in clear violation of the terms of the resolution quoted above. The Iraqi government's position in early 2003 was that it had long since destroyed all WMD. In support of that position it pointed to the fact that it had handed over thousands of pages of documentation and had allowed inspectors to travel throughout Iraq for years seeking weapons, which they had not found, and had thus complied with the resolution.[22] The UN never declared Iraq to be in compliance with Resolution 687 of 1991. In fairness, however, it should be noted that the United States would have been able to veto any such proposed declaration. On May 23, 1991, Secretary of State James Baker stated, in public testimony before the U.S. Congress, that his administration intended to keep UN sanctions in place as long as Saddam Hussein was in power. This statement, apparently never officially retracted, raises the question whether the UN Security Council, with the United States as a veto-wielding member, was capable of an unbiased judgment on the issue of whether or not Saddam's regime had in fact complied with the resolution.[23] If, as Baker and other high officials stated, the United States would never allow sanctions to be lifted while Saddam was in power, then Saddam had no rational incentive to do more than cooperate only as much as necessary to avoid war, since even full cooperation would not result in the sanctions being lifted.

Iraq's revised 1992 claims turned out to be incomplete, and quite false in at least one important respect. Weapons inspectors continued to make finds that raised suspicions, particularly concerning the existence of additional, unrevealed documentation that Iraq could use to revive its programs if sanctions were lifted. Dramatically, in July 1995, Iraq admitted (again under pressure) to having an offensive biological weapons program (but not weapons, which it stated had been destroyed in 1991). The newly-revealed material and facilities were then destroyed.[24] *However, no weapons were found after 1991, nor any clear evidence of chemical or nuclear programs. No clear evidence of any proscribed weapons or weapons programs at all was found after the mid-1990s.* On December 7, 2002, Iraqi made a declaration to the UN in which it admitted to several minor violations of Resolution 687, committed after the inspectors were expelled in 1998, that were not directly related to WMD themselves.[25]

Despite the complete lack of weapons discoveries noted above, and the complete lack of discoveries of weapons programs after the biological program was discovered in 1995, the Saddam regime's early lies, followed by a mixture of truth, lies, and piecemeal revelations under pressure from inspectors and defectors, made it hard to believe that Iraq under Saddam could be telling the truth in any particular situation. By March 2003, thanks to this convoluted history and the regime's claim to have destroyed weapons without outside witnesses or documentation, likely coupled with the regime's desire to hide the knowledge that would let it reconstitute those programs in the future, it was extremely difficult for Iraq to demonstrate conclusively, to the satisfaction of all, that it had in fact dismantled all its programs.[26] Even as highly qualified UN inspectors roamed freely through the country, guided by the best intelligence the U.S. government and other governments could provide, yet found nothing, it was still nearly impossible for Saddam's regime in early 2003 to "prove a negative." This fact was likely related both to the desire to protect other secrets, and to project an image of strength to neighboring countries.[27] That Saddam could not "prove his innocence" of harboring WMD is not, however, evidence of guilt. (For the Bush administration claim to be "enforcing" Resolution 687, see Chapters 5 and 6.)

Evidence Presented by Powell Was Weak

While Secretary Powell insisted in his UN speech that he was sharing "what the United States *knows* [emphasis added] about Iraq's weapons of mass destruction," there were strong indications within the speech itself not only that the U.S. government in fact did not "know" that its allegations were true, but also that its evidence was weak. Powell explained that his information came from U.S. government sources and those of other countries. "Some . . . are technical, such as intercepted telephone conversations and photographs taken by satellites. Other sources are people who have risked their lives to let the world know what Saddam Hussein is really up to."[28] These technical sources revealed vague conversations and fuzzy images that in fact were subject to other interpretations, as a touch of healthy skepticism showed many even at the time.

Beginning with the technical sources, look first at the recorded conversations. In one of the conversations Powell quotes, two senior officers express concern before UN inspectors arrive. One asks the other, "We have this modified vehicle. What do we say if one of them sees it?" This is followed by a short conversation about the "modified" vehicle, and then one says "We evacuated everything. We don't have anything left."[29] In the context of a search for hidden forbidden weapons, it is natural to think it likely that this is what the two officers were discussing. Powell put this interpretation on the conversation, and many were convinced at the time. However, it is simply unclear in the end what the two officers were talking about. How was the vehicle modified? What was "evacuated?" No one knew, and it is not even clear anyone knows now. These vague words, suspicious as they sounded, actually proved nothing at all.

Powell then spoke of satellite images that are "hard for the average person to interpret, hard for me." He then pointed to a series of "features" in the satellite photos that were "sure signs" of chemical weapons storage. "How do I know? How can I say that? Let me give you a closer look. Look at the image on the left. On the left is a close-up of one of the chemical bunkers. The two arrows indicate the presence of sure signs that the bunkers are storing chemical munitions. The arrow at the top that says security points to a facility that is a signature item for this kind of bunker. Inside that facility are special guards and special equipment to monitor any leakage that might come out of the bunker. The truck you also see is a signature item. It's a decontamination vehicle in case something goes wrong." He then shows a later picture of the same facility "as the UN inspection team is arriving." "The bunkers are clean when the inspectors get there," Powell states, "they found nothing."[30] As with the conversation, this set of "sure signs" and "signature items" struck skeptical listeners and observers as not so sure (and we should all be skeptical when war is possible and a government is pushing it[31]). All viewers really saw was the shape of some kind of bunker, or some feature of a bunker, and some kind of vehicle nearby. There can be more than one reason for a certain shape. There can be innocent but unknown reasons for a vehicle to be parked near a bunker. Any of these reasons could be connected, as just one possibility, to legitimate, non-proscribed military activities by Iraq. The regime could have had legitimate reasons to keep it secret. Another question that should have come up in this case is whether it is actually possible to clean up a chemical weapons site so thoroughly in a short time that sophisticated instruments of UN inspectors picked up nothing whatsoever. One more question was whether there was any actual evidence that the Iraqis had been warned in this case that the inspectors would arrive, and if so, how long beforehand. If inspectors "found nothing," one possibility that needed to be honestly considered was that there really was just that—nothing. Yet Powell in effect proposed that the fact nothing was found was actually evidence that something was there, and that there was an effort to hide it. This is simply flawed logic.

Powell also cited a number of reports by defectors, who were "in a position to know," or who "supervised . . . facilities" to produce biological weapons. Pollack, in his 2002 book *The Threatening Storm*, has some useful comments on defectors.

> To some extent, these sources are suspect because they . . . have reasons for telling us what they want to believe and what they want us to believe. . . . In early February 1991, I tried to write a piece suggesting that Iraqi morale might be starting to erode across the board, but General Colin Powell himself shot it down with the angry rebuke that we should never write intelligence based on defector reporting because defectors can never be trusted. General Powell wasn't entirely wrong.[32]

It should always be obvious that a defector, who tells you a dictator you hate is doing something you want to catch that dictator doing, is likely to be treated well. Defectors have to be thoroughly and carefully vetted—as does any source of "intelligence." Defectors, and any "raw" intelligence, may be gold—or garbage. Powell claimed that there was corroboration "by many sources, some of them sources of the intelligence services of other countries."[33] (By itself, this sounded like a good reason to believe Powell, and ordinarily this would have been the case. However, there were powerful reasons, available to the ordinary citizen and reader, to doubt the integrity of the entire process that produced

Powell's speech—see "Other Contemporaneous Reasons to Doubt the Official Case.")

As stated in Chapter 2, witnesses should be thoroughly cross-examined before their testimony is accepted, by people with real independence from the group that gathers the evidence. Not only was Powell not cross-examined, he himself was not even one of the primary witnesses who needed to be questioned. Interpreters can misunderstand recorded voices, or intentionally or unintentionally distort what they hear, but even if they do not, a conversation shared by two people may not be understood by a third even if the third speaks the language. Photographs too can be misinterpreted. Untrustworthy defectors can be accepted at face value. No evidence was presented that the defectors who "risked their lives" had demonstrated that their testimony was trustworthy, and the danger that they were in fact telling Western powers stories those powers wanted to hear was clear. When you are looking very hard for something in a place that you can't see very clearly, you have a tendency to find it. This tendency to see what is not there has to be guarded against by building some kind of skepticism into the process. There was little evidence that the Bush administration had done this, and the evidence noted below (again, see "Other Contemporaneous Reasons to Doubt the Official Case") strongly suggested at the time that it had not. However, what is disheartening, and the reason for Powell's evident later shame over his testimony, is that a man with a reputation for honesty and straightforward speech, in a position of authority with the ability to test assertions against actual evidence, presented a case whose flaws were only obvious to the already suspicious. There is a natural, understandable tendency to believe those in authority, especially if they have reputations for honesty. Powell's personality and reputation made a weak, one-sided case sound convincing to those who were not following more skeptical accounts closely. That was an abuse of all those who trusted him or trusted their government.

Although this is not an exhaustive account of the Powell speech, Powell's claim that there were massive discrepancies in the Iraqi accounting for the various items used in weapons production should be briefly addressed. Powell joked: "Dr. Blix has quipped that, quote, 'Mustard gas is not marmalade. You are supposed to know what you did with it.'" While the real Iraqi records were surely better for mustard gas than for marmalade, "the best-laid plans of mice and men gang aft agley," something true even for dictators' records.[34] Completely perfect record-keeping does not exist. Accounting discrepancies raised questions, and might have even pointed toward violations, but they did not amount to proof.

Other Contemporaneous Reasons to Doubt the Official Case

Besides the inherent weaknesses in Powell's testimony, there were several other extremely strong reasons at the time for doubting the Bush Administration claim that it "knew" Iraq had WMD. First was the entire UN inspection process from 1991 to 1998. Scott Ritter, a retired U.S. Marine Corps Captain who worked as a UN weapons inspector for most of that time, summarizes the work:

"Overall, UNSCOM (the United Nations Special Commission, for Iraq) carried out nearly 300 discrete inspection missions, and thousands of monitoring inspections."[35] The UN's flaws are well known. It does, however, get some things done, and at least some of them quite well. By all accounts the teams chosen by the UN for this work consisted of professionals who knew their business, had strong financial backing for the equipment, personnel, and travel they needed, were determined to uncover any hidden Iraqi weapons or weapons development systems, and most of all, were being supplied with intelligence by Western powers, including the United States, the United Kingdom, Germany, and Israel. In other words, the UN inspections were not random walks through Iraqi buildings. Based on intelligence supplied from defectors and technical sources, the very sources Powell cited to the UN, the inspectors made thousands of surprise visits to sites of interest to Western intelligence services, including those of the U.S. government. Early on, they made real discoveries of enormous embarrassment to Saddam's regime. First, by insisting on an aggressive program of inspections, they showed Saddam and his circle that they could not hide the weapons and programs they had. Then, ongoing inspections and aggressive use of intelligence from other countries enabled the inspectors to go after the documentation trail. The inspectors' work on biological weapons forced the Iraqis to reveal and destroy that program. When Saddam's son-in-law Hussein Kamal defected to Jordan (making him available to Western intelligence officials), the regime was so much on the defensive that it dumped an entire archive of written material documenting the WMD programs on Kamal's property, led UN inspectors to it, and attempted to blame it on Kamal. After that, the inspectors continued an aggressive effort to follow up on evidence of concealment by the Iraqis, with the ultimate aim of discovering whether or not there were in fact any ongoing programs.[36] However, the last discovery of significant evidence of an ongoing program came in the summer of 1995, when Iraq's offensive biological weapons program was revealed.[37] In the next three years, there were no significant finds demonstrating an ongoing program.[38] (After a CIA-sponsored coup attempt against Saddam that was stopped by his intelligence services in 1996, and in the midst of evidence of U.S. government spying on his regime through the UN inspection process, Saddam expelled the inspectors in 1998.[39]) Although there were loose ends, the highly intrusive inspections, with occasional access to very high-level Iraqi defectors and all the intelligence Western powers could share, found no evidence of an ongoing program after the summer of 1995.

A second, very strong piece of evidence casting doubt on Colin Powell's case for war was the new inspections program (undertaken by UNMOVIC, the UN Monitoring and Verification Commission, a successor to UNSCOM) at the end of 2002, after the passage of UNSCR 1441 on November 8, 2002. That new inspections program, again staffed by professionals, well-supplied with both resources and intelligence, was led by Hans Blix. Blix made the following powerful report to the Security Council in early February: "Since we arrived in Iraq, we have conducted more than 400 inspections covering more than 300 sites. All inspections were performed without notice, and access was almost always provided promptly. In no case have we seen convincing evidence that the

Iraqi side knew in advance that the inspectors were coming."[40] These inspection sites, obviously, were based on the intelligence from governments of countries such as the United States. Note that one of the satellite photos Powell cited showed inspectors arriving. Yet not one of those 400 site visits yielded a single piece of evidence of a program to produce weapons of mass destruction. An analogy: consider a policeman who gets a search warrant based on "sure intelligence" that someone is hiding drugs on an estate. He takes the warrant, makes a surprise visit to the estate, and inspects four hundred sites there–and finds nothing. Will anyone after that find it credible if the source states that, regardless of the failure to find anything so far, after all his looking, he still "knows" there are drugs hidden on the estate?

Those final inspections produced significant results. Dr. Mohamed El Baradei, the director general of the International Atomic Energy Agency, reported to the UN Security Council on January 27, 2003: "We have to date found no evidence that Iraq has revived its nuclear weapons program since the elimination of the program in the 1990's. . . . we should be able within the next few months to provide credible assurance that Iraq has no nuclear weapons program."[41] El Baradei reported back again in February, with the same report on WMD in general: much had been checked, but there was no evidence to date of any violations. A later summary of that report states: "Three weeks later, he returned and stated even more emphatically that Iraq's weapons capabilities had deteriorated badly since the time of the Desert Fox raid [in 1998]. 'During the past four years,' he told the security council, 'at the majority of Iraqi sites industrial capacity has deteriorated substantially.'"[42] All of this was public testimony, whether it was widely read or not.

One more extremely powerful reason at the time to doubt the February 6 Powell testimony was evidence that it included at least some falsehoods (however they made their way into his material), and some assertions that were doubtful. First, in his testimony Powell cited "the fine paper that the United Kingdom distributed yesterday, which describes in exquisite detail Iraqi deception activities." But a February 7 BBC news story revealed that the UK paper, actually included "large chunks" taken from several previously published articles, one using information a dozen years old.[43] The story in the UK paper the *Independent*, February 9, stated that the dossier "was largely copied—complete with poor punctuation and grammar—from an article in last September's *Middle East Review of International Affairs* and two articles in *Jane's Intelligence Review*. But the Downing Street compilers also rounded up the numbers and inserted stronger language than in the original. In a section on a movement called Fedayeen Saddam, members are, according to the original, "recruited from regions loyal to Saddam." The Government dossier says they are "press-ganged from regions known to be loyal to Saddam." On Fedayeen Saddam's total membership, the original says 18,000 to 40,000. The dossier says 30,000 to 40,000.[44] Knowing that Powell was relying in part on a flawed and doctored UK intelligence dossier, should responsible Americans not at the least have asked for time to sort out what else in his testimony was not true?

Powell had also spoken of aluminum tubes that he said "most U.S. experts think . . . are intended to serve as rotors in centrifuges to enrich uranium."[45] He added that Iraq "is attempting to acquire magnets and high-speed balancing machines; both items can be used in a gas centrifuge program to enrich uranium."[46] On January 27, El Baradei had told the Security Council that the tubes' "purpose appeared to be as claimed by the Iraqis, to reverse engineer conventional rockets. . . . On March 7, El Baradei went further, stating that . . . his nuclear experts had found 'no indication' that Iraq had tried to import high-strength aluminum tubes or specialized ring magnets for enrichment of uranium."[47] On the same date, El Baradei cast doubt on the documents President Bush relied on for his statement in his January 30, 2003, "State of the Union" address that "[t]he British government has learned that Saddam Hussein recently sought significant quantities of uranium from Africa." A *Washington Post* story on these doubts stated: "Knowledgeable sources familiar with the forgery investigation described the faked evidence as a series of letters between Iraqi agents and officials in [Niger]. . . . The forgers had made relatively crude errors that eventually gave them away—including names and titles that did not match up with the individuals who held office at the time the letters were purportedly written."[48] If El Baradei had access to the problems with these documents before the war started, the same information was certainly available to U.S. intelligence agencies and high officials. As noted below, those doubts were also published.

An article appearing January 28, 2003, called "A Case for Concern, Not a Cause for War,"[49] had cited a great deal of expert testimony calling into question parts of the U.S. and British case against Saddam, some of which was included in Powell's testimony a week later. Powell cited discrepancies in Iraq's accounting for its anthrax stocks, but the article pointed out that the U.S. government case assumed that none of the "growth media" had been lost, damaged, or destroyed, as Iraq claimed. The article also cited testimony by "Middle East military expert Anthony Cordesman of the Center for Strategic and International Studies . . . in a 1998 report" that "the shelf-life and lethality of Iraq's weapons is unknown, but it seems likely that the shelf-life was limited. In balance, it seems probable that any agents Iraq retained after the Gulf War now have very limited lethality, if any." Any leftover growth media "would long since have passed its expiry date by 1999."[50] The article also noted strong evidence against Bush administration claims that Iraq had been attempting to buy uranium ore in Africa in the 1990s, or had retained VX nerve agent, as then-National Security Advisor Condoleezza Rice had claimed January 23. The article notes that "the Iraqi government has long had a survivalist strategy, by projecting an image of strength exercised to the . . . benefit of its support base. . . . It is not at all apparent how the retention of proscribed weapons could serve this survivalist strategy. If inspectors uncover non-conventional weapons, then this would lead to the government's ouster." The article points out that "habits of secrecy are not the same as continuing programs of illicit armament." The survivalist strategy included instilling fear in the neighbors, and confidence in the regime's supporters, both of which ends are served by secrecy concerning dangerous weapons or the lack of them.[51]

Circumstantial Evidence for Doubting the Administration's Case

In addition to these very solid reasons to doubt the Bush administration case, there was a set of circumstantial reasons for those who had followed news about Iraq over the years, involving the way the threat was announced. Suddenly in the fall of 2002 major administration figures from the President on down said that Saddam had to go, that he was a danger to the United States. U.S. government policy before that time had been clear: he was not a danger to the United States. In early 2001, for example, Powell said sanctions "have worked" and Saddam Hussein was not a threat. "He has not developed any significant capability with respect to weapons of mass destruction. He is unable to project conventional power against his neighbors." Also, Powell said, everyone he spoke with in the Middle East told him the U.S. government needed to work to improve sanctions.[52] However, there were no startling revelations of new misdeeds by Saddam or capabilities he had developed. The first thing announced was the new conclusion: Saddam must go. The reasoning and purported evidence came later, in bits and pieces, and each piece of it was seriously and credibly challenged as it came out.

There was also evidence that the WMD threat was not taken very seriously by the Bush administration itself. One such piece of evidence was the widely reported statement of White House Chief of Staff Andrew Card, on the timing of speeches in the fall of 2002 concerning the urgency of Iraq, "From a marketing point of view, you don't introduce new products in August."[53] That is not the approach of people seriously concerned about the safety of their country. Jacob Hornberger asks, about efforts to involve the UN and a coalition of other nations, "if a foreign nation was really about to attack the United States, especially with WMDs, would any president spend any time whatever going to the UN to seek permission to attack that nation first or spend time to round up a group of countries to participate in a 'coalition of the willing'? . . . Indeed, if an enemy nation was really about to attack the United States, would the president even be talking about the importance of enforcing UN resolutions? Who in his right mind would care about the importance of enforcing UN resolutions if another nation was about to fire nuclear, biological, or chemical weapons at our country? All that would matter would be taking out attacking missiles immediately."[54]

Conclusion Concerning WMD

Many of the doubts raised about Iraq's possession of WMD were real and solid ones, based on testimony by genuine experts that conflicted with that of Colin Powell. Anyone who read about these doubts did not need to be a scientist to see that there were real questions, at least, concerning the U.S. government case. Where serious doubts are raised, does a just system execute an accused person? Surely not. How then could it be just to launch a war based on questionable intelligence? After all, the evidence raised against the Powell case was from people with authentic expertise, and it was not built of desperate, clutching-at-straws fantasies. The situation was closer to the opposite—the Powell case was not built on a single piece of undoubted physical evidence. Despite the existence of a robust inspection process, the Powell case rested on subjective interpretations of fuzzy photographs and recordings of ambiguous bits of conversations, and unverified, unexamined testimony of unknown people. In addition, it had been mixed with obvious falsehoods, a fact revealed just days later. At the least, a delay to sort out the truth about the various claims would have been necessary for a just cause case to be built on claims of an Iraqi WMD program.

Saddam's Character

Saddam's admittedly reckless, evil, and aggressive character did not constitute the risk alleged, when considered in context (including U.S. government actions over the years). Solzhenitsyn reminds us all in the Gulag Archipelago that "the line separating good and evil passes not through states, nor between classes, nor between political parties either, but right through every human heart, and through all human hearts." We should be very wary of proclaiming ourselves or our friends the absolute embodiment of good, or our enemies the absolute embodiment of evil. Nonetheless, with that caveat in mind, it is indeed reasonable to characterize Saddam Hussein as reckless, evil, and aggressive.

However, the question is whether this demonstrated character constituted such a grave risk as to constitute a reason for war. In this section evidence will be presented that Saddam's recklessness fell short of irrationality; that his use of WMD, while deplorable, was calculated, rational, and limited; that there was an important element of hypocrisy in Bush administration attacks on Saddam's reckless and aggressive character; that there is little evidence of Saddam's hatred for the United States as such; and that even where future clashes with a (possible) stronger Saddam were predicted, the evidence was very strong that he could have been deterred.

Saddam Was Not a Maniac

The evidence is against the idea that Saddam was some kind of maniac. Pollack, who wrote *The Threatening Storm* to make the case in favor of an invasion of Iraq, admits this in an article extracted from the book, saying Saddam was "not . . . insane."[55] In *The Threatening Storm* itself, in the chapter "The Dangers of Deterrence," he writes "Saddam Hussein is not irrational." Saddam connected ends and means, Pollack believed. (Of course, it is hard to become leader of a country without some kind of rationality.) "Neither is Saddam suicidal, as far as we can tell," Pollack continues. "Unlike Adolf Hitler, he does not have an apocalyptic conception of himself or of Iraq." (In fact, Saddam has been characterized as following a "survivalist" strategy.) "Finally, there is some evidence that Saddam has a crude understanding of deterrence logic and has been successfully deterred in the past." To back up this point, Pollack notes Saddam's launching of Scud missiles with conventional warheads at Israel in 1991— hoping on the one hand to provoke Israel into replying with conventional weapons (in order to gain Arab sympathy), but also careful not to provoke Israel to respond with its own WMD.[56] Pollack also points out that in 1990, after a British weapons designer working for Iraq was assassinated ("almost certainly by the Mossad") Saddam threatened massive retaliation against Israel if it struck Iraq. Privately, however, he assured the U.S. and Israel governments through the Saudi ambassador to the United States that he had no intention of attacking Israel, and asked for Israeli assurances that it would not attack Iraq, which it eventually provided.[57] These are hardly the acts of a semi-suicidal madman.

John Mearsheimer and Stephen Walt point out that Saddam "dominated Iraqi politics for more than 30 years," during which time he started two wars against his neighbors. "Saddam's record in this regard is no worse than that of neighboring states such as Egypt or Israel, each of which played a role in starting several wars since 1948."[58]

Saddam's attacks on Iran and Kuwait were very serious miscalculations, but they were not evidence of insanity. Saddam had been forced to cede territory to the Shah in the 1970s, and the new revolutionary Iranian regime was seriously provoking the Iraqi regime, attempting to stir revolt and assassinate senior officials. Mearsheimer and Walt summarize the Iraqi move thus:

> Facing a grave threat to his regime, but aware that Iran's military readiness had been temporarily disrupted by the revolution, Saddam launched a limited war against his bitter foe on September 22, 1980. His principal aim was to capture a large slice of territory along the Iraq-Iran border, not to conquer Iran or topple Khomeini. "The war began," as military analyst Efraim Karsh writes, "because the weaker state, Iraq, attempted to resist the hegemonic aspirations of its stronger neighbor, Iran, to reshape the regional status quo according to its own image."[59]

The following account of the immediate issues before the war began supports an interpretation of Iranian aggressiveness against Iraq:

> Despite the Iraqi government's concern, the eruption of the 1979 Islamic Revolution in Iran did not immediately destroy the Iraqi-Iranian rapprochement that had prevailed since the 1975 Algiers Agreement. As a sign of Iraq's desire to maintain good relations with the new government in Tehran, President Bakr sent a personal message to Khomeini offering "his best wishes for the friendly Iranian people on the occasion of the establishment of the Islamic Republic." In addition, as late as the end of August 1979, Iraqi authorities extended an invitation to Mehdi Bazargan, the first president of the Islamic Republic of Iran, to visit Iraq with the aim of improving bilateral relations. The fall of the moderate Bazargan government in late 1979, however, and the rise of Islamic militants preaching an expansionist foreign policy soured Iraqi-Iranian relations.
>
> The principal events that touched off the rapid deterioration in relations occurred during the spring of 1980. In April the Iranian-supported Ad Dawah attempted to assassinate Iraqi foreign minister Tariq Aziz. Shortly after the failed grenade attack on Tariq Aziz, Ad Dawah was suspected of attempting to assassinate another Iraqi leader, Minister of Culture and Information Latif Nayyif Jasim.[60]

Concerning the invasion of Kuwait in 1990, Mearsheimer and Walt write "a careful look shows Saddam was neither mindlessly aggressive nor particularly reckless." Explaining that Iraq believed it was entitled to some reciprocal help from Kuwait after it "helped protect Kuwait and other Gulf states from Iranian expansionism," they note Iraq's anger over Kuwait's refusal to loan Iraq $10 billion and to write off debts Iraq had incurred with it during the war.

> Saddam reportedly decided on war sometime in July 1990, but before sending his army into Kuwait, he approached the United States to find out how it would react. In a now famous interview with the Iraqi leader, U.S. Ambassador April Glaspie told Saddam, "[W]e have no opinion on the Arab-Arab conflicts, like your border disagreement with Kuwait." The United States may not have intended to give Iraq a green light, but that is effectively what it did.[61]

Then, as others have done, the writers show how Saddam's hanging onto Kuwait in the face of U.S. government threats can be seen to have made political sense, in context, at the time. "Saddam undoubtedly miscalculated, but . . . history . . . is full of cases where leaders have misjudged the prospects for war. No evidence suggests Hussein did not weigh his options carefully. . . . he was facing a serious challenge . . . he had good reasons to think his invasion would not provoke serious opposition."[62]

Saddam's WMD Use Was Evil but Limited

Saddam's use of chemical weapons was despicable and unjustified. However, he did not use WMDs in an irrational or unlimited manner. Iraq's population is far smaller than Iran's, and Iran had the advantage of many more "martyrs" who could be sent on basically suicidal missions against Iraq. In the Kurds, despite very natural and well-justified sympathies for them, Saddam faced a persistent rebellion that he could not break. In the 1991 struggle against the United States and its allies over Kuwait, Iraq did not use its WMD, neither against Israel (which it struck with Scud missiles with conventional warheads) nor against the U.S. forces or those of its allies. For more on this point, see the section on deterrence below.

Attacks on Saddam's Aggressive Character Were Hypocritical

Evidence of Saddam's aggressiveness rests, as Mearsheimer and Walt point out, on his starting of two wars. Yet after Saddam began one of those wars, against Iran, there is one country that offered Iraq tremendous material and diplomatic support, which lasted throughout the conflict: the United States. That support began and continued after the Iraqi aggression, and was not even diminished by credible reports that Saddam was using chemical weapons, as noted in the section on "Hypocrisy and WMD." In 1982, two years into the war, the United States supplied Iraq with sixty helicopters capable of military uses, according to noted military historian John Keegan.[63] In *The Threatening Storm*, Pollack has a long section on how "U.S. support for Iraq blossomed throughout the war."[64] The U.S. government support continued during Iraq's attacks against its rebel Kurds during that war. Joost Hiltermann, in "The Men Who Helped the Man Who Gassed His Own People" cites evidence that the U.S. government, knowing that chemical attacks on the Kurds had been launched by Saddam, publicly accused Iran of being partly responsible for the attack on the Iraqi Kurdish town of Halabja. He further states that "Declassified State Department documents show that when [then-Special Envoy to the Middle East Donald Rumsfeld] had an opportunity to raise the issue of chemical weapons with the Iraqi leadership in 1983, he failed to do so in any meaningful way."[65] It is hypocritical to condemn something that one strongly supported without admitting to being wrong about that support (and given ten years of support, it would make sense to repeat that admission more than once).

Little Evidence of Saddam's Hatred for the United States As Such

Saddam's rhetoric has often been strongly anti-United States. However, U.S. administrations caused Saddam's regime a great deal of harm at times, as well as strongly supporting the government of Israel, which had hostile relations with Saddam's regime. Lieutenant General Brent Scowcroft, National Security Advisor to President Ford and the first President Bush, wrote in August 2002 in the *Wall Street Journal*, "There is little evidence to indicate that the United States itself is an object of [Saddam's] aggression. Rather, Saddam's problem with the U.S. appears to be that we stand in the way of his ambitions."[66] Saddam has not struck directly at U.S. citizens or forces, except on his own territory, in the immediate vicinity of Iraq during war by the United States against Iraq, and perhaps, once outside of wartime, on territory neighboring Iraq. CIA analyst Pollack began his 2002 book with these words:

> As best we can tell, Iraq was not involved in the terrorist attacks of September 11, 2001. American intelligence officials have repeatedly affirmed that they can't connect Baghdad to the attacks despite Herculean labors to do so. "There's not a drop of evidence" linking Iraq to the attacks, one senior intelligence official told the Los Angeles Times. Iraq's ties to Usama bin Ladin's al-Qa'eda terrorist network were always fairly limited. Saddam generally saw bin Ladin as a wild card he could not control and so mostly shied away from al-Qa'eda . . . Likewise, bin Ladin detested Saddam for his lack of piety . . . the evidence that has been produced to claim an Iraqi link to the 9/11 attacks has failed to measure up.[67]

Later in the same book he dismisses claims that Iraq was connected to the first attack on the World Trade Center in 1993.[68]

Saddam is often accused of sending assassins to kill former President Bush in 1993 in Kuwait. Pollack, in *The Threatening Storm*, mentions this alleged Iraqi attempt in five places (listed in the index of that book), but does not address the questions journalist Seymour Hersh raised in November of that same year about the alleged plot. Hersh noted serious questions by noted experts about technical details of the plot, as well as the propensity of the Kuwaiti authorities to manufacture stories in their favor and of the Kuwaiti police to torture suspects into confessing.[69] Pollack writes "Iraqi tradecraft proved so incompetent and the Mukhabbarat's security so inadequate that the operation was quickly rolled up and Iraq's culpability was easily proven."[70] But this is the same Saddam who Pollack alleges is wary of supporting international terrorists because their efforts could be traced back to him. For Saddam, soon after a crushing defeat in Kuwait, to send a team of incompetents to assassinate the former leader of the world's only superpower would be far more foolhardy than anything else he is alleged to have done, with little positive return likely even if, or especially if, they succeeded. Hersh demonstrates that the assassination attempt is at least in doubt.

The Iraqi regime also fired on U.S. aircraft many times during the 1990s. While this is true, it should be noted that these were U.S. military aircraft flying over Iraqi airspace against the express wishes of the Iraqi government, and engaged, often, in attacking Iraqi military installations. They were not in international airspace, far less over the United States. The "no-fly zones" are discussed in Chapter 9, but the limited point here is that these actions are better evidence of an attempt to reassert sovereignty and turn Arab opinion in Saddam's favor and against the U.S. government than of hatred and hostility, given the circumstances. All in all, the evidence simply does not justify the President's claim of "deep hatred" of the United States by Saddam Hussein.

The Evidence Is Strong That Saddam Could Have Been Deterred

The President, the Secretary of State, and authors such as Pollack raised the specter of a future, nuclear-armed Iraq that could not be deterred. Both the consideration of an attack with yet-to-be-developed future weapons and the question of whether Saddam could reasonably have been deterred even when armed with them are considered below in the next chapter, under "preemption." Saddam's rationality, demonstrated here, tends to argue already that unless he were at least as well armed as the United States (highly unlikely in the conceivable future), he would be able to be deterred by clear threats concerning lines he must not cross. Nothing in Saddam's behavior indicates that he was more insane or less rational than the Soviet rulers, and while U.S. administrations fought a number of proxy wars with the Soviets, and perhaps both sides were less careful at times than they should have been, overall the tacit agreement "we will not fight you directly, but only through proxies on the territory your allies control" did not lead to catastrophe. Given our far greater military as well as economic strength, and Israel's impressive advantage in terms of nuclear weapons and mastery of conventional warfare, it is hard to see why deterrence should have been unworkable.

The Misleading Terrorism Threat

The President's statement concerning Saddam's support for terrorism, that he "has aided, trained, and harbored terrorists, including operatives of Al Qaeda," was vague and misleading, of doubtful validity, and inflated. In addition, there was other contemporaneous evidence that the threat of terrorism from Iraq was, at the very least, under control. With these weaknesses, the President's statement did not provide a convincing part of a just cause for an American attack on Saddam's Iraq.

The President's Statement Was Vague and Misleading

To begin with, there is no single, official U.S. government definition of terrorism.[71] To begin a war on a regime based on its alleged support for a tactic which the accuser has not carefully defined raises issues. Next, there was no attempt in the President's speech to identify whether he meant terrorists who had committed terrorism in the past or who were simply identified as such because they belonged to terrorist organizations. Moreover, there was no attempt to differentiate between terrorists who attacked (or meant to attack) other countries or the United States. This is important because terrorism, as practiced by non-State actors, is the tactic of the weak against the strong, and as such is quite widespread. While the mention of Al Qaeda appeared to invite listeners to think of the attacks of September 11, 2001, and see a connection, it appears to be a reference to persons who had no demonstrated connection with the attack on the United States. It seems wrong to proclaim to Americans that their country is going to war without making clear whether it is going to war on their behalf or on behalf of citizens of other countries.

The Statement's Validity Was Doubtful

While Secretary Powell's remarks at the UN extended to the training of Palestinians, his focus was on "the potentially much more sinister nexus between Iraq and the al Qaeda terrorist network headed by Abu Musab Al Zarqawi." Powell began by stating that Al Zarqawi's camp was located "in northeastern Iraq." A few sentences later, he noted rather indirectly that "Those helping run this camp are . . . operating in northern Kurdish areas outside Saddam Hussein's controlled Iraq."[72] After Saddam was repelled from Kuwait in 1991, the Kurdish areas of northern Iraq rebelled. Saddam's attempts to reassert control of these areas were repelled by direct U.S. government aid to the Kurds, movement of U.S. forces into some of the areas, and warnings to Saddam, such that Saddam's regime failed to control most of these areas, including the one in question, for the rest of its existence. Since Saddam did not control the area he could hardly be accused of being the host of this Al Qaeda camp. Powell attempted to avoid this obvious conclusion by claiming that Saddam "has an agent in the most senior levels" of the organization that controlled the area, and that various Al Qaeda agents moved "freely" in and out of Baghdad. This was obviously weak, as even "having an agent" in an organization shows no control over it, and gives no insight into what that agent's assigned task was. Next, Powell's argument had to be based on either defectors or captured persons whose testimony could have been shaped by many factors, and was difficult to corroborate. Finally, the nineteen plane hijackers of 9/11 moved "freely" indeed through U.S. cities, and it is well known that some of them had been reported to the FBI, and were being tracked by them. Obviously that does not prove U.S. government collaboration with Al Qaeda. Powell went on to note allegations of Saddam's "secret, high-level Iraqi intelligence service contacts with Al Qaeda." These allegations suffer the usual problems of sourcing: what factors, possibly including torture, shaped the testimony of these sources? But in addition, contacts in themselves prove nothing. If contacts proved threat and complicity, then CIA contacts with any number of nasty organizations over the years would prove U.S. government intent to overthrow dozens of regimes. Would such contacts justify attacks on the United States by these regimes? Surely not.

The Statement Was Inflated

That the President's statement was inflated is especially true of the suggestion that "operatives of Al Qaeda" were "aided, trained, and harbored" by Saddam's regime. No evidence was provided for the assertion that "operatives of Al Qaeda" were "aided" and "trained" by Saddam's regime. The only thing remotely qualifying for "harboring" is the training camp "in northeastern Iraq," but as Powell himself noted indirectly, the area was not controlled by Saddam, making it a serious exaggeration to imply that Saddam "harbored" the Al Qaeda operatives there. An even greater stretch would be to claim that because certain Al Qaeda agents moved "freely" in and out of Baghdad, Saddam harbored them. As noted, the 9/11 hijackers moved freely through the United States.

Other Contemporaneous Evidence

Serious analysts, many with access to classified information, had already weighed in publicly on this question. In an August 2002 *Wall Street Journal* article, Brent Scowcroft, a hard-headed realist with no affection for Saddam, wrote:

> But there is scant evidence to tie Saddam to terrorist organizations, and even less to the Sept. 11 attacks. Indeed Saddam's goals have little in common with the terrorists who threaten us, and there is little incentive for him to make common cause with them. He is unlikely to risk his investment in weapons of mass destruction, much less his country, by handing such weapons to terrorists who would use them for their own purposes and leave Baghdad as the return address. Threatening to use these weapons for blackmail—much less their actual use—would open him and his entire regime to a devastating response by the U.S. While Saddam is thoroughly evil, he is above all a power-hungry survivor . . . There is little evidence to indicate that the United States itself is the object of his aggression.[73]

Conservative columnist Bob Novak had in May 2002 dissected the evidence against a claimed meeting between "suicide hijacker Mohammed Atta" and "an Iraqi secret service operative in Prague." Noting that the Iraqi spy's "alleged presence in Prague is the solitary piece of evidence that could link Saddam Hussein's dictatorial regime to the carnage at the World Trade Center," Novak showed convincingly that the evidence against any such meeting having occurred was far stronger than any evidence in its favor.[74]

CIA analyst Pollack, in his 2002 book *The Threatening Storm: The Case for Invading Iraq*, had a great deal to say about Saddam and terrorism. The extensive quotation from that book, in the section "Little Evidence of Saddam's Hatred for the United States As Such," shows that the CIA had severe doubts about the connection between Saddam and terrorism. These words appear to have contradicted in advance, both with evidence and logic, much of Secretary Powell's later UN testimony. Pollack's introduction continues:

> So far, the evidence that has been produced to claim an Iraqi link to the 9/11 attacks has failed to measure up. The claimed "smoking gun" was a reputed meeting between the 9/11 mastermind, Muhammed Atta, and an Iraqi intelligence official in Prague during April 2001. However, the Czechs have changed their story on this meeting several times, and U.S. intelligence officials are skeptical that the meeting took place. Even if they did meet, since no one knows what they said and there is no other evidence to implicate Iraq, the fact of the meeting itself doesn't allow us to make the case that Saddam was behind 9/11. Likewise, stories have emerged that Iraq has supported an Iraqi Kurdish group with strong ties to al-Qa'eda, initially called Jund al-Islam but later called Ansar al-Islam, as a proxy against the Patriotic Union of Kurdistan (PUK)—one of the two main Iraqi Kurdish factions. Although the claims come from prisoners of the PUK and therefore should be treated with caution, they may be valid. Nevertheless, even if it does turn out to be true that Saddam has supported a small faction of pro-al-Qa'eda Iraqi Kurds against the other Kurdish militias, this is still a far step from demonstrating that he was behind al-Qa'eda terrorist operations against the United States. Both the United States and Iran supported the Bosnian Muslims during the 1990s, but that doesn't mean the United States was behind Iranian terrorist operations.[75]

Pollack returns a number of times to this theme. It should be remembered that in this book published in 2002, Pollack was attempting to build a case for the invasion of Iraq. In his chapter "The Threat," Pollack restated the obvious: "[Saddam] seems to recognize that a terrorist attack on the United States under current circumstances would only give Washington a *casus belli* to employ military force to remove his regime."[76] Later in the chapter he notes that the claim that Iraq was behind the 1993 bombing of the World Trade Center "is now looking like a red herring."[77] Moving on, Pollack claims that "Iraq's principal terrorist activity is supporting local groups against its regional adversaries" such as Turkey, Iran, and Israel. He qualifies even that, stating for instance that Saddam "continues to provide a home" for "old-line Palestinian rejectionists," but "they have largely been prevented from conducting operations for more than fifteen years."[78] Pollack states, "Since the outbreak of the Al Aqsa *intifadah* in the fall of 2000, Iraq has also begun providing support to Hamas and other Palestinian terrorist groups." However, "he has tried to walk a fine line, giving moral and some material support but refraining from actual operational involvement."[79] (Later Pollack states more explicitly that Saddam was "paying $25,000 apiece to the families of Palestinian suicide bombers, thereby encouraging more."[80])

If anti-Saddam CIA analyst Pollack is correct, Saddam was well aware that any confirmed act of terrorism against the United States would have provided

the U.S. government with solid reasons to remove him, and he acted accordingly. Although Pollack writes in terms of support for terrorist groups, the only
concrete act of which he accuses Saddam in recent years is making after the fact
payments to families of suicide bombers. Not planning, not ordering, not master-
minding, but paying money to (unspecified numbers of) family members after
the fact. This is hardly the reckless supporter of terrorism whose portrait Secretary Powell painted for the UN.

An Inflated Claim of Danger

The danger of an attack on the United States in the near to medium term
was quite low, and far-off, possible dangers cannot provide a just cause to attack
other nations. The very term "danger" makes little sense except in the near to
medium term. No predictions are likely to be true in the long term other than
sweeping generalizations ("in the long run we are all dead," "change is coming"), but those are unlikely to be useful. Thus, it is impossible to justify an attack on another nation on a moral basis on the grounds that ten years from now it
may be much stronger than it is today and attack us (see Chapter 5 for more development of this idea). The heart of the Bush administration case, as expressed
by the President and the Secretary of State, was that due to the conjunction of (a)
Saddam's possession of some WMD and attempt to obtain others, (b) his reckless and aggressive character, and (c) his support for terrorism, there was a nearly immediate danger to the United States. Saddam's regime itself was "a grave
and gathering danger" as the President characterized it in a speech to the UN in
September 2002.[81] This summation was shared by the U.S. Congress, which in
its "Authorization for Use of Military Force Against Iraq Resolution of 2002"
authorized the President to "defend the national security of the United States
against the continuing threat posed by Iraq."[82] Pollack's threat description went
beyond both the President and Congress rhetorically, seemingly evoking the
demonic Dark Lord of Tolkien's *Lord of the Rings*: "the ugliest of things would
be to hide our heads in the sand while Saddam Hussein [Sauron Hussein?] ac-
quires the capability to kill millions of people and hold the economy of the
world in his cruel hand."[83] (Pollack earlier evoked, for me at least, Frank Her-
bert's science fiction/fantasy novel *Dune*, writing that if Saddam acquired nuclear weapons "we would have to work hard to convince Saddam that we would
really fight a nuclear war amid the oil fields of the Persian Gulf to defend Kuwait"—in other words, Saddam could blackmail the world, as *Dune*'s dark hero
Paul Atriedes blackmailed the universe, with the threat to destroy its most vital
commodity.)[84]

If (a) plus (b) plus (c) = (d), deadly and immediate danger, and (a), (b), and
(c) when examined fall short, then (d) does not constitute the danger advertised.
If the arguments presented here are correct, there was insufficient evidence that
the WMD threat, or the maniacal dictator, or the menace of terrorism were anything like what was stated or implied in the official case.

Although the case for danger in the President's address rests on the three factors just listed, there was expert testimony available to reinforce the opposite proposition, which was rather easily verifiable: not only was Saddam no military danger to the United States, he was no military danger to any other country in his own region, largely due to the tremendous economic and military weakness brought on by over a decade of sanctions. First, Colin Powell in February 2001, on his first tour of the Middle East as Secretary of State, said containment and sanctions, "have worked," and Saddam Hussein was not a threat. "He has not developed any significant capability with respect to weapons of mass destruction. He is unable to project conventional power against his neighbors. So, in effect, our policies have strengthened the security of the neighbors of Iraq. . . . Everyone I spoke to said, you've got to go down this track of improving sanctions."[85] That fall, after September 11, Powell repeated his well-informed assessment to a reporter: "Iraq isn't going anywhere . . . It's in a fairly weakened state. It's doing some things we don't like. We'll continue to contain it."[86]

Here is CIA analyst Pollack, in the months before the war: "As the doves argued, Iraq truly was a small, weak state and the threat it represented was always a longer term one."[87] A bit later: "Iraq today is a shadow of its former self. . . . [Saddam is] weaker because he has been deprived of the military strength that made him a regional power." Further along: "By 1990, Iraq's military had developed a range of limited capabilities that made it a formidable force by regional standards, though still very poor by first-world standards. As a result of its catastrophic defeat during the Gulf War and the long period under U.N. sanctions, however, Iraq has lost many of the elements of this limited capability."[88] Pollack goes on to analyze Saddam's military weakness in great detail. Many more pre-war quotations on this theme could be supplied.

OBJECTIONS

Objection One: War Was Part of a Just, Global War on Terror

Objection: What about the "War on Terror" or the "Global War on Terror"? Isn't it clear that Saddam was part of a terrorist support network, and that terrorists struck the United States on 9/11? As Neuhaus wrote, "But a careful reading of [the book *Knowing the Enemy*] . . . leaves no doubt that millions of people possessed of lucidly lethal intentions in obedience to what they believe to be the commands of God have declared war on us, and therefore we are, not by choice, at war."[89]

Reply: This book focuses on the war against the concrete, visible regime of Saddam Hussein. First, the President explicitly claimed that Saddam's history of support for terrorism was one of the keys to the Bush administration case that it was justified in attacking Saddam's regime. Those claims have been carefully examined here, and found to be weak. Second, if a presumed just, wider war is given as the reason for attacking a regime, then that regime's connection to the wider cause must be demonstrated, through strong evidence, to be beyond reasonable doubt. In other words, if war against Iraq was to be justified on the basis of the just war case for a wider "war on terror," then the evidence against Iraq concerning terrorism would have to be strong enough to stand on its own at any rate. Thus, a merely presumed connection to a wider war adds nothing to a just war cause against Iraq.

As for Neuhaus' statement from April 2006, first, the number has nothing concrete to back it up. Millions may indeed say they "hate America," or perhaps hate American secular democracy, or what the United States does in the world, yet how many of these are people who know nothing of the wider world, and have no way of doing anything concrete against the strongest military power in the history of the world, the United States? Neuhaus does not say. How many millions of people in the world hated communism in the 1950s and 1960s? Perhaps many millions, yet surely they were not much of a concrete threat to the Soviet Union and China. Finally, it was a relative handful of people who launched the 9/11 attacks, not "millions" of Muslims. Thus, "millions have declared war on us" is a statement with no concrete reference point, and no evidence to back it up. To speak of hostile feelings and beliefs as "declaring war" is at best a metaphor. Yet Neuhaus here equates hatred of the United States (or its actions) by millions of Muslims with a United States invasion of a Muslim country, using the same word, "war," to describe both.

Objection Two: Saddam Hussein Acted As If He Had WMD

Objection: Saddam Hussein acted as if he had WMD. Since he created that impression, the Bush administration was not to blame if it believed him.

Reply: First, Saddam stated publicly that he did not have WMD.[90] Second, what if Saddam at times acted as if he had WMD, contrary to the public declaration that he did not? Consider the following, previously cited quotation: "the Iraqi government has long had a survivalist strategy, by projecting an image of strength exercised to the . . . benefit of its support base." Attempting to reassure supporters, and put fear into possibly aggressive neighbors, might call for looking tougher than you are. At the same time it is worth remembering that, as the article quoted also notes, "It is not at all apparent how the retention of proscribed weapons could serve this survivalist strategy. If inspectors uncover nonconventional weapons, then this would lead to the government's ouster." In addition, "habits of secrecy are not the same as continuing programs of illicit armament." If Saddam "acted tough," or even was reported (whether credibly or not) to have told his generals he had WMD, such actions could have been explained in other ways (connected to the regime's desire to stay in power) besides actual possession of WMD, especially in light of his public denial of having them.

Objection Three: Saddam Smuggled the WMD into Syria

Objection: Saddam Hussein must have smuggled the WMD into Syria, which is ruled by the same Ba'ath Party Saddam belonged to in Iraq, when it became apparent U.S. government forces were going to invade.

Reply: The argument here is that the evidence for Saddam's possession of WMD was weak, and weak evidence is not a strong enough basis on which to go to war. The assertion that Saddam sent these hypothetical weapons to Syria simply ignores the documented fact that the evidence that he had WMD at all was weak.[91] Concerning the party name, the Soviet Union and China were both ruled by entities called "the Communist Party" during the Cold War, which did not prove in any way that they cooperated on every issue—using the same party name does not mean that two groups have the same interests.

Anyone who wishes to believe that the WMD were smuggled into Syria in the final days before the U.S.-led invasion can believe it—or anything at all, for that matter. But given that the CIA had every incentive to find evidence for such an assertion, and immense resources at its disposal to find that evidence, and failed to do so (Appendix B), this belief is a kind of faith without any evidence behind it.

Objection Four: The Administration Had Bad Intelligence

Objection: Because the intelligence services did a poor job, the administration cannot be blamed for launching the war. As Neuhaus wrote:

> "I believe that military action in removing . . . Saddam Hussein and his regime in Iraq could be morally justified on the basis of what was known then. Some of what almost all informed people thought they knew then has turned out not to be the case. Saddam Hussein's presumed possession of and ability to use weapons of mass destruction is the most obvious instance. What is known in retrospect has led to long second thoughts, and not only about the competence of the intelligence services."[92]

Reply: Neuhaus was not the only one to have blamed the intelligence services for the fact that "almost all informed people" (in his view) thought they knew Iraq possessed WMD. (President Bush himself said "the intelligence failure in Iraq" was "the biggest regret of all the presidency," a formulation that takes no responsibility for the result.)[93] As pointed out elsewhere, skepticism toward a government that wants to make war is always a good idea, and a skeptical approach to administration claims when they were made, as well as awareness of published evidence to the contrary, should have made thoughtful observers aware that "what was known" was dubious at best. However, there is more to be said about the use of intelligence pre-war. It seems Neuhaus, in the quotation above, assumed that the incompetence of the intelligence services led to Neuhaus' false "knowledge." Yet Neuhaus and others who felt the same relied on intelligence and intelligence summaries that had been publicly released, not the actual intelligence, to which they had no access. What Neuhaus appears to ignore in this statement is that the public release of intelligence and intelligence summaries is a political, not an intelligence, decision, and is always shaped by political considerations. This means that the competence of those who actually analyzed the intelligence cannot be easily judged by what is released. Political manipulation is always possible. In fact, as a little thought will indicate, the question of what intelligence to release is usually, in most governments, a primarily political decision, and the criterion for what to release is typically: "what will help us politically?"

The most fundamental problem with this account of an "intelligence failure" is that it does not take into account the political pressure on the intelligence agencies themselves from the stream of speeches and public statements from President Bush and high Bush administration officials calling Saddam a direct threat to the United States. Would not such numerous, strongly worded comments cause most intelligence analysts to hesitate even to look for evidence that might contradict the President's policy? How much courage would it take to write an analysis indicating that Saddam was not a threat, or that the evidence for the existence of weapons of mass destruction was weak? An analogy: Neuhaus edited for years a magazine, *First Things*, which generally follows a strongly pro-life line. Do not the statements of Neuhaus and the senior editors at the magazine indicate that pushing a pro-choice stance at *First Things* is a poor way to get promoted, but a good way to have one's loyalty to the magazine questioned? The difference is that a magazine has every right to take a stance on such an issue, but an administration that takes a strong public stance on a question of fact by that very stance encourages intelligence officials charged with discovering the truth to "get with the program," to direct their efforts to supporting administration conclusions, rather than seeking the truth.

If there were convincing evidence that high administration officials showed an awareness of the political pressure they were creating and made real efforts to counteract it (even quietly) by encouraging analysts and other intelligence officials to disregard the public statements and provide dispassionate analysis, that might suggest that the administration was not guilty of what it gave every appearance of doing. Instead, a number of accounts testify to the existence of an effort, directed from a level higher than the CIA and the other intelligence agencies (but supported in many cases by top officials in those agencies), to manipulate intelligence. The manipulation in many cases involved taking any "raw intelligence" that supported the views of high administration officials, and the President's apparent determination to go to war against Iraq, and passing it to officials who leaked it to media sources or used it to support their views, regardless of whether the raw intelligence was verified or corroborated. It is the job of the intelligence services to verify and corroborate, among other things, such raw intelligence, indicating whether it is likely to prove reliable and thus worthy of inclusion in an assessment of possible threats to the country. The bypassing of that process ignored, at the least, the entire purpose of having and paying intelligence analysts—or indeed, the whole Washington intelligence machinery. This politically directed or inspired manipulation was almost sure to produce bad intelligence—and it appears to have done so. Before criticizing "the competence of the intelligence services," the critics need to wrestle with these accounts, many of them carefully sourced.

Since May 1, 2005, there is a very different suggestion from "competence of the intelligence services" in a leaked British memo (dated July 23, 2002) whose authenticity has not been denied by the UK government, namely that war had already been decided upon at least by July 2002 at the highest levels in Washington. According to the memo, the chief of British intelligence told Tony Blair and his cabinet in July 2002, after a trip to Washington in which he had met senior U.S. officials, certainly including George Tenet and other high officials, that "Bush wanted to remove Saddam, through military action, justified by the conjunction of terrorism and WMD. But the intelligence and facts were being fixed around the policy."[94] It must be stressed that this was the understanding of the chief of British intelligence in July 2002, according to the memo. The British government, then, believed that the intelligence was not being used by the Bush administration as a tool to discover the truth about Iraq, but as a tool to supply justifications for a policy of war that had already been determined, regardless of the intelligence.

But that was not the first time this story was reported. For example, a story about Douglas Feith, entitled "Top Pentagon Policy Aide To Quit," includes the following sentence:

> Feith has stirred considerable controversy during his four years at the Pentagon. He oversaw the Office of Special Plans, which critics said fed policy-makers uncorroborated prewar intelligence on Saddam Hussein's Iraq, especially involving purported ties with the al Qaeda terror network.[95]

This piece of the puzzle was widely reported elsewhere, and long before, although perhaps not as widely in the U.S. press until later. For example, on July 17, 2003, the British newspaper *The Guardian* ran a story by Julian Borger entitled, "The spies who pushed for war." Here are some quotations from that story:

> According to former Bush officials, all defence and intelligence sources, senior administration figures created a shadow agency of Pentagon analysts staffed mainly by ideological amateurs to compete with the CIA and its military counterpart, the Defence Intelligence Agency.

> The agency, called the Office of Special Plans (OSP), was set up by the defence secretary, Donald Rumsfeld, to second-guess CIA information and operated under the patronage of hard-line conservatives in the top rungs of the administration, the Pentagon and at the White House, including Vice-President Dick Cheney. . . .

> Mr. Tenet has officially taken responsibility for the president's unsubstantiated claim in January that Saddam Hussein's regime had been trying to buy uranium

in Africa, but he also said his agency was under pressure to justify a war that the administration had already decided on. . . .

The White House counter-attacked yesterday when new chief spokesman, Scott McClellan, accused critics of "politicizing the war" and trying to "rewrite history." . . .

The president's most trusted adviser, Mr. Cheney, was at the shadow network's sharp end. He made several trips to the CIA in Langley, Virginia, to demand a more "forward-leaning" interpretation of the threat posed by Saddam. When he was not there to make his influence felt, his chief of staff, Lewis "Scooter" Libby, was. Such hands-on involvement in the processing of intelligence data was unprecedented for a vice-president in recent times, and it put pressure on CIA officials to come up with the appropriate results. . . .

In the days after September 11, Mr. Rumsfeld and his deputy, Paul Wolfowitz, mounted an attempt to include Iraq in the war against terror. When the established agencies came up with nothing concrete to link Iraq and al-Qaida, the OSP was given the task of looking more carefully.

William Luti, a former navy officer and ex-aide to Mr. Cheney, runs the day-to-day operations, answering to Douglas Feith, a defence undersecretary and a former Reagan official.

The OSP had access to a huge amount of raw intelligence. It came in part from "report officers" in the CIA's directorate of operations whose job is to sift through reports from agents around the world, filtering out the unsubstantiated and the incredible. Under pressure from the hawks such as Mr. Cheney and Mr. Gingrich, those officers became reluctant to discard anything, no matter how far-fetched. The OSP also sucked in countless tips from the Iraqi National Congress and other opposition groups, which were viewed with far more skepticism by the CIA and the state department. . . .

"They surveyed data and picked out what they liked," said Gregory Thielmann, a senior official in the state department's intelligence bureau until his retirement in September. "The whole thing was bizarre. The secretary of defence had this huge defence intelligence agency, and he went around it."

In fact, the OSP's activities were a complete mystery to the DIA and the Pentagon. . . .

The OSP absorbed this heady brew of raw intelligence, rumor and plain disinformation and made it a "product," a prodigious stream of reports with a guaranteed readership in the White House. The primary customers were Mr. Cheney, Mr. Libby and their closest ideological ally on the national security council, Stephen Hadley, Condoleezza Rice's deputy.

In turn, they leaked some of the claims to the press, and used others as a stick with which to beat the CIA and the state department analysts, demanding they investigate the OSP leads.[96]

Chapter 12 of James Bamford's book *A Pretext for War* repeats substantially the same allegations in the *Guardian* story, quoting many sources who worked in the OSP or directly with OSP officials.[97] In the following chapter, Bamford quotes an unnamed CIA official who said his boss stated in a meeting, "if Bush wants to go to war, it's your job to give him a reason to do so." The official went on, "he said it to about fifty people. And it's funny because everyone still talks about that."[98]

American military historian Gabriel Kolko has made some remarks that illuminate "intelligence failures" in a more general way. Kolko was asked, "But if there are critical voices in the military, why are they ignored?" His response:

> Like the CIA, the military has some acute strategic thinkers who have learned from bitter experiences. The analyses of the US Army's Strategic Studies Institute—to name one of many—are often very insightful and critical.
>
> The problem, of course, is that few (if any) at the decisive levels pay any attention to the critical ruminations that the military and CIA consistently produce. There is no shortage of insight among US official analysts—the problem that policy is rarely formulated with objective knowledge is a constraint on it. Ambitious people, who exist in ample quantity, say what their superiors wish to hear and rarely, if ever, contradict them. Former CIA head George Tenet is the supreme example of that, and what the CIA emphasized for the president or Donald Rumsfeld was essentially what they wanted to hear. While he admits the CIA knew far less regarding Iraq than it should have, Tenet's recent memoir is a good example of desire leading reporting objectively. The men and women who rise to the top are finely tuned to the [negative] relationship between ambition and readiness to contradict their superiors with facts. The entire mess in Iraq, to cite just one example, was predicted. If reason and clarity prevailed, America's role in the world would be utterly different.[99]

It should be clear to all with hindsight what was clear enough to anyone who has worked in a bureaucracy at the time: if the tone at the top of the administration toward intelligence regarding Iraq had been, "give us the truth, and we will make our decisions accordingly," the "intelligence" produced by our intelligence agencies would have been completely different. To push hard against what is obviously the desire of the President and his team is to ask to be ignored, treated as a non-team player, and passed over at promotion time. Kolko states that many took that risk, with the result that they had no influence on the intelligence "product" that was passed up to their political superiors. Those who appear to have shaped the intelligence to satisfy those political superiors are of course blameworthy. But if blame is being discussed, surely those in high places who indicated the desired conclusions rather than calling for the unalloyed truth are even more to be blamed. The message publicly communicated by President Bush and administration's leaders in the run-up to the Iraq war was not "let the chips fall where they may, we want the unalloyed truth." Absent that message, and especially in light of the evidence that whole offices bypassed the normal intelligence vetting process, the implicit message to everyone in the intelligence community was, "the desired conclusion is clear. Contradicting it will get you nowhere."

Objection Five: Saddam's Irrationality Was Risk Enough

Objection: Even if Saddam was not technically insane, as argued here, the scope of his "miscalculations" was so huge, and their results were so disastrous for Iraq, that he might as well have been insane. The United States could not afford to take the risk that he would not attack this country.

Reply: As David Gordon notes,

> The key passage [is this]: "Iran is a rational state actor, which, like most other countries in the world—including American allies—will eagerly cooperate with the United States when their interests coincide with ours. . . . To know that a country and its leaders act rationally is to take a huge and critical step toward realizing that that country—no matter how internally repressive it might be— cannot and will not be a threat to the U.S." Greenwald's argument is a simple one: Because of the overwhelming military might of the United States, no other country can attack us without facing utter destruction. Other countries, wishing rationally to advance their own interests, grasp this fact. Accordingly, they will neither attack us nor threaten us.[100]

Iraq did attempt to hold onto Kuwait against U.S.-led resistance, and to assert Iraqi sovereignty in the "no-fly" zones which the UN did not authorize. (The assertion of an Iraqi assassination attempt against the first President Bush appears dubious, and the notion that Saddam was behind the first World Trade Center attack in 1993 has now been abandoned by intelligence analysts.) Despite those clashes, nothing Saddam ever did constituted a direct attack on or threat to the United States itself. Even when Iraq was under attack by U.S. forces that were enforcing Resolution 678, its own responses were carefully controlled— note the non-use of chemical and biological weapons, which Iraq possessed, against the U.S. forces or Israeli cities in 1991. Miscalculating what the U.S. government might do in response to an invasion of a third country, Kuwait, which had no defense treaty with the United States, is one thing. Miscalculating that it could attack the United States and get away with it would be different by orders of magnitude. Saddam never gave the slightest indication that he might make that kind of miscalculation.

NOTES

1. *Summa*, II-II, 60, 2. The quotation continues, "First, when it is contrary to the rectitude of justice, and then it is called 'perverted' or 'unjust': secondly, when a man judges about matters wherein he has no authority, and this is called judgment 'by usurpation': thirdly, when the reason lacks certainty, as when a man, without any solid motive, forms a judgment on some doubtful or hidden matter, and then it is called judgment by 'suspicion' or 'rash' judgment."

2. Bush, "The War Begins," in *Iraq War Reader*, 503-4.

3. Bush, "The War Begins," in *Iraq War Reader*, 503-4.

4. Colin Powell, "Presentation to the U.N. Security Council: a Threat to International Peace and Security," in *Iraq War Reader*, 465.

5. Powell, "Presentation to the UN," in *Iraq War Reader*, 477.

6. "OPCW Member States," *Organization for the Prohibition of Chemical Weapons*, http://www.opcw.org/nc/about-opcw/member-states/?tx_opcwmemberstate_pi1% 5Bsort Field%5D=0&tx_opcwmemberstate_pi1%5BsortReverse%5D=0&tx_opcwmemberstate_ pi1%5Bpointer%5D=3 (accessed January 19, 2009).

7. The bulk of the information in this quotation and the preceding paragraph is derived from the United States Chemical Convention Website, http://www.cwc.gov (accessed September 30, 2007).

8. "Geneva Protocol," *Federation of American Scientists*, http://www.fas.org/nuke/ control/geneva/intro.htm (accessed June 20, 2009).

9. "U.S.-Iraq ProCon.org," ht tp://www.usiraqprocon.org/wmdchart.html (accessed September 30, 2007).

10. Kenneth Pollack, *The Threatening Storm: The Case for Invading Iraq* (New York: Random House, 2002), 210. Note that this book is advertized as "A Council on Foreign Relations Book," with jacket endorsements from editors of both *Foreign Affairs* and *Newsweek*.

11. "Weapons of Mass Destruction: Nuclear Non-Proliferation Treaty [NPT]," *Federation of American Scientists*, http://www.fas.org/nuke/control/npt (accessed October 2, 2007).

12. "Status of Nuclear Weapons States and their Nuclear Capabilities," *Federation of American Scientists*, http://www.fas.org/nuke/guide/summary.htm (accessed April 18, 2008).

13. "The Atomic Bombings of Hiroshima and Nagasaki," *Atomicarchive.com*, http://www.atomicarchive.com/Docs/MED/med_chp10.shtml (accessed April 18, 2008). Bias, if any, on this U.S. government-funded site would presumably be toward a lower number of casualties.

14. David Brown, "Study Claims Iraq's 'Excess' Death Toll Has Reached 655,000," *The Washington Post*, October 11, 2006, http://www.washingtonpost.com/wp-dyn/content/article/2006/10/10/AR2006101001442_pf.html (October 2, 2007). A survey by Iraqi physicians overseen by epidemiologists at Johns Hopkins University's Bloomberg School of Public Health, and published by the respected British medical journal the *Lancet*, produced an estimate of 655,000 additional deaths due to the war between the invasion in March 2003 and the summer of 2006. Although this study produced only an estimate, and has generated controversy, it is widely acknowledged to have used the standard methodology for attempting to take measurements in a difficult and insecure environment where accurate data are not being collected by any government or central organization.

15. Michael Dobbs, "U.S. Had Key Role in Iraq Buildup/Trade in Chemical Arms Allowed Despite Their Use on Iranians, Kurds," *The Washington Post*, December 30, 2002, http://www.washingtonpost.com/ac2/wp-dyn/A52241-2002Dec29?language=prin-ter (accessed October 10, 2007). According to the story, "U.S. involvement with Saddam Hussein in the years before his 1990 attack on Kuwait . . . included large-scale intelligence sharing, supply of cluster bombs through a Chilean front company, and facilitating Iraq's acquisition of chemical and biological precursors. . . . A review of thousands of declassified government documents and interviews with former policymakers shows that U.S. intelligence and logistical support played a crucial role in shoring up Iraqi defenses against the 'human wave' attacks by suicidal Iranian troops.

The administrations of Ronald Reagan and George H.W. Bush authorized the sale to Iraq of numerous items that had both military and civilian applications, including poisonous chemicals and deadly biological viruses, such as anthrax and bubonic plague."

16. "Military: Iran-Iraq War (1980-1988)," GlobalSecurity.org, http://www.globalsecurity.org/military/world/war/iran-iraq.htm (October 2, 2007). See section "The Tanker War, 1984-1987."

17. Joost R. Hiltermann, "The Man Who Helped the Man Who Gassed His Own People," in *Iraq War Reader*, 42. The *Washington Post* article above states that: "Declassified documents show that Rumsfeld traveled to Baghdad at a time when Iraq was using chemical weapons on an 'almost daily' basis in defiance of international conventions."

18. Hiltermann, "The Man Who Helped the Man," *Iraq War Reader*, 43.

19. "Fact Sheet," Bureau of International Security and Nonproliferation (ISN), *U.S. Department of State*, April 20, 2006, http://www.state.gov/t/isn/rls/fs/64874.htm (accessed October 3, 2007).

20. "Appendix 1: Key U.N. Resolutions," in *Iraq War Reader*, 644-45.

21. Scott Ritter, *Iraq Confidential: The Untold Story of the Intelligence Conspiracy to Undermine the UN and Overthrow Saddam Hussein* (New York: Nation Books, 2005), 38.

22. Chief UN weapons inspector Hans Blix did not consider war necessary: see "Hans Blix's briefing to the security council," *The Guardian*, February 14, 2003, http://www.guardian.co.uk/Iraq/Story/0,2763,895882,00.html (accessed October 4, 2007). Blix stated on February 14, 2003 that "it seemed from our experience that Iraq had decided in principle to provide *cooperation on process*, most importantly *prompt access to all sites* and assistance to UNMOVIC in the establishment of the necessary infrastructure. This impression remains, and we note that *access to sites has so far been without problems*, including those that had never been declared or inspected, *as well as to Presidential sites and private residences*" [emphasis added]. However, he did not state the Iraq was granting full "cooperation on substance," which he defined as requiring "immediate, unconditional and active efforts by Iraq to resolve existing questions of disarmament—either by presenting remaining proscribed items and programmes for elimination or by presenting convincing evidence that they have been eliminated." In other words, Iraq's cooperation at the end, while it was active and placed no significant obstacles before the inspectors, could have been more proactive. While Blix is surely right that Iraq, if it was not doing so, should have cooperated in the way he describes, from the tex of Resolution 687 it does not seem that cooperation at this superlative, proactive level was legally imposed on Iraq in it (although it was in Resolution 1441 of 2002). In addition, Resolution 687 did not state that Iraq must rid itself of the capability to produce WMD—how could it? If it has smart scientists and money, any country can produce WMD. It appears that Blix was using tough language to try to force as much cooperation as possible from Iraq, a laudable objective. Perfect cooperation, like perfect anything, is not likely in this world, and is never a just human standard. A war should never be started on account of lack of perfect cooperation, although a demand for perfection may be acceptable as a negotiating stance if it is remembered that it is just that, a negotiating position. The difficulty is remembering the fact.

23. Ritter, *Iraq Confidential*, 5. See also Martin Fletcher and Michael Theodoulou, "Baker Says Sanctions Must Stay as Long as Saddam Holds Power," *The Times* [UK], May 23, 1991, http://globalpolicy.igc.org/security/issues/iraq/history/1991baker.htm (accessed October 3, 2007). In his prologue to *Iraq Confidential*, Ritter makes the case, with considerable evidence, that the first Bush administration, in negotiating Resolution 687,

was aiming not at disarmament of Iraq but at regime change. The case that both the first Bush administration and the two Clinton administrations aimed at regime change in Iraq is based largely on public statements by high officials in those administrations, including U.S. Presidents.

24. Iraq Survey Group, "Comprehensive Report of the Special Advisor to the DCI on Iraq's WMD (September 30, 2004) [also known as "the Duelfer Report"]," September, 2004, https://www.cia.gov/library/reports/general-reports-1/iraq_wmd_2004/chap6.html (accessed October 4, 2007). That Saddam's regime admitted the existence of and destroyed this weapons program is stated in the Chapter "Biological Warfare," under "Key Findings": "Iraq eventually owned up to its offensive BW program later that year [1995] and destroyed the remaining facilities in 1996 under UN supervision." While the word "remaining" is an after-the-fact judgment (by a U.S. government official), the Iraqi declaration and destruction of biological weapons facilities in 1995 and 1996 was widely reported at the time.

25. Glen Rangwala, Nathaniel Hurd, and Alistair Millar, "A Case for Concern, Not a Cause for War," quoted in *Iraq War Reader*, 462. (The article first appeared in Middle East Report Online, January 28, 2003.) "From 1999-2002, Iraq pushed at boundaries only indirectly related to the proscribed weapons. Iraqi weapons program personnel extended the al-Samoud missile range and imported missile engines and raw material to produce solid missile fuel. The Iraqi government acknowledged these transgressions in its December 7 declaration, and . . . has agreed to halt these programs." The word "only" in this quotation was a judgment call by the authors on January 28, 2003, the date of publication of their article.

26. Although the use of post-war information is involved, it is important to note the following: with the benefit of hindsight, and of the U.S. government being able, with very little hindrance, to search all of Iraq after the U.S.-led invasion of March 2003, the evidence indicates that the regime destroyed at least the vast majority of its WMD in 1991, or as the CIA's Duelfer Report put it: "Iraq's WMD capability . . . was essentially destroyed in 1991." That does not mean Saddam did not try to retain information, personnel, and facilities for reviving these programs in the future—he did. But from Duelfer's official report (see Appendix B), after the mid-1990s Iraq had no credible chemical, biological, or nuclear weapons, or programs in support of them, that violated UNSCR 687. The later defectors' tales of extensive chemical and biological weapons programs with mobile labs, dramatically proclaimed to the world by Colin Powell in his speech to the Security Council, seem to have no demonstrable basis in fact. In the words of Washington Post journalist and author Thomas Ricks, "The official, bipartisan conclusion of the Senate Select Committee on Intelligence's review of the prewar handling of intelligence was, 'Much of the information provided or cleared by the Central Intelligence Agency for inclusion in Secretary Powell's speech was overstated, misleading, or incorrect.'" (Thomas Ricks, *Fiasco: The American Military Adventure in Iraq* [New York: The Penguin Press, 2006], 90.) Given the failure of U.S. forces to find evidence of existing weapons or ongoing weapons programs, that is an understatement. Powell said in a September 2005 television interview that the speech was "'painful' for him personally and would be a permanent 'blot' on his record" (see Steven Weisman, "Powell Calls His UN Speech a Lasting Blot on His Record," *The New York Times*, September 9, 2005 http://www.nytimes.com/2005/09/09/politics/09powell.html?ex= 1283918400&en=e450abcc095582d7&ei=5090&partner=rssuserland&emc=rss (accessed December 21, 2006).

27. In addition, as Ritter points out, the paperwork that might have proven that Iraq did in fact destroy all its WMD was interwoven with some of Iraq's most secret security

arrangements, *Iraq Confidential*, 145. Although Ritter's book was published after the current war began, the fact that WMD documents and regime security were interwoven was clear enough to thoughtful analysts at the time. As Rangwala, Hurd, and Millar pointed out in January 2003 in "A Case for Concern," 462, "The Iraqi government has long had a survivalist strategy, by projecting an image of strength exercised to the patrimonial benefit of its support base." Revelations of sensitive security arrangements harmed that "image of strength" on which the government relied.

28. Powell, "Presentation to the U.N.," 465.

29. Powell, "Presentation to the U.N.," 466.

30. Powell, "Presentation to the U.N.," 468.

31. See for example, MacArthur, "Remember Nayirah, Witness for Kuwait?" 135-37, which discusses the fact, revealed after the 1991 war, that Nayirah, with her testimony of having seen Iraqi soldiers dump Kuwaiti babies on the floor as they stole the incubators, was actually the daughter of the Kuwaiti Ambassador to Washington, and quite unlikely to have witnessed any such act (and the story was almost certainly false). For a similar example, see Thomas Fleming, "The Historian Who Sold Out," *George Mason University's History News Network*, 6-09-03, http://hnn.us/articles/1489.html (October 16, 2007), about British war propaganda during WWI. For more recent examples, look up claims of mass graves in Kosovo created by murdering Serbs, and then look up the exposes after the war. The pattern is very widespread. Propaganda is not just used by totalitarians or dictators.

32. Pollack, *Threatening Storm*, 346. (Note: the quotation continues: "but he also wasn't entirely right.")

33. Powell, "Presentation to the U.N.," 469.

34. You should also know where a billion dollars goes. A billion dollars is not minor moolah. Unfortunately, in the case of U.S. government work to reconstruct Iraq, there are apparently many, many billions missing: they can't be accounted for. See, for example: "Audit: U.S. lost track of $9 billion in Iraq funds: Pentagon, Bremer dispute inspector general's report," *CNN.com*, January 31, 2005, http://edition.cnn.com/2005/WORLD/meast/01/30/iraq.audit/ (accessed October 10, 2007).

Millions of dollars worth of weapons are also apparently missing. See: "Audit finds many missing U.S. weapons in Iraq Government report: About 14,000 weapons—1 in 25—unaccounted for," *Associated Press*, October 29, 2006, http://www.msnbc.msn.com/id/15474042/ (accessed October 10, 2007). I have cited examples from the U.S. government effort that became known since the war, but the fallibility of all human projects was clear at the time as well.

35. Ritter, *Iraq Confidential*, xii. Ritter decided that by the end of his time with the UN, the US government in particular had politicized the inspections, placing its own interests ahead of the UNSCOM mission to uncover the truth about Iraqi weapons and weapons systems. He made this conclusion clear in speeches and articles before the current war began.

36. Pollack, *Threatening Storm*, 61-63, and see index p. 493 for listing of related pages. Pollack admits that UNSCOM created much more trouble for Saddam than the Iraqis had expected, and achieved truly significant results. His claims (in 2002) of parts of programs being hidden were impossible to verify at the time, before the March 2003 invasion, and have since been shown to be either false or completely unverifiable by the Duelfer Report.

37. Ritter, *Iraq Confidential*, 109. The story was also covered in contemporary news articles.

38. Ritter, *Iraq Confidential*, 229. The defection of Saddam's son-in-law Hussein brought new revelations of ongoing concealment schemes by the regime, and attempts to penetrate that scheme in order to be certain that more weapons and programs had not been concealed. (Note: as in the preceding footnote, I am quoting accounts published after the war, but the facts were published at the time as well.)

39. Ritter covers the coup attempt in *Iraq Confidential*, Chapter 13, and states that it attempted to piggyback on the inspections, see p. 167. Ritter was not the first to tell this story. For coup attempts, see also Pollack, *Threatening Storm*: "the Bush and Clinton administrations authorized the ouster of Saddam Hussein [by the CIA]" p. 284; a CIA-backed effort to overthrow Saddam began in 1992, p. 287; the CIA-backed 1995 coup, p. 72; which was betrayed to Saddam's forces and "rolled up" in June 1996, p. 288. For use of intelligence assets placed in Iraq by UNSCOM but used by the U.S. government for its own purposes (a betrayal of the trust UNSCOM demanded of Saddam's regime), see Susan Wright, "The Hijacking of UNSCOM" (1999) in *Iraq War Reader*, 186, and extensive references to this by Ritter in *Iraq Confidential*: e.g. pp. 138, 153, 167, 216-217, 220-221. Wright in her article points to evidence that information gathered "under cover of UNSCOM" appears to have been used "to define targets for the December [1998] bombing raids during Operation Desert Fox" (p. 188). Ritter also heard (Australian) UNSCOM chief Richard Butler saying he wanted to "have a crisis" in Iraq by May 8, 1998, in order to provide justification for a planned U.S. bombing campaign that would end on the 15th, a Muslim religious holiday that year (*Iraq Confidential*, 272), in what Ritter described as "nothing less than total collusion between a United Nations official . . . and the USA, over military action that had not been sanctioned by the Security Council."

40. "Hans Blix's briefing to the security council" (see note 22 above).

41. Khidhir Hamza with Jeff Stein, "Behind the Scenes with the Iraqi Nuclear Bomb" (see "editor's postscript"), *Iraq War Reader*, 195.

42. Ricks, *Fiasco*, 94.

43. "Iraq Dossier Solid—Downing Street," *BBC News*, February 7, 2003, http://news.bbc.co.uk/1/hi/uk_politics/2735031.stm (accessed December 7, 2007).

44. Paul Lashmar and Raymond Whitaker, "MI6 and CIA: The New Enemy Within," in *Iraq War Reader*, 481.

45. Powell, "Presentation to the U.N.," 473.

46. Powell, "Presentation to the U.N.," 474.

47. Editors' postscript, Khidhir Hamza with Jeff Stein, "Behind the Scenes with the Iraqi Nuclear Bomb," *Iraq War Reader*, 195.

48. Joby Warrick, "Some Evidence on Iraq Called Fake," *The Washington Post*, March 8, 2003, http://www.globalpolicy.org/security/issues/iraq/unmovic/2003/0308someevid.htm (accessed April 19, 2008).

49. Rangwala, Hurd, and Millar, "A Case for Concern," 457.

50. Rangwala, Hurd, and Millar, "A Case for Concern," 460-61.

51. Rangwala, Hurd, and Millar, "A Case for Concern," 462.

52. Ricks, *Fiasco*, 27. Ricks does not state in his endnotes where the Powell statement was reported at the time.

53. William Schneider, "Marketing Iraq: Why Now?" *CNN. com: InsidePolitics*, September 12, 2002, http://archives.cnn.com/2002/ALLPOLITICS/09/12/schneider.iraq/index.html (accessed October 10, 2007).

54. Jacob Hornberger, "They Lied About the Reasons for Going to War," *LewRockwell.com*, October 24, 2006, http://www.lewrockwell.com/hornberger/hornberger106.html (accessed October 10, 2007).

55. Pollack, "Can We Really Deter a Nuclear-Armed Iraq?," in *Iraq War Reader*, 403. Note: while Pollack in this essay called Saddam "one of the most reckless . . . risk-tolerant . . . leaders of modern history," who is "often delusional" and "driven by paranoia," Pollack's examples show miscalculation, not insanity.

56. Pollack, *Threatening Storm*, 248.

57. Pollack, *Threatening Storm*, 31.

58. John Mearsheimer and Stephen Walt, "An Unnecessary War," in *Iraq War Reader*, 415 (the article was originally published in the January/February 2003 issue of *Foreign Policy*).

59. Mearsheimer and Walt, "An Unnecessary War," *Iraq War Reader*, 416.

60. "Military: Iran-Iraq War (1980-1988)," *GlobalSecurity.org*, http://www.global security.org/military/world/war/iran-iraq.htm (accessed October 2, 2007). See section "Iraqi Offensives, 1980-82." (Clearly U.S. administrations are sometimes supportive of armed responses to attempts by a country's neighbors to assassinate its high officials.)

61. Mearsheimer and Walt, "An Unnecessary War," *Iraq War Reader*, 417.

62. Mearsheimer and Walt, "An Unnecessary War," *Iraq War Reader*, 418.

63. John Keegan, *The Iraq War* (New York: Alfred A. Knopf, 2004), 67. Keegan writes: "[the U.S. government] did send sixty military helicopters designated as crop-sprayers, which Saddam peremptorily had adapted to fire anti-tank missiles." Keegan's characterization here appears naïve. It is hard to believe high U.S. officials were surprised when military helicopters "designated" as crop-sprayers were "peremptorily" modified back to fulfill their original military function (during a war!). The best evidence of the lack of official surprise is that there were no serious negative repercussions for Saddam in response to this quite predictable act.

64. Pollack, *Threatening Storm*, 18 ff.

65. Hiltermann, "The Man Who Helped the Man," *Iraq War Reader*, 41-42.

66. Brent Scowcroft, "Don't Attack Saddam," in *Iraq War Reader*, 295-96. The original article appeared in *The Wall Street Journal* on August 15, 2002.

67. Pollack, *Threatening Storm*, xxi.

68. Pollack, *Threatening Storm*, 156.

69. Seymour Hersh, "Did Iraq Try to Assassinate Ex-President Bush in 1993? A Case Not Closed," in *Iraq War Reader*, 140 (originally published in the November 1, 1993 edition of *The New Yorker*).

70. Pollack, *Threatening Storm*, 156.

71. See endnote in Chapter 2 on this subject.

72. Powell, "Presentation to the U.N.," 475.

73. Scowcroft, "Don't Attack Saddam," 295.

74. Robert Novak, "No Meeting in Prague," in *Iraq War Reader*, 266, 267. (Novak's syndicated columns are published widely. This one appeared on May 13, 2002.)

75. Pollack, *Threatening Storm*, xxi and xxii.

76. Pollack, *Threatening Storm*, 149.

77. Pollack, *Threatening Storm*, 156.

78. Pollack, *Threatening Storm*, 156.

79. Pollack, *Threatening Storm*, 157.

80. Pollack, *Threatening Storm*, 379.

81. George W. Bush, "A Grave and Gathering Danger," September 12, 2002, in *Iraq War Reader*, 316.

82. Quoted in *Iraq War Reader*, 382. (The resolution was passed in October 2002.)

83. Pollack, *Threatening Storm*, 424.

84. Pollack, *Threatening Storm*, 415.

85. Ricks, *Fiasco*, 27. Ricks does not state his source for this quotation.

86. Ricks, *Fiasco*, 31. According to Ricks, this statement was made to "Bill Keller of the *New York Times.*"

87. Pollack, *Threatening Storm*, 106.

88. Pollack, *Threatening Storm*, 158.

89. Neuhaus, "The Two-Hundred-Year-War," *First Things* no. 162 (April 2006): 67. To continue the reply in the main text, earlier in the article Neuhaus points to "feckless American responses to jihadi attacks in Beirut, Somalia, and elsewhere," without ever stating what gave American soldiers the right to exert force against local groups in those places before the jihadis attacked them. Neuhaus does not address the possibility that instead of being members of a world-wide "jihadi" conspiracy actively working to destroy America, these attackers were local fanatics angered by the activities of U.S. military forces in their backyards. If that is the case, the solution could be as simple as leaving them alone in their own backyards. Then they would have to compete for local power against other local would-be leaders.

The attacks of 9/11 touched home in the United States. Yet, how many Muslims lost their lives at the hands of U.S. forces attempting to impose the will of the U.S. government thousands of miles from American shores in the ten or so years before some 3,000 Americans lost their lives? When President Clinton's Secretary of State Madeleine Albright was asked on the television program *60 Minutes* about the UN estimate that there had been a half million preventable deaths of Iraqi children in the aftermath of the "Desert Storm" war with Iraq, the well-informed Albright did not bristle with indignation at the implication that sanctions kept in place by a U.S. veto could have contributed to so many children's deaths. She simply replied that it was "worth it" (see Chapter 9). To note this is not to justify 9/11, but it is to situate it in history. It is necessary to imagine how Americans might feel if Muslim forces on a regular basis for a decade dropped bombs on American soil, or occupied American territory, or imposed sanctions that harmed American civilians, or appeared to exert humiliating pressure on an American government. It is then necessary to transfer the resulting understanding to how some Muslims have felt and feel. To continue the thought experiment, what if all American resistance to and anger against the foreign occupying force were seen as proof of American desire to rule the world? Yet if the occupiers went away, is it not possible, in this thought experiment, that "hate-filled" Americans would simply get on with their lives? Neuhaus does not appear to face the possibility that a global "war," such as it is, might simply fizzle out if American governments stopped attempting to impose their will on Muslim countries. This is, perhaps, a failure of the imagination.

One major attack planned and executed by a small group operating in a primitive country that could not defend them for three months does not constitute a 200-year war. If such a war exists in the fantasies of some Muslims, or some Americans, it does not mean it has to exist in reality.

90. Saddam Hussein, "Iraq Has No Interest in War," *Iraq War Reader*, 464 (originally broadcast through the auspices of Associated Press Television News in February 2003). Also note that in Iraq's December 7, 2002, declaration, it admitted to having extended the range of Al-Samoud missiles, but to no other violations of any UN resolutions. See Rangwala, Hurd, and Millar, "A Case for Concern," *Iraq War Reader*, 462.

91. Since this is an "after-the-fact" objection, it is fair to add some additional after-the-fact evidence in reply. Despite ample opportunity for the U.S. government to investigate, there is still no convincing evidence that Saddam ever had any WMD after 1991, much less that he sent them to Syria. See Appendix B, "Quotations from the

Duelfer Report."

92. Neuhaus, "Internationalisms," *First Things*, no. 148 (December 2004): 66.

93. Famously, Bush stated in an interview with Charlie Gibson on ABC:

> BUSH: I don't know—the biggest regret of all the presidency has to have been the intelligence failure in Iraq. A lot of people put their reputations on the line and said the weapons of mass destruction is a reason to remove Saddam Hussein. It wasn't just people in my administration; a lot of members in Congress, prior to my arrival in Washington D.C., during the debate on Iraq, a lot of leaders of nations around the world were all looking at the same intelligence. And, you know, that's not a do-over, but I wish the intelligence had been different, I guess.
>
> GIBSON: If the intelligence had been right, would there have been an Iraq war?
>
> BUSH: Yes, because Saddam Hussein was unwilling to let the inspectors go in to determine whether or not the U.N. resolutions were being upheld.

Bush's apparent lack of awareness that Saddam allowed the inspectors to go anywhere they wished in Iraq is odd, to say the least. See "Transcript: Charlie Gibson Interviews President Bush," http://abcnews.go.com/print?id=6356046 (accessed December 26, 2008).

94. "The secret Downing Street memo," *TIMESONLINE*, May 1, 2005 http://www.timesonline.co.uk/tol/news/uk/article387374.ece (accessed October 17, 2007).

95. Joel Roberts, "Top Pentagon Policy Aide To Quit: Douglas Feith Has Been A Driving Force Behind Iraq War Planning," *CBSNews.com*, Jan. 27, 2005 http://www.cbsnews.com/stories/2005/01/27/politics/main669785.shtml (accessed October 17, 2007).

96. Julian Borger, "The spies who pushed for war," *The Guardian*, July 17, 2003, http://www.guardian.co.uk/Iraq/Story/0,2763,999737,00.html, (accessed October 19, 2007).

97. James Bamford, *A Pretext for War: 9/11, Iraq, and the Abuse of America's Intelligence Agencies* (New York: Random House, 2004), 283.

98. Bamford, *A Pretext for War*, 333-34.

99. Gabriel Kolko, quoted in "Historian Interview: The U.S. Will Lose War Regardless What it Does," in *Spiegel Online International*, http://www.spiegel.de/international/world/0,1518,504865,00.html, accessed October 19, 2007.

100. David Gordon, "A Tragic Legacy: How a Good vs. Evil Mentality Destroyed the Bush Presidency," *The Mises Review*, http://www.mises.org/misesreview _detail.aspx?control=319 (accessed October 10, 2007). Gordon's article is a review of Glenn Greenwald's *A Tragic Legacy: How a Good vs. Evil Mentality Destroyed the Bush Presidency*. The remainder of this endnote consists of a continuation of that review:

> Of course the Bush administration does not see matters this way. How can one account for this clear failure to think rationally? Greenwald contends that the president and his advisors are gripped by a Manichean mentality. Like the ancient Manichees, Bush sees this world as a struggle between absolute good and evil:
>
> > The term Manichean refers in its most literal sense to a religion founded in the third century by the Persian prophet Manes . . . its

central precept was that the entire world could be cleanly divided into two opposing spheres—God and Satan in the world of the eternal, and a corresponding battle of Good and Evil playing out on earth . . . the historical fate of the Manichees is of far less interest than is contemporary reliance on their religion's central moral tenets. In the overwhelming majority of President Bush's significant speeches and interviews throughout his political career—but particularly since the 9/11 attacks—he evinces a dualistic worldview lodged at the core of his belief system. (p. 46)

Here it is important to avoid misunderstanding. Greenwald does not argue as a moral skeptic, denying that any distinction can be drawn between good and evil. Rather, what concerns him is the readiness with which the Bush administration views other countries as so dominated by evil that they cannot be expected to act rationally. . . . A possible objection to Greenwald's thesis is that if he is right about Bush's policy, does this not show that at least one nation, our own, does not act rationally? But if one, why not others? How, then, can Greenwald be so sure that Bush's antagonists will act rationally? But this objection fails. Bush's policies, however bad, do not threaten the United States with complete destruction; and the avoidance of destruction is the only requirement of rationality that Greenwald needs for his argument.

Chapter Five

Just Cause II: Preemption, UN Resolutions, and a New Iraq

Before it is too late to act, this danger will be removed. . . . Under resolutions 678 and 687, both still in effect, the United States and our allies are authorized to use force.

—George W. Bush[1]

I know there is . . . a reasoned expectation that successful action will weaken Islamist enemies of civilization and strengthen the Muslim forces of decency and freedom. The U.S. plans for changing the politics and culture of the Middle East, including Palestinian-Israeli relations, are indeed ambitious.

—Richard John Neuhaus, "The Sounds of Religion in a Time of War"[2]

Introduction:

This chapter analyzes the second half of the Bush administration's case that in attacking and invading Iraq under Saddam Hussein, its cause was just. The heart of the case made by the administration, analyzed in the preceding chapter, was clearly that there was "no doubt" that Saddam's regime possessed WMD, that the regime had a history of aggression and strong ties to terrorists, and that aggressive action by that regime through the provision of WMD to terrorists was likely.

Bush and other administration officials, by adding that the U.S. government "will not and cannot accept that risk to the American people," as Powell put it, implicitly argued that the United States had a right to preemptively "remove" the danger posed by Saddam's regime. Adding to the core case of preemptive self-defense, Bush and his officials claimed that "under resolutions 678 and 687, both still in effect, the United States and our allies are authorized to use force in ridding Iraq of weapons of mass destruction," and, as a kind of afterthought, promised to help Iraqis build a "new Iraq" if a war occurred.

As the just cause claim was introduced in detail in the previous chapter, only the sections relevant to these additional justifications will be repeated here.

DETAILED CLAIM OF A JUST CAUSE (2)

The President's March 17 Speech

On March 17, 2003, President Bush gave a speech, televised from the White House, in which he announced the end of his efforts to gain a second UN resolution and gave Saddam Hussein and family forty-eight hours to leave Iraq or face war. The second part of that speech is quoted below, with the second group of the main causes announced in the speech numbered as in the preceding chapter:

> (5) The United States and other nations did nothing to deserve or invite this threat, but we will do everything to defeat it. Instead of drifting along toward tragedy, we will set a course toward safety. Before the day of horror can come, before it is too late to act, this danger will be removed. . . . (6) Under resolutions 678 and 687, both still in effect, the United States and our allies are authorized to use force in ridding Iraq of weapons of mass destruction. This is not a question of authority, it is a question of will. . . . Many nations, however, do have the resolve and fortitude to act against this threat to peace, and a broad coalition is now gathering to enforce the just demands of the world. The United Nations Security Council has not lived up to its responsibilities, so we will rise to ours. . . . Saddam Hussein and his sons must leave Iraq within 48 hours. . . . (7) If we must begin a military campaign . . . As our coalition takes away [the regime's] power we will deliver the food and medicine you need. We will tear down the apparatus of terror. And we will help you to build a new Iraq that is prosperous and free. In a free Iraq there will be no more wars of aggression against your neighbors, no more poison factories, no more executions of dissidents, no more torture chambers and rape rooms. The tyrant will soon be gone. The day of your liberation is near."[3]

Summarizing these statements gives the following:

5. The Right of Preemption: The United States, possessing "sovereign authority to use force in assuring its own national security," and faced with a clear future danger either to itself or some other country may (and will) strike "before the day of horror," and in fact before any concrete evidence of Iraqi plans to act, i.e. preemptively.

6. The UN: The United States is also justified in acting in that it is enforcing earlier UN resolutions: United Nations authority continues to exist for the United States to forcibly rid Iraq of WMD. (Note: this summary ignores "other nations," which seems to have little to do with the justice or lack of justice of the cause. If a cause is legal and just, it is so for a single enforcing nation; if it is unjust, adding a hundred nations would not change that fact.)

7. Liberation: *If* the United States and others act (which they will unless Saddam and his sons leave), the coalition will also provide humanitarian relief, liberate Iraq from a tyrant, help rebuild the country, and so forth. (This point is clearly not part of the main justification of the action, since it will not happen if "Saddam and his sons" leave Iraq in forty-eight hours. If Saddam's failure to leave had been followed by an actual declaration of war, this ambiguity would have been avoided.)

This second part of the case presented by the President, then, is that due to the danger posed by Saddam's regime, the United States was justified in removing him preemptively in order to avoid future danger to itself and possibly other countries. As an additional reason, the President added that UN resolutions were still in force, and other countries would help enforce them. Finally, as a kind of addendum, the President added that if military action were to take place, the coalition would end tyranny in Iraq and help Iraqis build a better country. This is not a part of the core of the announced reasons for the war, as Bush stated that if Saddam and his sons left Iraq, there would be no invasion. (He could have said, but did not say: "We must liberate Iraq: tyranny such as Saddam's and that of his political party must not stand.")

THE BUSH ADMINISTRATION FAILED TO MEET THE JUST CAUSE CRITERION

This second half of the administration's complex case for war failed, on the basis of knowledge available at the time, to meet "the strict conditions" of the "just cause" criterion, when subject to the "rigorous consideration" the theory requires. Continuing the argument from the previous chapter: (5) Preemptive attack of the kind proposed is not warranted under just war theory (which, however, implies deterrence). (6) The attempt to justify the attack under United Nations resolutions was, when examined in detail, seriously flawed. (7) The belief that the United States would be in a position to help Iraqis "build a new Iraq" after removing its government by force rested on culpable ignorance of well-known facts concerning Iraq's people, history, and culture.

EVIDENCE THE JUST CAUSE CRITERION WAS NOT MET

Preemptive Attack Unwarranted under Just War Theory

Preemptive attack of the kind proposed is not warranted under just war theory (which, however, implies deterrence).

For the American historical context, consider two quotations on the subject of preemptive war. First: "All of us have heard this term 'preventive war' since the earliest days of Hitler. I recall that is about the first time I heard it. In this day and time . . . I don't believe there is such a thing; and, frankly, I wouldn't even listen seriously to someone who came in and talked about such a thing." That was President Dwight Eisenhower's reaction in 1953 when presented with plans to wage preventive war to disarm the Soviet Union, which had acquired nuclear weapons in 1949. Second: "Our position is that whatever grievances a nation may have, however objectionable it finds the status quo, aggressive warfare is an illegal means for settling those grievances or for altering those conditions." That was from the opening statement of Supreme Court Justice Robert Jackson, the American prosecutor at the Nuremberg trials, to the Nuremberg tribunal.[4]

President Bush said very little in his pre-war speech to justify preemption as a doctrine; he simply assumed it: "Before the day of horror can come, before it is too late to act, this danger will be removed." But he had made several speeches in the run-up to the war, most important the one at West Point in June 2002, in which he had laid out the new doctrine. In the wake of the attacks of September 11, the President said:

> The gravest danger to freedom lies at the perilous crossroads of radicalism and technology. When the spread of chemical and biological and nuclear weapons, along with ballistic missile technology—when that occurs, even weak states and small groups could attain a catastrophic power to strike great nations. Our enemies have declared this very intention, and have been caught seeking these terrible weapons. They want the capability to blackmail us, or to harm us, or to harm our friends—and we will oppose them with all our power.
>
> For much of the last century, America's defense relied on the Cold War doctrines of deterrence and containment. In some cases, those strategies still apply. But new threats also require new thinking. Deterrence—the promise of massive retaliation against nations—means nothing against shadowy terrorist networks with no nation or citizens to defend. Containment is not possible when unbalanced dictators with weapons of mass destruction can deliver those weapons on missiles or secretly provide them to terrorist allies.
>
> We cannot defend America and our friends by hoping for the best. We cannot put our faith in the word of tyrants, who solemnly sign non-proliferation treaties and then systematically break them. If we wait for threats to fully materialize, we will have waited too long. . . .

The war on terror will not be won on the defensive. We must take the battle to the enemy, disrupt his plans, and confront the worst threats before they emerge. In the world we have entered, the only path to safety is the path of action. And this nation will act. . . .

All nations that decide for aggression and terror will pay a price. We will not leave the safety of America and the peace of the planet at the mercy of a few mad terrorists and tyrants. We will lift this dark threat from our country and from the world. . . . There can be no neutrality between justice and cruelty, between the innocent and the guilty. We are in a conflict between good and evil, and America will call evil by its name.[5]

This is the same conjunction of threats the President warned about on March 17, 2003: terrorists and tyrants with WMD. President Bush warned of two threats that could no longer be dealt with by "Cold War doctrines": terrorist networks, and "unbalanced dictators." As he noted, it does seem that deterrence against terrorists (if hosted by ignorant and fanatical rulers such as the Taliban) is not an option, because they themselves are in many cases willing to die, and their hosts may not even understand what they are doing. Threats to destroy the terrorists' relatives or fellow citizens or co-religionists (not to mention Internet rumblings such as "nuking Mecca") are simply threats to commit more grave injustices in return, something repugnant to just war theory (as well as to all systems of ethics outside the Nietzschean ones), and not obviously sure to deter, either. (With the exception of U.S. forces in Muslim countries, the United States has been struck by a mere handful of Muslims in recent years—would the United States really want to start an all-out war against all the world's Muslims because of that handful that attacked?) However, deterring tyrants who wish to survive certainly is an option–and so is deterring them from giving the worst of their weapons to terrorists. As noted above, deterrence in fact worked against Saddam when everyone knew he had some WMD. The President stated, "containment is not possible when unbalanced dictators with weapons of mass destruction can deliver those weapons on missiles or secretly provide them to terrorist allies." But the idea of delivering WMD on missiles assumes tyrants with either missile-capable submarines or ballistic missile technology who also do not care if they are killed and have their regimes destroyed, an extremely rare combination. The concern about tyrants secretly providing WMD to terrorist allies has also been discussed above. (In passing, it appears that this sentence of President Bush applies more closely to North Korea than it did to Iraq, yet the United States did not go to war against that country. One of the likeliest reasons for this is the fact that North Korea's deterrence capabilities against U.S. interests were far greater than Iraq's. The reason does not seem to be that there is less to fear from North Korea.)

But the heart of the claim is that "we will confront the worst threats before they emerge." Again there is no particular discussion of the morality of this mode of action; it is simply stated or assumed to be the only possible "path to safety." Furthermore, "if we wait for threats to fully materialize, we will have waited too long." This is indeed a new idea in terms of just war theory, the teaching of confronting with armed force "threats" before they even "emerge" or "fully materialize," meaning they are not even fully in existence. A war fought under this justification would fully deserve President Eisenhower's description of "preventive war."

Preemptive attack, for excellent and rather obvious reasons, is not warranted under just war theory, except under carefully limited and strictly defined circumstances. Preventive war is not sanctioned at all under the theory. To see why, consider an analogy based on a hypothetical small town in Texas where most adults have weapons. Suppose you live in such a town, and a man in that town appears to hate you. Consider two situations. In situation one, the man who appears to hate you is a brutal man who beats his wife and has often been in trouble with the law. You believe he is about to purchase an accurate, high-powered rifle with an excellent hunting scope, a great sniper's weapon. Are you justified in gunning him down yourself in the street, after you hear this news? Clearly not. One reason is that such justification, applied generally as a rule, would justify many, many people in the town killing many, many others. The rule would create chaos. (In such a town, which is rather like the world we live in, there are threats all around, yet there is no "path to safety." Complete safety does not exist. It would obviously be impossible to "kill all the evil people in town" with weapons. Attempting to removing threats "before they fully materialize" would be a path to bloodshed and destruction, not safety.)

In situation two, the same brutal man has sworn publicly to kill you (although the wording of such an oath would be important: "that SOB is going to die" might not be enough, because he might reasonably be understood to be predicting rather than threatening). Having sworn publicly and clearly to kill you, he walks onto your ranch, against your standing orders, with a rifle in his hand, and hulking friends beside him with rifles in their hands. The reckoning of justice here is clearly different. You now have a right to shoot him first, even from behind a rock or tree, and with no warning, if you are able. His action—threatening you and then entering your property against your orders, and armed—may be justly considered an assault on you, even if you then fire the first shot. (If he merely spat on the street as you passed, or insulted you, these would not in themselves constitute assaults, even by an armed man.) In order to isolate the issue of preemptive attacks from all other issues, Saddam needs to be situated carefully in an extended analogy: Saddam, a brutal man and a convicted criminal, had served time for his crimes in early 2003, and was still on probation. (There was a real issue about the impartiality of the probation board, however, since the only way to get off probation would have been for the U.S. government, his sworn enemy, to agree—see "Objection 2" below.) The U.S. government was, in this analogy, a fellow citizen, not the sheriff. There was no sheriff, only a sort of citizens' court (the UN)—a "court" dominated, it should be noted, by five citizens of the town (the Security Council) who traditionally held most of the firepower. Saddam had never threatened the United States, had never come near the U.S. ranch. He had taken potshots at representatives of the United States (firing at warplanes in the "no fly" zones), but that was always on his ranch (and he had never hit one, whereas the U.S. representatives on his ranch, the warplanes, had killed quite a few of Saddam's). Saddam had just stated he did not want a war.[6]

It is tempting to propose the rule "good people are allowed to kill bad people, but bad people are not allowed to kill good people." But as Solzhenitsyn noted, no one on earth is pure evil or pure good, and we change over time. How would we decide who is good enough, and who bad enough, for such a rule? Each person will say he is good, and his enemy evil. Furthermore, how do we know people are good or evil? By their actions, unless we claim some direct insight into their hearts, which will not work because everyone can claim such insight, and the insights will contradict each other. If the rule is "a good nation may attack an evil nation without any concrete evidence that it is threatened by that evil nation," what nation would admit to being evil, or what tribunal would be qualified to judge? On the other hand, the rule "attacking a nation without concrete evidence that that nation threatens you is an evil act" is capable, albeit with difficulty, of objective analysis.[7] It seems different rules for action by "the good" and "the bad" would not work. By the same token, it would be nice if we could say "democracies may attack tyrannies if they believe they are threatened, but not vice versa." But is such a rule at all practicable? Would Americans like to have a World Court of some kind adjudicating whether the U.S. Supreme Court made the right decision in its review of the Florida Supreme Court's decision about spoiled ballots in 2000, and therefore whether U.S. democratic bona fides were or were not in order? Or whether the existence of the Electoral College, or the Senate with its two votes for Wyoming and two votes for California, does not prove that "one person one vote" does not exist in the United States? Surely not, yet if Americans are unwilling to submit to an arbiter, how could the United States ask other nations to do so? As a matter of history, governments of countries with democratic forms have attacked other countries,[8] and committed atrocious brutalities against persons within their borders. Morality requires one set of rules for all countries, just as it requires one set of laws for all individuals in a country.

George Weigel appears to call for an international outlaw status, so to speak, for "rogue nations," such that they may be attacked at will if they do not bow to unspecified demands. As he put it in 2008 (slightly softening what he wrote in January 2003):

> New weapons capabilities and outlaw or rogue states require a development of the concept of defense-against-aggression. To take the obvious example: it makes little moral sense to suggest that the United States must wait until an enemy [originally: "a North Korea or Iraq or Iran"] actually launches a ballistic missile tipped with a nuclear, biological, or chemical weapon of mass destruction before the U.S. can, with moral legitimacy, do something about it. This instinctive moral intuition raises an important and delicate question: In the hands of certain kinds of states, does the possession of weapons of mass destruction constitute an aggression or, at the very least, an aggression-waiting-to-happen?[9]

Weigel's question above clearly invites a "yes" from the reader. In practice, this suggestion would justify "preventive war" as follows: Aggression constitutes permission under universally accepted international law, as well as almost every version of just war theory, for the aggressed-upon or any friendly nation to attack the aggressor. Thus, the suggestion that the possession of WMD by "rogue states" should be defined as aggression would be like the "Althing" in medieval Iceland proclaiming someone an outlaw—he could then be killed by anyone, without legal penalty. (Such outlaw status was usually the result of committing murder.) Under Weigel's plan, it would be "open season," all the time, for any nation that cared to hunt, on "rogue states." Unfortunately, rather than an objective definition of the term "rogue state," Weigel offered in the following paragraph only the idea that "This regime factor is crucial in the moral analysis, for weapons of mass destruction are clearly not aggressions-waiting-to-happen when they are possessed by stable, law-abiding states. No Frenchman goes to bed nervous about Great Britain's nuclear weapons . . . Every sane Israeli, Turk, or Bahraini, on the other hand, is deeply concerned about the possibility of an Iran [original: "Iraq or Iran"] with nuclear weapons and medium-range ballistic missiles."[10] Regardless of how many Turks and Bahrainis Weigel actually knows, and regardless of whether he is right about what Frenchmen and Turks and Israelis think, he is offering merely his own personal judgment of who is "sane," as well as of what states are "rogue," rather than attempting an objective definition. That is surely not acceptable for the definition of a key term in an important new development of a theory.

In addition, Weigel appears to offer a false dilemma here. There are surely many possible ways to differentiate between British nuclear weapons and North Korean ones short of stating that "the mere possession of weapons of mass destruction" by the latter would "constitute an aggression," or even, to quote another undefined term of Weigel's, "an aggression-waiting-to-happen." Nor, surely, is Weigel quite serious about his prescription: states, rogue or not, that actually have even minor armories of nuclear weapons have never in fact been attacked by the United States—precisely because of their possession of nuclear weapons. (North Korea is the latest evidence here. The differing U.S. treatment of Iraq and North Korea by the Bush administration can be interpreted as offering an ugly implicit lesson to the leaders of nations like Iran: get nuclear weapons, as insurance against attack.) Finally, like the Bush administration, Weigel is here lumping together possession of nuclear weapons with the possession, possibly, of very small numbers of chemical warheads. Having a handful of the latter, which might kill a few hundred or a thousand people if the wind were right, a number dwarfed by the number killed in a month of modern conventional warfare, would constitute "possession of WMDs."

Johnson would like to see just war theory evolve to accept preemptive attacks in certain cases. He writes: "I have gradually moved to the position that there is a serious case for preemption when an avowed enemy has WMD, and all other means of dealing with this threat offer no hope of removing him."[11] Johnson takes no note here of the fact that this proposed rule, had it been widely accepted, would have justified a preemptive strike either by the United States or by the Soviet Union against the other for a good thirty years. Nor does he note that the United States was an avowed enemy of Saddam, and the United States possessed WMD, and Saddam had no "other means of dealing with this threat" (of U.S. enmity and hostile actions). In other words, to put it in black and white, this proposed rule, as written, would have justified Saddam in preemptively striking the United States at any time during the 1990s or the early years of this century. Objectively speaking, there is a stronger case for considering the U.S. government "an avowed enemy" of Saddam's regime than vice versa. U.S. military forces repeatedly struck at Saddam's regime, on Iraqi soil, whereas Iraq never struck at U.S. forces, persons, or property on U.S. soil. In terms of verbal hostility, without attempting to weigh the two sides, it is clear that the U.S. government showed quite a bit of it to Saddam's regime. But Johnson, having noted his personal opinion on the case for preemption when "an avowed enemy" has WMD, immediately continues (with understatement): "But I think there is no moral consensus on this."

The statements above come near the conclusion of the section "Problems with the Focus on Preemption" of Johnson's book *The War to Oust Saddam Hussein*, written in 2005. This section follows a lengthy discussion of two pre-war critiques of the plan to attack Saddam's Iraq. (There is a longer discussion of this and some of Johnson's other thoughts on just war theory, in Chapter 11.) Johnson claimed that the "focus" on preemption "has been misguided":

> In the terms of moral analysis, the problem with an argument for preemption is centrally this: preemption is not inherently wrong or right, but it is extremely difficult to justify. For it to be justified, there must be a clear and present danger. While the administration and others favorable to the use of military force against Saddam Hussein's regime made a powerful case as to the danger itself, they did not demonstrate clearly, even with Secretary of State Colin Powell's forceful U.N. presentation, that the danger was present, in the sense of an attack definitely intended and in the process of preparation. We now know that the danger was not present, but again, the debate was about the prospect, and that is where moral decision has to take place. That the danger is present, as I suggested earlier, is hard to demonstrate in cases like this because the necessary knowledge may be available only through sensitive intelligence sources.[12]

It is not entirely clear, but it appears, based on the problems Johnson presents with the administration's case, that when he writes about the focus on preemption being misguided, he means it was misguided both in the writings and speeches of those in favor of the war and of those against it. For the first group, he believes the administration and its allies failed to show a "clear and present danger," rendering preemption difficult to use convincingly as justification. For the second group, Johnson believes preemption can play a legitimate part in a just war case, but only on conditions, and most anti-war writers apparently ignored those conditions, in his view. It would seem, though, that if an administration is campaigning for a war largely on the basis of an explicit doctrine of preemption, and failing to meet necessary conditions for preemption, it makes perfect sense for those opposed to the war to "focus" on that proposed ground of war, whether or not they did it well.

As noted in Chapter 2, the burden of proof is on those proposing war. Johnson implicitly admits this principle above by stating that preemption is only justified in the case of a clear and present danger, and that Secretary of State Powell did not demonstrate that the danger was present. The administration, in other words, failed to justify preemption in this case.

It is important to note, contra Johnson, that in the official case for war as made by the President and Secretary of State, preemption is not so much a "focus" as the lynchpin of the case, the piece that tied it together: Saddam's alleged possession of WMD plus his reckless and aggressive character plus his alleged support for terrorism equaled a future danger to the United States. There are always possible future dangers just about everywhere, but they are rarely said to provide an immediate cause for a just war. In this case, however, preemption of that future danger was given as the major justification of the war.

According to Johnson, then, just war theory allows preemption only on strict conditions of an attack "definitely intended and in the process of preparation." However, just war theory does imply deterrence. Since just war theory explicitly authorizes defensive wars, preparation for such wars is allowed if there is any danger that they will be necessary. Such preparation (think Switzerland before World War II) puts an enemy on notice that any attack will be costly at the least. Furthermore, since the theory authorizes war in other circumstances if the cause is just, preparations for such wars may also be justly made. Clearly this type of military preparedness, along with an announced willingness to overturn or punish an egregiously evil action, can function as a deterrent to obvious wrongdoing. (Nuclear deterrence is beyond the scope of this book, as it is not necessary for the discussion of whether the U.S. government acted justly in launching the Iraq war. Deterrence in general has a place within the bounds of just war theory, while preemption in general does not.)

To sum up: the usual statements justifying preemption of uncertain future threats, when generalized, end up justifying any nation attacking any other armed nation that dislikes it. As this is a recipe for endless war, it cannot be part of just war theory. Even a theorist who believes preemption can be legitimate under just war theory, such as Johnson, believes those making such a case must demonstrate that there is a "clear and present danger," in the sense of an attack "definitely intended and in the process of preparation," but neither the President nor the Secretary of State even claimed that was the case. The official Bush administration case for war hinged on preemption, but that preemption failed even the somewhat permissive just war reasoning of Johnson.

The Flawed Case for Enforcing UN Resolutions

The Bush administration's attempt to justify the invasion of Iraq under United Nations resolutions was, when examined in detail, seriously flawed. The President claimed that Resolutions 678 and 687 were not only "still in effect," but that "the United States and our allies are authorized to use force" under them "in ridding Iraq of weapons of mass destruction." A close examination will cast severe doubt on this case.

Bush's Appeal to UN Resolutions Concerned Legality, Not Justice

As Johnson notes (see Chapter 3), "The authorization to use force implies the ability to control and cease that use, that is, a well-constituted and efficient chain of command." Johnson states that the UN does not possess these attributes. Although Johnson clearly believes that the UN authorization was important in establishing that more than one country saw Iraq as an obstacle to justice and peace in the area, the implication of Johnson's words is that the UN cannot function properly as a sovereign authority that can authorize the use of force according to just war theory. If that is the case, then a UN resolution authorizing force can be legally relevant, but cannot in itself establish the justice of a decision to use force. Even if Johnson is not correct and the UN does possess sovereign authority, there is still a distinction to be noted between the legal force of a ruling and the justice of that ruling. We maintain this distinction when we speak of unjust laws (e.g., Jim Crow laws) or unjust rulings by courts (e.g., the *Dred Scott* decision).

The President's appeal was clearly to the legal authority UN resolutions convey, rather than to their moral force. Iraq, by signing the UN Charter, obliged itself to abide by the terms of the Charter, including acceptance of UN Security Council resolutions. Presumably, however, just as the United States reserves the right to self-defense, regardless of a hypothetical resolution that would deny it that right, Iraq also reserved the right to self-defense regardless of any resolution that could be interpreted to the contrary. If a hypothetical resolution called for the removal of a government, presumably the inherent right of each state to defend itself would trump any such resolution. Although it is not often noted, the resolutions of early 1991, beginning with Resolution 686, of March 2, regularly used the phrase "affirming the commitment of all Member States to the independence, sovereignty, and territorial integrity of Iraq and Kuwait," or similar language. No Security Council resolution ever authorized the removal of the government of Iraq.

Johnson states that the United States and the British see the United Nations within the common-law tradition, which

> influences the interpretation of what actually is the content of international law, including the status of the United Nations and . . . the black-letter provisions of the Charter. From this perspective . . . the United Nations is viewed as an organization of states that retain their sovereignty, not as a super-sovereign entity whose authority surpasses that of states, and the charter's treatment of the right of states to resort to armed force in Article 2 and Chapter VII . . . is understood through the prism of the sovereign state's right to protect its vital interests.[13]

If that is indeed the position of the U.S. government, then unless that government is explicitly hypocritical, that position acknowledges that the government of Iraq had these same rights, despite the plain "black-letter" meaning of resolutions to the contrary. (Johnson apparently uses an egregious double standard: Iraq may be held to the smallest jot and tittle of the "black-letter law" of resolutions, but the great powers like the United States are not bound even by the "black-letter" of the more fundamental rule of the Charter itself.)

While Iraq's UN membership obliged it to accept UN resolutions, in a similar way U.S. membership in the UN officially acknowledged the exclusive right of the UN Security Council to authorize the use of force, other than in self-defense. For the United States, as well as all UN member states, the Charter carries the force of a duly signed treaty, and has created the legal obligations as well as rights that any such treaty creates. (For the U.S., such a treaty is on the level of the Constitution itself, see Chapter 12.) It would be absurd for the United States to expect to exercise its rights under the Charter without acknowledging its obligations under the same Charter, including the obligation to interpret UN resolutions in an impartial manner. Analogously, a policeman may only enforce the law while operating under police department regulations. The moment a police officer tortures a suspect, or gives an order unconnected with the law, or interprets the law falsely, he is no longer "enforcing the law." The very law that gives him authority limits that authority.

What the Resolutions Authorized

In light of this, it is clear that any U.S. government justification of an action on the basis of UN resolutions could only have legal force if it was a legitimate interpretation of such resolutions in light of valid legal principles. To determine if this was the case, the language of the resolutions must be examined. The President claimed that two resolutions, UNSCR 678 of November 29, 1990, and Resolution 687 of April 3, 1991, were "still in effect."

Two Situations, Two Key Resolutions

Resolutions are often casually quoted without situating them in their contexts. But the context of statements is often crucial to their understanding. In this context, two very different situations led to two different UNSC resolutions:

Situation One (late 1990): Iraq has invaded Kuwait, and despite considerable efforts at a peaceful resolution of the situation, and many warnings from the U.S. government and from the Security Council, Iraq refuses to remove its forces from Kuwait.

Response One (November 29, 1990): The Security Council issues Resolution 678 (1990). In this resolution, it authorizes the use of force ("all necessary means") against Iraq, if Iraq does not take actions mandated in its resolutions beginning with Resolution 660 (1990), most importantly, withdrawal from Kuwait, adding "and to restore international peace and security in the area." It does not authorize the overthrow of Saddam's regime.

Situation Two (early 1991): Iraqi forces have been utterly defeated in Kuwait, and Iraqi infrastructure has been devastated by bombing by U.S.-led coalition forces. Iraq, acknowledging its defeat on the battlefield, has accepted a temporary battlefield cease-fire and indicated a willingness to comply with UN lutions.

Response Two (April 3, 1990): The Security Council issues Resolution 687 (1991), "affirming the commitment of all Member States to sovereignty, territorial integrity and political independence of Kuwait and Iraq," and laying down the conditions for a permanent cease-fire between Iraq and the "Member States cooperating with the government of Kuwait." These conditions include the earlier ones laid down in resolutions concerning Iraq and Kuwait after Resolution 660 (1990), and also many additional conditions, especially those related to the acknowledgment and destruction (under international supervision) of Iraq's WMD. There is no authorization of the use of force in this resolution. However, the Security Council, both by stating that it is acting under Chapter VII of the UN Charter, and by its statement that it "Decides to remain seized of the matter and to take such further steps as may be required for the implementation of the present resolution and to secure peace and security in the region" makes clear two things: one, that it can authorize the use of force again, if it so chooses due to an unacceptable degree of non-cooperation, and two, that it is the body authorized to take any such decisions. (Note: Chapter VII of the Charter includes language about the use of force, but also concerns non-military measures. Some writers have written as if a reference to Chapter VII points exclusively to the use of force, which is a false inference.)

Situation One never returned. Iraq did not invade Kuwait, nor any other country, after the authorization to use force was granted.

Situation Two also did not return. However, its aftermath continued until the U.S.-led invasion of early 2003. Throughout the interim period, there was partial Iraqi compliance with the second resolution noted above, Resolution 687 (1991), but that compliance was never and was never acknowledged to be complete. Nonetheless, it should be emphasized that the Security Council did not at the beginning of Situation Two, in Resolution 687 (1991), authorize the use of force to enforce that resolution, nor did it do so at any subsequent point. It reserved and often emphasized its right to do so, but never chose to exercise that right.

Major Purpose of 678 (1990): Driving Iraqi Forces from Kuwait

UNSCR 678 of November 29, 1990, authorized "member states cooperating with the government of Kuwait . . . to use all necessary means to uphold and implement resolution 660 (1990) and all subsequent relevant resolutions and to restore international peace and security in the area." The forces of the United States and its allies then drove Saddam's forces out of Kuwait in early 1991. The UN Security Council clearly believed that the major actions called for in UNSCR 678 had been accomplished when on April 3, 1991, after Saddam's forces were expelled from Kuwait, it passed Resolution 687. That resolution begins by "welcoming the restoration to Kuwait of its sovereignty, independence, and territorial integrity and the return of its legitimate government."

Resolution 678 also called for the "Member States cooperating with the Government of Kuwait" to "restore international peace and security in the area." The cease-fire resolution, 687 of 1991, did not state that it had been restored, rather that the Council was "bearing in mind its objective of restoring international peace and security in the area as set out in its recent resolutions." However, it is clear from the actions of all concerned that the major part of this restoration had been accomplished with the defeat of Iraqi forces and their removal from Kuwait. If that were not the case, there would have been no reason to accept a cease-fire in the field between coalition forces and Iraq, something done by General Schwarzkopf with U.S. government approval, and without any complaint from the Security Council.

It is immediately clear, then, that the earlier resolution, 678 of 1990, was at least in part no longer "in effect" as early as April 3, 1991, because the major purpose of the resolution, that of "restor[ing] to Kuwait . . . its sovereignty, independence, and territorial integrity and the return of its legitimate government" had been accomplished, and no further use of force was needed to achieve it. This was by far the most important demand of the group of resolutions cited in Resolution 678 ("resolution 660 (1990) and all subsequent relevant resolutions" concerning Iraq's occupation of Kuwait—see Objection 1 in this chapter for a list of those resolutions and summaries of what they called for). In the paragraph of Resolution 678 that authorized the use of force, the authorization is "to uphold and implement resolution 660 (1990) and all subsequent relevant resolutions and to restore international peace and security in the area." The emphasis is on Resolution 660 and international peace and security. The demand in Resolution 660 is "that Iraq withdraw immediately and unconditionally all its forces to the positions in which they were located on 1 August 1990." Looking at the other demands in those resolutions, which are not even mentioned individually in Resolution 678, it is difficult to believe the Security Council would have authorized the use of force to enforce any of them. To repeat, the enforcement of Resolution 660 and the major part of the "restoration of international peace and security in the area" had been accomplished by April 3, 1991.

Resolution 687, in a New Situation, Created a Formal Cease-Fire

After welcoming the restoration of Kuwait's sovereignty and independence, Resolution 687 goes on to repeat demands for compliance with some of the previous resolutions not yet fully enforced, and to add some new and different demands.

Three things need to be emphasized here. First, Paragraph 33 of the resolution states that upon Iraq's notification to the Council of its acceptance of the resolution's provisions, a formal cease-fire "is effective between Iraq and Kuwait and the Member States cooperating with Kuwait in accordance with resolution 678 (1990)." In other words, with Iraq's formal acceptance of the resolution, the hostilities are formally proclaimed to be over. Thus, with Resolution 687, the UN (with full U.S. government concurrence) formally proclaimed the end of fighting between Iraq and the countries that had undertaken to forcefully end its occupation of Kuwait. Before the cease-fire, the states fighting to reverse the occupation of Kuwait were entitled to continue fighting until the goals of the UN resolutions were achieved, without any further input from the Security Council. But the cease-fire put a formal end to that earlier authorization (in Resolution 678 of 1990) to begin or continue that fighting. That is not to say that the authorization could not be revived, but a formal cease-fire by definition suspends earlier authorizations to use force, with the expectation and hope that these will not be revived. The governments of the United States and its allies took their authorization to use force against Iraq from the Security Council: that authorization was no longer in force, because a cease-fire was in effect.

Resolution 687 Made No Provision for the Use of Force

Second, while the Security Council noted in both the earlier resolution, 678 of 1990, and in resolution 687 of 1991, that it was acting under Chapter VII of the UN Charter, entitled "Action with respect to threats to the peace, breaches of the peace, and acts of aggression," the cease-fire resolution, 687 of 1991, makes no provision whatsoever for the use of force against Iraq by any member state, either for the new demands it contains or for the earlier demands it repeats. Provisions for the use of force, which are exceptional by nature, need to be explicit, as was the case in Resolution 678.

The statement that the Council was acting under Chapter VII when it passed Resolution 687 indicates the continuing gravity of the situation as perceived by the Council: the situation had not yet been completely "put right." But that statement does not indicate the Council's wishes as to how possible non-compliance would be addressed. Note that Article 39 of Chapter VII states, in full, that "The Security Council shall determine the existence of any threat to the peace, breach of the peace, or act of aggression and shall make recommendations, or decide what measures shall be taken in accordance with Articles 41 and 42, to maintain or restore international peace and security." Thus, a variety of measures are possible under Chapter VII, and it is up to the Security Council to decide what those might be. Chapter VII continues with Article 40 and 41:

Article 40
    In order to prevent an aggravation of the situation, the Security Council may, before making the recommendations or deciding upon the measures provided for in Article 39, call upon the parties concerned to comply with such provisional measures as it deems necessary or desirable. Such provisional measures shall be without prejudice to the rights, claims, or position of the parties concerned. The Security Council shall duly take account of failure to comply with such provisional measures.

Article 41
    The Security Council may decide what measures not involving the use of armed force are to be employed to give effect to its decisions, and it may call upon the Members of the United Nations to apply such measures. These may include complete or partial interruption of economic relations and of rail, sea,

air, postal, telegraphic, radio, and other means of communication, and the severance of diplomatic relations.

Only with Article 42 does Chapter VII go on to discuss measures using armed force. Thus it should be absolutely clear that for the Security Council to state that it is acting under Chapter VII is not in itself in any way an authorization to use force.

687 Stated That the Security Council Would Deal with Violations

Third, Paragraph 34 states that the Council "decides to remain seized of the matter and to take such further steps as may be required for the implementation of the present resolution and to secure peace and security in the region." In other words, this last sentence shows that the Council decided to continue to follow the issue and to take further decisions as it saw fit. Truces do not always last, and if one side or the other violates them seriously, responses are necessary. Some violations are more serious than others. However, violations of a cease-fire agreement are not generally held to plunge the parties automatically back into conflict, any more than violations of a treaty are automatic causes for war. In either case, mechanisms are often in effect for dealing with such problems without resorting to the use of force. In the case of this cease-fire, the resolution itself established that mechanism: the Security Council itself would consider the matter, decide what to do, and take further steps as it deemed necessary and appropriate. By proclaiming a cease-fire between "Iraq and Kuwait and the Member States cooperating with Kuwait," Resolution 687 created obligations on the U.S. government and the coalition it led as much as it created obligations for Saddam and his government. One of those obligations on the U.S. government was to bring cease-fire violations to the attention of the Council, and, clearly enough, to abide by any resulting decision of the Council.

More Evidence That Any Decision Was for the Security Council

It is obvious enough that Resolution 687 (of 1991) left the decision as to what possible "further steps" might be needed with the Council, not with any member state, not only from the dispute resolution mechanism built into 687, but from the very nature of the case. A body that can take a decision is inherently qualified and empowered to decide whether the decision is being properly enforced, unless there is a higher body empowered to oversee it, or unless it delegates that power to some other group or person. Consider a legislature, or a board of directors, or a high court. When any of these makes a decision, except in the case of one of the exceptions mentioned above, the body that made the decision has the right to consider whether to revisit it, and no member of that body has the right to speak for the entire body, or interpret the will of that body on its own. If an individual Senator decides that a Senate decision is not being honored, or a board member tells the world on her own authority that the board is being thwarted, or if one Justice says the Supreme Court's decision in a case is not being enforced, these members clearly do not have the authority of the bodies of which they are part. The United States, as a single "Member State," had no credible claim to be a higher body than the UN Security Council, nor had the Security Council delegated its authority to the U.S. government, nor could the U.S. government speak on behalf of the UN, or judge with the UN's authority whether a decision was being implemented or not. Imagine, for example, a case in which Russia or China decided that UNSCR 242 (November, 1967), which "*emphasiz[es]* the inadmissibility of the acquisition of territory by war," and calls for "withdrawal of Israel armed forces from territories occupied in the recent conflict,"[14] was not being fulfilled and that Russia or China must enforce it. Not only would the Russian or Chinese interpretation be hotly denied, but the argument made above would be forcefully brought into play: a Member State has no right to enforce UNSCRs unless invited explicitly (as in Resolution 678) to do so. The Bush administration had every right to an opinion on whether UN resolutions were being honored or flouted, and to decide on its own what to do about that (consistent with its own treaty obligations under the Charter), but no legal (or logical) right to make any judgment on behalf of the UN on the issue.

In addition, the language of Chapter VII, the legal authority of which Resolutions 678 and 687 claim, reinforces the fact that both the determination and the authorization of further steps rests with the Council, not the member states. As quoted above, Article 39 of Chapter VII reads: "The Security Council shall determine the existence of any threat to the peace, or act of aggression and shall make recommendations, or decide what measures shall be taken in accordance with Articles 41 [non-military measures] and 42 [military measures], to maintain or restore international peace and security." These powers, to determine the existence of a threat and decide how to meet it, are fundamental to the Council itself as defined in the Charter, which the United States and all other members signed when they joined the United Nations. Any action taken by a member state without Security Council authorization, regardless of any claim to be "enforcing UN resolutions," clearly lacked the legal authority of the UN. If the Bush administration believed that Saddam's failure or alleged failure to comply with any provisions of the cease-fire instrument (Resolution 687) constituted a threat to "international peace and security," then according to the Charter, which the United States signed, it was the responsibility of the Council, not of any member state, including the United States, to "decide what measures [should] be taken."

The purposes of Resolution 678 of 1990, which authorized the use of force against Saddam's regime, were fundamentally accomplished by the liberation of Kuwait from Saddam's forces (even if additional demands were placed on the regime by this resolution and the subsequent Resolution 687). The Security Council authorized the use of force for a specific purpose: that purpose accomplished, the Security Council announced that a formal cease-fire was in effect. The Security Council's authorization to use force was then no longer in effect, and could only be renewed by the Security Council.

In conclusion, neither of the two resolutions cited by the President remained fully in effect (despite the fact that the obligations on Saddam's regime laid out in them had not been lifted, nor proclaimed to be fulfilled), and the limited authorization in one of the two resolutions to use force had expired. The authorization in Resolution 678 (1990) of "member states cooperating with the government of Kuwait . . . to use all necessary means to uphold and implement resolution 660 (1990) and all subsequent relevant resolutions and to restore international peace and security in the area," which called especially for the expulsion of Iraqi forces from Kuwait, expired with the cease-fire proclaimed in the second of the two resolutions, 687 of 1991. (With the U.S. and coalition forces militarily beyond challenge, the Security Council would surely not have called for a cease-fire if the major purposes for which it called for the use of force had not been accomplished.) While the latter resolution laid many obligations on Saddam's regime, some of which it failed to fulfill in subsequent months and years, (1) the Council did not authorize the use of force to ensure their fulfillment, and (2) the determination of what "further steps" needed to be taken in accordance with that resolution, as well as the authorization of those steps, remained (a) according to the language of the resolutions themselves (approved by the U.S. government), (b) by the nature of the case, and (c) under the UN Charter (signed by the United States), the responsibility of the Security Council, not of any other body or person. Even if the Bush administration claimed authority under the UN resolutions, it would clearly not want this kind of enforcement authority to be assumed by any other power, demonstrating that it does not believe there is a general rule in favor of this kind of enforcement. The President had no legitimate legal claim to be enforcing these UN resolutions.

"Building a New Iraq" Was Unlikely to Succeed

The belief that the United States would be in a good position to help Iraqis "build a new Iraq" after removing its government by force rested on culpable ignorance of well-known facts concerning Iraq's people, history, and culture. This assertion will be supported in some detail in subsequent chapters, especially in Chapter 10, "Reasonable Chance of Success." Here are a few of the relevant, well-known facts. First, invasions of countries with sharply different cultures from those of the invader, however well-meaning the invaders claim to be, have a history of leading, often, to bitter insurgencies. In the twentieth century, the British occupation of Iraq after World War I, the Israeli invasion of Lebanon in 1982, and the U.S. invasion of the Philippines at the beginning of the century spring to mind, but there are numerous other examples. The idea that Iraq as a whole would quietly accept being ruled by foreigners for an indeterminate length of time ran counter to its history and culture.

Second, Iraq's internal divisions made it difficult even to envisage a workable and democratic system of government for the country, much less put one into place. George H. W. Bush (president from 1989 to 1993), in his book written with his National Security Advisor Brent Scowcroft, *A World Transformed*, mentioned Iraq's division into "the Shiites in the south and the Kurds in the north . . . [and] the Sunni population of central Iraq."[15] Bush and Scowcroft did not mention in that passage that the Sunni Arabs, a small minority, have been the dominant group in Iraq for hundreds of years, but they did not need to: it is well known among those with a smattering of knowledge of Iraq and its history. After discussing their desire not to see Iraq broken up, they go on in the same passage to assert: "Had we gone the invasion route, the United States could conceivably still be an occupying power in a bitterly hostile land."[16] They seemed to see the state of Iraq as a kind of Humpty-Dumpty that they didn't want to break for fear of having to shoulder the impossible responsibility of putting it back together again—or running away and leaving chaos. The fear that Iraq, with its deep fault lines, would not be easy to hold together was an obvious one that experts often expressed, even if officials from the administration of the second President Bush and think-tank gurus claiming to be Iraq experts often lightly glossed over the notion. A real expert on a country, at a minimum, speaks the language of the people involved and has spent some time living among them. The administration was responsible for finding such real experts and at the least listening seriously to their advice.

OBJECTIONS

Objection One: The Word "Subsequent" in UNSCR 678

Objection: As Pollack wrote in *The Threatening Storm*:

> Some nations argue that . . . resolution [678]'s reference to "all subsequent relevant resolutions" meant only those on the books prior to the passage of 678. However, the United States has employed a more literal interpretation—namely any resolution regarding Kuwait passed after, and derived from, its actions during and after the invasion of Kuwait. We are also not the only nation that subscribes to this interpretation.[17]

Pollack was stating that the authorization to use force in Resolution 678 of 1990 was not only for the purpose of removing Iraqi forces from Kuwait, but to allow the enforcement of resolutions not only subsequent to Resolution 660 of 1990, but of those passed after the war, such as Resolution 687 itself, with its calls for Iraq to declare and destroy its WMD, and Resolution 688 of April 5, 1991, which condemned "the repression of the Iraqi civilian population in many parts of Iraq" and demanded that Iraq "immediately end this repression."

Reply: As of the passage of Resolution 678 on November 29, 1990, the already existing resolutions "subsequent" to 660 (which was passed August 2, 1990) and "relevant" to it were the following (all labeled "Iraq—Kuwait"[18]):

- 661 (August 6): imposes a trade and financial dealings ban on Iraq;
- 662 (August 9): responding to Iraq's official annexation of Kuwait, calls on member states and international organizations not to do anything that would lend support to that action;

- 664 (August 18): demands that Iraq allow the departure of "third country nationals" from Kuwait, and ensure they are not harmed;
- 665 (August 25): calls on States "cooperating with Kuwait" with naval forces in the area to help halt all shipping to and from Iraq, except humanitarian supplies;
- 666 (September 13): goes into more detail on the trade embargo and humanitarian issues;
- 667 (September 16): (acting under Chapter VII of the UN Charter) condemns Iraqi incursions into diplomatic premises in Kuwait, and repeats the demands in 664;
- 669 (September 24): passes to a committee the task of looking into requests for economic assistance related to Iraq's invasion of Kuwait;
- 670 (September 25): reaffirms earlier resolutions, and calls on all states to prevent air traffic (other than humanitarian) between Iraq and other countries;
- 674 (October 29): condemns the taking of hostages by Iraqi forces;
- 677 (November 28): condemns "attempts by Iraq to alter the demographic composition of Kuwait and to destroy civil records" there.

One thing is certain: when Resolution 678 referred to "all subsequent relevant resolutions" it referred to those on this list, for they were both "subsequent" to 660, and relevant to Iraq. The claim that 678 referred in addition to future resolutions not in existence at that time, which might or might not be passed, containing language that the nations approving 678 had never seen, is a dubious one. This is especially plain given the gravity of any resolution authorizing the use of force. Is it likely that members of the Security Council meant to write a blank check for any nation to go to war at will to enforce future, unwritten resolutions, resolutions that would be passed in many cases by other nations (since the non-permanent members of the Security Council would rotate out of it)? This seems unlikely, to say the least. (It is hard to imagine any U.S. administration, or indeed any government, knowingly voting for a resolution that would authorize other nations to use force, in an unlimited time frame, based on unknown future resolutions.) It is a general principle of legal interpretation to prefer the clear and straightforward interpretation over the unclear, strained, or merely possible interpretation.

But if all this were not enough, consider the use of "subsequent" in the preceding paragraph in the resolution. Pollack is quoting paragraph 2, which "authorizes Member States co-operating with the Government of Kuwait, unless Iraq on or before 15 January 1991 fully implements . . . the above-mentioned resolutions, to use all necessary means to uphold and implement resolution 660 (1990) and all subsequent relevant resolutions and to restore international peace and security in the area." But the preceding paragraph also uses the same phrase: "1. [The Security Council] *Demands* that Iraq comply fully with resolution 660 (1990) and all subsequent relevant resolutions, and decides, while maintaining all its decisions, to allow Iraq one final opportunity, as a pause of good will, to do so." In other words, the Council called on Iraq to comply, during a "final opportunity," a mere "pause" (between November 29, 1990 and January 15, 1991), to comply with "resolution 660 and all subsequent relevant resolutions." (No "Iraq-Kuwait" resolutions between 678 and the start of the war are shown on the UN website list of Security Council resolutions.) The fact that the Council demanded that Iraq comply in a mere six weeks with the "subsequent" resolutions or face war, and passed no more resolutions before the war began, appears to demonstrate rather conclusively that the intended reference was to the resolutions between 660 and 678 of 1990—to call on Iraq to comply immediately with resolutions that had not yet been passed would have been absurd. Since the same phrase is used in paragraph 2, which authorizes the use of force, it seems that the same interpretation applies in both paragraphs.

Note that Resolution 678 called almost exclusively, when the list of resolutions between 660 and 678 is carefully considered, for the withdrawal of Iraqi forces from Kuwait and the reversal of that immediate situation. It is this limited set of demands that the various members of the Security Council, after careful consideration, judged worthy of an "all means necessary" permission to "the Member States cooperating with Kuwait," the authorization to use force. For all the additional demands placed on Iraq by the Security Council after 678, including 687 and 688 (and 688, issued just two days after 687, did not even mention "acting under Chapter VII"), no such permission was granted. The logical conclusion is that the Security Council members who authorized these other demands saw them as so much less grave than the demand to reverse the invasion and annexation of Kuwait that they did not wish to authorize the use of force in order to reverse them.

Objection Two: Saddam's Truce Violations

Objection: In *The War to Oust Saddam Hussein*, Johnson writes: "In terms of the law of war, deliberate breaking of the terms of a truce reopened the conflict again at the point at which the truce was made, and gave the belligerent who was wronged the rights he had up to the point the truce was signed." Johnson believes that since Saddam broke the truce by repeatedly violating the terms of Resolution 687, this "justified resumed military action against the regime itself"[19] (although Johnson does not state by whom).

Reply: The main problem with this argument is that according to Resolution 687 the formal cease-fire was declared, not by Saddam's regime on the one hand and the U.S. government and its coalition on the other, but by Saddam's regime and the Security Council. The U.S. government and its allies took action against Saddam's regime under Security Council authorization (an authorization granted with heavy U.S. government involvement, and full U.S. government concurrence). And, it was the Security Council (again with U.S. government concurrence) that laid down the conditions for a cease-fire and declared that the cease-fire was in place. Thus, if truce-breaking justified "resumed military action," it was the Security Council's right, both as the party under the authorization of which the war was begun and as the party that proclaimed the truce, to make that decision. Furthermore, Johnson's phrase "the belligerent that was wronged" appears to miss an important point. Kuwait was hardly a belligerent, and the United States was not attacked by Saddam. As the parties themselves expressed the issue at the time, the wronged party was, in addition to Kuwait, the world community of nations, as represented by the Security Council. The Security Council never delegated to any U.S. administration the authority to determine on its behalf whether Saddam was in compliance with the cease-fire terms. On the contrary, with U.S. government concurrence, the Council clearly claimed that responsibility for itself.

A second problem with Johnson's argument is that the United States itself broke "the terms of the truce" almost immediately after it was declared, and went on doing so. Secretary of State James Baker, in testimony to the U.S. Congress on May 23, 1991, "stated as official policy that economic sanctions against Iraq would not be lifted, regardless of Iraq's compliance with its disarmament obligation, a policy which was in direct opposition to the letter and intent of resolution 687."[20] Through Baker's statement the U.S. government, although it had voted for the cease-fire, declared its intention not to comply with its terms less than two months later, and in fact prevented the UN from doing so. Even more gravely, without any authorization from the Council it claimed to be representing, and in complete violation of the agreed cease-fire, the U.S. government attempted several times, starting as early as 1992, to overthrow the regime through covert means.[21] The U.S. government also apparently used intelligence gathered by the UN weapons inspectors to guide its "Desert Fox" bombing campaign against Saddam's regime in 1998, a clear violation of the terms of the inspections laid out by the UN.[22] If the truce included the United States (and Johnson clearly thinks so), it is hard to see these multiple belligerent actions, none of them authorized by the UN, as other than truce-breaking.

Objection Three: Objectives of UNSCR 678 Were Never Met

Objection: As noted, UNSCR 678 (dated November 29, 1990) authorized "member states cooperating with the government of Kuwait . . . to use all necessary means to uphold and implement resolution 660 (1990) and all subsequent relevant resolutions and to restore international peace and security in the area." Granting for the sake of argument the interpretation here of "subsequent," it is still clear that, contrary to his agreement when he accepted UNSCR 687, Saddam remained a threat to "international peace and security in the area." Thus, force remained authorized to deal with that threat.

Reply: This objection is a subset of the objection above. In addition to the reply to that objection, consider the evidence in this chapter in the section "The Flawed Case for Enforcing UN Resolutions," that the authorization to use force was ended by the entering into force of the formal cease-fire. Despite the Security Council's concern that "international peace and security in the area" had not been fully restored, it would not have proclaimed a cease-fire without the belief that the major steps toward restoring that peace and security had been taken. That would have been absurd. The cease-fire resolution (687) did not make any provision for the use of force to impose the will of the Council on Saddam's regime, although it reserved the possibility of such future action (to itself) by acting under Chapter VII of the Charter. There are many parts of the world where international peace and security are not fully in effect, but, as Article 39 of Chapter VII points out, "The Security Council shall determine the existence of any threat to the peace, or act of aggression and shall make recommendations, or decide what measures shall be taken in accordance with Articles 41 [non-military measures] and 42 [military measures], to maintain or restore international peace and security."

With the formal cease-fire's entry into force, the claim of one country or a group of countries to be acting to enforce a prior resolution already dealt with by the Security Council could not legitimately claim the authority of the Security Council, which instead (with the concurrence of the U.S. government) had mandated a mechanism for dealing with violations: the Security Council itself would meet and act, in accord with its own wishes. While the UN actions or failures to act as the U.S. government wished were often distasteful to U.S. administrations, the decisions to sign the UN Charter, and in this case the additional decision to respond to the invasion of Kuwait in the UN framework, bound the United States (except in the case of clear self-defense) to abide by subsequent UN decisions.

Objection Four: Respect for the International Community

Objection: Saddam had defied the international community for over a decade, and failure to stop this defiance would have destroyed respect for the international community. As U.S. Permanent Representative to the UN at the time John Negroponte said to the Security Council on February 24, 2003:

Nearly 12 years ago, the Security Council passed Resolution 687. This resolution stated that Iraq continued to pose a threat to international peace and security at the close of the Gulf War and laid out a number of conditions intended to ensure that Iraq could no longer pose such a threat. Among its other provisions, Resolution 687 laid down a 45-day timeline for Iraq to disarm. Iraqi disarmament is now 4225 days overdue. Last November, this Council passed Resolution 1441, giving Iraq a final opportunity to comply. Regrettably, today, the story is still the same: No truth, no real cooperation, and most importantly, no disarmament.

We cannot allow ourselves to return to business-as-usual on Iraq. Over the past 13 years, a pattern has emerged. Each time that there is a renewed acknowledgment that a non-compliant Iraq poses a threat, political or military pressure mounts. The Council then calls on Iraq to disarm. Iraq offers minimal signs of cooperation on process until the political pressure subsides and then returns to its standard operating procedures of non-compliance and non-cooperation. Unfortunately, to anyone familiar with the Security Council debates of the 1990s on Iraq, the discussions we have had over the past several weeks sound terribly familiar. . . .

Iraq has also failed to cooperate fully and actively with the inspectors. Iraq has not accounted for biological and chemical materials that we know they had. And it declined to cooperate adequately or fully on interviews. It never showed the kind of active cooperation this Council demanded in 1441—the kind that is absolutely necessary to verify disarmament. We concluded, therefore, that Iraq was yet in further material breach of resolution 1441. . . .

Knowing as we do that what we have seen from Iraq is not active cooperation or compliance, let me cite just a few examples of Iraq's failures to comply with operative paragraphs of Resolution 1441:

- OP3—Iraq's December 7 Declaration was not currently accurate, full, or complete.

- OP5—Iraq has failed to allow all persons to be interviewed in the mode of UNMOVIC or the IAEA's choice.

- OP7—Iraq has failed to provide adequate lists of names of all personnel currently and formerly associated with Iraq's WMD programs.

- OP9—Iraq has failed to cooperate actively with UNMOVIC and the IAEA.[23]

Reply: Ambassador Negroponte's speech was given during the U.S./UK attempt to have the Security Council pass a second resolution with a "trigger," something similar to Resolution 678 (1990) that would obviously and automatically authorize the use of force in the absence of complete Iraqi compliance. The speech is reasonably accurate in what it says. What it leaves out is important, and the nations that refused to go along with the proposed resolution were well aware of it: the context of Iraqi non-cooperation, the imperfect but considerable cooperation Iraq did offer, and the lack of tangible evidence for the strongest claim the U.S. and UK governments were making: continued possession of WMD and a WMD program. "No truth, no real cooperation, and most importantly, no disarmament" was quite an inaccurate summary even based on what could be demonstrated at the time: there was a great deal of truth and cooperation from Iraq, even if imperfect, and the charge "no disarmament," in the light of the failure of weapons inspectors to find WMD over a decade, was simply baseless.

But all that is to some extent beside the point of this objection, which is about respect for the international community. That respect can only be based on the just rules of the community and their just execution. The nations that signed the UN Charter are the international community. The UN has its rules, which the United States helped establish. No U.S. administration can claim to enforce those rules on others while violating them itself and hope to see respect for the international community grow. What it loses by that kind of behavior is more fundamental: the respect of others. A police chief who sets aside the law in his eagerness to "get the criminals" becomes a law-breaker by doing so, and the purpose of respect for the law is lost.

Objection Five: The Legal Case for a Legal War

Objection: This claim that the UN resolutions do not provide a legal basis for war is contradicted by four legal experts at least. Attorney General Lord (Peter) Goldsmith of the United Kingdom presented an opinion to Parliament on March 17, 2003, that the war was legal in terms of international law. A similar argument was made by Christopher Greenwood, Professor of International Law at the London School of Economics and Political Science, in an article published in the *San Diego International Law Journal* in 2003. William H. Taft IV and Todd Buchwald, in an article published in July 2003 in the *American Journal of International Law*, also argued in favor of the war's legality. Mr. Taft was then the Legal Adviser of the United States Department of State; Mr. Buchwald was then Assistant Legal Adviser for Political-Military Affairs of the United States Department of State.

Reply: The arguments of these men are important enough that they must be considered in detail in the following chapter. When that is done, it can be seen that their arguments do not refute the arguments presented in this chapter.

NOTES

1. Bush, "The War Begins," in *Iraq War Reader*, 503-4.
2. Neuhaus, "The Sounds of Religion," 79.
3. Bush, "The War Begins," in *Iraq War Reader*, 503-4.
4. Quoted in Jonathan Schell, "Pre-Emptive Defeat, Or How Not to Fight Proliferation," March 3, 2003, quoted in *Iraq War Reader*, 506 (the article originally appeared in *The Nation* as "The Case Against the War" on the date cited).
5. Bush, "Remarks at West Point: 'New Threats Require New Thinking,'" June 1, 2002, in *Iraq War Reader*, 268.
6. Saddam Hussein (Interview with Tony Benn), "Iraq Has No Interest in War," February 4, 2003, in *Iraq War Reader*, 464 (originally broadcast through the auspices of Associated Press Television News).
7. It might be objected that the Bush administration and its backers claimed that the United States was threatened by Saddam's Iraq, while others disagreed. Not so: the President said the United States could not wait for "the threat" to fully materialize. By so saying, he admitted that the threat was not yet a reality. Colin Powell made the same claim in his UN presentation, quoted above, with the same clear implication: "Given [his] history of aggression, given what we know of his grandiose plans, given what we know of his terrorist associations and given his determination to exact revenge on those who oppose him, should we take the risk that he will not *some day* [emphasis added] use these weapons at a time and the place and in a manner of his choosing at a time when the world is in a much weaker position to respond?"
8. See Pat Buchanan, "The Democracy Worshipper," *LewRockwell.com*, June 20, 2007, http://www.lewrockwell.com/buchanan/buchanan60.html (accessed October 10,

2007).

9. Weigel, *Against the Grain*, 216. The essay quoted originally appeared as "Moral Clarity in a Time of War" in the January 2003 issue of *First Things*.

10. Weigel, *Against the Grain*, 216.

11. Johnson, *War to Oust*, 53.

12. Johnson, *War to Oust*, 51. It seems to me that Johnson's last remark is naive. If "sensitive intelligence sources" had really shown with any degree of certainty that the United States had been facing a clear and present danger, then as Jacob Hornberger pointed out (see Chapter 4, the section "Circumstantial Evidence for Doubting the Administration's Case"), it is extremely difficult to believe the U.S. government would have spent months trying to convince anyone else of that fact—it would have acted. Furthermore, if one is about to embark on a war, the "sensitive intelligence sources" are likely to be irrelevant for the future: highly placed double agents of Saddam, for example, would have no function after Saddam's overthrow. As far as technical sources go, Powell's UN testimony revealed clearly that U.S. intelligence agencies could listen in on conversations among Iraqi officers, and take satellite photographs of government installations (not that this should have surprised anyone). Johnson implies that human intelligence sources in need of protection will be needed to make a case, but he glides over the danger of sloppy or even fudged or manipulated intelligence addressed in Chapter 4, Objection 4. This latter danger always exists, which is one reason for my proposed rule in Chapter 2, IJWP 6: "Secret Justifications for War are Unacceptable."

13. Johnson, *War to Oust*, 127. At one point in this book (p. 63), Johnson writes that "[a]ccording to the older, moral understanding of sovereignty, though, [Saddam] forfeited the right to sovereign immunity and, indeed, the right to govern Iraq with his tyrannical exercise of government. In this conception, his crimes meant he could rightly be deposed." Unfortunately, Johnson never defines tyranny in any objective way, nor does he state where the authority resides to declare a government a "tyranny." Without a definition and an authority, how would one even begin to apply such an idea? Johnson gives a wide range of examples on the same page, from the removal of Pol Pot to the removal of Manuel Noriega. These examples all appear to be normative for Johnson, although I do not see that Johnson states this clearly at any point. He apparently assumes that all sane people are in agreement concerning which nations are tyrannies and which are not. Yet few nations (or perhaps none) are willing to give the blank check of approval in advance to the United States, or any other nation, to remove whatever governments the U.S. government may perceive as tyrannies.

14. "UN Security Council Resolution 242," November 22, 1967, http://www.un.org/documents/sc/res/1967/scres67.htm (accessed October 19, 2007).

15. George (H.W.) Bush and Brent Scowcroft, "Why We Didn't Go to Baghdad," in *Iraq War Reader*, 101 (article excerpted from their 1998 book *A World Transformed*).

16. Bush and Scowcroft, "Why We Didn't Go to Baghdad," 102.

17. Pollack, *Threatening Storm*, 369.

18. "Security Council Resolutions – 1990," *UN.org*, http://www.un.org/Docs/scres/1990/scres90.htm (accessed August 27, 2007).

19. Johnson, *War to Oust*, 56.

20. Ritter, *Iraq Confidential*, 5. See also Martin Fletcher and Michael Theodoulou, "Baker Says Sanctions Must Stay as Long as Saddam Holds Power," *The Times* [UK], May 23, 1991, http://globalpolicy.igc.org/security/issues/iraq/history/1991baker.htm (accessed October 3, 2007).

21. See Pollack, *Threatening Storm*, 287. (U.S. government coup plotting starts in 1992. For the 1996 coup attempt, see p. 79.) See also Ritter, *Iraq Confidential*, 162-69.

22. Susan Wright, "The Hijacking of UNSCOM," *Iraq War Reader*, 188. (The article was originally published in 1999.) The U.S. government also apparently attempted to use inspectors to provoke Iraq into action that would justify a military strike in 1996, see Ritter, *Iraq Confidential*, 153.

23. John Negroponte, "Negroponte Urges Prompt Adoption of New Iraq Resolution," 24 February 2003, http://www.globalsecurity.org/wmd/library/news/iraq/2003/Iraq -030224-usia10.htm (accessed December 22, 2007).

Chapter Six

Just Cause III:
The Legal Case

The present writer believes that those governments who resorted to force were right to conclude that they could rely on the authorization of military action in resolution 678, read together with resolutions 687 and 1441.

–Christopher Greenwood, "International law and the pre–emptive use of force"[1]

Yes, I have indicated it is not in conformity with the UN Charter, from our point of view and from the Charter point of view it was illegal.

—Kofi Annan, "Excerpts, Annan Interview"[2]

Introduction:

As noted in the preceding chapter, at least four well-qualified legal experts have argued that the UN resolutions provided a legal basis for war against Iraq. These four wrote extensively in defense of the claim that the war was a legal one, and their opinions may stand for those of others. Attorney General Lord (Peter) Goldsmith of the United Kingdom presented an opinion to Parliament on March 17, 2003, that the war was legal in terms of international law. A similar argument was made by Christopher Greenwood, Professor of International Law at the London School of Economics and Political Science, in an article published in the San Diego International Law Journal in 2003.[3] William H. Taft IV and Todd Buchwald, in an article published in July 2003 in the American Journal of International Law, also argued in favor of the war's legality.[4] Mr. Taft was then the Legal Adviser of the United States Department of State; Mr. Buchwald was then Assistant Legal Adviser for Political-Military Affairs of the United States Department of State.

In this chapter, the case made by these men will be examined. The three arguments will be outlined individually and then, because there is so much over-lap among them, the response will deal with all three together.

Goldsmith's Arguments:

Greenwood supplements Goldsmith's brief, March 17, 2003, statement with "a longer paper on the legal basis for action sent by the Secretary of State for Foreign and Commonwealth Affairs to the Foreign Affairs Committee of the House of Commons."[5] Two paragraphs from that longer paper are particularly relevant:

> 5. SCR 687 did not repeal the authorisation to use force in paragraph 2 of SCR 678. On the contrary, it confirmed that SCR 678 remained in force. The authorisation was suspended for so long as Iraq complied with the conditions of the ceasefire. But the authorisation could be revived if the Council determined that Iraq was acting in material breach of the requirements of SCR 687. Although almost twelve years have elapsed since SCR 687 was adopted, Iraq has never taken the steps required of it by the Council. Throughout that period the Council has repeatedly condemned Iraq for violations of SCR 687 and has adopted numerous resolutions on the subject. In 1993 and again in 1998 the coalition took military action under the revived authority of SCR 678 to deal with the threat to international peace and security posed by those violations.

> 7. On 14 January 1993, in relation to the UK/US military action the previous day, the then UN Secretary-General said: "The raid yesterday, and the forces which carried out the raid, have received a mandate from the Security Council, according to resolution 678, and the cause of the raid was the violation by Iraq of resolution 687 concerning the ceasefire. So, as Secretary-General of the United Nations, I can say that this action was taken and conforms to the resolutions of the Security Council and conforms to the Charter of the United Nations."

In Goldsmith's concise opinion made public March 17, 2003, he argued that from the "combined effect" of Security Council Resolutions 678 (1990), 687 (1991), and 1441 (2002), "authority to use force against Iraq exists."[6] Certain of Goldsmith's points are numbered below in order to provide a response that is easier to follow. (1) He pointed out that all three resolutions were adopted under Chapter VII of the UN Charter, "which allows the use of force for the . . . purpose of restoring international peace and security." (2) Noting that Resolution 687 imposed obligations on Iraq, he stated that the resolution "suspended but did not terminate the authority to use force under Resolution 678." (3) He next stated that "A material breach of Resolution 687 revives the authority to use force under Resolution 678." Furthermore,

> (4) The Security Council in Resolution 1441 gave Iraq "a final opportunity to comply with its disarmament obligations" and warned Iraq of the "serious consequences" if it did not. The Security Council also decided in Resolution 1441 that, if Iraq failed at any time to comply with and co-operate fully in the implementation of Resolution 1441, that would constitute a further material breach. It is plain that Iraq has failed so to comply and therefore Iraq was at the time of Resolution 1441 and continues to be in material breach. Thus, the authority to use force under Resolution 678 has revived and so continues today.

Goldsmith then responded (5) to the anticipated objection that in Resolution 1441, the Security Council "12. Decides to convene immediately upon receipt of a report [of Iraqi non-compliance] in accordance with paragraphs 4 or 11 above, in order to consider the situation."[7] He wrote: "Resolution 1441 would in terms have provided that a further decision of the Security Council to sanction force was required if that had been intended. Thus, all that Resolution 1441 requires is reporting to and discussion by the Security Council of Iraq's failures, but not an express further decision to authorise force."

The points numbered (3) and (4) above form a syllogism:

Major premise: material breaches automatically revive the authority to use force

Minor premise: the Security Council itself found Iraq in material breach by March 2003. (Although the Security Council, despite a finding in Resolution 1441 that Iraq was in material breach, gave it a final chance to avoid war by fully complying with 1441, absent that compliance, it stated, Iraq would be further in material breach. Iraq failed to fully comply, therefore it was in material breach.)

Conclusion: the authority to use force was revived.

Greenwood's Arguments:

Greenwood is arguing a wider case than simply Iraq, as may be seen from his title, "International Law and the Pre-emptive Use of Force: Afghanistan, Al-Qaida, and Iraq." In full agreement with Johnson, he spends some time arguing for a general right to preemptive self-defense, but only if the threat is "imminent." He quotes U.S. Secretary of State Daniel Webster's letter to the British in 1837 that recognized a right to anticipatory self-defense, but only if there is "a necessity of self-defense, instant, overwhelming, leaving no choice of means and no moment for deliberation."[8] This definition, he says, was used at the International Military Tribunals at Nuremberg and Tokyo, and is not controversial in international law. He argues that weapons of mass destruction, and their possible delivery by terrorists, would affect what could reasonably be seen as "imminent," but cannot remove the necessity of meeting that test. "In so far as talk of a doctrine of 'pre-emption' is intended to refer to a broader right of self-defense to respond to threats that might materialize at some time in the future, such a doctrine has no basis in law."[9]

Greenwood writes that the term "material breach" "has a special meaning in the law of treaties: . . . 'the violation of a provision essential to the accomplishment of the object or purpose of the treaty'. . . . The object and purpose of resolutions 687 and 1441 is plainly to restore international peace and security and a material breach of its terms is therefore one that involves a violation of a provision essential to the accomplishment of that object."[10] He does not mention any automatic result of a material breach in the law of treaties, such as an automatic authorization to use force in response. Summarizing the events of February and early March 2003, Greenwood describes briefings of the Council, and the "effective deadlock" of the Council by mid-March, as almost all members believed Iraq to be in material breach of Resolution 687 (1991), he writes:

> there were evident differences about the extent of that breach and about the best way in which to respond to it. . . . By March 16 . . . the United States, the United Kingdom, and a number of other States decided to take military action without a further resolution, relying on the authorization granted by resolution 678 (1990). That action began on March 20, 2003.[11]

On the legality of the ensuing war, Greenwood writes:

> it is plain that, at the date military action commenced, Iraq continued to be in material breach of resolution 1441 (2002) and resolution 687 (1991). The debate in the Council on March 7, 2003 showed that, with the possible exception of Syria, all the members of the Council accepted that this was the case. Moreover, that breach was no technicality but meant that, on the basis of the existing Security Council resolutions, Iraq posed a threat to international peace and security as determined by the Security Council.[12]

Greenwood makes clear his view that Resolution 1441 of 2002 did not in itself re-authorize the use of force against Iraq.

> In [the] circumstances, there is no doubt that the Council could lawfully have adopted a fresh resolution authorizing military action. Resolution 1441 (2002) did not, in and of itself, constitute such a fresh mandate. The text of that resolution made clear that any breach by Iraq was to be reported to the Council, which would then "convene . . . in order to consider the situation and the need for full compliance with all of the relevant Council resolutions in order to secure international peace and security." Moreover, several States made clear when the resolution was adopted that there was no "automaticity" involved, so that any violation by Iraq would have to be discussed by the Council before any recourse to force.[13]

Yet, Greenwood continued, such a re-authorization of the use of force was not necessary.

> A new resolution expressly authorizing military action was not, however, necessary as a matter of international law. The authorization to use "all necessary means" contained in resolution 678 (1990) had not been terminated by the Security Council. On the contrary, as demonstrated above, it was reaffirmed, as recently as November 2002, in the preamble to resolution 1441 (2002). Contrary to what is frequently suggested, resolution 678 was not solely about the liberation of Kuwait. The authorization for the coalition to use force went beyond the goal of liberating Kuwait by authorizing military action for the purpose of restoring international peace and security in the area.
> Resolution 687 (1991) then determined that the restoration of international peace and security required the partial disarmament of Iraq. Resolution 687, pa-

ragraph 1, affirmed resolution 678 except to the extent that the other provisions of resolution 687 expressly changed resolution 678. The text of resolution 687 contained nothing that expressly (or impliedly) indicated that the Council either considered that the mandate contained in resolution 678 had been discharged or that it could not be relied upon in the event of Iraq continuing to pose a threat to international peace and security. The imposition of a ceasefire by resolution 687 (1991) suspended hostilities and thus suspended the authority to use force but, by reaffirming resolution 678, resolution 687 left open the possibility of further military action to achieve the objectives of resolution 678 in the event of Iraqi violation of the ceasefire terms.[14]

Greenwood cites several other points to show that, in his view, military action was authorized. First, he writes that "the recent reaffirmation of resolution 678 (1990) in the preamble to resolution 1441 (2002) cannot be dismissed as mere verbiage; the only possible interpretation of that paragraph in the preamble was that the Council (unanimously) considered that the earlier resolution was still in force." Second, he continues immediately, "The principle that the authorization of force contained in resolution 678 could revive in the event of Iraqi violation of the ceasefire conditions in resolution 687 was relied on by the United Kingdom and the United States in January 1993. That action—and the legal justification advanced for it—received support from the Secretary-General of the United Nations."[15]

Finally, Greenwood states that:

> the requirement in paragraph 12 of resolution 1441 that the Council consider the matter, did not mean that no action could be taken under resolution 678 unless the Council decided on such a course. As the British government's statement on the legal basis for military action made clear: "Had that been the intention, [resolution 1441] would have provided that the Council would decide what needed to be done to restore international peace and security, not that it would consider the matter. The choice of words was deliberate; a proposal that there should be a requirement for a decision by the Council, a position maintained by several members, was not adopted. Instead the members of the Council opted for the formula that the Council must consider the matter before any action is taken" . . . The members were divided about what to do [about the continuing Iraqi material breach] with the result that no decision could be taken. In these circumstances, although it must be recognized that others have taken a different view, the present writer believes that those governments who resorted to force were right to conclude that they could rely on the authorization of military action in resolution 678, read together with resolutions 687 and 1441.[16]

In other words, Greenwood is stating here that while Resolution 1441 did not authorize military action, neither did it completely rule out military action in the absence of a second, follow-up resolution. The finding of material breach in 1441 is important to Greenwood, and adds in his view to the case for a revival of the authority to use force, but Greenwood had stated earlier that 1441 did not, in and of itself, constitute such a fresh mandate.

Taft and Buchwald's Arguments

Taft and Buchwald build their argument largely on the same lines as Goldsmith, with an added focus on Resolution 1441, which they see in stronger terms. They point out that Resolution 678 (1990) did not provide for "further determination" by the Security Council whether the final opportunity to comply had been met by Iraq, with the implication that Resolution 1441, which also did not call specifically for any further determination by the Council, also authorized force. Concerning the meaning of "material breach," they argue strongly that a finding of material breach, in Security Council parlance, authorizes the use of force:

> As a legal matter, a material breach of the conditions that had been essential to the establishment of the cease-fire left the responsibility to member states to enforce those conditions, operating consistently with Resolution 678 to use all necessary means to restore international peace and security in the area. On numerous occasions in response to Iraqi violations of WMD obligations, the Council, through either a formal resolution or a statement by its president, determined that Iraq's actions constituted material breaches, understanding that such a determination authorized resort to force.[17]

Like Greenwood, they cite the statement of the Secretary General of the UN in 1993 as evidence for the idea that a material breach automatically justified the use of force by coalition forces, stating:

> Indeed, when coalition forces—American, British, and French—used force following such a presidential statement in January 1993, then Secretary-General Boutros-Ghali stated that the "raid was carried out in accordance with a mandate from the Security Council under resolution 678 (1991), and the motive for the raid was Iraq's violation of that resolution, which concerns the cease-fire. As Secretary-General of the United Nations, I can tell you that the action taken was in accordance with the resolutions of the Security Council and the Charter of the United Nations."[18]

Building on this understanding of a "material breach," they write:

> The Council in effect decided [in adopting Resolution 1441] that, in view of the past behavior of Iraq, the threat it posed to others, and the fact that the opportunity it was being given to remedy its breaches was a final one, any such violations by Iraq would mean that the use of force to address this threat was consistent with Resolution 678.[19]

They also quote Goldsmith's interpretation of Resolution 1441, "Resolution 1441 would in terms have provided that a further decision of the Security Council to sanction force was required if that had been intended. Thus, all that resolution 1441 requires is reporting to and discussion by the Security Council of Iraq's failures, but not an express further decision to authorize force." In Taft and Buchwald's view, "nothing in Resolution 1441 required the Council to adopt any further resolution, or other form of approval, to establish the occurrence of the material breach that was the predicate for coalition forces to resort to force."[20]

They conclude, on this subject,

> the Council had already made the decision that violations described in paragraph 4—"false statements or omissions in the declarations submitted by Iraq pursuant to this resolution and failure by Iraq at any time to comply with, and cooperate fully in the implementation of, this resolution"—would constitute a material breach of Iraq's obligations, and thus authorize the use of force to secure Iraqi compliance with its disarmament obligations.[21]

The conclusion of their argument is that "striking" similarities between Resolution 678 (1990) and 1441 (2002) show that the latter resolution also "authorize[d] coalition forces" to use force:

> The similarities in this regard between Resolution 1441 and Resolution 678 are striking. Using the same terminology that it later adopted in Resolution 1441, the Council in Resolution 678 decided to allow Iraq a "final opportunity" to comply with the obligations that the Council had established in previous resolutions. The Council then authorized member states to use force "unless Iraq on or before 15 January 1991 fully implement[ed]" those resolutions. It was clear then that coalition members were not required to return for a further Council decision that Iraq had failed to comply; nor did they do so before commencing military operations. The language of Resolution 1441 tracked the language of Resolution 678, and the resolution operated in the same way to authorize coalition forces to bring Iraq into compliance with its obligations.[22]

Analysis

Non-Emergency Responses to Cease-Fire Violations Require Fresh Authorization, in This Case from the UN Security Council

Resolution 687 (1991) created a cease-fire. It is true, as these writers claim, that a cease-fire is generally seen as a suspension rather than a termination of the earlier authority (from whatever quarter) to use force. However, it is rarely the case, and certainly was not here, that a cease-fire violation authorizes either party to re-launch full-scale war unilaterally if it decides to do so. Generally, cease-fire agreements lay out specific mechanisms to determine what will take place if one side or the other violates terms of the agreement, whether through material breaches or otherwise, and the final words of Resolution 687 provided such a mechanism in the cease-fire it created. Many cease-fire agreements include monitoring committees that are charged with investigating alleged violations. Such mechanisms are created precisely so that breaches of the terms may be carefully investigated, rather than automatically leading to a resumption of war.

Shooting or military movement into forbidden territory by side A may provoke an immediate military reaction of self-defense by side B's forces in the immediate area, but even that would not necessarily return the two sides to full-scale war. With modern communications in place, it is hard to conceive of a violation by side A that would not cause side B's military to request instructions from its authorizing authority (generally, its government), even if it responded militarily, in a limited way, to the urgent situation developing at the front line.

But the authorizing authority in this cease-fire agreement is the Security Council, which both authorized force earlier, and suspended that authorization in Resolution 687 (1991).

With the Expulsion of Iraqi Forces in 1991, a Fundamentally Different Situation Emerged, As Resolution 687 (1991) Recognized

The fact that Resolution 687 (1991) established a cease-fire emphasizes that the world and the Security Council perceived that a fundamentally different situation was in place after the expulsion of Iraqi forces from Kuwait. When Resolution 678 (1990) was passed, Iraq held Kuwait, Iraq was defying the UN, and Iraq rejected Security Council demands. In April of 1991,

(1) Iraq was no longer in possession of Kuwait,
(2) Iraq had been defeated in battle, and acknowledged that defeat, and
(3) Iraq was no longer rejecting UN Security Council resolutions, but accepting its responsibility to fulfill them.

These new facts were the fundamental ends to achieve which the Council had originally authorized the use of force. If that had not been the case, there would have been no reason for a cease-fire. The coalition forces had overwhelming military superiority. The fact that the Council decided, despite this overwhelming superiority, to cease the use of force, is important in analyzing what the new resolution meant. The United States and the United Kingdom, to give an example, would clearly not have been allowed by Resolution 687 to return to war against Iraq a month later, claiming that Iraq had not taken sufficient steps or demonstrated sufficient sincerity in its compliance with the old and new demands included in the resolution. In Resolution 687 the Security Council took the use of force off the table, while clearly reserving to itself the possibility of putting it back there if it chose.

The Security Council could easily have framed Resolution 687 (1991) in the same or similar terms to Resolution 678 (1990). Resolution 687 could have stated that the Security Council

> demands that Iraq comply fully with the thirteen resolutions mentioned above, and decides, while maintaining all its decisions, to allow Iraq one final opportunity, as a pause of good will, to do so; authorizes Member States cooperating with the government of Kuwait, unless Iraq on or before July 1, 1991, fully complies with all demands in the thirteen resolutions mentioned above, to use all necessary means to ensure compliance with those resolutions and to fully restore international peace and security in the area.

If it had done so, it would have authorized the coalition to enforce its will concerning both the new demands and the remaining, unfulfilled demands on Iraq. It did not do so. In fact, the Council did not authorize the use of force at all in this resolution. Rather, it strongly warned Iraq, through multiple means, that *the Council* would take action, including a new authorization of force if it so chose, to ensure its new resolution was implemented. Instead of authorizing the use of force, the Council decided to keep various sanctions in place until Iraq complied with all its obligations.

In light of this new situation, any threat from a violation of the cease-fire agreement would be a new threat, not a revival of the old one, and would therefore require a new authorization of force, not a revival of the old one. A revival of the old one, which would have meant a revival of authority to use force to remove Iraqi forces from Kuwait, would no longer have made sense.

The Security Council's Original Authorization to Use Force Was Limited, and Did Not Authorize Overthrow of Saddam's Regime

Resolution 678 of 1990 grants to "member states co-operating with the Government of Kuwait" a limited authorization to use force. The object of the use of force is said to be "to uphold and implement resolution 660 (1990) and all subsequent relevant resolutions and to restore international peace and security in the area."[23] A glance at 660 and the subsequent resolutions will show that besides a reversal of the physical takeover of Kuwait and claim to have annexed it, the remainder of the demands concern relatively minor issues in comparison, such as an embargo on air traffic and shipping or respect for diplomatic premises in Kuwait. There is nothing in those resolutions about overthrowing the regime of Saddam Hussein. This interpretation of the expressed will of the Council is affirmed in resolution 686 and 687 of 1991, both of which include the preambular statement, "Affirming the commitment of all Member States to the independence, sovereignty, and territorial integrity of Iraq and Kuwait" (or in 687 "Kuwait and Iraq"). With minor variations, this statement is repeated in resolution 688 of 1991. Again in resolution 1441 of 2002 is the statement "Reaffirming the commitment of all Member States to the sovereignty and territorial integrity of Iraq, Kuwait, and the neighbouring States." To assert that a "revived" authorization to use force included authorization to overthrow Saddam's regime is to begin with an assertion of a revival of force to free Kuwait, which was in fact no longer occupied by Saddam's forces, and to go on to contradict multiple subsequent UN Security Council affirmations of Iraq's independence, sovereignty, and territorial integrity.

Resolution 687 (1991), Reserved and Emphasized the Security Council's Inherent Authority to Ensure Its Implementation

It would seem clear enough from the argument concerning cease-fires in general that absent a provocation that urgently required an immediate military response, the coalition forces, noting a violation of any kind by Iraq, would return to the Security Council for specific instructions as to how to respond to such a violation. (The question of the results of "material breaches" of a cease-fire resolution will be dealt with below.) There was nothing in Resolution 687 (unlike Resolution 678 [1990]) to suggest that coalition forces were entitled to determine the existence of violations themselves and respond as they wished. In fact, quite the opposite is indicated by the final words of Resolution 687, that the Council decided to "remain seized" of the matter and "take such further steps as may be required for the implementation of the present resolution and to secure peace and security in the region." This is reinforced by the fact that it is the Security Council in international law that is authorized to "determine the existence of any threat" and "make recommendations, or decide what measures shall be taken . . . to maintain or restore international peace and security" (UN Charter, Article 39).

In light of the UN Charter, even the inherent right of self-defense, individual or collective, under armed attack (see Article 51) is only held to continue

> until the Security Council has taken measures necessary to maintain international peace and security. Measures taken by Members in the exercise of this right of self-defense shall be immediately reported to the Security Council and shall not in any way affect the authority and responsibility of the Security Council under the present Charter to take at any time such action as it deems necessary in order to maintain or restore international peace and security.[24]

The right of "collective self-defense" recognized in the Charter is subordinate, after the immediate emergency of the armed attack, to actions taken by the Council.

In line with the gravity with which the Council continued to view the situation, and the evident fact that it did not recognize a full and complete restoration of peace and security in the area, the Council in Resolution 687 (1991) did at least three things that reminded Iraq (and the world) that the Council itself could authorize force again, if necessary: it mentioned Resolution 678 (1990), it cited Chapter VII, and it pointedly "Decide[d] to remain seized of the matter and to take such further steps as may be required for the implementation of the present resolution and to secure peace and security in the region."

Opinions of the UN Secretary-General Are Not Legally Binding

Paragraph seven in the paper from the UK Secretary of State for Foreign and Commonwealth Affairs looks to the support of the then Secretary-General of the United Nations. The ability of the holder of this office to speak for the Council with binding legal authority may be rather quickly disposed of with a related example. On September 16, 2004, Secretary-General Kofi Annan told a BBC reporter, concerning the current war, "it is not in conformity with the UN Charter, from our point of view and from the Charter point of view it was illegal."[25] Clearly the U.S. and UK governments have not considered *that* opinion binding. The function of the Secretary-General of the United Nations is laid out in Chapter XV of the Charter, and in particular in Articles 97 through 99. Article 97 states that "He shall be the chief administrative officer of the [UN] Organization."[26] There is no suggestion whatsoever that he makes official UN determinations of what is and is not in accord with the Charter or with Security Council resolutions.

Acting under Chapter VII Indicates the Gravity of the Problem, Not an Authorization to Respond with Force

Turning to Goldsmith's arguments, it should first be clear that for the Security Council to invoke Chapter VII of the UN Charter in no way constitutes an automatic authorization to use force. Chapter VII is not entitled "The Use of Force," but "Action with Respect to Threats to the Peace, Breaches of the Peace, and Acts of Aggression." Chapter VII begins with Article 39, which states in full:

> The Security Council shall determine the existence of any threat to the peace, breach of the peace, or act of aggression and shall make recommendations, or decide what measures shall be taken in accordance with Articles 41 and 42, to maintain or restore international peace and security.[27]

Articles 42 through 48 in Chapter VII concern the use of force, but Articles 40 and 41 speak of other measures that may be employed. Thus, for the Security Council to invoke Chapter VII actually emphasizes two things: the gravity of the situation, such that it may require force, and the authority of the Security Council itself to determine the existence of one of the serious problems listed above, and to "decide what measures" need to be taken.

Resolution 687 (1991) Does Not Mention "Suspension" of Authorization to Use Force; It Supersedes Resolution 678 (1990)

Next, Goldsmith stated that Resolution 687 (1991) "suspended but did not terminate the authority to use force under Resolution 678." There is no clear statement about "suspension" of the authority to use force in Resolution 687. It seems more accurate to state that Resolution 687 clearly superseded Resolution 678 (1990). In Resolution 687 (1991), the Council recognized a completely new situation (the end of the Iraqi occupation of Kuwait), and it both repeated old unfulfilled requirements on Iraq and imposed additional requirements on it, without authorizing the use of force for either set of requirements. However this situation is interpreted, though, the issue of the future use of force was specifically dealt with in the statement in the resolution that the Council "decides to remain seized of the matter and to take such further steps as may be required."[28] It is hard to see how this leaves any room for member states to unilaterally "help" the Council.

Security Council "Suspension of Authority," Even if Granted for Argument's Sake, Requires Security Council Revival of Authority

As pointed out, Resolution 687 (1991) emphasized the Security Council's authority to take decisions and act if necessary in the future. But even if we take Goldsmith's characterization as accurate, that it "suspended . . . the authority to use force," we are left with an obvious inference: If the Security Council authorized the action, and the Security Council suspended that authorization, who else could reverse that suspension but the Security Council? As pointed out, the Council's function under Article 39 of the Charter is as follows: "The Security Council shall determine the existence of any threat to the peace, breach of the peace, or act of aggression and shall make recommendations, or decide what measures shall be taken" in response. Given that fact, it seems that the Council's core Article 39 function of determining the existence of threats and deciding what measures to take would immediately come into play, especially in light of its strongly worded concluding decision in Resolution 687 to "remain seized of the matter and to take such further steps" as required.

"Material Breach" Has No Settled Definition for Security Council Resolutions, Consequences Not Defined in International Law

That leads to the question of what a "material breach" is and whether it has the kind of automatic result Goldsmith and others claimed it did. First, there is no clear, settled, and internationally agreed definition of "material breach" in the context of Security Council resolutions. The term "material breach" has a well-defined meaning in two contexts: contract law, and the law of treaties. There is no convention defining "material breach" of a Security Council resolution, which is neither a treaty nor a contract. It follows that there is no binding agreement among nations on the consequences of a material breach. The numerous statements by U.S. and UK legal sources that a "material breach" "revives the authority to use force" and so forth, do not appeal to the authority of an agreed convention, treaty, or other instrument that sets out the definition and consequences of such a breach in the case of a UN Security Council resolution.

In addition, in at least one Security Council Resolution, 1441 of 1990, the phrase material breach was used in a context that made it clear it did not automatically authorize the use of force. That Resolution states that Iraq is in "material breach" of Resolution 687 (1991), but warns that any case of further material breaches "will be reported to the Council for assessment" (paragraph four), and the Council "Decides to convene immediately upon receipt of a report in accordance with paragraphs 4 or 11 above, in order to consider the situation." As Michael Dorf, Professor of Law at Columbia University School of Law, pointed out on January 8, 2003:

> The Bush Administration and the news media have sometimes suggested that a finding of a "material breach" will automatically trigger war with Iraq. But in fact, Resolution 1441 states that in the event of a material breach or other Iraqi interference or failures to comply with disarmament obligations, the Security Council will "consider the situation and the need for full compliance with all of the relevant Council resolutions in order to secure international peace and security." That is, the resolution itself expressly considers material breach to be a trigger for further deliberation, not automatic war.[29]

Material Breaches in Contract Law

As noted, there are two contexts in which the term "material breach" has a well-defined meaning, contract law and the law of treaties. In contract law, it is a serious violation of the terms of a contract. Dorf writes that in contract law, "A material breach only occurs when one party so completely fails to hold up its end of the bargain that the other party is excused altogether from further performance under the contract."[30] Dorf goes on to point out that "when one party to a contract is in material breach, the other party has the option of terminating the contract, but is not required to do so. If our computer manufacturer believes that future shipments from the keyboard supplier are still a good deal, then notwithstanding a time-is-of-the-essence clause, it can continue the contract in force." In other words, a material breach in contract law allows the innocent party to obtain remedies, rather than imposing obligations or automatic results, unless those are defined in the contract—and even then, the innocent party may decline to impose or insist on the full remedy available.

Material Breaches in Treaty Law

The other context in which "material breach" has a clear definition is the law of treaties, according to Christopher Greenwood:

> The term "material breach" has a special meaning in the law of treaties. In Article 60 (3) of the Vienna Convention on the Law of Treaties, 1969, material breach is defined as: . . . "(b) the violation of a provision essential to the accomplishment of the object or purpose of the treaty." At the Security Council meeting that adopted resolution 1441, Ireland stated that it understood the term "material breach" in the resolution to have the meaning set out in this Article.[31]

Greenwood continued:

> Of course, resolution 687 is not a treaty but a unilateral act of the Security Council, more akin to a legislative instrument, which binds Iraq irrespective of its agreement. However, it is unlikely that anything will turn on this point. The object and purpose of resolutions 687 and 1441 is plainly to restore international peace and security and a material breach of its terms is therefore one that involves a violation of a provision essential to the accomplishment of that object. That includes the possession by Iraq of prohibited weapons, or the failure to cooperate actively with the inspectors, because the inspection mechanism is itself essential to the accomplishment of the purpose of the resolution.

Note that Greenwood says nothing about any automatic result of material breaches.

The *Encyclopædia Britannica*, under the entry "treaty," provides another look at "material breach," again providing an analogy to the situation under a Security Council resolution, which is not a treaty:

> Treaties may be terminated or suspended through a provision in the treaty (if one exists) or by the consent of the parties. In the case of a material breach— i.e., an impermissible repudiation of the treaty or a violation of a provision essential to the treaty's object or purpose—the innocent party of a bilateral treaty

may invoke that breach as a ground for terminating the treaty or suspending its operation. Multilateral treaties may be terminated or suspended by the unanimous agreement of all their parties. A party specially affected by a breach of a multilateral treaty may suspend the agreement as it applies to relations between itself and the defaulting state. In cases where a breach by one party significantly affects all other parties to the treaty, the other parties may suspend the entire agreement or a part of it.[32]

Material Breach: Applying the Treaty Law Analogy

Resolution 687 (1991) was at least analogous to a treaty, as it was an agreement between Iraq and the Security Council concerning conditions for suspension of hostilities. Note firstly, if the resolution is considered as analogous to a treaty in light of the *Encyclopædia Britannica* quotation, that there was indeed a "provision in the treaty" for possible termination or suspension: the Security Council decided to "remain seized" of the matter, meaning that it could, in accord with its inherent powers under Chapter VII, make decisions concerning breaches of the peace. This really should settle the issue of the proper response to a material breach of a Security Council resolution: it should be referred to the Security Council, which makes a decision (and whatever decision it makes, even if it is no decision, that is the authoritative response).

But, continuing with the analogy, if Resolution 687 (1991) is looked at as a bilateral agreement, then the "innocent party" is the Security Council (representing the world community of nations, or at least the community of UN Member States), not the United States or the UK, neither of which was attacked by Iraq, neither of which attacked Iraqi forces on its own authority in 1991, and neither of which concluded a separate, formal cease-fire agreement with Iraq to end the war. Resolution 678 (1990) "Authorizes Member States cooperating with the government of Kuwait" to enforce its earlier resolutions through all necessary means, and the member states that took action did so explicitly on that basis.

Considering the analogy of a multilateral treaty, as a legal matter there is no particular convincing way in which the United States or the UK could be said to be "specially affected" by any breach committed by Saddam's Iraq, which lies thousands of miles from their shores. (The claims of self-defense by the United States are a separate issue, addressed in earlier chapters.) But if it is considered as a multilateral treaty, then there is already in place an agreed mechanism (since all Member States have signed the UN Charter) for dealing with breaches of any kind that consist of threats to international peace and security: a return to the Security Council for a decision—and whatever decision the Security Council takes is the authoritative one in a legal context (unless immediate self-defense, a separate issue, is involved).

UN Representatives Explicitly Stated 1441 Did Not Authorize the Use of Force, Even in Case of Further Material Breaches

Resolution 1441 did not constitute authorization for the use of force, even in the event of future material breaches by Iraq. The resolution's text states that such material breaches "will be reported to the Council for assessment" which will cause the Council "to convene immediately . . . in order to consider the situation." The remarks of various Permanent Representatives to the UN, as reported in the press release after Resolution 1441 was passed,[33] add additional clarity. A sample:

> John Negroponte (United States) said . . . the resolution contained . . . no "hidden triggers" and no "automaticity" with the use of force. The procedure to be followed was laid out in the resolution. And one way or another, Iraq would be disarmed. If the Security Council failed to act decisively in the event of further Iraqi violation, the resolution did not constrain any Member State from acting to defend itself against the threat posed by that country, or to enforce relevant United Nations resolutions and protect world peace and security.

In this quotation, Negroponte explicitly denied that the resolution contained "automaticity" concerning the use of force, and implicitly acknowledged that the Security Council would decide on further steps. Rather than stating that 1441 provided a legal basis for the use of force, he instead claimed that if the UN "failed to act decisively" other Member States would have other justifications than 1441, namely self-defense and other "relevant . . . resolutions."

> Jeremy Greenstock (United Kingdom) said . . . there was no "automaticity" in the resolution. If there was a further Iraqi breach of its disarmament obligations, the matter would return to the Council for discussion. He expected the Council then to meet its responsibilities.

There is no hint here that 1441 already authorizes force. Greenstock strongly implies that the Council will make a decision in case of a material breach, and he "expected the Council" to "meet its responsibilities" when it took that decision. The decision, then, in his account, was the Security Council's to make.

> Jean-David Levitte (France) said . . . if the inspection authorities reported to the Council Iraq had not complied with its obligations, the Council would meet immediately and decide on a course of action. France welcomed the lack of "automaticity" in the final resolution.

Note the explicit French statement that in case of failure by Iraq to meet its obligations, the Council would "decide on a course of action." The Mexican, Irish, and Russian representatives repeat the same thought in various forms, in line with the language of the Charter itself.

> Adolpho Aguilar Zinser (Mexico) said . . . in case of failure to comply, the Council would act on determinations it would make on whether international peace and security was threatened. The Council decision preserved the legitimacy, effectiveness and relevance of the Council, in compliance with its mandate to maintain international peace and security. It strengthened the Council, the United Nations, multilateralism and an international system of norms and principles. Those who had advocated the automatic recourse to the use of

force had agreed to afford Iraq a final chance, he said. Iraq was now obliged to fully comply with its international obligations. The resolution had eliminated "automaticity" in the use of force as a result of material breach. He welcomed the acceptance of the two-stage approach, in accordance with which any failure to comply by Iraq should be taken on the basis of two prerequisites. There should be two time periods: a process of credible inspections of real Iraqi military capabilities; and the agreement of the Council on ways and means to be adopted should the inspection process detect a threat to international peace and security. . . .

Richard Ryan (Ireland) said . . . the resolution . . . provided for a clear, sequential process for Iraq compliance. Developments would be then examined by the Council itself, which had the primary responsibility to decide whatever action needed to be taken. . . .

Sergey Lavrov (Russian Federation) . . . emphasized that the resolution did not contain any provisions for the automatic use of force and underlined that the sponsors of the text had affirmed that today. He said it was of fundamental importance that there was clear confirmation in the resolution that all members respected the sovereignty and territorial integrity of Iraq.

There are more such individual statements, but these may suffice. In addition, the following statement by three permanent members of the Security Council[34] is very strong on this point. If the U.S. or UK representatives disagreed, it would have behooved them to make that disagreement public, immediately (which they did not do).

IRAQ/UNSCR 1441

Iraq—Joint statement by the People's Republic of China, France and the Russian Federation

New York, November 8, 2002

Resolution 1441 (2002) adopted today by the Security Council excludes any automaticity in the use of force. In this regard, we register with satisfaction the declarations of the representatives of the United States and the United Kingdom confirming this understanding in their explanations of vote, and assuring that the goal of the resolution is the full implementation of the existing Security Council resolutions on disarmament of Iraq's weapons of mass destruction. All Security Council members share this goal.

In case of failure by Iraq to comply with its obligations, the provisions of paragraphs 4, 11 and 12 will apply. Such failure will be reported to the Security Council by the Executive Chairman of UNMOVIC or by the Director General of IAEA. It will be then for the Council to take a position on the basis of that report.

Therefore, the resolution fully respects the competences of the Security Council in the maintenance of international peace and security, in conformity with the

Charter of the United Nations.

Summing Up "Material Breach"

To sum up this section, there is considerable ambiguity about the meaning of "material breach," and there is no international agreement that it triggers any particular response. The clearest thing the phrase seems to signal is a serious violation of a resolution, one that calls for Security Council consideration, which is followed naturally by a decision (of whatever nature) by the Security Council. If the Security Council states that there is a material breach, that term carries an implicit threat in this case to authorize the use of force, but use of the phrase includes no automatic authorization of force. This is clear from statements by the UN Representatives of major and minor countries, including the United States, the United Kingdom, and the other permanent members. The appeals by UK officials to their own government's previous contested actions, supported by their own government's interpretation, and to one endorsement by the Secretary General of the UN, do not appear to have any kind of finality, and contradict the most recent clear usage from the Security Council, as well as effectively depriving the Council of one of its explicit, core functions.

It would appear then that Goldsmith's syllogism is built on a flawed major premise. Since the party that negotiated and authorized the cease-fire, the Security Council, was still in existence, and empowered by the Charter to deal with precisely such issues as violations of cease-fire agreements, and had determined to do so, it is difficult to see how a "material breach" could be said with any authority to revive automatically an authorization to use force from an earlier resolution that dealt with an earlier situation (one that in this case was over a decade old).

What Is Not Ruled Out in 1441 Is Not Thereby Authorized

Goldsmith's final point, no. (5) above, does not claim that Resolution 1441 authorized the use of force. Instead, he states very carefully the limited point that Resolution 1441 did not expressly rule out the use of force in the absence of a follow-up resolution. While this is accurate, it ignores several facts. First, the Council's decision in Resolution 1441 regarding past material breaches was to give Iraq another opportunity to comply. Second, its decision regarding a possible future material breach was that it would "be reported to the Council for assessment." Representatives quoted above reinforced that language. The Bush administration and British assumptions that "material breaches" automatically authorized the coalition to resort to force involve a contradiction of these explicit statements by the Council. They also ignore the inherent powers of the Council. On the one hand, Goldsmith is correct: Resolution 1441 did not expressly rule out any use of force on any basis whatsoever. However, that left th ose arguing in favor of an existing authority to use force to make their case on other grounds, a case dealt with in other sections of this response.

Who Speaks for the Security Council?

Christopher Greenwood wrote that "at the date military action commenced, Iraq continued to be in material breach of resolution 1441 (2002) and resolution 687 (1991) . . . with the possible exception of Syria, all the members of the Council accepted that this was the case. Moreover, that breach was no technicality but meant that, on the basis of the existing Security Council resolutions, Iraq posed a threat to international peace and security as determined by the Security Council." But only the Security Council can speak for the Security Council. Furthermore, threats to international peace and security can come in a range of intensities, from weak to strong. Article 39 of the Charter settles the matter of who decides what to do about such a threat: "The Security Council shall determine the existence of any threat to the peace, breach of the peace, or act of aggression and shall make recommendations, or decide what measures shall be taken . . . to maintain or restore international peace and security." This power was not delegated to any other body.

Reference to Resolution 678 (1990) in the 1441 Preamble

Concerning the preamble to Resolution 1441, Greenwood wrote: "the recent reaffirmation of resolution 678 (1990) in the preamble to resolution 1441 (2002) cannot be dismissed as mere verbiage; the only possible interpretation of that paragraph in the preamble was that the Council (unanimously) considered that the earlier resolution was still in force." But that is not the only possible interpretation. A reaffirmation of a previous resolution can instead convey the importance of that earlier resolution as laying down fundamental principles that are still important in a situation. It can also reinforce the seriousness of a new resolution. Greenwood's implication that because the resolution "remained in force" the same coalition could use force against Iraq simply does not make sense. It would mean that the authorization to use "all necessary means" to compel Iraq to remove its forces from Kuwait remained in force, an absurd statement after April 1991.

Greenwood Is Strict on the Requirement for Imminence, Loose on the Council's Decision-Making Power

While Greenwood is, rightly, quite strict concerning the idea that "imminence" is absolutely required in preemptive self-defense, he is loose concerning the manner in which the Security Council decides to use its own, wider powers. He does not really address the fact that Article 39 empowers the Security Council, and not any other body, to "determine the existence of any threat to the peace, breach of the peace, or act of aggression" and to "make recommendations, or decide what measures shall be taken in accordance with Articles 41 and 42, to maintain or restore international peace and security." Nor does he address the fact that Resolution 687 (1991) alludes to that power when in it the Council "decides to remain seized of the matter and to take such further steps as may be required for the implementation of the present resolution and to secure peace and security in the region," a statement that would be absurd if the Council had meant the coalition to make its own determinations and take steps of its own choosing to enforce that resolution.

Strong Circumstantial Evidence That Resolution 1441 Did Not Authorize Use of Force

Taft and Buchwald's arguments have largely been dealt with, as they too overlap with or rely on Goldsmith's. Note that Taft and Buchwald basically argued, contrary to Greenwood and to Goldsmith, that Resolution 1441 authorized the use of force. A number of arguments against this position have been advanced. Here is one more: a strong piece of evidence, even if circumstantial, of the weakness of the attempt to claim that Resolution 1441 implicitly authorized the use of force, is that President Bush did not cite the Resolution directly in his pre-war speech. Given that he was clearly looking to build the strongest possible case for war, and used a wide variety of justifications for it, it is hard to see how he would not have cited this one unless his administration felt that the verbal assurances from high U.S. and UK officials about a lack of "hidden triggers" and "automaticity," perhaps coupled with the British failure to claim that Resolution 1441 itself authorized the use of force, were simply too strong to allow a claim that that Resolution 1441 authorized war in the absence of another follow-up resolution. A second powerful piece of circumstantial evidence of the weakness of the case that Resolution 1441 authorized war is the fact that the U.S. and UK governments pushed very strongly for the passage of such a follow-up resolution (although they failed to achieve it).

Striking Differences between Resolutions 1441 and 678

One final point of Taft and Buchwald's is the "striking" "similarities . . . between Resolution 1441 and Resolution 678." While there are some important similarities, the striking and obvious differences make it impossible to see these two resolutions as parallel. First, Resolution 678 set a date for full compliance, but Resolution 1441 did not. Second, the question of fact concerning compliance was, in the main, simple and unambiguous in Resolution 678—the presence of Iraqi military forces in Kuwait on or after January 15, 1991. On the other hand, the question of fact in Resolution 1441 was complex and many-faceted—"full cooperation" with UN demands. Third, Resolution 678 did not state that reports of non-compliance "will be reported to the Council for assessment," nor that the Council "decides to convene immediately upon receipt" of such a report, "to consider the situation," all of which Resolution 1441 did. Fourth, instead of such demands for further reports and further consideration, Resolution 678 simply "authorize[d] Member States . . . to use all necessary means" to enforce previous resolutions, "unless Iraq on or before 15 January 1991 fully implements" those resolutions. Resolution 1441 contained no such authorization, a loud and obviously a calculated omission. Finally, Resolution 1441 was accompanied by very clear statements clarifying and emphasizing that possible non-compliance would not trigger the use of force, something that, in the case of Resolution 678 was completely lacking, and also would have made nonsense of the plain meaning of the text of that resolution. These striking differences make clear that the two resolutions had different purposes.

NOTES

1. Christopher Greenwood, *International Law and the Pre-emptive Use of Force: Afghanistan, Al-Qaida, and Iraq*, 4 San Diego Int'l L.J. no. 7, 36 (2003). I gratefully acknowledge learning of Greenwood's article, as well as that of Taft and Buchwald, in an unpublished dissertation by Esther Wanjie, "The Use of Force in Iraq: An Analysis of Peaceful Disarmament Alternatives and the Potential Impact of Views about its Legality on the Position of Peaceful Dispute Resolution Provisions in the UN Charter."

2. Kofi Annan, "Excerpts: Annan interview," *BBC News*, September 16, 2004 (last update), http://news.bbc.co.uk/2/hi/middle_east/3661640.stm (accessed December 7, 2007).

3. Greenwood, *International Law and Pre-emptive Use of Force*.

4. William H. Taft IV and Todd F. Buchwald, *Preemption, Iraq, and International Law*, 97 American Journal of International Law no. 3 (Jul., 2003).

5. "MEMORANDUM BY THE FOREIGN AND COMMONWEALTH OFFICE: IRAQ: LEGAL BASIS FOR THE USE OF FORCE," *Information Commissioner's Office*, March 17, 2003, http://www.ico.gov.uk/upload/documents/library/freedom_of_ information/notices/annex_c_-_memorandum_by_foreign_and_commonwealth_office _17 0303.pdf (accessed April 19, 2008). I was led to this document by Greenwood's article.

6. "A case for war: Lord Goldsmith's published advice on the legal basis for the use of force against Iraq," *The Guardian*, March 17, 2003 http://www.guardian.co.uk/world/2003/mar/17/iraq2 (accessed December 8, 2007).

7. "Security Council Resolutions – 2002," *UN.org*, http://daccessdds.un.org/doc/UNDOC/GEN/N02/682/26/PDF/N0268226.pdf?OpenElement (accessed August 27, 2007).

8. Greenwood, *International Law and Pre-emptive Use of Force*, 13.

9. Greenwood, *International Law and Pre-emptive Use of Force*, 15.

10. Greenwood, *International Law and Pre-emptive Use of Force*, 29.

11. Greenwood, *International Law and Pre-emptive Use of Force*, 33.

12. Greenwood, *International Law and Pre-emptive Use of Force*, 33.

13. Greenwood, *International Law and Pre-emptive Use of Force*, 33-34.

14. Greenwood, *International Law and Pre-emptive Use of Force*, 34.

15. Greenwood, *International Law and Pre-emptive Use of Force*, 34.

16. Greenwood, *International Law and Pre-emptive Use of Force*, 35-36.

17. Taft and Buchwald, *Preemption, Iraq, and International Law*, 559.

18. Taft and Buchwald, *Preemption, Iraq, and International Law*, 559.

19. Taft and Buchwald, *Preemption, Iraq, and International Law*, 561.

20. Taft and Buchwald, *Preemption, Iraq, and International Law*, 562.

21. Taft and Buchwald, *Preemption, Iraq, and International Law*, 562.

22. Taft and Buchwald, *Preemption, Iraq, and International Law*, 562-63.

23. "Security Council Resolutions – 1990," *UN.org*, http://daccessdds.un.org/doc/RESOLUTION/GEN/NR0/575/28/IMG/NR057528.pdf?OpenElement (accessed August 27, 2007).

24. *UN Charter*, art. 51.

25. Kofi Annan, "Excerpts: Annan interview."

26. *UN Charter*, art. 97.

27. *UN Charter*, art. 39.

28. "Security Council Resolutions – 1991," *UN.org*, http://daccessdds.un.org/doc/ RESOLUTION/GEN/NR0/596/23/IMG/NR059623.pdf?OpenElement (accessed August 27, 2007).

29. Michael Dorf, "Is Iraq in 'Material Breach' of its Obligations under the U.N. Resolution? A Geopolitical Question, Not Simply a Legal One," *Findlaw's Writ: Findlaw Legal News and Commentary*, January 8, 2003, http://writ.news.findlaw.com/dorf/2003 0108.html (December 16, 2007).

30. Dorf, "Is Iraq in 'Material Breach' of its Obligations?"

31. Greenwood, *International Law and Pre-emptive Use of Force*, 29.

32. *Encyclopædia Brittanica*, "treaty," http://www.britannica.com/EBchecked/topic/ 603884/treaty (accessed February 27, 2008).

33. "Press Release SC/7564: Security Council holds Iraq in 'Material Breach' of Disarmament Obligations, Offers Final Chance to Comply, Unanimously Adopting Resolution 1441 (2002)," *UN.org*, November 8, 2002, http://www.un.org/News/Press/ docs/2002/SC7564.doc.htm (December 8, 2007).

34. "IRAQ/UNSCR 144: Iraq - Joint statement by the People's Republic of China, France and the Russian Federation," *Embassy of France in the United States*, November 8, 2002, http://www.ambafrance-us.org/news/statmnts/2002/iraq111302.asp (December 8, 2007).

Chapter Seven

Right Intention/The Aim of Peace

Evidence of your intention may be your words and acts. If these conflict, your acts carry more weight than your words.

—U.S. Internal Revenue Service[1]

Now in order that a choice be good, two things are required. First, that the intention be directed to a due end . . . Secondly, that man take rightly those things [i.e., the means] which have reference to the end: and this he cannot do unless his reason counsel, judge, and command aright, which is the function of prudence and the virtues annexed to it.

—Aquinas, *Summa*[2]

Introduction

We must judge intentions. If statements made by political actors were to be taken at face value in just war evaluations, the vast majority and perhaps all wars would meet this criterion, and the criterion would be meaningless.

"Right intention" may seem a rather vague criterion, especially in a theory that claims to be a practical as well as a moral guide to action. After all, intentions (or aims, or purposes) are in the mind. On the one hand, people proclaim their own intentions all the time—always good ones. Very few people in the history of the world have publicly proclaimed their bad intentions. On the other hand, we often suspect that others are lying about their intentions, whether to themselves or to us. It is difficult even to be sure about our own intentions at times, much less those of others. But as the quotation from Aquinas above suggests, for classic just war theory, intentions are strongly linked with means, and since means are visible, the link will provide important evidence concerning intentions.

Despite the difficulty in determining intentions, as Johnson reminds us, "right intention" is one of the core, primary, "deontological" criteria. In the quotation at the beginning of this chapter, Aquinas uses it as an example of how failure to meet just one criterion can render a war unlawful. Johnson lists some wrong intentions mentioned by Aquinas, taking them from the main article on war of the *Summa*.[3] The wrong intentions Aquinas lists, sometimes quoting Augustine, are "the passion for inflicting harm, the cruel thirst for vengeance, an unpacific and restless spirit, the fever of revolt, the lust of power, and such like things . . . motives of aggrandizement, or cruelty." Aquinas lists as right intentions "the advancement of good, or the avoidance of evil." He goes on: "True religion looks upon as peaceful those wars that are waged . . . with the object of securing peace, of punishing evil-doers, and of uplifting the good." These thoughts are reasonably comprehensive.

But knowing what aims to look for, how do we determine what is in the hearts and minds of a ruler or group of leaders who begin a war, since that is where intentions reside? Although each of the six just war criteria may be judged at least somewhat more clearly after the fact, this is especially true of intentions, because of their hidden nature. Because of this, we tend to judge intentions in two stages, before the action and after it. In the first stage, before an action is undertaken, it seems that we normally judge the intentions of the actor with some hesitation, and only in part based on what he says. We also factor in our judgment of the person's character, whether the justifications offered for a planned action appear to make sense, and what we can see of the plans and preparations to act. (Since judgments of the character of the United States President and others involved in decision-making vary widely, and are contentious, and because other evidence is available, that factor is ignored here.) In the second stage, judgments of intentions are always revisited and if necessary revised after the fact.

After that second stage, we are more confident about those revised judgments because we can see what the actual preparations and (sometimes) the actual plans were. When the measurable preparations and detailed plans match the original stated intentions, we judge the earlier statements to have been sincere. If, as happens often enough, we notice a mismatch, we tend to believe by the evidence (although it is not always proof) that the stated intentions were not sincere. We use the visible facts, now revealed, to judge the invisible motives and aims (even if we may never be able to prove we are right about them). This is because we know from experience that Aquinas' thought, in the second quotation at the beginning of this chapter, was right: to choose rightly we must not only "intend" the right result, we must also choose the means that will accomplish that result. Those means are generally visible, and they cast the only light we have on the deeper intentions of the mind or heart. Continuing to judge by others' stated intentions after contradictory facts have become available is simply naïve. Although partisanship has a tendency to push us to judge "our" side in this extraordinarily lenient way, we rarely do the same for the "other" side.

Because of this need to judge intentions in two stages, important parts of this chapter fall into pre-war and post-war halves. The post-war half of this chapter will be the only exception to the rule that the vast majority of the information in this book was available before the war.

We judge intentions based on positive preparations or the lack of them. If you drive around at night with burgling tools in a bag, and are caught, almost everyone will believe you have the intention of breaking into a house, (unless you are, perhaps, a policeman who has just arrested a burglar). Your statement of innocent intentions will not be believed. You can be convicted of a crime in the United States on this kind of evidence. Such examples could be multiplied. In addition, a lack of preparation will also give others powerful evidence of someone's real intentions. If you go on a three-week vacation and your family discovers you have come without any workout clothing, your intention, stated to the family beforehand, to "get in shape this vacation" will be severely doubted. We also judge intentions based on lack of preparation when someone is in charge of a complex activity and delegates various pieces. The planner for a large wedding reception may rent the hall herself, but is likely to delegate the cooking, the beverage orders, and the playing of music. If when the reception starts it turns out that only soft drinks were ordered, the only way to persuade sensible people that she intended to supply alcohol would be for her to show that she had given the order and it was ignored for some reason.

Furthermore, there is a serious moral dimension to being unprepared for an event which is a dangerous possibility but obviously reasonably likely, in the view of any intelligent person, to occur. A Girl Scout troop leader who takes a group of campers for a five-day wilderness hike without adequate preparation for possible rainfall will be considered liable if they are soaked and half of them catch pneumonia. If someone needs first aid and she has no kit, the same judgment applies.

Lack of needed preparation is even more powerful evidence of a lack of good intentions if the person in general prepares well, or is well prepared for a part of the activity. When a person is generally or usually unprepared, lack of preparation may be merely an indication of a lack of common sense, or carelessness. However, the more complex and important the activity, and the more planners involved, and the greater the possible dangers, the more we expect those responsible to have consulted with experts and anticipated and prepared for various possible problems based on a realistic assessment of the action to be taken, and the more we attach a moral judgment to failure to do so. Humans always make mistakes, but if planning was detailed, careful, and based on real-world assumptions, it is easier to forgive mistakes and see them as such. A complete lack of planning for some aspect of an activity, or planning based on assumptions that could easily have been checked against reality and found wanting, is usually judged morally deficient in a large-scale, complex activity with the potential to damage human lives. That would apply to a business started with other people's money, without an adequate business plan or marketing plan, for example. It applies much more to a war, with its certainty of destroying at least some human lives.

THE RIGHT INTENTION/ AIM OF PEACE CLAIM

President Bush clearly proclaimed, in his television address immediately before the war began, the good intentions of the United States, including the intention to liberate rather than subjugate Iraq: "The day of your liberation is near." In an earlier speech, he promised that U.S. forces would remain no longer than necessary: "We will remain in Iraq as long as necessary, and not a day more."

THE DETAILED CLAIM:
RIGHT INTENTION/AIM OF PEACE

As noted, the President's March 17 speech, from which the second of the quotations above is taken, functioned as a declaration of war under the delegated authority granted by the U.S. Congress on March 10, 2002. The speech contained important statements about Bush administration intentions, although it dealt with them quite briefly:

> Many Iraqis can hear me tonight in a translated radio broadcast. If we must begin a military campaign, it will be directed against the lawless men who rule your country and not against you. As our coalition takes away their power we will deliver the food and medicine you need. We will tear down the apparatus of terror. And we will help you to build a new Iraq that is prosperous and free. In a free Iraq there will be no more wars of aggression against your neighbors, no more poison factories, no more executions of dissidents, no more torture chambers and rape rooms. The tyrant will soon be gone. The day of your liberation is near.[4]

That speech, however, may be supplemented with statements from a public speech given by the President at the American Enterprise Institute on February 26, 2003, less than a month before:

> Rebuilding Iraq will require a sustained commitment from many nations, including our own: we will remain in Iraq *as long as necessary* [emphasis added], and not a day more. America has made this kind of commitment before—in the peace that followed a world war. After defeating enemies, we did not leave behind occupying armies, we left constitutions and parliaments. We established an atmosphere of safety, in which responsible, reform-minded local leaders could build lasting institutions of freedom. In societies that once bred fascism and militarism, liberty found a permanent home . . . The Nation of Iraq . . . is fully capable of moving toward democracy and living in freedom . . . A new regime in Iraq would serve as a dramatic and inspiring example of freedom for other nations in the region . . . Success in Iraq could also begin a new stage for Middle Eastern peace, and set in motion progress toward a truly democratic Palestinian state. The passing of Saddam Hussein's regime will deprive terrorist networks of a wealthy patron that pays for terrorist training, and offers rewards to families of suicide bombers. And other regimes will be given a clear warning that support for terror will not be tolerated . . . Without this outside support for terrorism, Palestinians who are working for reform and long for democracy will be in a better position to choose new leaders. True leaders who strive for peace; true leaders who faithfully serve the people.[5]

THE BUSH ADMINISTRATION FAILED TO MEET THIS CRITERION

The Bush administration failed to meet the Right Intention/Aim of Peace criterion. This contention is divided into two parts, pre- and post-war.

Pre-war, the announced Bush administration intentions in the weeks before the war raised justifiable suspicions which the final announcement of war (as well as subsequent announcements) failed to allay. The Bush administration aim, as officially stated before the invasion, was an immediate but undefined "liberation" to be followed by an indefinite but not permanent occupation that would serve U.S. government purposes in the wider Middle East. There were no announced, realistic plans to create a new Iraqi government and depart, nor an announced schedule for those events. "As long as necessary" was undefined. The openly announced plan for an indefinite occupation raised suspicions that the Bush administration harbored motives, in the words of Aquinas, of "the lust of power" or "aggrandizement." Such suspicions were understandable in the context of American attempts to shape the world through force and subterfuge of various kinds. They were especially understandable in light of post-World War II colonialism in the Middle East and Iraq's possession of oil. These justifiable suspicions did not prove the lack of a right intention.

The definitive test of intention in war, however, is the revelation, after the war begins, of concrete plans made before the war is launched. In classic just war theory, as exemplified by Aquinas, intention is defined as "the movement of the will to the end as acquired by the means." The evidence shows that: (1) Military planning was thorough, demonstrating that other planning at the same level was possible. (2) After the invasion, it became clear that detailed U.S. government plans to manage Iraq after conquering it simply did not exist. (3) There was a lack of informed, positive planning to take care of the economic needs of Iraqi citizens. (4) There was no realistic plan for creating a stable, unified government among Iraq's sharply disparate social, ethnic, and religious groups, simply a statement that the United States would do so. (5) There was no plan to deal with the virtual certainty of an eventual insurrection by at least some sectors of Iraqi society. In sum, the evidence shows a lack of the right intention necessary for a just war.

EVIDENCE THE CRITERION
WAS NOT MET

The Pre-War Announced "Liberation" Raised Suspicions

The President's announced aim for Iraq after the removal of Saddam Hussein was a reconstruction ("rebuilding Iraq") modeled on the postwar "reconstruction" of Germany and Japan after World War II. In those "reconstructions," there were no pre-announced deadlines for a withdrawal of U.S. troops, which in fact stayed for decades, although after some time they were no longer an occupying force. Nor were there pre-announced criteria for the end of this period of enforced tutelage in freedom: surrender at the end of the war by each country was effectively unconditional, and the United States (with allies who had at best a limited say in the matter) undertook both to shape the societies it had conquered and their politics, and to determine when that reshaping was complete. The model might be compared to a limited but indefinite criminal rehabilitation, presided over by a judge with nearly unlimited authority.

In addition, the President announced clearly that part of his intention in toppling Saddam's regime was to reshape the Middle East ("other nations in the region") by both providing a future positive example of liberty and by demonstrating the negative result of supporting terror. Included in the reshaping of the wider Middle East is Palestinian society, which is to receive the same set of positive and negative examples, as well as a cutting off of funding for terrorism. Although neither terrorism nor liberation is defined in the speeches, clearly liberation is conceived quite differently from, for example, the liberation of Norway or France during World War II—in those cases the liberation was from a foreign, occupying force, and there were quick handovers of authority to existing resistance movements. Also, with active resistance movements directed against occupation and with democratic traditions firmly in place, it was a simple matter to give power to the resistance movements, with the assurance that real elections would be held in a short time, based on existing, viable constitutions. No such conditions held in Iraq, and no such straightforward "liberation" was possible.

Significantly, there were no published or announced U.S. government plans giving details of the intended eventual handover to an Iraqi government, nor was there an announced road plan showing how or when or under what conditions this might be achieved. (As Senator Robert Byrd stated accurately on the Senate floor on February 12, 2003: "And yet we hear little about the [planned] aftermath of the war in Iraq. In the absence of plans, speculation abroad is rife . . . To whom do we propose to hand the reins of power after Saddam Hussein?"[6])

The post-war occupations of Germany and Japan were "indefinite" simply in the sense that no end date was defined. For the President to say "we will remain in Iraq as long as necessary, and not a day more" may have reassured many Americans of the good intentions of the U.S. government, but it should not be surprising that it did not reassure everyone. Literalists noticed that the term "necessary" was not defined, and that the President seemed to be reserving the power to define it to himself and his successors. The President was stating clearly that the control of the nation of Iraq, previously in the hands of Iraqis, for good or ill, since the British left, was to be taken over by the United States, and relinquished only when the United States decided to do so. This is an important aspect of the stated intention of the United States.

Again, the stated, pre-invasion intention of the Bush administration offered as a model for liberation not post-World War II France or Norway, but Germany and Japan. These "liberations" were not felt as such by many of the people of those countries, it is safe to say, and they were followed by long periods of occupation that ended only when the conquering nations decided to end them. It is odd the President and his advisors chose this model. The people of Germany and Japan, quite unlike the French and Norwegians, did not generally throw flowers in the paths of the American soldiers who marched into their countries during WWII. These were "liberations" that looked exactly like conquest and occupation, even if time showed the occupations to be rather benevolent. In addition, there were some sharp differences between Germany and Japan after World War II and Iraq in March 2003, differences that made the comparison a poor one. Most important, these two powers had just attempted to subjugate large portions of the world, an attempt that met with a catastrophic and overwhelming defeat. These two factors, not present in Iraq, were likely to provoke collective guilt or at least collective acceptance of temporary subjugation by an outside power. Not only had Iraq not tried to conquer the world or even build an empire (the two wars it had started were quite local), it had not crossed one border with aggressive intent in the dozen years before the war. Another factor to be considered is the homogeneity of German and Japanese societies relative to Iraq's. As Dilip Hiro pointed out, the Japanese emperor was able to proclaim the unconditional surrender of his country and have such a proclamation obeyed by his countrymen.[7] Japan is an island. Both Germany and Japan developed as political units through internal efforts (ignoring Napoleon's eventual effect on German unification) but Iraq was carved artificially out of a long-lived Ottoman Empire at the end of World War I. Given that in Iraq the vital factors that defined Japan and Germany after World War II were missing, it is difficult to see how saying, in effect, "we succeeded in Japan and Germany" should have given any hope for a successful "liberation" of Iraq beyond the immediate removal of Saddam's regime.

All of these problems with the stated intentions of the Bush administration raised immediate suspicions. One factor behind those suspicions is the long history of conquest of Middle Eastern lands by Western powers. This is not the proverbial millennia-long memory of the Middle East, but a matter of recent decades. Many Middle Easterners have grandparents who lived under Western occupation. They remember that the Western occupiers appeared in no hurry to depart, and often did so only when forced by violent insurgencies. In addition, U.S. administrations have openly professed an interest in controlling the oil fields of the Middle East. As Professor (and former colonel and West Point teacher) Andrew Bacevich notes:

> In January 1980, to forestall any further deterioration of the U.S. position in the gulf, [President Carter] threw the weight of American military power into the balance. In his State of the Union address, the president enunciated what became known as the Carter Doctrine. "Any attempt by any outside force to gain control of the Persian Gulf region," he declared, "will be regarded as an assault on the vital interests of the United States of America, and such an assault will be repelled by any means necessary, including military force."[8]

Iraq has the second largest oil reserves in the world.[9] This does not define the war as a "war for oil," but Africa, for example, has a number of dictatorships without oil or strategic importance that seem quite unlikely to be liberated by the United States any time soon. It must be acknowledged, on the one hand, that the United States has often had the military power to conquer a territory, and failed to use that power. Thus, an automatic belief that the United States intends to conquer and annex a territory during a war is not reasonable. On the other hand, the United States has conquered and occupied territories and countries, for its own benefit, annexing some permanently (the Southwest territories taken from Mexico, Hawaii), and others temporarily (Cuba and the Philippines after the Spanish-American War, for example). Thus, neither is it absurd to suspect that a U.S. administration may have impure motives in a given situation.[10] Given that the U.S. government has often acted in pursuit of its perceived interests, the presence of large oil reserves under Iraqi soil was likely to exacerbate any such suspicions.

Post-War Revelations of Administration Intentions

Thorough Military Planning vs. Other Planning

In the case of the U.S. government-led invasion of Iraq, the U.S. military was undeniably well prepared to overcome organized military resistance by the forces of Saddam's regime. While some have argued that the job could have been done more safely or with somewhat fewer casualties,[11] in fact the organized fighting was finished in a relatively short time, despite the proverbial uncertainties of war. Military preparations were excruciatingly thorough, and based on all of the best intelligence available about the military capabilities of the regime. Sufficient additional resources were available to overcome unforeseen capabilities of the enemy forces. Clearly the intention by those in charge of the war effort was to plan for all reasonable contingencies, and provide sufficient resources to overcome any difficulties along the way to the overthrow of the regime. This is an indication that the United States government is quite capable of careful planning and forecasting that takes reality, in massive detail, into account. Failure to plan for other eventualities, then, is not due to an inability to plan or lack of resources to use in planning.

Detailed Post-Invasion Plans to Manage Iraq Were Nonexistent

The lack of an announced "exit strategy" would have been seen as unwise, in retrospect, even if a realistic strategy had been ready—it was bound to create suspicion in Iraq and the wider world, and it did. However, it quickly became obvious that despite the enormously detailed planning for the military conquest of Saddam's forces, there was in fact no realistic plan to govern Iraq post-conquest, nor was there a realistic plan to move expeditiously to hand power over to Iraqis.

There is no need to write very much about this lack of planning. The facts are now widely acknowledged, including by those in favor of the war, but they have usually not made the vital connection between this lack of planning and the absolute necessity of planning if there is a sincere right intention to create "the peace of order," in a phrase of Augustine's. In other words, they have noted the lack of planning, but have not noted that it shows that a realistic right intention, a necessary criterion of just war theory for a just war, was simply missing.

Johnson accepts some blame for not emphasizing this aspect of just war theory in the pre-war debate, but insists "There is enough guilt here to go around."[12] If he means, as he seems to mean, that pro- and anti-war commentators share equal guilt on this issue, this conclusion does not follow. First, the burden of proof is on those making the case for war. Second, those with a deeper, better understanding of just war theory (which he clearly believes he and those who agree with him have) owe us a deeper and better application of it if they are going to write and speak about it. Third, there were many published pre-war critics who explicitly and carefully pointed out the likely costs of the war. Many of them are quoted extensively above. When Johnson writes "the rest of what might be required for establishing a peaceful society in Iraq after the removal of Saddam Hussein and his regime simply was not addressed in the debate over whether to remove that regime by force,"[13] he is simply wrong. These other requirements were thoroughly addressed by anti-war critics, who pointed out that they were missing from announced administration plans for post-conquest Iraq. It was the voices in favor of war that glided over and ignored these requirements.

Thomas Ricks, Pulitzer Prize-winning author of *Making the Corps* and the Washington Post's senior military correspondent, spends much of his 2006 book *Fiasco* making the detailed case, both from testimony and from events, that no real plan to govern Iraq had been drawn up before the war. Only a few points from this voluminous book will be cited below.

To begin, Ricks notes, the Defense Department was placed in charge of "postwar Iraq." Ricks quotes a later Rand Corporation study to summarize the problems with that decision: "the Defense Department lacked the experience, expertise, funding authority, local knowledge, and established contacts with other potential organizations needed to establish, staff, support and oversee a large multiagency civilian mission."[14] Next, the task force that was supposed to provide post-war planning "didn't produce a plan," according to Army Lt. Gen. Joseph Kellogg.[15] According to another source, the team "never produced a usable blueprint for running postwar Iraq."

Ricks goes on: "In mid-January, just eight weeks before the invasion, the lead in planning for the postwar situation was taken away from Central Command and moved to the Pentagon." Only at this point was retired Army Lt. Gen. Jay Garner recruited by Secretary of Defense Donald Rumsfeld to "lead postwar operations in Iraq—a task that was expected to be mainly humanitarian work, likely focused on aiding refugees and perhaps the civilian victims of Iraqi chemical or biological weapons."[16]

Ricks earlier describes an Army War College exercise in December 2002 designed to look at post-war Iraq, convened by the Pentagon and involving "about two dozen military experts, Middle East area specialists, diplomats, and intelligence officials at the Army War College." The report produced by the group stated: "The possibility of the United States winning the war and losing the peace is real and serious. . . . Thinking about the war now and the occupation later is not an acceptable solution. . . . Successful occupation will not occur unless the special circumstances of this unusual country" are heeded.[17]

Ricks then describes General Jay Garner's meeting on February 21 and 22 with

> experts from across the U.S. government to discuss postwar Iraq. The session was notable because, according to participants, it was the sole occasion before the war when all the warring factions within the U.S. government met. The official attendance list carries 154 names, but attendees remember many more. "This was the only time the interagency really sat down at the operator level with policy presence and discussed in detail the activities each of the pillar teams had planned," recalled [a participant] . . . The problems were clear. The group had been set up "far too late" . . . There weren't enough troops in the war plan "for the first step of securing all the major urban areas, let alone for providing an interim police function." Without sufficient troops "we risk letting much of the country descend into civil unrest, chaos whose magnitude may defeat our national strategy [sic] of a stable new Iraq."[18]

Perhaps the President was not informed of the problem. He promised, in his February 26 address to the American Enterprise Institute just four days later: "We will provide security against those who seek to spread chaos, or settle scores, or threaten the territorial integrity of Iraq."[19]

The war started less than a month later. When, as predicted in Garner's interagency meeting, there was widespread looting in Iraq, including of museums, hospitals, and other public buildings (except the Ministry of Petroleum), for which U.S. forces provided no protection, Donald Rumsfeld famously responded "stuff happens." Ricks comments: "the message sent to Iraqis . . . was that the U.S. government didn't care—or, even more troubling . . . that it did care but was incapable of acting effectively."[20]

CIA analyst Pollack, in his 2002 book *The Threatening Storm: the Case for Invading Iraq* spent much of his Chapter 11, "The Case for an Invasion," arguing for a massive force that would have at the least greatly alleviated this problem.[21] Pollack made a compelling case that if the U.S. government was concerned about the Iraqi people and the aftermath of the war, it needed to have a huge number of forces on hand in order to maintain security for them.

No Planning for Economic Needs of Iraqi Citizens

Detailed planning to meet the economic needs of ordinary Iraqis was clearly lacking, as the following quotations make terribly clear:

> On May 16, De-Baathification of Iraq Society was issued over [Presidential envoy and de facto governor of Iraq Paul] Bremer's signature as Coalition Provisional Authority [CPA] Order Number 1. It purged tens of thousands of members of the Baath Party—perhaps as many as eighty-five thousand.[22]

But on May 23, Bremer issued CPA Order Number 2, Dissolution of Iraqi Entities, formally doing away with several groups: the Iraqi armed forces, which
accounted for 385,000 people; the staff of the Ministry of Interior, which
amounted to . . . 285,000 people . . . and the presidential security units, a force
of some 50,000. "Abruptly terminating the livelihoods of these men created a
vast pool of humiliated, antagonized, and politicized men," noted Faleh Jabar,
an expert on the Baathist [sic] party . . . Many of these men were armed. . . .
Bremer's two orders threw out of work more than half a million people and
alienated many more dependent on those lost incomes.[23]

[Bremer] soon began pursuing a program aimed at moving Iraq toward a free-
market economy, beginning by shutting down unprofitable state-run industries.
This had the political effect of alienating the middle class, which already had
been hit hard by de-Baathification, and which was full of managers from those
inefficient industries.[24]

Such actions were noticed both by U.S. soldiers and by Iraqis. Ricks quotes
a Lt. Col. Holshek:

At Tallil there were eleven thousand [U.S. personnel], hundreds of millions of
dollars being spent, and not a goddamn thing being done for the people down-
town. So we looked like an occupation power. And we were—we behaved like
one. The message we were sending was, we didn't care much about the Iraqis,
because we didn't do what we needed to do on things like electricity.[25]

An Iraqi woman blogger, who says she lost her job after the invasion, wrote
on August 24, 2003:

Over 65% of the Iraqi population is unemployed. The reason for this is because Bremer made some horrible decisions. The first major decision he made
was to dissolve the Iraqi army. That may make sense in Washington, but here,
we were left speechless. Now there are over 400,000 trained, armed men with
families that need to be fed. Where are they supposed to go? What are they
supposed to do for a living? I don't know. They certainly don't know.
   They roam the streets looking for work, looking for an answer. You can
see perplexity and anger in their stance, their walk, their whole demeanor. Their
eyes shift from face to face, looking for a clue. Who is to answer for this mess?
Who do you think?
   Bremer also dissolved the Ministry of Information and the Ministry of Defense. No matter what the excuses, these ministries were full of ordinary people
with ordinary jobs—accountants, janitors, secretaries, engineers, journalists,
technicians, operators . . . these people are now jobless. Companies have been
asked to "cut down" their staff. It no longer has anything to do with politics.
The company my uncle works in as an engineer was asked by the CPA to get
rid of 680 of the 1,500+ employees—engineers, designers, contractors, mechan-
ics, technicians and the administration were all involved.
   Other companies, firms, bureaus, factories and shops shut down as a result
of the looting and damage done in the post-war chaos—thousands of other
workers lost their jobs. Where to go? What to do?[26]

No Political Plan for Creating a Stable, Unified Government

There was no realistic plan for creating a stable, unified government among Iraq's sharply disparate social, ethnic, and religious groups, simply a statement that the United States would do so. This is an extraordinary fact. To see why, consider the example of the United States. When the United States formulated its Constitution, the colonists were a relatively culturally homogenous group—at least among those who would be allowed to vote. In addition, the representatives of each colony, without outside direction, had just finished working together to achieve the difficult task of wresting their independence from the British. But even given those positive factors, writing the Constitution was still not a simple task, nor was it done by a group of wise men acting officially on behalf of the planned new nation as a whole. The Constitution was written by a group of men who were officially sent as representatives of their States. (Their assigned job, of course, which they ignored, was to propose an improved version of the Articles of Confederation, not to suggest a considerably more powerful central government, as they in fact did.) Each of those States saw itself as an independent political unit that had temporarily delegated some of its rights to the weak central government created by the Articles of Confederation. While each State had its own interests, the different regions or groups of States had their interests as well. Did these men vote on a Constitution, with numbers of votes based on the population of each State? Certainly not. They began by exploring the interests of each region, and suggested compromises, such as dividing the legislature between a House with numbers of seats based on population, and a Senate with two seats for each State, regardless of size. Were the States with large populations thrilled with that compromise? Definitely not, but if they had insisted on a single House, the small States would have rejected the Constitution.

President Bush told the American Enterprise Institute in February 2003, "[t]he United States has no intention of determining the precise form of Iraq's new government. That choice belongs to the Iraqi people. Yet we will ensure that one brutal dictator is not replaced by another. All Iraqis must have a voice in the new government, and all citizens must have their rights protected."[27] On the surface, the intention expressed in these words is excellent. But did the Bush administration have a plan to produce a constitution for Iraq that would protect regions with smaller populations against the will of the large-population regions? Did it have a plan to persuade the minority Sunni Arabs, who had been the rulers of modern Iraq throughout its history, and who had dominated the majority Shiites for hundreds of years, to accept political minority status? Apparently not. What the U.S. government finally did was simply to hold elections throughout Iraq, and then to have the winners sit together and draw up a constitution for the nation. In other words, unlike the U.S. case, during the drafting of the Constitution in 1787, complete domination of minorities by the majority was built into the rules that shaped the writing of the constitution itself.

Having midwifed a constitution in which minorities and low-population regions have no protection against domination by the majority, it seems the U.S. government continued pushing the resulting government of Iraq to devise power and revenue-sharing plans. Although this is certainly not how the United States dealt with such issues, somehow many in the United States expected "pressure" from the U.S. government to persuade the representatives of the majority (Shiite Arabs), who have been oppressed by the minority (especially Sunni Arabs, since the Kurds expect to maintain some kind of autonomy), to come up with equitable solutions that will protect the minority—against themselves! This was precisely the problem anticipated before the war by many experts, including those listened to by the first President George Bush, who wrote with Brent Scowcroft, after discussing their decision not to carry the war to Iraq: "Had we gone the invasion route, the United States could conceivably still be an occupying power in a bitterly hostile land."[28] Saying, "all Iraqis must have a voice in the new government" did nothing to solve the problem; in fact, it simply restated one of the oldest problems of political science.

Many of the quotations in earlier sections of this chapter from Ricks' book *Fiasco* concern the question of a plan to administer Iraq until it was handed over to a new government, but that is the smaller of the missing things. As Ricks eloquently describes the gradual worsening of the situation on the ground in the months and years following the invasion, he makes even more clear by his near silence the hugeness of the missing piece that had apparently barely been discussed, much less planned: the need to create a new Iraqi government in a deeply divided society. Ricks notes at one point that "according to an internal Army War College summary," the official U.S. Army plan for post-war operations in Iraq operated on an assumption "That an Iraqi government would quickly spring into being, permitting a quick handoff to Iraqi interim administration with UN mandate."[29] The fact is enormous, but not always mentioned in this context: the United States destroyed the existing government, without any plan to create a new one. The decision to go to war with Iraq was made and carried out without any plan for putting a new government in place.

No Plan for the Virtual Certainty of an Insurrection

As noted above in Chapter 5, in the section "Building a New Iraq was Unlikely to Succeed," the belief that the United States would be in a good position to help Iraqis "build a new Iraq" after removing its government by force rested on culpable ignorance of well-known facts concerning Iraq's people, history, and culture. First, invasions of countries with sharply different cultures from those of the invader, however well-meaning the invaders claim to be, have a history of leading to bitter insurgencies. In Chapter 5, the British occupation of Iraq after World War I, the Israeli invasion of Lebanon in 1982, and the U.S. invasion of the Philippines at the beginning of the twentieth century were cited as examples. A few more: Ethiopia under the Italians in the 1930s, Somalia under the UN in the early 1990s, Afghanistan under Russia in the 1980s. This list could go on and on. It might be easier simply to ask for a list of conquered, occupied countries where an insurgency did not take place. If such a list begins with Germany and Japan after World War II, then, again, the special circumstances already mentioned that applied in those two countries should be considered. In Eastern Europe under Soviet domination, there were numerous attempts by the people to assert their independence. Only after the brutal crushing of these movements did patriots desiring independence turn to other means of dissent. That would be a shameful model for the United States to have followed, and the eventual outcome could not have been encouraging even if it had been considered. The idea that Iraq as a whole would quietly accept being ruled by foreigners for an indeterminate time was always unlikely in light of recent world history, and also ran counter to Iraq's particular history and culture. A near certainty of an eventual insurgency or insurrection should have been part of pre-war U.S. government planning, especially given the well-known Iraqi pride and dislike of being dictated to by foreigners.[30]

OBJECTIONS

Objection One: Detailed Post-War Plans an Unrealistic Idea

Objection: Isn't it unrealistic to expect detailed post-war planning? After all, this would take enormous knowledge of the country, and deal with many unpredictable variables. Wasn't it a good enough intention to remove a dictator and then hand over power to the people?

Reply: But if it is realistic to expect an incredibly detailed plan to *conquer* a country, a huge undertaking, why not expect such planning for the ruling of a country, and the handover of power to its people? Just as it would be utterly irresponsible to launch a non-emergency war in the modern age without voluminous, detailed, reality-based plans for winning the military battles, it is clearly irresponsible not to have at least a similar level of planning for a post-war transition, if a war is to be fought at all. Secondly, power simply cannot be handed to "the people." Governance of a country as a whole is never performed by "the people" in some kind of homogeneous mass. There must always be mechanisms to determine how power is exercised, and people fight precisely over the control of these mechanisms. Only those who largely agree on the mechanisms for the exercise of power form a peaceful political body. Europe, America, Japan, and Australia have political cultures in which the vast majority of people agree that political power should be acquired at the polls and exercised through an existing constitutional arrangement. The Iraqi people clearly did not have such a culture in 2003, nor did they have a usable constitution. Without a plan to overcome this deficit, there was no short or medium-term likelihood of achieving a peaceful, stable Iraq. That is "the aim of peace," and failing to have a realistic plan to achieve it means failing to meet the "right intention" criterion. Plunging a society into war with no realistic plan to create stability later is not a just act.

Objection Two: What about Oil? Remaking the Middle East?

Objection: What about the belief of many that the Bush administration was seeking to ensure access to Middle East oil supplies? What about the President's claim that the war would cause dramatic positive changes in the wider Middle East's political culture? These issues have hardly been addressed here.

Reply: Seizing resources to ensure economic security is not a legitimate intention in just war theory. A case might be made that this was part of the Bush administration's intention. If so, however, the results indicate very poor execution of the plan. At the end of the Bush administration, the total direct financial cost was widely reckoned to be close to a half a trillion dollars, a figure that did not include such items as future medical care for wounded veterans or the higher price of oil.[31] Iraqi oil production in April 2009 was some 2.37 million barrels per day, while the prewar figure was 2.58 million barrels per day.[32] Although the early decision to secure the oil ministry buildings in Baghdad while providing security almost nowhere else in that city rang alarm bells in much of the world, that action is not in itself proof that the aim of the Bush administration was to seize Iraqi oil. However, demonstrating proof or even the likelihood of a wrong intention is not necessary here, only whether a right intention can be demonstrated. Without a right intention, a war is unjust, as Aquinas pointed out.

Concerning the project of remaking the Middle East, it could not possibly be just to make war in one country in order to "shape" another, even if that were possible. This fact may have influenced the decision not to mention this aim in President Bush's "declaration of war" radio address. Once again, however, it is not necessary to consider all possible intentions: the key intention needed was the aim of peace, the intention to create a stable, just society in the targeted country. If that had been present, it would have made a just war far more likely. Absent, like any of the other criteria, it made a just war impossible.

Objection Three: The Administration Trusted Its Experts

Objection: The Bush administration understandably trusted certain experts, who said Iraqis would welcome U.S. forces as liberators. One of those experts, Fouad Ajami, was quoted by the Vice President as saying "after liberation the streets in Basra and Baghdad are 'sure to erupt in joy in the same way the throngs in Kabul greeted the Americans.'" Other experts had different opinions. Choices must be made among experts.

Reply: It is true that Fouad Ajami is both an Arabic speaker and an academic, and certainly qualifies as a Middle East expert, and favored the war in Iraq. Other highly qualified academics, such as Bernard Lewis, also were in favor of the war, and gave reasons for that point of view. There is no need to deny the knowledge of such men, but nor is there any need to pit expert against expert in this case. It is enough to note two things: first, being greeted as a liberator is relatively easy—the twentieth century is full of invasions that are initially greeted, as least by part of the populace, as liberations. It is much more difficult to be seen as a liberator if you are still occupying a country six months after your arrival. If you have no plan to deal with that, you have not done your homework. Second, when the writings of the pro-war academics are examined in some detail, it seems they did not in fact offer such optimistic views as is often thought—and when they did, the details of how the optimistic outcome would arrive are extremely sketchy. These pro-war experts offered no road map for dealing with the likely problems noted in this chapter.

Shortly before the war Ajami offered a quite sober view of the likely response of the wider Arab world, writing in "Iraq and the Arabs' Future" in the January/February 2003 issue of *Foreign Affairs*:

> There should be no illusions about the sort of Arab landscape that America is destined to find if, or when, it embarks on a war against the Iraqi regime. There would be no "hearts and minds" to be won in the Arab world, no public diplomacy that would convince the overwhelming majority of Arabs that this war would be a just war. An American expedition in the wake of thwarted UN inspections would be seen by the vast majority of Arabs as an imperial reach into their world, a favor to Israel, or a way for the United States to secure control over Iraq's oil. No hearing would be given to the great foreign power. [It is interesting that Ajami apparently thought an "expedition" would follow something that never happened: Iraqi "thwarting" of inspections.]
>
> America ought to be able to live with this distrust and discount a good deal of this anti-Americanism as the "road rage" of a thwarted Arab world—the congenital condition of a culture yet to take full responsibility for its self-inflicted wounds. There is no need to pay excessive deference to the political pieties and givens of the region. Indeed, this is one of those settings where a reforming foreign power's simpler guidelines offer a better way than the region's age-old prohibitions and defects.
>
> Above and beyond toppling the regime of Saddam Hussein and dismantling its deadly weapons, the driving motivation of a new American endeavor in Iraq and in neighboring Arab lands should be modernizing the Arab world. The great indulgence granted to the ways and phobias of Arabs has reaped a terrible harvest—for the Arabs themselves, and for an America implicated in their affairs.[33]

At the least, Ajami was warning in the final weeks before the war that the welcome in the wider Arab world might be far from warm. In fact, he predicted a great deal of hostility, with no prediction of when it might end (and no reason why many Iraqis, who are also Arabs, would not share that hostility). It is hard to see how this widespread, ongoing hostility would not help derail the project of modernizing the Arab world and healing its "self-inflicted wounds." This passage also shows an apparent dripping, harsh contempt for the existing Arab world that might cause disquiet about Ajami as an expert—the contemptuous are right many times, but they are rarely the best guides to a subject. And is it not rather contemptuous to think the United States could "modernize the Arab world" by force? Certainly there appears to be more hubris than sober academic wisdom in the idea that one country's military could hope to transform an entire region in a positive way.

But this beginning was simply Ajami's prediction, correct as it turned out, of widespread hostility in the wider Arab world. Later in the article, Ajami applied this cautious approach to prediction to Iraq itself:

> Iraq should not be burdened, however, with the weight of great expectations. This is the Arab world, after all, and Americans do not know it with such intimacy. Iraq could disappoint its American liberators. There has been heartbreak in Iraq, and vengeance and retribution could sour Americans on this latest sphere of influence in the Muslim world.[34]

Most importantly, one looks in vain for Ajami's suggestions on how to overcome the deep divisions outlined by Hiro, or the pitfalls laid out so carefully by James Fallows (both quoted at length in the following chapter). Concerning Iraq itself, Ajami wrote again and again in this article "Iraq may . . . ," "Iraq might . . . ," "a more likely outcome . . . ." On the one hand, this assumes a unity of Iraq that Ajami should have known was an illusion. On the other hand, it shows that he had no confidence in the outcome of a U.S. invasion. He offered one hopeful comparison for the task of "repairing" or "detoxifying" Iraq's own political culture—the U.S. occupation of Japan from 1945 to 1952. He acknowledged that the heterogeneous Iraq differed from Japan, but devoted just one paragraph to the importance of "the Japanese precedent," and that paragraph had no detail whatsoever about Iraq.[35] In essence, then, Ajami made clear before the war that he saw it as a roll of the dice, with no guarantee even of a democratic Iraq as an outcome. Part of his conclusion reads as follows: "It is with sobering caution, then, that a war will have to be waged. But it should be recognized that the Rubicon has been crossed. Any fallout of war is certain to be dwarfed by the terrible consequences of America's walking right up to the edge of war and then stepping back, letting the Iraqi dictator work out the terms of another reprieve."[36] Those "terrible consequences" are simply not discussed in the article. This was not a just war analysis, it was not even risk analysis, and neither was it a confident prediction of a successful outcome.

Bernard Lewis is another pro-war academic whose predictions were actually more nuanced than his reputation would indicate. Like Ajami, Lewis gave little detail to back up his more optimistic assertions. Lewis had a tough-guy persona earned with lines from 2002 like: "Our anxious pleading with the fragile and frightened regimes of the region to join—or at least to tolerate—a campaign against terrorism and its sponsors has put the U.S. in a corner where it seems to be asking permission for actions that are its own prerogative to take."[37] Yet Lewis is not easy to put into a box. On imposing democracy, Lewis has said:

> Democracy is dangerous anywhere. Democracy is a very strong medicine which has to be administered in small, gradually increasing doses: Otherwise you risk killing the patient. We talk sometimes as if democracy were the natural human condition, as if any deviation from it is a crime to be punished or a disease to be cured. . . . Democracy . . . is the parochial custom of the English-

speaking peoples for the conduct of their public affairs, which may or may not be suitable for others. . . . Hitler came to power by a free and democratic vote.[38]

He has actually written, "the overwhelming majority of our terrorist enemies['] . . . main grievance against us is that, in their eyes, we are responsible for maintaining the tyrannical regimes that rule over them—an accusation that has, to say the very least, some plausibility."[39]

Looking carefully at Lewis' remarks made at an academic conference, entitled "The Regional Implications of Pursuing 'Regime Change' in Iraq" (made in October 2002), one finds a picture rather similar to Ajami's emerging: Lewis shares reservations and generalized predictions, not detailed analyses. It is a witty speech: "One view holds that the Arabs and other Middle Eastern peoples are not like Westerners. They are incapable of running free and democratic institutions. Whatever we do, they will be governed by odious tyrants . . . this is known as the pro-Arab attitude." But when Lewis comes to the meat of the speech, there is not much beef: "The Middle East is a region of great, ancient civilizations with talented and ingenious people, and I have no doubt at all that they can create free societies. We cannot do it for them. The most that we can do is to remove obstacles. Among these obstacles are regimes such as that of Saddam Husayn." He goes on to raise the parallel of—what else? Post World War II Germany and Japan. "Following the end of that war, American and other Allied forces entered both countries, but not with the intention of conquering and dominating them. The Allied intention was, first, to remove a major menace, and second, to give them the opportunity to redeem themselves and to restore or create their own freedom." Lewis goes on to state that he is optimistic about Iraq because of its fine educational system. He concludes: "For this and other reasons, there is general hope. The main task is not creating opportunities, but removing obstacles."[40]

So, while Lewis has plenty of expertise to draw on, his only examples of "obstacles removed" that turned out well are—Japan and Germany. Once again, there were factors at work in those two instances that did not apply to Iraq, but Lewis ignored that fact. Secondly, the United States did not simply "remove obstacles" in Japan and Germany—it began an extensive, forceful tutelage that went on for years. Is it even possible for a conqueror simply to "remove obstacles," without favoring one native group or another for at least an interim period? But regardless of what Lewis may have had in mind when he used this phrase, it is clearly not compatible in any normal sense with leaving 100,000 or more troops in the country for months (much less years) after the conquest. That is an ongoing occupation, whether benevolent or not. Lewis did not provide any good reason for an occupation by the United States to turn out well in Iraq. His general optimism seemed to be based largely on the character of the educated Iraqis he met. That is very positive, but it is surely not a balanced point of view backed up by a wide-ranging analysis.

It appears that people like Ajami and Lewis lent their names and reputations to the war effort, as was their right, but did not provide detailed analyses that took the reality of the situation into account. Instead, they provided generalizations and hope.

Objection Four: Why Plan for Looting after Liberation?

Objection: How could the looting have been predicted? Weren't the Iraqis simply more violent and lawless than we expected, and how could the American government have expected that?

Reply: The looting should not have been a surprise. When the existing government was removed in Kosovo, widespread ethnic cleansing and so-called "revenge killings" took place, despite the presence of NATO troops. When Mobutu's government fell, in slow motion, in Zaire in 1997, as his troops retreated from each region there was looting before the rebels arrived. In the late 1960s in the United States, power outages in "ghettos" led to looting. The instances are legion. Wherever there is a government based on coercion rather than one that evolved from a sense of social cohesion (or even, in the U.S. case, a government that does not have the respect of a significant portion of the populace), and such a government is even temporarily removed, looting takes place. If you deliberately remove a government, and you are responsible, you will have detailed plans and resources in place to stop the expected looting. Surely the U.S. government was responsible to research the question of what was likely to happen when a government was removed. (In fact, the experts predicted "chaos"—even President Bush was aware of these predictions, saying the United States would ensure it didn't happen, see above.)

Objection Five: Intention and Planning Are Separate Issues

Objection: Even if the Bush Administration failed to plan carefully for the aftermath of war, that does not mean it failed to show right intention. That judgment is too harsh. Intentions need to be considered separately from the question of detailed planning. In the account given here, there is no room for mistakes. While mistakes were made, as a number of senior Bush administration officials have admitted, they nonetheless meant well, and that is what "right intention" is surely about.

Reply: No less an authority than Aquinas makes it clear that this sharp division between planning (the choice of means to an end) and intention (the willing of that end) is incorrect. Aquinas provides a positive answer to the question "Whether intention of the end is the same act as the volition of the means?" (The entire section is well worth reading.) In his "On the contrary" section, he writes clearly: "Therefore in things pertaining to the will, the intention of the end is the same movement as the willing of the means."[41] He continues:

> The end, considered as a thing, and the means to that end, are distinct objects of the will. But in so far as the end is the formal object in willing the means, they

are one and the same object. . . . Accordingly, in so far as the movement of the will is to the means, as ordained to the end, it is called "choice": but the movement of the will to the end as acquired by the means . . . is called "intention."

To translate that into less philosophical language, only an aim for which means have been chosen can be definitely shown to have been intended in the sense that classic just war theory uses the word. Someone who takes only enough fuel to cross the first 100 miles of the Sahara Desert cannot be shown to have "intended" to cross the whole Sahara unless he had other, realistic plans for acquiring fuel along the way. Failure to choose the necessary means is a failure to intend the stated end.[42] Detailed planning that was wrong ("willing the wrong means") would be another issue altogether. Had that been present, it would be useful to talk about mistakes, and such mistakes might not have nullified a right intention. But in many cases outlined in this chapter, there is no evidence of any serious planning at all for vital purposes: no means were chosen for the stated end of "liberation" and enabling a peaceful, well-governed society, leading inescapably to the conclusion that the stated intentions did not qualify as "right intentions" under just war theory.

For classic just war theory, "intention" is not a good thought that sits in a ruler's mind without having any effect, nor is it the pious expression of that thought coming out of his mouth. It is an internal fact that is fleshed out in the real world by the choice of means that will lead to the stated end.

Objection Six: What about Simple Miscommunication?

Objection: What about simple miscommunication? It appears to many people that Bush had the right intention, to liberate Iraq and help Iraqis establish a decent and stable society, but the intention got lost in the bureaucracy. He surely gave orders, but he couldn't be everywhere to see that they were enforced.

Reply: The President, as he famously said, was the "Decider." As such, he bears ultimate responsibility for what took place, not only because of the office, but because the authority and resources of the office of the presidency are such that he could have easily ensured that the right planning did take place and that the resources were available. President Bush has a Master's degree in Business Administration. One of the keys to management is to know the various categories of actions needed, to ensure that each one is delegated to a competent person with the resources to ensure that it is accomplished, and then to follow up periodically and ensure that each of the necessary actions is proceeding according to plan. If a manager simply "delegates" responsibility to a planner, then the manager intends whatever that person comes up with, for good or ill.

The only possible escape from responsibility would be if a manager chose someone with a great reputation and track record, followed up to attempt to ensure that the person was making progress, and finally discovered after the fact that the person chosen somehow failed to do what was required. However, any manager who discovers on the day a new factory is opened that some vital delegated piece of equipment is missing will probably not give a big hug to the person left in charge of that piece. More likely, the manager will let everyone know that he or she not only intended to have everything in place, but also chose someone, provided resources, and followed up—with someone who turned out to be incompetent or a crook. George Bush, on the other hand, granted the Presidential Medal of Freedom on December 2, 2004, to former CIA Director George Tenet, who directed the provision of the bad intelligence that helped justify the war, former General Tommy Franks, who oversaw the plan for conquest that had no provision for a transition to civilian Iraqi rule, and L. Paul Bremer III, who quickly fired over half a million Iraqis without making any provision for them to find work.[43] These actions in no way appear to be the deeds of a man who intended something other than what was done.[44]

Objection Seven: Perhaps Bush Changed His Intention Later

Objection: Perhaps the Bush administration did not fulfill this criterion at the outset of the war. However, anyone can see that administration officials realized their errors, and took very many steps to attempt to establish a peaceful and just Iraq, as well as organizing elections and then handing over power to the new government that was formed. The fullness of a "right intention" seems to have developed late, but surely not too late.

Reply: This objection, or query, begins with an admission that the war was launched without a right intention. We need to begin by recalling that Aquinas says a war without a right intention is unjust. It is gravely immoral to start an unjust war, which is equivalent to an aggressive war. The immorality of one action is not removed by beginning to act morally afterward.

Moving from the corporate to the personal level by way of illustration, if someone does something gravely immoral to a person, does it become moral if the intention changes after the initial deed? What if a man, believing his neighbor is mistreating his wife, breaks into the house and shoots the neighbor in the leg. Surely the first thing demanded by a realization that the act was wrong is an apology, not for mistakes in performance, but for the immoral act itself. Without at least the apology, who would be inclined to forgive, on a personal level? And the apology must be followed by a commitment to do whatever is necessary to right the wrong. If that is true on the personal level, why should it be different on a corporate level?

In addition, it is simply not clear that changing intention after an invasion would turn an unjust into a just war, even if all the other criteria had been met. (As IJWP 5 in Chapter 2 points out, all criteria need to be met for a just war.) The damage done by an invasion without a right intention may be impossible to repair. Property is destroyed, but worse, people have died, and are wounded and maimed and blinded. An existing government is gone, with no clarity about how a new one is to be established. How would all that become right with a simple change in intention?

Of course, it's better to have a late right intention than never, but it is not clear whether even that can be demonstrated. Perhaps the later intention was only to look as good as possible in a politically difficult situation. The analysis of all administration actions from a given point onward (and how would that point be chosen?) to see if a right intention had been demonstrated at that point would be far more difficult than showing a right intention from the beginning. At any rate, unless the other five criteria prove to have been met, the question is a theoretical one. The issue of what the country that launches an unjust war should do when the realization sets in will be revisited at the end of Chapter 12.

Objection Eight: Missing Essential Element in Just War Idea

Objection: the respected (and clearly pro-war) Just War commentator Johnson stated in 2005 that the Bush administration "missed an essential element in the just war idea." This appears to be different from failing to meet the criterion.

But another of the core just war concepts, which must always be honored, is that the aim of such force must include the establishment of peace. . . . one is obligated, if one uses force to remove an evildoer from power, to replace his government with one that exercises sovereign authority for good, not evil, and that can create an order that serves justice and peace. . . . In retrospect, the need to have this treated more importantly in the public debate looms even larger because of the practical obligations it carries for American involvement in the reconstruction of the Iraqi public order. The possibility of long-term American involvement should have been part of our general consideration of the argument for regime change, for political good typically does not come without some other political sacrifice. . . . I would have had the Bush administration argue more forwardly for making this commitment in advance. . . . After Bosnia, Kosovo, and Afghanistan, it was obvious that, in such cases, a relatively robust military presence is needed to maintain general order by deterring most outbreaks of force [sic] and punishing those which occur . . . These cases, especially the older ones from the former Yugoslavia, also show how difficult it is to carry this out and how much time and effort are required to succeed. Regime change is not accomplished merely by removing the evil regime; it also requires some such restorative process as this. . . . Remarkably, all that this requirement [establishing peace] might entail was utterly neglected [sic] in this moral debate. . . . Arguments were put forward that looked back to Iraq's brief experience with democracy following the end of the British mandate, but they neglected to take account the repression and systematic efforts at thought control characteristic of the intervening decades or the fact that many talented and independent-minded Iraqis had simply fled the country to escape this regime. . . . Liberty is not the only virtue of a good society. . . . Establishing liberty does not assure peace. . . . If we are to take seriously that a justified resort to force must intend the establishment of peace, then not addressing what this meant in concrete terms is to miss an essential element in the just war idea.[45]

Reply: First, Johnson's statement that the issues involved were "utterly neglected" in the pre-war debate is inaccurate. As shown in this and the following chapter, precisely these issues were raised again and again by those opposed to the war, from Brent Scowcroft on the "realist right" all the way to the other end of the American political spectrum. In addition, the factors he cites as likely to create difficulties in the effort are not the most important ones: if they had been, many Middle Eastern countries would be flourishing democracies today, since they have not suffered under tyranny like Saddam's. He is quite right, however, that there are many, easily accessible recent examples of the effort needed to succeed at "the establishment of peace."

Secondly, Johnson speaks of the Bush administration "miss[ing] an essential element in the just war idea." Here Johnson nearly admits, but somehow neglects mentioning, the vital fact. Aquinas stated: "in order for a war to be just, three things (one of which was right intention, including the aim of peace) are necessary." If these necessary elements are not present, then the war, for Aquinas, is not just. Johnson implies at least that the Bush administration did "not address" what [the establishment of peace] "meant in concrete terms." Johnson almost seemed to see that this meant failing to meet one of the core criteria, with the resulting verdict, "an unjust war." To say "missing an essential element in the just war idea" in effect dodges that essential point.

NOTES

1. U.S. income tax instructions, form 2555, 2008, second page.
2. Aquinas, *Summa*, I-II, 58, 4.
3. Johnson, *War to Oust*, 38.
4. Bush, "The War Begins," 503-4.
5. Bush, "Iraq is Fully Capable of Living in Freedom" (speech at the American Enterprise Institute), February 26, 2003, in *Iraq War Reader*, 558, 559.
6. Senator Robert Byrd, "Sleepwalking through History" (Senate speech), February 12, 2003, quoted in *Iraq War Reader*, 484. The State Department's "Future of Iraq" project, which existed at the time but was not public, did not have the blessing of the White House (and, at any rate, did not give clear guidance on the shape of the future government). For the intra-agency feuding over the shape of a future Iraqi government, see Ricks, *Fiasco*, 78-81 and 101-111. At the time, the only thing apparent was that there was no announced plan with any detail whatsoever. The "Future of Iraq" notes were released as a result of a Freedom of Information Act (FOIA) request, and are available at *The National Security Archive*, 2006, http://www.gwu.edu/~nsarchiv/NSAEBB/NSAEBB198/index.htm (accessed October 11, 2007).
7. Dilip Hiro, "The Post-Saddam Problem," in *Iraq War Reader*, 563.
8. Andrew Bacevich, "The Real World War IV," *Syracuse University*, http://faculty.maxwell.syr.edu/merupert/BACEVICH%20The%20Real%20World%20War%20IV.pdf (accessed January 23, 2008) (Note: article first appeared in the *Wilson Quarterly*, Winter 2005). Bacevich continues: "From Carter's time down to the present day, the doctrine bearing his name has remained sacrosanct. As a consequence, each of Carter's successors has expanded the level of U.S. military involvement and operations in the region. Even today, American political leaders cling to the belief that skillful application of military power will enable the United States to decide the fate not simply of the Persian Gulf proper but of the entire greater Middle East."
9. "According to the US Energy Information Administration (EIA), 'Iraq holds more than 112 billion barrels of oil—the world's second largest proven reserves. Iraq also contains 110 trillion cubic feet of natural gas, and is a focal point for regional and interna-

tional security issues.'" Quoted in "Iraq: Oil and Economy," *About.com: U.S. Government Info,* http://usgovinfo.about.com/library/weekly/aairaqioil.htm (accessed October 11, 2007).

10. Cf. Stephen Kinzer, *Overthrow* (New York: Times Books, 2006) which details the overthrow of 14 regimes by the United States in 110 years. Whether or not one agrees with the details of Kinzer's analysis, the facts do appear to indicate a U.S. government willingness to use force that is at least questionable in many cases, and at worst in obvious violation of international law and justice, in pursuit of perceived U.S. interests.

11. See Ricks, *Fiasco,* 118-19.

12. Johnson, *War to Oust,* 67.

13. Johnson, *War to Oust,* 65.

14. Ricks, *Fiasco,* 78.

15. Ricks, *Fiasco,* 79.

16. Ricks, *Fiasco,* 80.

17. Ricks, *Fiasco,* 72-73.

18. Ricks, *Fiasco,* 101.

19. Bush, "Iraq is Fully Capable," 557.

20. Ricks, *Fiasco,* 136.

21. Pollack, *Threatening Storm,* 332-34.

22. Ricks, *Fiasco,* 160.

23. Ricks, *Fiasco,* 162-63.

24. Ricks, *Fiasco,* 165. The question is not whether such industries in the long run needed to be shut down, though surely that was an Iraqi rather than an American decision. The question is whether it was done in a way that showed concern for the needs of ordinary Iraqis. As these decisions were taken, huge contracts in Iraq were going to American companies.

25. Ricks, *Fiasco,* 200.

26. Riverbend, "Baghdad Burning," *Riverbendblog,* August 24, 2003, http://riverbendblog.blogspot.com/2003_08_01_riverbendblog_archive.html (accessed October 11, 2007). (Note: while there is some debate on the internet concerning the blogger's identity, alluding to the high quality of her English [there is speculation that she lived in the United States for a time], there is every reason to believe that a young Iraqi woman might want to blog anonymously. The facts she cites concerning the situation in Iraq are not at all farfetched, and the opinions reflect those of other Iraqis who have spoken for attribution.)

27. Bush, "Iraq is Fully Capable," 557.

28. Bush and Scowcroft, "Why We Didn't Go to Baghdad," 102.

29. Ricks, *Fiasco,* 110.

30. See for example Hiro, "The Post-Saddam Problem," 561, but many other sources are available.

31. See for example Lawrence B. Lindsey, "What Iraq will cost the U.S.," *Fortune,* http://money.cnn.com/2008/01/10/news/economy/costofwar.fortune/ (accessed February 12, 2008). Lindsey is a former White House economist who left the White House after his public estimate that the war might cost up to $200 billion displeased his bosses. On January 31, 2009, the estimate of direct costs of the war by the "National Priorities Project," showed a total cost to date in excess of $593 billion. "Cost of War," *National Priorities Project,* http://www.nationalpriorities.org/costofwar_home (accessed January 31, 2009).

32. "Iraq: Key Figures since the war began," *The Associated Press,* May 1, 2009, http://www.google.com/hostednews/ap/article/ALeqM5j1bBjr_tTTXaVRXckza_PUyGPf EwD97TP36G0 (accessed May 31, 2009).

33. Fouad Ajami, "Iraq and the Arabs' Future," *Foreign Affairs*, January/February 2003, Volume 82 No. 1, 2.

34. Ajami, "Iraq and the Arabs' Future," *Foreign Affairs*, January/February 2003, Volume 82 No. 1, 11.

35. Ajami, "Iraq and the Arabs' Future," 15.

36. Ajami, "Iraq and the Arabs' Future," 18.

37. Bernard Lewis, "A War of Resolve," *The Wall Street Journal*, April 26, 2002, http://www.opinionjournal.com/editorial/feature.html?id=105001985 (accessed October 22, 2007).

38. Lewis, quoted in Saul Singer, "Domino Democracy: an interview with Bernard Lewis" *The Jerusalem Post*, April 21, 2002, http://lists.topica.com/lists/saulsinger/read/message.html?mid=802506841 (accessed October 22, 2007).

39. Lewis, "At War: Time for Toppling: The arguments against regime change are backward," *The Wall Street Journal*, September 28, 2002, http://www.opinionjournal.com/editorial/feature.html?id=110002355 (accessed October 22, 2007).

40. Lewis, "The Regional Implications of Pursuing 'Regime Change' in Iraq (Part I)," The Washington Institute for the Middle East, Weinberg Founders Conference, October 2002 http://www.washingtoninstitute.org/templateC07.php?CID=114 (accessed October 22, 2007).

41. Aquinas, *Summa*, I-II, 12, 4.

42. I am indebted to my friend, Thomas Aquinas College tutor John Nieto, for steering me toward this observation by Aquinas.

43. "Presidential Medal of Freedom Recipient L. Paul Bremer III," *The Official Site of the Presidential Medal of Freedom*, http://www.medaloffreedom.com/PaulBremer.htm (accessed December 19, 2008).

44. In a strange interview on December 15, 2008, Bush, when reminded by the interviewer that Iraq only became "one of the major theaters against al Qaeda" after the United States invaded, responded, "So what? The point is that al Qaeda said they're going to take a stand. Well, first of all in the post-9/11 environment Saddam Hussein posed a threat. And then upon removal, al Qaeda decides to take a stand." It is an extraordinary answer in light of the use of Saddam's supposed links to Al Qaida to justify the overthrow of Saddam. The lack of interest in the sequence of events makes it appear that what actually happened, including to the country of Iraq, had little interest for him. That casts an unpleasant light on the question of Bush's intentions. "Bush On Al Qaeda Not Existing In Iraq Before Invasion: 'So What?'," *Think Progress*, http://thinkprogress.org/2008/12/15/bush-so-what/ (accessed December 26, 2008). (Note: I first saw this interview referred to on the LewRockwell.com blog.)

45. Johnson, *War to Oust*, 63-65.

Chapter Eight

Proportionality of Ends

Is the political objective we seek to achieve important, clearly defined and understood? . . . Will military force achieve the objective? At what cost? Have the gains and risks been analyzed? How might the situation that we seek to alter, once it is altered by force, develop further and what might be the consequences?

—Colin Powell, "Questions policymakers should ask"[1]

Introduction

Here we take leave of the "deontological" criteria, the ones that directly concern the morality of the choice, according to Johnson, and begin the "prudential" criteria. If examination of the first three criteria gives us the preliminary result that a war would be just, we must still examine the next three criteria. Even if it is conceptually just in the abstract, in the real world a war might or might not lead to more evil than the evil we mean to punish or avoid (proportionality of ends). It might or it might not be possible to achieve the same result without going to war (last resort). It might appear likely or unlikely that war can even achieve the just result we are seeking (reasonable chance of success). Decision-makers and anyone thinking about a proposed war must give rigorous consideration to each of these questions.

In fact, it is clear that "right intention," the last of the "deontological" criteria, involves a great deal of prudential thinking. It seems to be a kind of bridge between the first and second groups of criteria. The last four criteria may be rearranged as follows: after determining that it has a just cause and sovereign authority, a country considering war must then make realistic plans based on an in-depth assessment of the situation that includes a reality-based assessment of the risks involved. Those plans must aim, via suitable means, at the peace of justice and order (the "right intention" criterion). With reality-based plans to achieve the good and desired aim in place, the next three questions that must be asked are: is it highly probable that the good produced by executing these force-ful plans will outweigh the evil (proportionality of ends)? If so, proceed to the next question: is there in fact another way to achieve the desired result short of war (last resort)? If there is no other reasonable way, the final question is, are the war plans likely to succeed (reasonable chance of success)? If the answers to the last three questions are yes, no, and yes, then going to war is just. Put this way, it is clear that all of the last four criteria depend completely on a realistic set of plans, based on a realistic assessment of the situation, including a realistic as-sessment of the risks of action and inaction. All four, when legitimately per-formed, are connected by these same realistic plans and risk assessments.

Proportionality of ends calls, in particular, for a painstaking, realistic calcu-lation of the damage likely to be caused in the entire course of a war. Such a calculation must include all the likely or reasonably possible consequences of war, and not merely those in some brief "shooting phase." The war is only over when "success" is achieved, a topic to be dealt with more fully in a later chapter. To the credit of the Bush administration, "removing Saddam" was never the official statement of success before the war, and as of December 2008, his final full month in office, President Bush was still talking about "winning" the war as a goal that lay in the future.[2] Success is clearly the achievement of the hoped-for new peaceful, orderly, stable situation aimed at from the beginning of the con-flict (if it meets just war criteria) by the party making war. A proper "proportio-nality of ends" calculation needed to include all the costs to be incurred until that success was achieved. Many of the difficulties the administration faced in Iraq were in fact anticipated, and the costs of overcoming them should have been part of the calculation of overall damage likely to be caused by the war and its after-math. The costs to be considered needed to include human lives likely to be lost and damaged, property losses, and monetary costs. Such relative intangibles as instability needed to be factored in as they contributed to other costs.

The first thing to note about proportionality of ends is that this is not a natu-ral way for human beings to think. All of us prefer to think in terms of simple good and evil, even absolute good and evil. When we go to war, we tend to speak of some terrible evil that if not eradicated or at least stopped now will take over the world. We don't tend to think much about the damage our country's wars may cause, because we tend to consider them absolutely necessary. Then, after our country's military acts in a faraway place, our press reporting of the resulting damage tends to be minimal and quickly over. We simply move on.

President Bush's March 17 speech addressed the evil to be avoided: "The danger is clear. Using chemical, biological, or, one day, nuclear weapons, ob-tained with the help of Iraq, the terrorists could fulfill their stated ambitions and kill thousands or hundreds of thousands of innocent people in our country or any other."[3] He did not even mention, however, the evils certain to be brought on by a war if the United States started one: accidental deaths and maiming of civilians by the hundreds at least (or thousands, or perhaps hundreds of thousands, and possibly millions), the deaths and maiming of soldiers on all sides, temporary chaos that allows some soldiers and non-soldiers to deliberately kill, rape, and rob civilians with impunity, the destruction of property, the expense of a great deal of money. Almost every war in history has entailed these kinds of costs. Nor did he mention what many, many wars have led to: the unleashing of civil strife, leading to thousands more intentional and accidental deaths, and even possible further wars. His February speech to the American Enterprise Institute[4] contains only this on the subject of possible costs:

> Protecting those boundaries [of "civilized behavior"] carries a cost. If war is forced upon us by Iraq's refusal to disarm, we will meet an enemy who hides his military forces behind civilians, who has terrible weapons, who is capable of any crime. The dangers are real. . . . The work ahead is demanding. It will be difficult to help freedom take hold in a country that has known three decades of dictatorship, secret police, internal divisions, and war. It will be difficult to cultivate liberty and peace in the Middle East, after so many generations of strife.

There is really not even a guess about the costs, which shifted quickly and subtly in the speech into "dangers," i.e., possible costs, rather than likely ones, and "difficulties," which are simply problems to be overcome.

Secretary of State Colin Powell, in his February 2003 presentation to the UN Security Council, mentioned in great detail the terrible things Saddam's presumed weaponry could do to the United States or others, but did not mention any of the damage war was certain to do to Iraq. The United States Congress, in its October 10, 2002, resolution authorizing the use of force against Iraq, mentioned the dangers Iraq was believed to pose to the United States and others, but made no mention of the possible costs of war.[5] Secretary of Defense Donald Rumsfeld said during a radio interview in November 2002:

> Now, transport yourself forward a year, two years, or a week, or a month, and if Saddam Hussein were to take his weapons of mass destruction and transfer them, either use them himself or transfer them to the al Qaeda, and somehow the al Qaeda were to engage in an attack on the United States, or an attack on U.S. forces overseas, with a weapon of mass destruction you're not talking about 300, or 3,000 people potentially being killed, but 30,000, or 100,000 human beings.[6]

While Rumsfeld was estimating the (possible, worst-case scenario) cost of *not* fighting, a legitimate thing to do in itself, again there is no mention of the costs to others of a war waged by the U.S. Vice President Cheney said in August 2002, "the risks of inaction are far greater than the risk of action,"[7] but he said nothing about what the "risk of action" was.

There appears to be no pre-war official U.S. statement that assesses the likely costs of a war in Iraq. Certainly such statements are missing from the places one would most hope to find them, that is, official U.S. declarations and formal testimony. This forces me to use a statement by a non-official source, for the first and only time in this book, as the initial statement of the case that the war met this criterion.

THE PROPORTIONALITY OF ENDS CLAIM

"What about Muslim reaction? What about civilian casualties? . . . I know that possible consequences have been considered, day and night for many months, by competent parties. I know there is a determination to minimize damage to innocents, and a reasoned expectation that successful action will weaken Islamist enemies of civilization and strengthen the Muslim forces of decency and freedom."[8]

DETAILED CLAIM OF PROPORTIONALITY OF ENDS

As noted above, I have found no pre-war official U.S. statement claiming that the likely costs of war had been studied and determined to be proportionate. Therefore, here is a quotation instead from priest, writer and editor Father Richard John Neuhaus, from an essay published in May 2003:

> In the debate leading up to military action, there was much understandable talk about the terrible consequences of war. The question of consequences bears strongly, of course, on the just war criterion of proportionality. One was struck by the ways in which the Bush Administration addressed the Iraq crisis with explicit reference to just war doctrine, including proportionality. . . . Ranking ecclesiastics took up the time of U.S. decision makers, badgering them about whether they had thought of this possible consequence or that. What about Muslim reaction? What about civilian casualties? The simple answer is that such consequences are unknowable and therefore unknown, except to God. I know that possible consequences have been considered, day and night for many months, by competent parties. I know there is a determination to minimize damage to innocents, and a reasoned expectation that successful action will weaken Islamist enemies of civilization and strengthen the Muslim forces of decency and freedom. The U.S. plans for changing the politics and culture of the Middle East, including Palestinian-Israeli relations, are indeed ambitious. Nobody can know for sure what will happen, but religious leaders should bring more to the discussion than their fears. Nervous hand-wringing is not a moral argument.[9]

THE ADMINISTRATION FAILED TO MEET THE PROPORTIONALITY OF ENDS CRITERION

There is no evidence that the United States made any good faith effort to create an official, objective assessment of possible costs of the war, making an official, objective assessment of proportionality of ends impossible. Warnings from responsible, well-informed sources showed that likely costs of war far outweighed the likely benefits of war, and were worse than the likely costs of not acting. Therefore, the United States failed to meet the "proportionality of ends" criterion, a failure that was clear at the time.

EVIDENCE THE PROPORTIONALITY OF ENDS CRITERION WAS NOT MET

There appear to be no official, public pre-war statements comparing a realistic assessment of likely costs, including likely civilian and military deaths on both sides, likely property damage, and likely monetary, military, and political costs (deaths of and injuries to U.S. soldiers, possible instability, possible civil war, etc.) to the benefits the Bush administration hoped to achieve. In many cases, U.S. officials went on the record only to state that the future was unknowable, or to predict optimistic outcomes. It is possible that such a detailed calculation was made, and is still classified. It is extremely unlikely that such an official detailed calculation exists and shows benefits outweighing costs: if it did exist, it would have been released (at least in an edited version protecting secret sources) to provide political cover for the Bush administration when the costs began to mount. In an important sense, this lack of a detailed estimate already proves the case that the Bush administration failed to meet this criterion. However, the case can also be made in more detail.

The Administration Failed to Calculate Likely Costs

The Administration Rejected the Idea of Calculation
Douglas Feith, the Department of Defense's Undersecretary for Policy, was in charge of day-to-day post-war (that is, post-conquest) Iraq policy.[10] In testimony before the Senate Foreign Relations Committee in February 2003, Feith was asked about the number of troops required, the cost of the planned war, what allies might join the United States in the war. "Senator, it's hard to answer a lot of these what-ifs because a lot depends on, you know, future events that we don't know." Asked how long the occupation might last, Feith demurred: "I don't think I want to venture into the prediction business."[11] This suggests a frightening attitude high in the administration: the aim had been chosen, and there was no attempt at calculation of the costs because they simply didn't matter.

Failure to Account for Likely Insurgency, Fighting Among Iraqis
An insurgency was deemed completely unlikely by Vice President Dick Cheney, who said in a speech, "As for the reaction of the Arab 'street,' the Middle East expert Professor Fouad Ajami predicts that after liberation the streets in Basra and Baghdad are 'sure to erupt in joy in the same way the throngs in Kabul greeted the Americans.'"[12] Deputy Defense Secretary Paul Wolfowitz fore-

saw an invasion that went very well indeed. In February 2003 he told the Detroit News, "Our principal target is the psychological one, to convince the Iraqi people that they no longer have to be afraid of Saddam . . . And once that happens I think what you're going to find, and this is very important, you're going to find Iraqis out cheering American troops." As Ricks notes, "he was dismissive of the notion that a U.S. intervention might unleash fighting among Sunnis, Shiites, and Kurds. 'I think the ethnic differences are there in Iraq but they're exaggerated,' he said."[13] Yet these opinions were not supported by any in-depth analysis. On the other hand, there were well-informed analysts who predicted that in the short to medium term an insurgency would begin, and that fighting among ethnic and religious communities for control of Iraq was almost sure to break out—some of these analysts are cited below.

Failure to Account for Likely Long, Large Troop Deployments

Career soldier General Eric Shinseki, testifying before Congress in late February 2003, was asked how many soldiers would be needed for the occupation. Basing his estimate on the number of troops needed in Bosnia and the number of troops used in Germany and Japan after World War II, Shinseki, when pressed to name a range, replied that "something on the order of several hundred thousand soldiers" would be needed. Wolfowitz, however,

> told senior Army officers around this time that he thought that within a few months of the invasion the U.S. troop level in Iraq would be thirty-four thousand, recalled . . . the Army general then at headquarters. Likewise, another three-star general, still on active duty, remembers being told to plan to have the U.S. occupation force reduced to thirty thousand troops by August 2003.[14]

Wolfowitz went on to publicly and sharply rebuke Shinseki: "some of the higher-end predictions that we have been hearing recently, such as the notion that it will take several hundred thousand U.S. troops to provide stability in post-Saddam Iraq, are wildly off the mark." He said it was "hard to conceive that it would take more forces to provide stability in post-Saddam Iraq than it would take to conduct the war itself. . . . hard to imagine . . . One should at least pay attention to past experience," Wolfowitz continued, explaining that Bosnia in his view was the wrong comparison. "I am reasonably certain that they will greet us as liberators, and that will help us keep the requirements down."[15] (As noted below, CIA analyst Pollack was not so optimistic. Neither was a pre-war study by the Army War College's Strategic Studies Institute, which concluded that even if "the war is rapid with few civilian casualties . . . most Iraqis and most other Arabs will probably assume that the United States intervened in Iraq for its own reasons and not to liberate the population. Long-term gratitude is unlikely and suspicion of U.S. motives will increase as the occupation continues."[16])

As it turned out, U.S. troop levels in Iraq were about 150,000 on May 1, 2003, the date Bush declared "Mission Accomplished." The number dropped in the following months to a Bush administration low of 115,000 in February 2004, but thereafter stayed between 120,000 and 160,000 until July 2007. The peak of

171,000 was in October 2007. Although the numbers dropped after that, they never fell below 140,000 for the remainder of Bush's term in office.[17] Five years after the invasion, in other words, the number of troops in place was roughly the same as the number that invaded. The number was still 140,000 in February 2009, just after Barack Obama's inauguration.[18] These high numbers, expensive as they were to maintain, were in no way high enough to provide stability and prevent the incredible devastation that took place during those years (although perhaps no practicable troop levels could have done so).

Failure to Account for Likely High Financial Costs

Wolfowitz later told the House Budget Committee that Iraq could "really finance its own reconstruction" with its oil wealth. Smacking down a report from an anonymous official who said the war and its aftermath "could cost as much as $95 billion," Wolfowitz said "I don't think he or she knows what he is talking about."[19]

Perhaps the nadir of optimistic predictions, says Ricks, was U.S. Agency for International Development director Andrew Natsios' firm prediction to Ted Koppel on Nightline that the total cost to the United States of reconstructing Iraq would be $1.7 billion. Koppel pushed back, but Natsios stood firm. Other countries would chip in, "[b]ut the American part of this will be $1.7 billion."[20]

Because there was no plan in place to set up a government and withdraw from Iraq, however, there was no good reason to believe these optimistic financial estimates. As it turned out, they were wildly wrong. At the end of the Bush administration, the total direct financial cost was widely reckoned to be close to a half a trillion dollars, a figure that did not include such items as future medical care for wounded veterans or higher costs for oil in the years after the invasion.[21]

Failure to Account for Likely U.S. and Iraqi Deaths

Commendably, CIA analyst Pollack, in *The Threatening Storm*, made careful estimates of the likely number of U.S. troop deaths in an invasion of Iraq. In a worst case scenario, he wrote, "the United States could suffer as many as 10,000 combat deaths. . . . [But] in [the] most likely case, the campaign would probably last four to eight weeks and result in roughly 500 to 1,000 American combat deaths."[22] Interestingly, while he laid out many of the costs involved with some accuracy, and pleaded for the United States not to invade "on the cheap," he did not include a chapter entitled "The Costs of an Invasion." But *The Threatening Storm* was not an official policy statement. Pollack's straightforward attempt to warn Americans about the likely costs (even simply to the United States) was not matched by U.S. officials. Neither Pollack nor, as far as I can discover, any U.S. official, discussed in public the likely costs to Iraqi soldiers, or to ordinary Iraqis and their property, yet that is surely absolutely necessary to a "proportionality of ends" discussion. Nor is there a classified estimate that has come to light, even in edited form.

A Range of Critics Offered Rough, Realistic Cost Estimates

A Senator's Tough Questions

While the Administration failed to assess likely costs, a wide range of critics did so—and others pointed out the lack of a risk assessment. Senator Robert Byrd, on the Senate floor shortly before the war, criticized that chamber of Congress for not insisting on answers: "To contemplate war is to think about the most horrible of human experiences . . . as this nation stands at the brink of battle . . . this Chamber is, for the most part, silent—ominously, dreadfully silent. There is no debate, no discussion, no attempt to lay out for the nation the pros and cons of this particular war. There is nothing."[23]

A little later in the same speech, Senator Byrd asked about post-war planning, and the risks of the war itself:

> This administration has not finished the first war against terrorism and yet it is eager to embark on another conflict with perils much greater than those in Afghanistan. . . . Have we not learned that after winning the war we must always secure the peace? And yet we hear little about the aftermath of war in Iraq. In the absence of plans, speculation abroad is rife. Will we seize Iraq's oil fields, becoming an occupying power which controls the price and supply of that nation's oil for the foreseeable future? To whom do we propose to hand the reins of power after Saddam Hussein? Will our war inflame the Muslim world resulting in devastating attacks on Israel? . . . Will the Jordanian and Saudi Arabian governments be toppled by radicals, bolstered by Iran which has much closer ties to terrorism than Iraq? Could a disruption of the world's oil supply lead to a world-wide recession? Has our . . . bellicose language and our . . . disregard of the . . . opinions of other nations increased the global race to join the nuclear club and made proliferation an even more lucrative practice for nations which need the income?

Not all of Senator Byrd's concerns have become realities, but many of the changes in the world that apparently were influenced by the war are as bad as Senator Byrd's nightmare list. To name just one: Iraq, which before the war had very little connection with active, ongoing terrorism, became for a time the focus of anti-U.S. efforts by terrorists.[24] War is known to unleash startling changes, and attempts to think these through beforehand are simply mandatory. There is little evidence the administration thought through the likely negative results of a war.

"Radical" Critics Asked Realistic Questions

In addition to political figures such as Senator Byrd, there were many writers, coming from a variety of political standpoints, who had considered these risks and likely costs in some detail, and had, like Senator Byrd, called for a national discussion of them. (Quotation marks have been placed around these political labels because they are so highly debatable, and hard to define. Whatever the meaning of these words may be, if they even have consistent meanings in the United States, the articles cited were so calm, well-researched, and well-reasoned that they could not be easily dismissed by thoughtful people.) On the "radical" side, perhaps, Jonathan Schell, in an article originally titled "The Case Against War"[25] asked if any circumstance was more likely to provoke Iraq to use its claimed forbidden weapons than an attack aimed at overthrowing the regime, and noted that the Bush administration had said it would consider the use of nuclear weapons in response, making actual use of WMD more likely in the case of an attack on Iraq. He pointed out that democracy is no barrier to "going nuclear": "The world's first nuclear power, after all, was a democracy, and of nine nuclear powers now in the world, six—the United States, England, France, India, Israel, and Russia—are also democracies."

Still at the "radical" end of the spectrum, and also in *The Nation*, Dilip Hiro, a journalist with some experience in the Middle East, began by pointing out that the U.S.-sponsored "Iraqi Open Opposition Conference" in London in December 2002 had just a single Sunni Arab leader in attendance, although "the Sunnis . . . have ruled Iraq since 1638."[26] He then did exactly what the Bush administration needed to do, and to present to the world: he assembled three scenarios, "optimistic, pessimistic, and in-between." The optimistic:

> The Pentagon's optimistic scenario envisages the bulk of Saddam's military surrendering or deserting en masse at the end of two to three weeks of continuous bombing, the operation costing $1.5 billion to $3 billion a week, with the population welcoming the "liberating" American soldiers. The brevity of the conflict insures unity in opposition ranks. The loss of Iraqi oil—now 2-2.5 percent of the global total—is amply compensated for by Saudi Arabia, with its spare capacity amounting to 6 percent of the world aggregate, and Iraq's oilfields will remain unharmed.[27]

Hiro then pointed out that much of this optimistic scenario relied on defectors' testimonies, which, as pointed out above, are shaped to what the recipients want to hear. He went on to note

> two pre-eminent facts of recent Iraqi history. One, Iraqis have a strong nationalistic sense that was enhanced . . . [by the] eight-year war with Iran. Two, almost invariably, Iraqi civilians blame Washington for the sanctions, which have reduced them to penury. Judging from the opinions expressed to me by ordinary citizens during my visit to Iraq in 2000, so deep is the resentment and hostility toward America and Americans that for the bulk of Iraqis, it is unimaginable that any good can come to them from Washington—especially if that would be at the end of a massive bombing campaign of their weakened country and society.[28]

It should be noted that Hiro was not alone in this sentiment. The pro-war Pollack, while arguing that some evidence in 1991 pointed to pro-U.S. sentiment inside Iraq, acknowledged that fierce hatred of the United States was not uncommon in Iraq at that time, and maintained that U.S. forces should not be too optimistic about being welcomed.[29]

In his consideration of the pessimistic scenario, Hiro emphasized the differences between Japan in 1945 and Iraq in 2003.

Despite the fact that policing was left to the Japanese authorities, Washington deployed 100,000 troops for more than six years to implement reform in Japan. By contrast, U.S. planners now envisage the stationing of 75,000—100,000 troops at the cost of $16 billion a year. This is unrealistic. In Northern Ireland, with a population of 1.7 million [cf. Iraq at about 24 million in 2003[30]], the British government . . . commit[ed] 60,000 troops and armed police [note: this comparison would argue for almost 850,000 troops in Iraq, if one hoped to do "as well" as the British in Northern Ireland] to tackle about 1,000 members of the Irish Republican Army, most of them in jail at any one time. . . . *Unlike highly homogenous Japan, Iraq is a heterogeneous society. The traditional religious, ethnic, and tribal animosities will break out in postwar Iraq once the iron hand of Saddam is removed, with civil conflict erupting along ethnic and sectarian lines, the deadliest one being between Sunnis and Shiites who share the Mesopotamian plain* [emphasis added]. . . . Last, Japan lacks natural resources and does not share land borders with neighbors. By contrast, Iraq, possessing the second-largest oil deposits in the world, is surrounded by six intrusive neighbors, each with its own agenda, and is located in a region that has been the most volatile and violent since World War II.[31]

"Liberal" Critics Listened to Soldiers and Spies

Yet it was far from only the "radical" journals that carried this kind of discussion. The somewhat "liberal" *Atlantic Monthly*, in November 2002, carried an article by James Fallows, who interviewed "spies, Arabists, oil-company officials, diplomats, scholars, policy experts, and many active-duty and retired soldiers," in order to answer the question: after Saddam is conquered, "What then?"[32] Fallows wrote that he began his research reluctantly accepting the Hitler analogy many administration officials were using, but eventually concluded that World War I would be a better comparison. The dangers he, through his sources, foresaw included (1) *No Quick Exit:* for logistical reasons alone, U.S. military forces could not leave quickly after removing Saddam, as Afghanistan was then demonstrating. (2) *Possible Civil War:* "It is quite possible that if we went in, took out Saddam Hussein, and then left quickly, the result would be an extremely bloody civil war . . . That blood would be directly on our hands," one source, who had fought as a Marine in Vietnam, told Fallows. (3) *The Burden of Occupation:* "Conquered Iraqis would turn to the U.S. government for emergency relief, civil order, economic reconstruction, and protection of their borders." (4) *The Need to Restore Infrastructure:* "Because you started the war, you have accepted a moral responsibility for [these needs]," another source stated. (5) *The Responsibility to Stop Vengeance:* "When the lid comes off after a long period of repression, people may be grateful and elated, but they may also be furious and vengeful, as the post-liberation histories of Romania and Kosovo [and many others!] indicate." (6) *Getting Caught in the Middle, Unable to Communicate:* another source, who ran an Iraqi refugee camp after the first Iraq war, spoke of the dangerous necessity of interfering in inter-Iraqi problems without understanding them. "And when that happens, you have no idea what kind of vendetta you've just fallen in the middle of." And so forth.

"Conservative Realists" Counted Costs to the War on Terror
On the more conservative side, as mentioned previously, Brent Scowcroft, a "conservative realist," warned in August 2002, in the far-from-liberal *Wall Street Journal*, "Don't Attack Saddam."[33] Scowcroft's main point was that the war would divert attention from, and make more difficult by alienating allies, the global war on terror.

"Paleoconservatives" Pointed Out Dangers
Congressman Ron Paul, a 2008 GOP Presidential candidate whose website said "as a Congressman, Dr. Paul tirelessly works for limited constitutional government, low taxes, free markets, and a return to sound monetary policies,"[34] also weighed in against the war in a speech September 10, 2002,[35] and on other occasions, warning of likely costs that the administration had not addressed. (Paul has been associated with libertarians as well.) Well-known paleoconservative Pat Buchanan also warned of the risks of war. Less than a week before the war began, on March 12, 2003, in "First and Last War of the Bush Doctrine?" Buchanan wrote that President Bush's proclamation of "a new strategic doctrine that mandates pre-emptive wars on any rival powers that seek to acquire weapons we already have was an act of hubris."[36] This was the latest in a long series of Buchanan articles critical of the war decision on moral and prudential grounds, often warning of high, and unexamined, costs.[37]

It is fair to say that critiques of and serious questions about the planned war, while many Americans may have heard them faintly if at all, came from a range of political viewpoints, and were published.

Pro-War "Conservatives" Later Lament Lack of Cost Discussion
Johnson, in Chapter 3 of *The War to Oust Saddam Hussein*, implicitly criticized the administration for failing to plan thoroughly for the achievement of this aim. He wrote:

> One is obligated, if one uses force to remove an evildoer from power, to replace his government with one that exercises sovereign authority for good . . . We should have—and always should—identified the goods and the sacrifices, then decided whether the sacrifices were worth making and, in practice, were likely to be made, given the other obligations our society has to its own people and to other nations.[38]

Johnson is stating here, by a strong implication, that this calculation was simply not made. As Johnson appears to be, for the most part, a staunch defender of the war, this is a damning accusation. By writing in effect that no proportionality of ends calculation was made before the war, he implied that it was impossible for the administration to claim that this criterion was met as the nation went to war.

What a Proportionality Calculation Would Have Looked Like

A war launched without a calculation of likely costs is foolish and unjust. Because of that, critics of a planned war who do not see that a calculation of costs has been made, or who see that important factors are being overlooked, are performing a service to the country by calling attention to those facts, even if they do nothing else. In the absence of a realistic case that benefits will outweigh costs, no war should be started. That does not mean that the critiques of a proposed action should always carry the day. It means simply that a full calculation was needed, of the costs and benefits of a war, and of the costs and benefits of doing nothing. This is an attempt to provide the kind of calculation that could have been made at the beginning of 2003, based on what was publicly known at that time.

Saddam was a dictator. While dictators can sometimes be relatively harmless, Saddam and his regime tortured opponents, and killed many of them unjustly. While he had started wars in the past, the 1991 war against him and the truce conditions imposed at that time should be considered the internationally approved punishment of Saddam and his regime. It should be remembered that in 1990, Saddam did not attack the United States, but Kuwait. The United States fought to remove his forces from Kuwait under the banner of the United Nations, and much as U.S. politicians and others wanted him removed from power, this was never the judgment of the United Nations. In fighting under the UN banner, the U.S. government accepted the more limited war aim of removing Iraqi forces from Kuwait. Whether he failed to meet the cease-fire conditions and, if so, what to do about it, were questions for the United Nations to decide, since the cease-fire was not between Saddam and the United States, but between Saddam and the UN. Saddam proved he could be deterred: neither the United States nor any other country tried to deter him from attacking Kuwait, but he was deterred from using WMD against U.S. forces, and apparently from giving them to terrorists (if he even wanted to do so). His support for terrorism had dwindled in the 1990s to something exceedingly meager at the worst. The vast majority of the deaths caused directly by Saddam's regime are connected with the war against Iran, during which the U.S. government supported Saddam, or with rebellions against his rule. For the last full year of his rule, 2002, Amnesty International, which was strongly anti-Saddam, summed up his government's annual (very negative) record thus:

> Scores of people, including possible prisoners of conscience, were executed. A general amnesty for prisoners was announced, but the fate of tens of thousands of people who "disappeared" in previous years remains unknown. Non-Arabs, mostly Kurds, in the Kirkuk region continued to be forcibly expelled to Iraqi Kurdistan. Relatives of opposition activists continued to receive threats.[39]

Thus the benefit to be gained from overthrowing Saddam was the removal of a dictator, no longer a serious threat to his neighbors, who continued to torture and kill political opponents, to the level of "scores" in one recent year, and whose forces practiced a certain amount of ethnic cleansing. (The regime's huge, and despicable, persecutions of ethnic minority regions were for the most part in abeyance, since the rebellions that provoked them were over or had reached, in the north, and with the help of U.S. force, a relatively stable *modus vivendi*.) In itself, this benefit looks real and significant.

But just war theory reminds us that we are not angels who are ranked purely on the side of good, nor are we able to separate good and evil cleanly and efficiently, nor can we remove evil at no cost. That does not mean we should despair of ever doing good through the use of force, but we need a way to count up the goods and evils, the benefits and costs, and we need to be realistic about what we hope to achieve through the use of force, as outsiders. I have lived in six countries in the Middle East and Africa, working with the Peace Corps, an American business, a humanitarian relief organization, and the State Department, over a total time span of almost fifteen years in the Middle East, and over seven years in Africa. I have visited many more countries. The U.S. government is not perfect, but the regimes of many of the countries I lived in or visited were far less perfect. Many were rather ugly in some ways; a few were terrible in many ways. These experiences did not extinguish idealism, but they did a great deal to encourage a realistic attitude about what is humanly achievable. Spreading democracy and freedom is a stirring goal, often supported by soaring rhetoric, but without the kind of real-world calculations attempted here, such attempts often end up doing more harm than good.

This rough calculation, then, concerns what evils might properly be healed or cured with the very crude instrument of war, and thus is only a very rough guide to other kinds of moral or legal calculation. Let us begin with the economists' concept of "sunk cost." What is spent is spent, and should not be considered in the present calculation. When considering what to do with a stock you own, the question to ask about is not "how much did I spend," but "what can I get for it, now, or in five years." You may have paid fifty dollars a share for a hot bank stock in 2007, but if in 2009 it is worth ten dollars a share, you need to forget what you paid and think about what you can get between the present moment and 2014. By a very rough analogy, old crimes should be set aside in any calculation that involves war. We might like to punish through war various regimes in the world for crimes ten and twenty and fifty years old, but there are so many evils to be punished the effort would destroy the world (and we would have to consider our own human rights violations in that period). If invasion of a neighboring country is to be punished, and five years or more later the aggressor nation is no longer holding any territory of that country, then punishment is probably too late. (It might be a different question if the aggressor nation were still holding part or all of a nation against the will of those occupied, but absent ongoing genocide, even there a limit must be in place. War cannot cure or right old evils.)

Realism calls for a look at the recent past, the present, and the near future. Let us posit, not as a hard and fast rule, that a realistic calculation should generally be limited to five years in the past, and five years in the future (somewhat arbitrary figures, perhaps, but the more distant past is extremely problematic, as argued above, and calculations of any kind beyond five years in the future are notoriously unreliable). In other words, the calculation should deal with evil and good in the past five years, ongoing evil and good, and likely evil and good in the next five years.

Admittedly, that this cuts off from consideration the greatest evils by Saddam's regime. Not only were they old in 2003, but as noted before, consideration of Saddam's evil in relation to the war in Iran would be rank hypocrisy since the U.S. government firmly supported Saddam throughout the conflict, implicitly confirming his own estimation that he was acting as a protective bulwark for the Arab Gulf nations against Iran. Consideration of the evil of his attacks on the rebels in 1991 would be hypocritical in the United States, for two main reasons. First, the U.S. government often speaks softly if at all concerning vicious suppression of rebellions by governments in power, and there have been many of them. This is in part due to practicality—to give just two examples, how could the United States possibly have stopped the Soviet Union or China from crushing their various rebellions, odious and disgusting as those acts of suppression were, without plunging the world into hideous, full-scale war? Nor did the United States try hard to stop the British suppression of the Mau Mau rebellion in Kenya, the French suppression of Algerians seeking their freedom— the list could go on and on. Perhaps there is also an element of bad conscience: to my knowledge, the United States government has never officially condemned or deplored the blatant, widespread attacks on civilians by Federal forces in the South under Abraham Lincoln. (Of course slavery, a desperate evil, needed to end, but in no way does a good end justify a means that is pure evil, and indiscriminate attacks on civilians were just that.) Secondly, and more powerfully, the U.S. government encouraged the Iraqi rebellions in question in 1991, and then, with a massive army a few miles away, stood by as they were crushed, doing nothing to help them. To claim a dozen years after one did nothing to stop an abuse that one is now punishing those who perpetrated it smacks strongly of hypocrisy.

In the case of a contemplated regime change, the present evil of a regime should be weighed against the present good of the same regime. An attempt to put a new regime in place through force should only be made if you can be reasonably confident that the balance of good and evil in the future regime, MINUS the evil involved in war, scores higher than leaving the existing regime in place (including expected goods and evils over the next five years).

Here is a far from exhaustive summary of Iraq in March 2003:

Existing evils of Saddam's regime, March 2003:

- Dictatorship—lack of political choice for citizens
- Killings of political opponents, at the rate of perhaps a hundred or fewer a year
- Torture (rate unknown, but surely significantly lower than during the rebellions)

- Ethnic cleansing (hundreds per year? Dozens?)
- Threats (and probably worse in some cases) to relatives of "opposition activists"
- A history of creating and using chemical and biological weapons, and scientists with expertise in creating and deploying them
- A history of seeking nuclear weapons

That is an ugly score sheet. Looking five years out, without U.S. intervention, such a situation was likely to continue, also an ugly and regrettable situation. In addition, as administration figures pointed out, the world was weary of sanctions, and the political pressure on the United States to allow them to expire was growing. Even if the evidence for Iraqi possession of WMD was weak in early 2003, the supposition that it could develop some kind of WMD in the near future, at the least chemical and biological weapons, was not far-fetched. But we must consider the goods of Saddam's regime also.

Existing goods of Saddam's regime, March 2003:

- Relative stability of life for citizens
- Some economic goods for most citizens (And much of the privation could be traced to UN-enforced sanctions—which could have been removed instantly if the U.S. government had allowed it—they were kept in place almost entirely by U.S. government veto power in the Security Council.)[40]
- Relative religious freedom and religious tolerance on a day-to-day basis (In other words, you were unlikely to be arrested and abused simply for being a Shiite unless your region was in rebellion or you were a Shiite leader suspected of plotting against Saddam. Christians and other minorities were, unlike in the years following the U.S. invasion of 2003, relatively safe from persecution. Iraq was a secular state whose identity did not depend on Islam. Random killings on the basis of religion were unknown. Intermarriage among religious groups was relatively common, and many neighborhoods were extremely mixed without undue friction between religious groups.)
- Very little threat to neighboring countries (this assumes ongoing U.S. government interest in "containing" Saddam, a rather easy assumption to defend).
- Women's freedom vis-à-vis men's. Women were free to work in a wide variety of jobs, without any fear of persecution for wearing what Westerners would consider modest clothing, i.e., showing hair, ears, arms and lower legs did not subject women to harassment and reprisals.

Thus, while this was a nasty little regime in many ways, and morally deplorable, with an awful past, it was far from the worst in the world. Most people lived relatively decent lives, had jobs, got married, had children. Fear of being obliterated for no reason was relatively rare. For the most part, all religions, and atheism, were tolerated. Was a new, much better regime likely to be achieved through the forceful removal of the existing one by an outside power, and what were the likely costs in such an effort?

No Good Reason to Believe a Stable Democracy Was Likely

First, what was there to give the Bush administration any confidence that it could put a new regime in place that was better than the old one and would be stable and lasting? Again and again, the President and his officials cited Germany and Japan as their examples of earlier U.S. successes. As pointed out in Chapter 7, there were enormous contrasts between these two countries after World War II and Iraq in 2003. Those examples were clearly not good enough to make sober, knowledgeable observers optimistic. Why not remedy that deficiency? Why didn't the Bush administration show a previous example of a Western power putting a democratic regime in place by force in the Middle East, a huge region where examples should abound? Why didn't the Bush administration cite the Israeli successes at molding the West Bank and Gaza and South Lebanon, or the French and British colonial successes in producing democratic regimes in the vast stretches of the Middle East that they governed as colonies in the twentieth century? What about the Russian success in shaping Afghanistan to its liking? To ask these questions is to answer them: the Middle East's history, modern as well as ancient, suggested and suggests that a conqueror with another culture simply has no reason to hope to be able to shape a Middle Eastern country in a desired direction. It can reasonably hope to crush, in the short term at least, but not to shape as it desires. It can establish a regime and maintain it with military force, but no post-colonial Middle Eastern state has been set up as a democracy by an outside power and then remained convincingly democratic after the departure of the outside power's military forces. With no positive examples of success in the past to point to, surely a prudent evaluation of the likelihood that the conquest of Iraq would lead to a stable democracy would have stated, "highly unlikely at best."

And That Alone Should Have Settled the Question

This consideration alone should have ended consideration of "proportionality of ends." When there is no reasonable confidence in your ability to put a better regime in place, then except in extraordinary circumstances, without even weighing the likely risks of war, the likely evils of attempted regime change outweigh the likely goods. Wars always bring evils (see Chapter 11 for Augustine's agreement with this point). A non-defensive war such as this one could only be justified if the likely outcome is so much better than the existing setup that the improvement outweighs the almost certain evils of war. If the outcome is most likely to be at best about the same, then the evils of war—death, destruction, rape, looting, maiming—clearly outweigh the benefits of a regime change.

But in Addition, Risks of War Were Huge, Benefits Uncertain

To summarize, the near-term benefits of removing Saddam appeared worthwhile in themselves. However, it is important to remember that Saddam's regime allowed a reasonably peaceful and prosperous life to the vast majority of its citizens, despite its odious nature. As the range of critics quoted above demonstrated, with thoughtful, realistic references to Iraqi history and culture, the risks of beginning a war and removing Saddam's regime were immense. Resistance was very likely, and the possibility of chaos was huge. In contrast, the hoped-for benefit of a stable and just Iraqi society emerging, especially if a democracy with political rights for all is one of the descriptions of such a society, was extremely unlikely to be achieved.

OBJECTIONS

Objection One: It Is Right to Trust Government

Objection: Wasn't it right for American citizens simply to trust their government, as Father Neuhaus apparently did? Isn't it right simply to trust it now? Shouldn't citizens believe that the calculations were made, and are still being kept secret?

Reply: Neuhaus certainly implied that religious leaders and others should simply trust the United States government: to do otherwise is to bring only fear to the discussion, to "badger" the "decision-makers," to engage in "nervous hand-wringing." The magazine Neuhaus edits, *First Things*, devotes article after article, month after month, to disagreeing with and often questioning the United States government on various issues. In fairness, however, perhaps what struck Neuhaus about the criticisms was not the questioning of decision-makers, but a perceived refusal by the critics to provide their own accounting of the likely results. Yet, first, many of those who "badgered" the government did provide rough calculations of likely results, which presumably differed from Neuhaus' ideas of what was likely. Second, as argued in Chapter 2, those in favor of war bear the responsibility to make the case for war, and not vice versa.

Note also Neuhaus' statement that, "one was struck by the ways in which the Bush Administration addressed the Iraq crisis with explicit reference to just war doctrine, including proportionality." Here Neuhaus appears to show greater appreciation for reference to the terms of just war theory than for use of it. As demonstrated in this chapter, many critics of the proposed war, by offering rational analysis of likely consequences of a U.S. invasion, were in fact practicing the theory by seeking to identify likely costs, something absolutely necessary for any estimate of proportionality of ends. The fact that the administration was not publicly identifying the likely costs and its plans to deal with the problems very likely to arise was a sign it was not applying just war theory, regardless of its rhetoric.

More broadly on the question of "trusting one's government," in the United States at least few do it consistently, or more than occasionally. If all Americans did it, no American would have voted for Bush over Gore, or for Clinton over Bush's father, and so on, all the way back to the revolt against George the Third of England. Many of those who, like Neuhaus, urged Americans to trust their government in the run-up to the war later attacked the State Department, the CIA, the Pentagon, or some other branch of the U.S. government, for allegedly leading administration leaders astray. There appears to be no consistency here. It is unlikely there is a single published, known commentator, of average or greater intelligence, who consistently trusts the government, from one year and one administration to the next. (Neuhaus himself showed very little trust in the Clinton administration's intentions or motives, as a glance at his remarks at the time of the Kosovo war makes clear.)

When we are urged to do something in a strongly inconsistent manner, the urging tends to be discredited by that very fact. The government, in a democratic society that raises just war objections to a proposed war, should make at least rough calculations known, or it opens itself to a justified accusation that it appears unconcerned with proportionality of ends. The case for proportionality is part of the case that a government in favor of war needs to make, at least in a rough way. Finally, there is a huge amount of evidence that governments generally, including American administrations, are quick to reveal facts that tend to vindicate them. This makes the existence of secret pre-war calculations highly unlikely.

Objection Two: The Future Is, in Fact, Unknowable

Objection: But as Neuhaus points out, humans can't see the future. As he says "the simple answer is that such consequences are unknowable and therefore unknown, except to God." If you leave out "except to God," an agnostic or atheist can agree as well: the future is simply unknowable.

Reply: Yet Neuhaus continues, in his next sentence, "I know that possible consequences have been considered, day and night for many months, by competent parties." One cannot eat one's cake and then have it too: if consequences are completely unknowable by humans, then it is meaningless that "competent parties" (or indeed any parties) are considering them. But consequences should indeed be considered, in order to estimate what, in all likelihood, they will be, something that should affect our subsequent decisions. That is what we should do before every serious decision, whether buying a car, marrying, starting a business, or taking a trip: we should gather information, consider likely risks and benefits, and estimate the consequences. Our estimates will not be perfect, but prudent people put a great deal of effort into producing them, and the more so the more serious the decision.

In fact, this statement that "consequences are unknowable" effectively strips the prudential criteria of any meaning, because each one of these three criteria depends on an estimation of likely future outcomes. This statement turns the "prudential criteria" into the "pious hope" or "faith and prayer" criteria. When Neuhaus censures theologians and other clerics for "taking up the time of decision-makers, badgering them about whether they had thought of this possible consequence or that," he criticizes them precisely for seeking to discover whether or not the "rigorous consideration" due to the just war criteria called for in the *Catholic Catechism* had taken place. Not only that, but immediately above that quotation in his essay, Neuhaus writes, concerning critics of the United States, "one might consult the history of, say, the last hundred years." That is just what the radical, moderate, and conservative war critics quoted above were doing— considering recent history for lessons to be learned about a possible invasion of Iraq. Neuhaus meant that the United States has often acted magnanimously and generously, and he is right about that—but that is not the only lesson history offers.

Objection Three: Without War, Things Would Be Worse

Objection: The thrust of this argument is that at the time of the war, the risks of allowing Saddam to remain in power were less than the risks of removing him. But there is very little here about the longer-term risks of allowing Saddam to remain in power: the likelihood that all international support for the sanctions would erode, and that Saddam would then be able to export oil in whatever quantities he liked, allowing him to rebuild his conventional military capacity as well as his WMD, this time free from worry about any kind of inspection regime. Both Pollack and Duelfer considered this a very likely scenario, Pollack based on what he saw before the war and Duelfer based on the evidence gathered by the Iraq Survey Group (see Appendix B).

Reply: There was indeed a range of longer-term predictions for what Saddam's regime might do if it escaped sanctions, and some of them were dire. However, this situation was built into the first Iraq war by the legal basis of that war and its ending: the UN Security Council resolutions discussed at length in Chapters 5 and 6. The potential always existed for Iraq to re-arm, which is simply saying, to rejoin the community of nations on a normal basis. There would be nothing surprising in this, based on the history of the twentieth century. Many unpleasant regimes have weapons, including WMD.

But long-term predictions are a poor way to deal with the future in general. The farther into the future we look, the less likely we are to be correct in a given prediction. Other unforeseen factors are likely, indeed almost certain, to spring up. A glance at science fiction from twenty years ago makes this abundantly clear. As recently as 1980, only a handful of "experts" predicted the fizzling out of communism. How many predicted that China would be an economic powerhouse, and Japan mired in endless economic doldrums, and the dollar at all-time lows? Long-term predictions are simply inherently unreliable, and as such cannot form the basis of the just use of force against another country—especially not when deterrence is an obvious alternative.

In addition, to make dire long-term predictions into the basis for military action is to open Pandora's box. One can easily come up with such dire predictions about a dozen countries, without trying hard. There is a real potential at the time of the writing of this book that Pakistan will slip into chaos in the near future: should the United States invade that country, with its various fanatical factions, and try to put a lid on its politics? Remove its nuclear weapons (but leave those of its rivals India and China)? Long-term, the stability of Saudi Arabia can certainly be questioned, and if an "Islamist" government took over, it might be hostile to the United States and other Western countries. The same could be said for Egypt and Jordan. What about future, likely hostile governments in China and Russia? "Long-term preemption" is simply a recipe for endless war.

Objection Four: Average Citizens Cannot Use This Criterion

Objection: The average educated citizen does not have time to learn the culture and history of the Middle East, nor of other parts of the world where leaders may call for a war. Yet wars are sometimes justified. How can citizens possibly put themselves in a position to judge their governments before the fact? Given that inability, isn't this a criterion for the elite?

Reply: The point is well taken. In fact, even the experts must rely on other experts as soon as they move out of the narrow circles of their own expertise. But that does not mean the ordinary citizen has no guidelines available at all, nor should such a person despair. In the case of a proposed war, first, ask whether those proposing the war or arguing in favor of it have offered an analysis of the likely costs to all sides. If such an analysis is available in some detail, then the beginning of a "proportionality of ends" discussion is in place, and that can only be positive. If such an analysis actually proposes a range of numbers, in terms of lives and economic costs, that is more good evidence that this criterion is in use. If those proposing the war are not using this criterion, then the war should not be supported.

Second, read sources on more than one side of the debate. Are major points made by one side consistently ignored or misrepresented by the other? Both sides may do this, but one may be worse than another. This effort is difficult. The human tendency is to reject whatever we personally disagree with—and once we find a single statement we dislike in an analysis, and especially if we find an ad hominem attack against a politician we favor, or a favorable reference to someone we dislike, that makes it even harder to note anything truthful in such news or analysis. Yet thoughtful people can listen to those with whom they disagree, and identify strong as well as weak points in their arguments. A public discussion of this criterion would certainly have a positive effect on a pre-war debate. Certainly the overall lack of detail from the pro-war side,[41] in the face of detailed concerns based on Iraqi history and culture, should have given pause at the least to pro-war citizens with any interest in just war theory. Perhaps it did for some. Next time, armed with a better understanding of how just war theory can be applied, surely more might insist on a reckoning—if they have escaped from partisanship (towards either side) as a guide for political action.

Objection Five: This Is Partisan, Pessimistic Analysis

Objection: Great weight is given here to pessimistic pre-war statements of those who opposed the war, but the analysis is unconvincing now that the surge has worked and Iraq is far more stable. In addition, there is an air of partisanship not only in the quoting of pessimistic writers in this chapter, but also in the weight given to their predictions.

Reply: The weight given to those statements is based on the strength of their appeals to cultural realities, history, and logic. The statements on both sides can be measured against these criteria for realism. A close look at the predictions by Ajami and Lewis, the experts quoted on the pro-war side, shows they were in fact nearly as realistic about the likelihood of failure as the anti-war experts, but somehow encouraged the administration to invade regardless. No pro-war expert seems to have made a detailed case as to why the war would succeed and why the likely benefits outweighed the likely costs.

As for the "surge" working, to focus on the situation this month or this year is to take a short-term view. In mid-2009, Iraq was better off in many ways than under Saddam in the early years of the twenty-first century, but it was also less stable and more violence-prone. It is not legitimate to compare two post-invasion situations and say, for example, that the invasion was justified because August 2008 was a less bloody month than August 2005. To take a short-term view is also to ignore the huge number of Iraqi deaths that have occurred, Iraqi refugees forced from their homes, the wounded, maimed and raped, the billions of dollars worth of Iraqi property destroyed. By one estimate, by 2008 over a million Iraqis had died due to the conflict. Over four million Iraqis were living outside their homes in late 2008, about half of them outside the country. Massive ethnic cleansing took place during the years of the worst strife that followed the U.S. invasion. All of these results of the U.S. invasion are briefly discussed in the concluding chapter of this book. Is this part of the calculation for the one objecting? If not, it should be.

Looking to the future from the standpoint of mid-2009, what is the evidence that there will be a stable Iraq in the next few years? It may indeed happen that U.S. troops will withdraw by the end of 2011, as Barack Obama indicated in his first months in office, and Iraq will become more stable than it is and remain so. However, there is no guarantee in mid-2009 that this will be the case. Only after U.S. troops have been gone for several years will it make sense to claim some kind of "success" for the U.S. invasion—but as this book is going to print, there is simply no guarantee that it will happen—and whatever success is achieved will have to be weighed against the immense human losses that have already occurred.

Although some of the negative predictions of anti-war writers have come about, others have not, as noted. The emphasis here was placed on the need for careful consideration of possible dangerous outcomes, which is what prudence is all about. It is possible to succeed after ignoring prudence, through sheer luck or, perhaps, tremendous perseverance in digging oneself out of the hole one has dug. Such "success" does not negate the original folly of ignoring prudence, nor does it retroactively make the original decision just.

Objection Six: Pessimistic Predictions Stifle Action

Objection: All great undertakings involve risk. If the kind of analysis advocated here had been used, they would simply not have been begun, to the detriment of mankind. Consider the building of the Panama Canal, the U.S. Apollo mission to the moon, or the building of any great cathedral or railroad for that matter. All of these involved enormous risks. Concerning wars, would the United States have taken on Hitler's Germany and Tojo's Japanese military clique if this kind of analysis had been used?

Reply: This objection actually reinforces the point that great projects that succeed involve incredibly detailed planning. Even if there were cost overruns or unanticipated difficulties, the extensive planning that did take place surely helped those executing the plans to deal with the unexpected. While great non-military projects can lead to ruined lives if they fail (a reason planning is a moral requirement for them), the ruin is sometimes indirect, whereas war always kills human beings. Concerning wars, the U.S. planners of World War II were well aware of U.S. steel production, labor force size, and the other factors of the industrial production of weapons, which helped them decide that the United States could emerge victorious. But Iraq should not be endlessly compared to World War II. How many disastrous wars would have been avoided if the kind of careful analysis called for here had been performed? World War I provides just one example: would it not have been a huge gain for the nations of Europe and the United States to have avoided that war?

It is true that an analysis can err by way of being too pessimistic, but it is dangerous to begin a great undertaking with a too optimistic analysis. It is also morally wrong to do so if a balanced analysis is possible. Again, what is striking here is how few careful, detailed analyses with an optimistic conclusion are available from any source (and there appear to have been no official ones). Compare one thorough "optimistic" analysis, that of Pollack in *The Threatening Storm*, with the more pessimistic analyses quoted above. Even Pollack gives no detailed proposals for how the deep divisions in Iraqi society and its historical animosity to invaders could have been overcome by a U.S. invading force.

NOTES

1. Colin Powell, 1992 (Questions policymakers should ask and answer before committing our forces to war. Quoted in op-ed Mark Danner, "A Doctrine Left Behind," *The New York Times*, November 21, 2004). http://www.nytimes.com/2004/11/21/opinion/21danner.html (Powell was a general when he formulated this prudential rule).

2. "'The war is not over,' Bush said, but 'it is decisively on its way to being won.'" Jennifer Loven, *AP*, "Bush: Iraq war is not over, more work ahead," http://news .yahoo.com/s/ap/20081215/ap_on_go_pr_wh/bush (accessed December 15, 2008).

3. Bush, "The War Begins," 503.

4. Bush, "Iraq is Fully Capable," 557-59.

5. "Authorization for use of Military Force Against Iraq Resolution of 2002 (H.J. Res.114)" (Joint Resolution of Congress, October 16, 2002), in *Iraq War Reader*, 378-83.

6. Donald Rumsfeld, former US Secretary of Defense, in a radio interview on November 14, 2002, with Infinity CBS Radio, in "Did Saddam Hussein and his regime pose an immediate threat?," *US - Iraq ProCon.org*, http://usiraq.procon.org/viewanswers .asp?questionID=891 (accessed January 24, 2009).

7. (Vice President) Dick Cheney, "The risks of inaction are far greater than the risk of action," in *Iraq War Reader*, 298.

8. Neuhaus, "Sounds of Religion," 79.

9. Neuhaus, "Sounds of Religion," 79.

10. Ricks, *Fiasco*, 78.

11. Ricks, *Fiasco*, 86.

12. Dick Cheney, "The risks of inaction," 299.

13. Ricks, *Fiasco*, 96.

14. Ricks, *Fiasco*, 97.

15. Ricks, *Fiasco*, 98. On the following page, Ricks quotes Andrew Bacevich for the underlying issues behind the Shinseki/Wolfowitz debate: "'Liberation' would leave loose ends. Unexpected and costly complications would abound. In effect, Shinseki was offering a last-ditch defense of the military tradition that Wolfowitz was intent on destroying, a tradition that saw armies as fragile, that sought to husband military power, and that classified force as an option of last resort. The risks of action, Shinseki was suggesting, were far, far greater than the advocates for war had let on."

16. Conrad C. Crane and Andrew Terrill, "Reconstructing Iraq: Insights, Challenges, and Missions for Military Forces in a Post-Conflict Scenario," *Strategic Studies Institute: United States Army War College*, Febr uary 2003, http://www.strategicstudiesinstitute .army.mil/pdffiles/PUB182.pdf (accessed July 14, 2007).

17. "Iraq Index: Tracking Variables of Reconstruction and Security in Post-Saddam Iraq," *Brookings*, February 26, 2009, 24 http://www.brookings.edu/saban/~/media/Files/Centers/Saban/Iraq%20Index/index20090226.pdf (accessed June 7, 2009).

18. Jason Campbell, Michael O'Hanlon, Jeremy Shapiro, and Amy Unikewicz, "Op-Chart: The States of Iraq and Afghanistan," March 19, 2009, *The New York Times*, http://www.nytimes.com/2009/03/20/opinion/20ohanlon.html (accessed May 1, 2009).

19. Ricks, *Fiasco*, 98.

20. Ricks, *Fiasco*, 109. Natsios may have acted merely as a spokesman with this pronouncement. It nonetheless reflects the thinking of delegated decision-makers in the administration.

21. See for example Lawrence B. Lindsey, "What Iraq will cost the U.S.," *Fortune*, http://money.cnn.com/2008/01/10/news/economy/costofwar.fortune/ (accessed February 12, 2008). Lindsey is a former White House economist who left the White House after his

public estimate that the war might cost up to $200 billion displeased his bosses. On January 31, 2009, the estimate of direct costs of the war by the "National Priorities Project," showed a total cost to date in excess of $593 billion. "Cost of War," *National Priorities Project*, http://www.nationalpriorities.org/costofwar_home (accessed January 31, 2009).

22. Pollack, *Threatening Storm*, 351.

23. Byrd, "Sleepwalking through History" 482.

24. "Report: Global terrorism up more than 25 percent," CNN.com, April 30, 2007, http://www.cnn.com/2007/US/04/30/terror.report/index.html (accessed January 24, 2009). The story cites a State Department study reporting that global terrorism was up 25 percent in 2006 compared with the previous year, and "incidents in Iraq accounted for nearly half of the 14,000 attacks and about two-thirds of the more than 20,000 fatalities worldwide. The number of deaths blamed on attacks increased by about 40 percent."

25. Jonathan Schell, "Pre-emptive Defeat, or How Not to Fight Proliferation," in *Iraq War Reader*, 506-509. The article was originally published in *The Nation* on March 3, 2003 as "The Case Against War."

26. Hiro, "Post-Saddam Problem," 560.

27. Hiro, "Post-Saddam Problem," 561.

28. Hiro, "Post-Saddam Problem," 561.

29. Pollack, *Threatening Storm*, 382.

30. "Frontline: Beyond Baghdad: Map: Iraq's People and Politics," *PBS.org*, http://www.pbs.org/wgbh/pages/frontline/shows/beyond/etc/map.html (accessed January 24, 2009). This map shows the rough divisions of Iraqi society and where different groups live.

31. Hiro, "Post-Saddam Problem," 563.

32. James Fallows, "The Fifty-First State?," in *Iraq War Reader*, 535. This article first appeared in *The Atlantic Monthly* in November 2002.

33. Scowcroft, "Don't Attack Saddam," 295-97.

34. "Who is Ron Paul?" Hope for America, *Ron Paul 2008*, http://www.ronpaul 2008.com (accessed October 20, 2007).

35. Congressman Ron Paul, "Questions That Won't Be Asked About Iraq," in *Iraq War Reader*, 304.

36. Pat Buchanan, "First and Last War of the Bush Doctrine?" *The American Cause*, March 12, 2003, http://www.theamericancause.org/patfirstandlastwar.htm (accessed October 17, 2003).

37. Another conservative, Democratic House Representative Ike Skelton, of Missouri, longed as a young man to go to West Point, a dream he had to give up when he was stricken with polio as a teenager. His deep interest in military affairs continued, however, culminating in his position as the leading Democrat on the House Armed Services Committee in 2003. Although Skelton's doubts may not have been broadcast as widely as some of those mentioned above, in September 2002 he wrote a letter to the President, after a meeting in which he asked, "What are you going to do once you get it [meaning 'do with Iraq' once U.S. troops have occupied it]?" The President, according to Skelton, answered, "we've been giving some thought to it." In Skelton's follow-up letter, he "quoted the Prussian military theorist Karl von Clausewitz, to remind the White House of the requirement in war 'not to take the first step without considering the last.' He also invoked the other great philosopher of strategy, Sun Tzu, who had observed, 'To win victory is easy, to preserve its fruits, difficult.'" Later in the letter, Skelton made the homely comparison, "But like the proverbial dog chasing the car down the road, we must consider what we would do after we caught it." He was worried, he wrote, about the "extreme difficulty of occupying Iraq with its history of autocratic rule, its balkanized ethnic

tensions and its isolated economic system," and wanted to see "detailed advance occupation planning." He also wanted to hear about "the form of a replacement regime . . . and *the possibility that this regime might be rejected by the Iraqi people, leading to civil unrest and even anarchy.* . . . The American people must be clear about the amount of money and the number of soldiers that will have to be devoted to this effort for many years to come [emphasis added]." Ricks, *Fiasco*, 36, 59.

38. Johnson, *War to Oust*, pp. 63, 64.

39. *Amnesty International: Report 2003*, New York: Amnesty International Publications, 2003, 134.

40. It is true that Saddam could and should have used more resources for the benefit of his people, and some of the privations suffered under sanctions can be traced to Saddam—but not all. Without the sanctions, far more resources would have been available to Iraq, and the people would have benefited. In addition, the combination of the destruction by coalition bombing of water treatment facilities and sanctions that prevented the import of water treatment chemicals must be acknowledged as extremely destructive of the health of many poor Iraqis.

41. Pollack's *The Threatening Storm* does not suffer from this deficiency—yet even Pollack did not provide a list of likely costs to Iraq of a U.S.-led invasion. Something similar could be said for Ajami.

Chapter Nine

Last Resort

First of all, do no harm.

—traditional, ascribed to Hippocrates[1]

Is the political objective we seek to achieve important, clearly defined and understood? Have all other nonviolent policy means failed?

—Colin Powell[2]

Introduction

To some, it will seem self-evident that the "last resort" criterion was not met. For others, it just as clearly was met. The President specifically addressed this criterion, making the case that the war was in fact undertaken as a last resort. That case needs to be considered.

One misunderstanding should be removed. Something can always be done besides war. Weigel is right to point out that the "last resort" criterion is not meant to be understood in "quasi-mathematical terms: the use of proportionate and discriminate armed force is the last point in a series of options, and prior, non-military options (legal, diplomatic, economic, etc.) must be serially exhausted before the criterion of last resort is satisfied."[3] Instead, Johnson's remarks are a balanced positive expression of what is required: "Determination must be made at the time of the decision to employ force that no other means will achieve the justified ends sought."[4] There is not a requirement that every possible alternative shall have been tried. However, the "determination" Johnson speaks of must be based on evidence.

187

THE LAST RESORT CLAIM

President Bush stated in his pre-war speech: "For more than a decade, the United States and other nations have pursued patient and honorable efforts to disarm the Iraqi regime without war. . . . Peaceful efforts . . . have failed."[5]

THE DETAILED LAST RESORT CLAIM

President Bush made a detailed claim in his pre-war March 17, 2003, speech that war was a last resort for the United States and its allies:

> For more than a decade, the United States and other nations have pursued patient and honorable efforts to disarm the Iraqi regime without war. That regime pledged to reveal and destroy all its weapons of mass destruction [WMD] as a condition for ending the Persian Gulf War in 1991. Since then the world has engaged in twelve years of diplomacy. We have passed more than a dozen resolutions in the United Nations Security Council. We have sent hundreds of weapons inspectors to oversee the disarmament of Iraq. Our good faith has not been returned. . . . Peaceful efforts to disarm the Iraqi regime have failed again and again because we are not dealing with peaceful men.[6]

THE ADMINISTRATION FAILED TO MEET THE LAST RESORT CRITERION

The Bush administration failed to meet the Last Resort criterion: (1) Iraqi cooperation with UN inspectors in the months before war was begun was very good. (2) The efforts to disarm Iraq of weapons prohibited it under Resolution 687 were not always peaceful and patient, and included covert and overt force as well as diplomacy. Many of these efforts were not authorized by the United Nations and appear to have contravened that same resolution, which proclaimed a cease-fire for both sides. (3) There was a great deal of evidence that the inspections had in fact succeeded in depriving Saddam's regime of the prohibited weapons. There was only sparse, poor-quality evidence that they had failed. (4) With no imminent threat to any country, peaceful efforts could easily have continued, and would certainly have clarified, for all reasonable observers, the status of claims about WMD programs and a threat to the United States.

EVIDENCE THE LAST RESORT CRITERION WAS NOT MET

In the Months before War, Iraqi Cooperation Was Very Good

On February 14, 2003, Hans Blix, the head of UNMOVIC (the United Nations Monitoring, Verification and Inspection Commission), began his report to the Security Council with the following words:

> Since I reported to the Security Council on 27 January, UNMOVIC has had two further weeks of operational and analytical work in New York and active inspections in Iraq. This brings the total period of inspections so far to 11 weeks. Since then, we have also listened on 5 February to the presentation to the Council by the US Secretary of State and the discussion that followed. Lastly, Dr. ElBaradei and I have held another round of talks in Baghdad with our counterparts and with Vice President Ramadan on 8 and 9 February.
>
> Let me begin today's briefing with a short account of the work being performed by UNMOVIC in Iraq.
>
> We have continued to build up our capabilities. The regional office in Mosul is now fully operational at its temporary headquarters. Plans for a regional office at Basra are being developed. Our Hercules L-100 aircraft continues to operate routine flights between Baghdad and Larnaca. The eight helicopters are fully operational. With the resolution of the problems raised by Iraq for the transportation of minders into the no-fly zones, our mobility in these zones has improved. We expect to increase utilization of the helicopters. The number of Iraqi minders during inspections had often reached a ratio as high as five per inspector. During the talks in January in Baghdad, the Iraqi side agreed to keep the ratio to about one to one. The situation has improved.
>
> Since we arrived in Iraq, we have conducted more than 400 inspections covering more than 300 sites. All inspections were performed without notice, and access was almost always provided promptly. In no case have we seen convincing evidence that the Iraqi side knew in advance that the inspectors were coming.
>
> The inspections have taken place throughout Iraq at industrial sites, ammunition depots, research centres, universities, presidential sites, mobile laboratories, private houses, missile production facilities, military camps and agricultural sites. At all sites which had been inspected before 1998, re-baselining activities were performed. This included the identification of the function and contents of each building, new or old, at a site. It also included verification of previously tagged equipment, application of seals and tags, taking samples and discussions with the site personnel regarding past and present activities. At certain sites, ground-penetrating radar was used to look for underground structures or buried equipment.
>
> Through the inspections conducted so far, we have obtained a good knowledge of the industrial and scientific landscape of Iraq, as well as of its missile capa-

bility but, as before, we do not know every cave and corner. Inspections are effectively helping to bridge the gap in knowledge that arose due to the absence of inspections between December 1998 and November 2002.

More than 200 chemical and more than 100 biological samples have been collected at different sites. Three-quarters of these have been screened using our own analytical laboratory capabilities at the Baghdad Centre (BOMVIC). The results to date have been consistent with Iraq's declarations.

We have now commenced the process of destroying approximately 50 litres of mustard gas declared by Iraq that was being kept under UNMOVIC seal at the Muthanna site. One-third of the quantity has already been destroyed. The laboratory quantity of thiodiglycol, a mustard gas precursor, which we found at another site, has also been destroyed.

The total number of staff in Iraq now exceeds 250 from 60 countries. This includes about 100 UNMOVIC inspectors, 15 IAEA inspectors, 50 aircrew, and 65 support staff. Mr. President,

In my 27 January update to the Council, I said that it seemed from our experience that Iraq had decided in principle to provide cooperation on process, most importantly prompt access to all sites and assistance to UNMOVIC in the establishment of the necessary infrastructure. This impression remains, and we note that access to sites has so far been without problems, including those that had never been declared or inspected, as well as to Presidential sites and private residences.[7]

Although Blix went on to urge Iraq to provide more assistance in clearing up past problems, such as accounting discrepancies concerning earlier declarations of weapons and weapons components in its possession, it is clear from this report that there were no significant complaints regarding Iraq's allowing UN inspectors to do their work unimpeded.

Patient, Honorable, Peaceful Efforts and Diplomacy—No

The President's case began with assertions that the United States and others had engaged in a dozen years of "patient and honorable efforts to disarm the Iraqi regime without war." There were "twelve years of diplomacy." "Peaceful efforts to disarm the Iraqi regime have failed again and again." Unfortunately, this picture is either incomplete or false, depending on how it is interpreted. Either way, it is seriously inaccurate.

In considering those "twelve years of diplomacy," it is useful to begin with then-Secretary of State James Baker's announcement, made on May 23, 1991, that the sanctions would not be lifted no matter what Iraq did, as long as Saddam was in power.[8] This announcement unilaterally changed the sanctions, which were announced and approved by the UN, not the United States. The UN resolution announcing the sanctions stated that if Saddam's regime did x, y, and z, the sanctions would be lifted. Political suicide by the regime was not one of the requirements of the UN sanctions. Baker's announcement, which was never denounced or denied by the U.S. government, made a mockery of that: no matter what the government of Iraq does, if Saddam is in place, the sanctions will remain in place, Baker said. The sanctions became, instead of a temporary measure to be lifted when compliance was in place, as the majority of those voting for them appeared to intend, a permanent punishment of Saddam's regime and of the Iraqi people, kept in place largely by one country, the United States (through its veto power), rather than the body that imposed them, the Security Council. Johnson states that truce-breaking by one side of an agreed truce frees the other from its obligations. To agree solemnly to truce terms, and then add additional terms unilaterally, is to break a truce. In spirit Baker's announcement did just that.[9]

Unfortunately the United States and its allies took other actions that were far from peaceful. The beginning of one of these occurred during the war: the destruction of water purification facilities in Iraq, contrary to the Geneva Convention, which the United States has signed.[10] Following the war, the sanctions then prevented the importation of the chemicals and equipment that would have allowed these water treatment plants to function properly.[11] This amounted to a conscious decision to deny clean drinking water, not to the regime, but to the people of Iraq. This was a contributor to the estimated half million preventable deaths of children in the aftermath of that first war with Iraq. When President Clinton's Secretary of State Madeleine Albright was asked on the television program *60 Minutes* about this UN estimate of the number of children's deaths, she said it was "worth it."[12]

The non-peaceful record goes on. One element of this record is the southern "No-Fly Zone." The two no-fly zones were added by the United States, the United Kingdom, and France (which later dropped its cooperation in their enforcement). They were never specifically authorized by the UN, although the U.S. government claimed to find authorization in UN Resolution 688,[13] which condemned "the repression of the Iraqi civilian population in many parts of Iraq" and demanded that Iraq "immediately end this repression." While the northern zone functioned to prevent Saddam's forces from crushing the Kurds, the southern zone did almost nothing to prevent the crushing of the Shiite rebellion in southern Iraq, even in the brief weeks that rebellion lasted. Despite this failure to achieve or later to have any connection with its stated purpose, the southern zone was kept in place by U.S. and UK forces for the next twelve years, and involved consistent firing of missiles at Iraqi air defenses, often leading to the deaths of Iraqi military personnel and occasionally civilians. These were hardly peaceful acts. As noted in Chapters 5 and 6, Resolution 687, unlike 678, makes *no* provision whatsoever for the use of force against Iraq by any member state. Paragraph 33 of the resolution states that upon Iraq's notification of the Council of its acceptance of the resolution's provisions, a formal cease-fire "is effective between Iraq and Kuwait and the Member States cooperating with Kuwait in accordance with resolution 678 (1990)." Iraq did notify the Council of its acceptance of the resolution, leading to a "formal cease-fire." Given that the UN never authorized the U.S. or UK governments to patrol the skies of Iraq after the "truce" of Resolution 687, these acts of force appear to be acts of aggression. Whether aggressive or not, they were certainly not *peaceful* acts.

Soon after the war, it became clear that Saddam might survive the Kurdish and Shiite rebellions (which were encouraged but not effectively helped by the U.S. government at the time), as well as the ongoing sanctions. The first decision in favor of covert action was taken three months after the end of the 1991 fighting in Iraq and Kuwait.[14] This was followed by at least two widely-reported coup attempts.[15] The Congress of the United States then effectively declared war on Saddam's regime in 1998, with the "Iraq Liberation Act," which states (in Section 3): "it should be the policy of the United States to support efforts to remove the regime headed by Saddam Hussein from power in Iraq and to promote the emergence of a democratic government to replace that regime."[16] Justified or not, it is hard to describe this as a peaceful act, or an act of patient diplomacy. It was followed by the air attacks of "Desert Fox" as President Bill Clinton faced impeachment in the U.S. Senate. These attacks were said to be in response to the expulsion of UN inspectors by Saddam's regime. Yet, with the admission by prominent U.S. players in the drama of those days that the U.S. government had indeed subverted the inspection process to gather intelligence for the purpose of overthrowing Saddam's regime, something reported at the time, but never contemplated in the UN resolutions, it is clear that the expulsion of the inspectors was hardly the aggressive act of non-cooperation it is often portrayed as—it looks more like an act of self-defense by the regime. Once again, like the Congressional declaration authorizing the overthrow of the regime, the "Desert Fox" attacks were aggressive, non-peaceful acts, whether justifiable or not. (And, of course, although ostensibly in "enforcement" of UN resolutions, they were not approved by the UN, nor had the UN declared the cease-fire of Resolution 687 null and void.)

In this entire series of acts following Secretary Baker's declaration that the U.S. government would never lift the sanctions with Saddam in place, the U.S. government took aggressive action not authorized by the UN, yet continued to appeal to the "truce" of Resolution 687 as something that bound Saddam. Somehow this resolution was not held to bind the U.S. government, but only Saddam's regime. Surely this would be a stronger case if the UN had authorized these actions by the United States, since U.S. government justification was always explicitly the enforcement of UN resolutions. However the UN did not authorize these acts. Therefore, in the context of UN Resolution 687 as a cease-fire agreement, it is hard to see them as other than truce-breaking acts.

Whether or not these actions were honorable (a quality difficult to define objectively), they were certainly not patient, nor consistently peaceful. "Twelve years of diplomacy" is a very poor description of efforts that included repeated military attacks neither authorized in the cease-fire terms, nor by subsequent decisions of the UN, despite the fact that the U.S. government consistently appealed to such decisions in order to justify its actions.

There Was Good Evidence Inspections Had Succeeded Long Ago

Bush's justification for all these U.S. actions was simply "the disarmament of Iraq." Hundreds of weapons inspectors did indeed go to oversee that disarmament. After some time, they were informed that all the weapons had been destroyed—but, contrary to the decision of the UN, in the absence of weapons inspectors.[17] However, the UN did not choose to go to war again over this breach, but instead to seek other means to deal with it. Rather than calling for the overthrow of Saddam's regime, the UN continued the inspections. The inspectors, in the following years, were provided access to some of those destroyed weapons.[18] Over the years they accepted the surrender of huge numbers of documents. The biological weapons program, after its existence was denied for years, was revealed in July 1995, "after a year-long investigation by the UN-SCOM biological weapons team which involved close cooperation with the intelligence services of both Israel and Germany."[19] When Saddam's son-in-law Hussein Kamal defected to Jordan in 1995, and was allowed to be interviewed by Western intelligence officials, Saddam's regime turned over huge numbers of documents on Iraq's earlier WMD programs, attempting to blame the hiding of the weapons on Kamal.[20] Kamal, even in the safety of Jordan and with his wife and children with him, told his interrogators that the regime had destroyed all its weapons due to the pressure of inspections (but "kept blueprints and moulds" for future production).[21] After the existence of a biological weapons program (but *not* of weapons) was revealed, *no* WMD and *no further evidence* of an ongoing WMD program was discovered by the inspectors. This was despite ongoing inspections guided by the best intelligence available to the governments of the United States, Germany, the United Kingdom, and Israel, among others. Throughout this process Iraq provided reluctant, imperfect, coerced, but nevertheless real and significant cooperation to the inspectors. Thus, from 1991 to 1998, there was considerable evidence that the inspections achieved success in their aim of ensuring that Saddam's regime got rid of its WMD and WMD programs. There was no proof that Saddam was hiding WMD in 1998, and considerable evidence (in the form of not finding anything no matter how much "intelligence" was received about the supposed weapons, and no matter how much the inspectors searched) that they were in fact gone.[22]

Fast forward to Bush administration threats in the fall of 2002. The President, in a September 12 address to the UN, called this third-rate, broken country, much of which was being bombed at will (the two no-fly zones, never explicitly authorized by the UN, cover the majority of the country) "a grave and gathering danger," and gave a long list of conditions for Iraq to meet "if the Iraqi regime wants peace."[23] This was belligerent language: Iraq was not threatening to do anything to any country at the time, but the President was implicitly but clearly offering war if Iraq failed to meet his conditions. The U.S. Congress continued the verbal belligerency in October with its "Authorization to Use Force" resolution, authorizing the administration to use force to "defend the national security" against this militarily weak regime that the United States had tried to overthrow several times in the previous ten years, even using UN inspections as cover for intelligence collection.[24] Despite the abuse of the inspections process by the U.S. government in the 1990s, Iraq again allowed inspections beginning in November 2002 after Resolution 1441 of that year. After some initial problems, and despite the highly intrusive nature of the searches, there was excellent cooperation at almost all times from the government of Iraq.[25] The inspectors were guided by the best intelligence available to the UN, as provided by the governments of the United States and its allies. Although extremely minor violations of Resolution 687 were admitted by Iraq before the inspectors even arrived (missiles had been modified to fly slightly farther than the 150 kilometers allowed under the resolution), no further violation was discovered, great or small, despite highly intrusive inspections that included 400 site visits. Once again, in those 400 site visits of late 2002 and early 2003, neither a single piece of evidence of an ongoing chemical, biological, or nuclear weapons program, nor one such weapon, was discovered.

No Imminent Threat; Peaceful Efforts Were Easy to Continue

Efforts to disarm Iraq were often not peaceful, and included force as well as diplomacy. The peaceful efforts that did take place (backed by the threat of force, of course) could not be absolutely proven to have succeeded, but gave a great deal of evidence of success. The official Bush administration statement that inspections "had failed" could not be substantiated. Even the President, by saying "the danger is clear. . . . the terrorists *could* fulfill their stated ambitions and kill thousands or hundreds of thousands in our country or any other. . . . Before the day of horror *can come*, before it is too late to act, this danger will be removed [emphasis added]"[26] admitted that there was no imminent threat from Saddam's regime to any other country. Thus, there was no necessity of going to war at the time, and other means, such as continued inspections, could easily have been used to deal with the concern over possible WMD.[27] The Just War Theory criterion of "Last Resort" was clearly not met by the Bush administration.

OBJECTIONS

Objection One: A Dozen Years of Lies Is Long Enough

Objection: Saddam still had not "come clean" with complete intelligence on his weapons and programs after a dozen years. Even at the end he did not do so completely. A dozen years is long enough.

Reply: This objection emphasizes the lack of compliance by Saddam's regime in accounting for the weapons and weapons-related material it stated it had destroyed. First, as demonstrated, the UN Security Council wrote the resolution that imposed these obligations on Iraq, and therefore, it was the UN Security Council that had the right to determine how much compliance Iraq had demonstrated and what the consequences should be. Second, there is a kind of Manichean assumption built into this objection, that some nations comply perfectly with UN obligations, and others fail to be perfect in their compliance and therefore fail completely, automatically justifying war as a result. The reality is that all compliance with and failure to comply with rules takes place on a scale, and the depth of non-compliance must be considered when the appropriate response is chosen. It is true that Saddam's compliance was never perfect in terms of his accounting for the WMD left at the end of the first Gulf War (and that may have involved hiding information he was obligated to share, at least under Resolution 1441). But the heart of the original obligations laid on Saddam's regime was the obligation to get rid of those WMD, not to account for them perfectly. As noted, there was no solid evidence that he still had any WMD. Given that fact, it is hard to see how going to war over incomplete accounting could ever have been a proportionate response. But the Bush administration claimed to go to war not over accounting issues and lies, but because there was "no doubt" that Iraq possessed WMD. In this objection, however, the accounting issues and lies justify war in themselves.

Objection Two: Without War, WMD Development Was Sure

Objection: Without the U.S.-led invasion, Saddam would simply have done whatever he could to get out from under sanctions. Then he would have used his wealth to rebuild his military capabilities, including WMD, making him a huge threat to his neighbors and international peace and order.

Reply: First, Resolution 687, which the U.S. government helped draft, and certainly approved, did not lay eternal sanctions on Saddam Hussein and Iraq. The objector wants to eat his cake (claim the authority of Resolution 687, which laid obligations on Saddam's regime) and have it too (ignore the rights of Saddam's regime under Resolution 687). Note that 687, along with other resolutions in this series, affirmed "the commitment of all Member States to the territorial integrity and *political independence* of Kuwait *and Iraq*" [emphasis added]. The resolution laid tough obligations on Saddam, with the clear understanding that if he met those particular obligations, the sanctions would be lifted. Once they were lifted, of course Saddam would have been free to rebuild his country's economy and its military. That was the bargain the U.S. government-endorsed resolution created. But second, the resolution called in paragraph 10 for the Secretary General of the UN to "develop a plan for the future ongoing monitoring and verification of Iraq's compliance with the present paragraph," meaning its destruction of existing WMD and commitment not to develop new WMD. The sanctions could have been lifted and the monitoring mechanism left in place, in view of Iraq's faulty accounting. It is true that at some future point Iraq could have demanded and perhaps forced the removal of all inspections—but no present action can possibly remove all future dangers. The Bush administration's war did not do that either.

Objection Three: Saddam Was Simply Too Dangerous

Objection: Regardless of the details of the UN resolutions cited, Saddam was simply too much of a danger to the region and to the United States to leave in place. That was clear after a dozen years of low-level conflict.

Reply: First, the idea that Saddam formed an undeterrable danger was dealt with in Chapter 4. Second, the United States freely and solemnly bound itself to respect the Security Council's role and abide by its decisions when it joined the United Nations, which it helped form. Successive U.S. governments endorsed and built their policies around UN resolutions concerning Iraq. This objection makes light of those solemn commitments, the very same kind of commitments for the breaking of which, it was claimed, Saddam's government had to be removed.

NOTES

1. This phrase, often attributed to Hippocrates, seems to be an echo of similar statements in his works: "'First, do no harm': Not in the Hippocratic Oath," *Time and the River: an Editor's Scrapbook*, 2006, http://www.geocities.com/everwild7/noharm.html (accessed June 7, 2009).
2. Colin Powell, in Danner, "A Doctrine Left Behind."
3. Weigel, *Against the Grain*, 220.
4. Johnson, *War to Oust*, 38.
5. Bush, "The War Begins," 503.
6. Bush, "The War Begins," 503.
7. Hans Blix, "Hans Blix's briefing to the security council."
8. Ritter, *Iraq Confidential*, 5. See also Martin Fletcher and Michael Theodoulou, "Baker Says Sanctions Must Stay as Long as Saddam Holds Power," *Times* (UK), May 23, 2001, http://globalpolicy.igc.org/security/issues/iraq/history/1991baker.htm (accessed October 3, 2007).
9. Elaine Sciolino, "Plan Would Let Baghdad Sell Oil," *New York Times*, July 23, 1991, http://query.nytimes.com/gst/fullpage.html?res=9D0CE1D6113DF930A15754C0A 967958260&sec=health&spon=&pagewanted=print (accessed October 3, 2007). Sciolino notes that "on May 7, Robert M. Gates, the deputy national security adviser and the nominee for Director for Central Intelligence, said in a speech that 'Iraqis will pay the price while he is in power.' Mr. Gates added: 'All possible sanctions will be maintained until he is gone.' On May 20, [President] Bush acknowledged to reporters that while there are some instances in which Iraq must sell its oil to comply with United Nations resolutions, 'my view is we don't want to lift these sanctions as long as Saddam Hussein is in power.'"
10. Thomas Nagy, "The Secret Behind the Sanctions: How the U.S. Intentionally Destroyed Iraq's Water Supply," *CommonDreams.org*, 2001, http://www.commondreams .org/views01/0808-07.htm (accessed October 11, 2007).
11. Nagy, "The Secret Behind the Sanctions."
12. Madeleine Albright, "Madeleine Albright – 60 Minutes," *Youtube.com*, May 12, 1996, http://www.youtube.com/watch?v=FbIX1CP9qr4&feature=related (accessed Janu-

ary 31, 2009). (Albright later apologized for this startling remark, but the damage, to the reputation of the United States, not just the Clinton administration, was done.) The combination of the destruction followed by sanctions that made repair impossible is rarely discussed in the major U.S. media.

13. Sarah Graham-Brown, "No-Fly Zones: Rhetoric and Real Intentions," Middle East Report, February 20, 2001, http://www.merip.org/mero/mero022001.html (accessed October 11, 2007). According to the U.S. military website *Defend America*, "Operation Southern Watch enforces the no-fly zone south of the 33rd parallel in Iraq and monitors compliance with United Nations Security Council Resolutions 687, 688, and 949." "IRAQ No-Fly Zone Violations," *Defend America*, http://www.defendamerica.mil/iraq/iraq_nofly.html (accessed October 11, 2007). According to the UN website chronology of the Iraq monitoring mission UNSCOM, on "15 Oct 1994: Security Council Resolution 949 (1994) demands that Iraq 'cooperate fully' with UNSCOM and that it withdraw all military units deployed to southern Iraq to their original positions. Iraq thereafter withdraws its forces and resumes its work with the Commission." "UNSCOM: Chronology of Main Events," *United Nations Special Commission: UNSCOM*, http://www.un.org/Depts/unscom/Chronology/resolution949.htm (accessed October 11, 2007). While in resolution 949 the Security Council declared it was "acting under Chapter VII" of the UN Charter, the resolution made no provision for the use of force, such as the Council used in resolution 678, much less a permanent monitoring and enforcement mechanism such as the U.S. government made out of "Operation Southern Watch."

14. Andrew Cockburn and Patrick Cockburn, "We Have Saddam Hussein Still Here," in *Iraq War Reader*, 91.

15. See footnotes in Chapter 4, in section "Other Contemporaneous Reasons to Doubt the Official Case."

16. Pollack, *Threatening Storm*, 91. For the text of the "Act," see "The Iraq Liberation Act of 1998," October 31, 1998, *www.findlaw.com*, http://fl1.findlaw.com/news.findlaw.com/hdocs/docs/iraq/libact103198.pdf (accessed October 11, 2007).

17. Ritter, *Iraq Confidential*, 35-38.

18. Ritter, *Iraq Confidential*, 41-42.

19. Ritter, *Iraq Confidential*, 109.

20. Ritter, *Iraq Confidential*, 109-14.

21. Ritter, *Iraq Confidential*, 113.

22. Ritter argues (especially in the second half of *Iraq Confidential*) that after Kamal's defection, the only rational purpose of continuing with inspections (rather than declaring, as Kamal insisted and the evidence strongly suggested, that Iraq was indeed free of WMD and WMD programs) was to follow up the "concealment mechanism" that had hidden the documents that came to light at that time, in order to ensure it had not been used to conceal weapons or programs. When this rationale was abandoned under Richard Butler, Ritter argues, inspections had become in effect merely a harassment tool wielded by the U.S. government against Iraq through compliant UN officials, as well as a way for the U.S. to gather intelligence. Indeed, when inspections had turned up no conclusive evidence of any kind of an ongoing WMD program or weapons, a fair process would have declared Iraq in compliance with 687, allowing sanctions to end, and then kept only monitors in place (as 687 called for). To impose ever more intrusive inspections, without offering evidence of violations or hope of an end to sanctions, looks more like harassment than enforcement.

23. Bush, "A Grave and Gathering Danger," 313-18.

24. "Authorization for Use of Military Force Against Iraq Resolution of 2002," 382.

25. Blix, "Hans Blix's briefing."

26. Bush, "The War Begins," 503.

27. Note Scowcroft's advice in "Don't Attack Saddam": "if he did [accept intrusive inspections], inspections would serve to keep him off balance and under close observation, even if all his weapons of mass destruction capabilities were not uncovered." Scowcroft, "Don't Attack Saddam," 297. As Senator Byrd said on the Senate floor on February 12, 2003: "War must always be a last resort, not a first choice. . . . This war is not necessary at this time. Pressure appears to be having a good result in Iraq. Our mistake was to put ourselves in a corner so quickly. Our challenge now is to find a graceful way out." Byrd, "Sleepwalking through History," 485.

Chapter Ten

Reasonable Chance of Success

Suppose a king is about to go to war with another king. Will he not first sit down and consider whether he is able with ten thousand men to oppose the one coming against him with twenty thousand? If he is not able, he will send a delegation while the other is still a long way off and will ask for terms of peace.

—Jesus[1]

You break it, you own it.

—Colin Powell[2]

Introduction

Discussion of the "reasonable chance of success" criterion has been clouded at times by lack of clarity over what constitutes "success." Some writers seem to assume that initial military success is all that is envisaged by this criterion. Johnson, in a chart laying out the criteria,[3] suffers from no such confusion: "Prudential calculation must be made of the likelihood that the means used will produce the justified ends sought." "Success," then, is the achievement of the desired aim, the "aim of peace," that which we intend (right intention) to achieve. Military success is only one small component of the picture. To the Bush administration's credit, success was defined broadly in its initial public statements, including the presidential statement that functioned as a declaration of war. However, instead of offering any kind of calculation showing that there was a reasonable chance of success, that presidential statement appeared to assume that success was all but certain.

THE REASONABLE CHANCE OF SUCCESS CLAIM

"And we will help you to build a new Iraq that is prosperous and free. In a free Iraq there will be no more . . . poison factories, no more executions of dissidents, no more torture chambers and rape rooms. . . . The day of your liberation is near."[4]

DETAILED CLAIM OF REASONABLE CHANCE OF SUCCESS

President Bush spoke of the kind of success his administration hoped to achieve in Iraq in a speech at the American Enterprise Institute on February 26, 2003:

> The first to benefit from a free Iraq would be the Iraqi people, themselves. Today they live in scarcity and fear, under a dictator who has brought them nothing but war, and misery, and torture. Their lives and their freedom matter little to Saddam Hussein—but Iraqi lives and freedom matter greatly to us.
> Bringing stability and unity to a free Iraq will not be easy. Yet that is no excuse to leave the Iraqi regime's torture chambers and poison labs in operation. Any future the Iraqi people choose for themselves will be better than the nightmare world Saddam Hussein has chosen for them. . . .
> The United States has no intention of determining the precise form of Iraq's new government. That choice belongs to the Iraqi people. Yet, we will ensure that one brutal dictator is not replaced by another. All Iraqis must have a voice in the new government, and all citizens must have their rights protected.
> Rebuilding Iraq will require a sustained commitment from many nations, including our own: we will remain in Iraq *as long as necessary* [emphasis added], and not a day more. America has made this kind of commitment before—in the peace that followed a world war. After defeating enemies, we did not leave behind occupying armies, we left constitutions and parliaments. We established an atmosphere of safety, in which responsible, reform-minded local leaders could build lasting institutions of freedom. In societies that once bred fascism and militarism, liberty found a permanent home. . . .
> The Nation of Iraq . . . is fully capable of moving toward democracy and living in freedom. . . .
> A new regime in Iraq would serve as a dramatic and inspiring example of freedom for other nations in the region.
> It is presumptuous and insulting to suggest that a whole region of the world—or one fifth of humanity that is Muslim—is somehow untouched by the most basic aspirations of life. Human cultures can be vastly different. Yet the human heart desires the same good things, everywhere on earth. In our desire to be safe from brutal and bullying oppression, human beings are the same. In our desire to care for our children and give them a better life, we are the same. For these fundamental reasons, freedom and democracy will always and everywhere have greater appeal than the slogans of hatred and the tactics of terror.

Success in Iraq could also begin a new stage for Middle Eastern peace, and set in motion progress toward a truly democratic Palestinian state. The passing of Saddam Hussein's regime will deprive terrorist networks of a wealthy patron that pays for terrorist training, and offers rewards to families of suicide bombers. And other regimes will be given a clear warning that support for terror will not be tolerated. . . .

Without this outside support for terrorism, Palestinians who are working for reform and long for democracy will be in a better position to choose new leaders. True leaders who strive for peace; true leaders who faithfully serve the people.[5]

Directly before the war, in his pre-war radio address President Bush summed up the hoped-for success in these words:

Many Iraqis can hear me tonight in a translated radio broadcast. If we must begin a military campaign, it will be directed against the lawless men who rule your country and not against you. As our coalition takes away their power we will deliver the food and medicine you need. We will tear down the apparatus of terror. And we will help you to build a new Iraq that is prosperous and free. In a free Iraq there will be no more wars of aggression against your neighbors, no more poison factories, no more executions of dissidents, no more torture chambers and rape rooms. The tyrant will soon be gone. The day of your liberation is near.[6]

THE ADMINISTRATION FAILED TO MEET THIS CRITERION

The Bush administration failed to meet the Reasonable Chance of Success criterion. Official U.S. statements before the war show clearly that despite Presidential statements, there was no detailed attempt to define "success" other than in military terms. Iraq was and is a deeply divided nation with no history of democracy. The discussion of a new government for Iraq avoided all the difficult details of the reality that is Iraq. Since "success" was not defined in any detail, it was impossible to calculate whether there was a reasonable chance to achieve "success." The examples offered of successful transplanting of democracy after conquest, Germany and Japan, were distinctly different from Iraq. No other examples were offered, especially not in the Middle East, despite numerous conquests by Western powers that could have led to the implanting of democracy.

EVIDENCE THIS CRITERION WAS NOT MET

In the planning of the war, in terms of Just War theory "success" had to be understood in terms of the Aim of Peace: the intention to put in place in Iraq a better government than it had. The "end" of a just war is to restore or establish peace. Everyone knows, and the President frankly admitted, that overthrowing an existing regime does not automatically establish peace.[7] "Removing Saddam's regime" could not be a legitimate definition of success in itself. What good is removing something bad if something worse takes its place? Is it responsible to "remove a bad government" without considering the results? Success, then, had to be defined in terms of Iraq and the Iraqis.

First, success needed to be defined in terms of Iraq's history. Modern Iraq was a country carved out of the Ottoman Empire after World War I, by agreement between the French and British, when the Ottoman Empire was clearly defunct. The new country consisted of three provinces of that Empire (one of which, Basra, included what is now Kuwait, although British backing had allowed the rulers of Kuwait to achieve de facto local autonomy—at the price of British rather than Ottoman control of their foreign policy).[8] Although the region has been the heartland of a number of Empires throughout history, it does not have the relative homogeneity of a country like the UK or France or Germany. It did not, like those countries, become a modern nation through internal developments leading to a shared language and a long history as a political unit. Instead, it was made a nation largely by outsiders. It had never in 2002 been a convincing democracy, and it remains deeply divided.

The people of the north, about 20 percent, are Kurds, who speak an Indo-European language with a closer relationship in its basic structure to French and English than to Arabic, although Kurdish includes many more Arabic loan words than French or English. The rest of the people of the country are ethnically and linguistically Arabs, but here again there is a deep division. About three quarters of these Arabs (60 percent of the total population) are Shiites, belonging to the same religious sect as the majority of Iranians. The other quarter of the Arabs, or 20 percent of the total population, are Sunnis (like the majority of Arabs in the world). As Dilip Hiro pointed out in January 2003, "the Sunnis . . . have ruled Iraq since 1638."[9]

There is a long history of bitter struggles among Sunnis and Shiites, often as bad as anything between Protestants and Catholics in Ireland, to use an analogy. Although both sides are Muslims, there are striking differences in approach. Imagining how an old-fashioned Baptist or Presbyterian feels about reciting memorized prayers, invocation of saints, burning incense in church, and statues of Mary gives a very rough idea how Sunnis feel about Shiites. Imagining how Northern Irish Protestants traditionally felt about Irish Catholic rule adds a political dimension to the picture. The Ottoman Empire was a Sunni empire. The ruling family the British imposed on newly created Iraq was a Sunni Arab family from the Hijaz, in what is now Saudi Arabia. After the British left Iraq, it was Sunni Arabs who dominated the independent government. Saddam was a Sunni Arab, and although he had quite a few members of minorities in his government (including at least one Christian, Foreign Minister Tariq Aziz), the Sunnis were clearly in charge under Saddam.

Thus, to go back to an earlier Bush administration and an earlier war, the question that was publicly raised and discussed among those interested in the second half of 1990 was, if Saddam is removed from power in Iraq, how will Iraq be ruled? Several facts were obvious: first, democracy was an idea that had never been convincingly tried in Iraq, and had no deep roots in people's minds. Second, power-sharing according to democratic formulas had never worked in Iraq, and is rare and fragile at best in the Middle East. Third, any elections would produce overwhelming Shiite victories, such that Shiites could easily dominate government as completely as they wished. Fourth, that the Sunnis would have a very difficult time accepting this. As a small minority, they had nonetheless been the dominant power in what is now Iraq for hundreds of years, and had ruled modern Iraq through its whole history. They had not done so by being nice people with a fine-tuned sense of respect for the wishes of others. They had done it some of the time as the agents of outside imperial powers, and some of the time through cleverness and brute force.

Why not break up such a star-crossed, accidental state into three countries? After all, the British in effect carved what is now Kuwait from the same piece of the Ottoman Empire, and the non-Arab group, the Kurds, have wanted out of Iraq since it was formed. But to make things more complicated, neighbors Iran, Syria, and especially Turkey have significant Kurdish minorities, and none of these countries wants to see an independent Kurdistan, which would be sure to support Kurdish rebels in their territories, at least by providing a haven for such rebels. The Saudis and the Arab Gulf countries, some of which have significant Shiite minorities (or even majorities) but all of which are ruled by non-Shiite Arabs who fear Iran, had no interest in a Shiite-dominated Iraq, nor in a pure Shiite mini-Iraq in the south, and as neighbors could be counted likely to object strongly and to interfere. (In fact, the most oil-rich portion of Saudi Arabia has a majority Shiite population, raising the stakes considerably.) Perhaps most of all, the center of the country, around Baghdad, is thoroughly mixed up among Shiites and Sunnis, and the borderlands of the Kurds are a mixture of Kurds and Arabs (and other ethnic/religious minorities). A breakup was likely to lead to massive ethnic cleansing, not a peaceful parting of the ways. The world saw this in India at its independence, at the breakup of Yugoslavia, and in many other parts of the world. (If the United States had resolved its racial diversity issues peacefully, instead of via civil war and decades of struggle, perhaps Americans would be entitled to be snooty toward the rest of the world on this issue—but it did not.)

This, then, was the problem in 1990 and 1991: Saddam, representing a small minority, held a deeply divided country together through clever divide-and-conquer tactics and brute force. None of the neighbors wanted the country broken up, and doing so could provoke additional wars in the struggle to redraw the boundaries, especially as neighbors plunged in to help groups similar to them, or to balance groups they did not like. Remove the ruler, and what happens? A struggle for power, obviously, with no clear end in sight, perhaps leading to a civil war lasting decades that spread to all the neighbors, or at the least that drew various neighbors into the conflict.[10] An outside country could impose itself as ruler, but that would bring out Iraqi nationalism and xenophobia (and the one thing that could unite them as Muslims would be a Christian invader). This was obviously a riddle of incredible difficulty, a Gordian knot. Removing Saddam was not going to be hard—but replacing him with a better system was going to be horribly difficult. The problem was so daunting that the first President Bush simply avoided it. Many Americans would have been very happy to see coalition forces "march on Baghdad" in 1991, but they had not studied Iraq. The first President Bush listened to experts who had studied it, and decided to avoid plunging into a quagmire.

The problem was exactly the same in 2002 and 2003 as it had been in 1990 and 1991. It may be startling, but it is clear from the second President Bush's February 26, 2003, speech at the American Enterprise Institute that no solution was proposed to the problem:

> Bringing stability and unity to a free Iraq will not be easy. Yet that is no excuse to leave the Iraqi regime's torture chambers and poison labs in operation. Any future the Iraqi people choose for themselves will be better than the nightmare world Saddam Hussein has chosen for them. . . . The United States has no intention of determining the precise form of Iraq's new government. That choice belongs to the Iraqi people. Yet, we will ensure that one brutal dictator is not replaced by another. All Iraqis must have a voice in the new government, and all citizens must have their rights protected.[11]

How would all Iraqis "have a voice in the new government"? This is not always so easy—minority groups in many lands often feel they have a vote but not much voice. How would all citizens "have their rights protected," given the deep divisions in Iraq, and the lack of a democratic tradition, and the likelihood of a civil war if democracy were imposed? There is no blueprint at all for achieving these good goals, nor was there in other speeches by administration officials. The Bush administration team decided to remove the existing glue of Iraq with hope and confidence, perhaps even with faith, but without any actual plan for dealing with the harsh realities of a bitterly divided country. If a detailed and realistic but secret plan existed at the time, and guided administration efforts post-conquest, it would surely have been released at some later date in order to improve the administration's image.

As administration officials from the President down put it, they were the idealists in the debate. In Bush's words, from the speech quoted above:

> It is presumptuous and insulting to suggest that a whole region of the world—or one fifth of humanity that is Muslim—is somehow untouched by the most basic aspirations of life. . . . Yet the human heart desires the same good things, everywhere on earth. In our desire to be safe from brutal and bullying oppression, human beings are the same. In our desire to care for our children and give them a better life, we are the same. For these fundamental reasons, freedom and democracy will always and everywhere have greater appeal than the slogans of hatred and the tactics of terror.[12]

In other words, those who doubted that these universal aspirations could be effectively imposed by an outside force actually looked down on the Arabs and

Muslims of Iraq. They were "presumptuous," speaking on behalf of Arabs and Muslims without the right to do so, and "insulting," since their position implied, according to the President, that Arabs or Muslims are inferior.[13] But surely it is flawed idealism to try to impose a good thing (democracy) without understanding how to avoid causing a civil war along the way. Surely it is not really pro-Muslim to crush a Muslim government, killing large numbers of Muslims in the process, in a move likely to lead to a Muslim civil war, without a detailed plan to avoid such a war, and with no guarantee of success in imposing democracy.[14]

In addition, the President and his experts pointed to Germany and Japan as examples of what the United States could easily do if it put its mind to it. In Chapter 7, some reasons were given for the poverty of that comparison. To summarize: either Germany or Japan or both had the following factors in favor of cooperation with a U.S. occupation and ability to come out of such an occupation united:

- Relative social homogeneity,
- A prior attempt to subjugate large portions of the world (likely to provoke collective guilt or at least collective acceptance of temporary subjugation by an outside power),
- Experience of a catastrophic and overwhelming defeat, after attacking or declaring war on the United States,
- An Emperor who was able to proclaim the unconditional surrender of his country and have such a proclamation obeyed by his countrymen (Japan), and
- A history of developing as political units through internal efforts.

Iraq had none of these factors in favor of acceptance of a long-term, open-ended U.S. occupation.

But in addition, given that post-war Germany and Japan were in highly unusual situations, and obviously poor countries to compare with Iraq, why not show others? As pointed out in Chapter 8, there simply do not appear to be any good examples in the Middle East of such U.S.- or Western-transformed countries.

OBJECTIONS

Objection One: The "First Iraq War" Succeeded

Objection: As Weigel noted in January 2007, there have actually been four Iraq Wars, and the first of them, the war to overthrow Saddam's regime, was in fact fully and swiftly successful. As Weigel wrote:

How, if at all, is America to help secure the peace in Iraq after the conclusion of
what was then called, somewhat innocently, the "major combat" phase of the
war? . . .

Framing that debate correctly in just-war terms means recognizing that
there have been, in fact, four Iraq Wars since a U.S.-led coalition invaded Iraq
in March 2003.

The first was the war to depose Saddam Hussein's regime and create the
political and military conditions for the possibility of responsible and responsive government in Iraq; it was quickly concluded at a very low cost in coalition military and Iraqi civilian casualties. The second—the war against Baathist
recalcitrants and other Saddamist die-hards—erupted shortly after a decisive
military victory had been achieved in the first war; both coalition and civilian
casualties increased significantly. As jihadists like the late, unlamented Abu
Mussab al-Zarqawi of "al-Qaeda in Iraq" flooded into the country, they deliberately created a third Iraq war, whose aims included not only driving the infidels from Mesopotamia but also destabilizing the fragile Iraqi democracy they
regarded as an offense against Islam. The fourth war, between Sunni "insurgents" (terrorists, in fact) and Shia death squads and militias, broke out in earn-
est after the bombing of a major Shia shrine, the Golden Mosque of Samarra, in
February 2006; a decisive event in which al-Qaeda operatives seem to have
played a part. The second, third, and fourth wars obviously overlapped at several points, making the situation on the ground more complex, more lethal, and
more difficult to understand.[15]

Reply: First, it is difficult to see how to take Weigel's assertion that the
United States fought an entire war (the "first" war) simply to "create the political
and military conditions for the possibility of responsible and responsive government in Iraq." No Bush administration official ever framed the goal, at the
time or since, as creating *conditions* for a *possibility*. It would have been political suicide to do so. And given the realities of widespread looting, massive un-
employment, lack of a constitution, and lack of any recognized Iraqi government
in the immediate aftermath of "major combat," in what sense were the "political
and military conditions for the possibility of responsible and responsive government in Iraq" in place immediately after the conquest of Saddam's forces?
Most political theorists would list order and widespread agreement on how to
form a legitimate government as among the necessary conditions.

Second, it is hard to reconcile Weigel's statement that the first war was
"concluded" after the initial military victory with the facts. Country A, which
heavily outguns Country B, invades it, promising to "liberate" it and to stay "as
long as necessary, and not a day more," with "necessary" undefined.[16] Country
A's troops seize Country B's capital, and the government of Country B is nowhere to be seen on April 7,[17] but there is no government surrender—then or
later. Country A troops do not depart, nor announce when they might depart. On
April 27, a hand grenade is thrown out of a crowd at Country A's troops.[18] On
April 28, a hostile demonstration (perhaps mixed with insurgents, although
many Country B citizens were armed, and there are conflicting accounts of who
fired first) meets with shooting from Country A's troops.[19] No Country B gov-
ernment-in-exile takes over, rather, a former Country A General is appointed as

some kind of governor (the details of his job are not very clear). [20] In early May, that General is replaced by another high-ranking official of Country A, with a new job title.[21] No timetable has been set for a handover of power to Country B leaders. Country A's announced goals are obviously far from being achieved. Country A has not withdrawn its troops nor announced when, even approximately, it will do so. Unless Country A plans a permanent military occupation, its war is not over.

Third, Weigel contradicts explicit statements from the U.S. president, the "Decider" who effectively declared war. In his pre-war speech, President Bush announced that "If we must begin a military campaign . . . we will help you to build a new Iraq," a promise he had elaborated on in his earlier, previously quoted speech at the American Enterprise Institute. Clearly President Bush's announced war aim was a radical transformation of the Iraq that existed under Saddam, and that is what he defined as "success." If this was all accomplished by the overthrow of Saddam, and the creation of "conditions" for a "possibility," why didn't U.S. troops then leave? If troops were to stay "not a day longer" than was "necessary," then in some sense they remained "necessary" in the view of the Bush administration (necessary for what if no resistance was in place, or foreseen?). Paul Bremer, the head of the CPA, wrote that he told Shiite politician Ahmed Chalabi in June 2003 that "the President has been very clear. We will stay in Iraq until the job is done, and not a day longer."[22] The U.S. leadership did not regard "the job" as finished in June, much less in April. When it is announced that war aims are not accomplished, and the invading troops remain in place, and the old government has never surrendered, and no group clearly representing the people is in place, a war is not over.

Fourth, Weigel seems to assume that an indefinite U.S. military occupation of Iraq after the invasion and overthrow of its government was a natural and legitimate state of affairs, whereas Iraqis or Muslims from nearby countries trying to remove that occupation was an unnatural, surprising, and illegitimate development. What Weigel calls the second, third, and fourth wars were not only entirely predictable, (and in fact predicted by experts), they occurred as a direct result of the removal of Saddam. Each is either a continuation or a new stage of the conflict that began with the U.S. invasion of Iraq, the struggle for dominance in that country. Weigel's "second war" was an attempt to reverse by guerrilla warfare the overthrow of the regime. Since the Iraqi forces never had a hope of defeating U.S. forces on the battlefield in a conventional fight, this looks more like a continuation of the earlier resistance to the U.S.-led invasion, not a "new war." The "third war" depended on a "flood" of what Weigel calls "jihadists," which Saddam never allowed, and who only gained access to Iraq due to the relative chaos that followed Saddam's ouster, coupled with widespread Iraqi anger against being occupied by U.S. forces. Since their most basic motivation was to remove a non-Muslim government from the heart of the Middle East, they would have had no motivation to come into Iraq under Saddam. Americans, who heavily supported the *mujahideen* of the entire Muslim world who "flooded" into Afghanistan when that country was in effect invaded by a non-Muslim state, the USSR, should not have been surprised by the same development occurring in Iraq. Weigel states that these "jihadists" aims "included not only driving the infidels from Mesopotamia but also destabilizing the fragile Iraqi democracy they regarded as an offense against Islam." Foreign fighters began to enter Iraq before any kind of Iraqi democracy was in place, so Weigel's belief that they aimed to "destabilize the fragile Iraqi democracy" is not well supported. Weigel notes obliquely, with his statement "driving the infidels from Mesopotamia," that they found a de facto U.S. occupation of Iraq "an offense against Islam," surely the fundamental offense in their view. He also states their goals in purely negative terms, an unhelpful approach in terms of understanding. In positive terms, Islamic "jihadists" wanted to throw out the U.S. military and the then-current fractured, not-yet-sovereign Iraqi "government" (which did not control the military forces operating in the country, and which, by standards easy to understand, could have been called a treacherous puppet government through its cooperation with invading and occupying forces) in order to establish what they saw as an Islamic government. The "fourth war," the civil war between Sunni and Shiite militants, was never allowed to break out under Saddam, and broke out precisely as a result of the instability that followed his removal (and the diminution of Sunni power that was seen as inevitable under a heavily Shiite government). With Saddam's regime gone, there was a struggle for power both within and outside of the flawed "democratic government" of Iraq, which could point to elections that put it in place, but not to any agreed, legitimizing mechanism for sharing power among the ethnic/religious factions in Iraq.

Fifth, and perhaps most important, this kind of analysis, far from assisting in "framing that debate correctly in just-war terms," in fact shatters the inner cohesion of just war theory. In the theory four of the six criteria—"right intention" and the three prudential criteria—all depend on one key element, an end or purpose for which a war should be fought, an end which must be supported by realistic planning to achieve it. Only this end can rightly be called "success." Weigel's analysis removes that end or purpose. Johnson states, in the chart mentioned at the beginning of this chapter, that the "aim of peace" is "the establishment of domestic and international stability, security, and peaceful interaction." Until they are established, the aim is not achieved, the "end" not accomplished—and therefore success in the war as such is lacking. And without this kind of reasonably complete success to aim for, neither "right intention" nor "last resort" nor "proportionality of ends" nor "last resort" has a point of reference, and all become useless as criteria.

Weigel's statement appears to be a rhetorical gambit, the chief benefit of which is the avoidance of the conclusion that the Bush administration failed to meet the "Reasonable Chance of Success" criterion. By claiming that the administration achieved success, as planned, in the "first" war, and that the rest of the struggle was simply the result of unforeseen problems that arose later, Weigel can claim implicitly that the criterion was met.

Objection Two: As of Late 2008, the War Had Succeeded

Objection: The implied premise here is that success could not be achieved. In fact, although the exact date of success is unclear, by late 2008 it was obvious that success had been achieved. A functioning democracy was in place, and it was dealing with the frictions among the various ethnic and religious groups through negotiations and legislative horse-trading rather than civil war. The proof of the strength of that fledgling democracy is that it even insisted on a date for departure from Iraq in its negotiations with the Bush administration. A democratic government with the maturity to insist that its liberators leave is a clear sign that success has been achieved.

Reply: First, the premise was not that success was impossible, but that a realistic assessment in early 2003 would have shown it to be unlikely, and thus the "reasonable" chance of success criterion was not met. It is not, after all, called the "possibility of success" criterion. Second, as noted in the reply to Objection 5 in Chapter 8, to focus on the immediate situation is not decisive in a just war analysis. As this book goes to print in 2009, U.S. troops are still heavily involved in Iraq. No one knows what will happen if they are fully withdrawn as planned. Going further, no one can be sure in 2009 what the situation will be in Iraq in 2011. If it does in fact become a stable, democratic, and just state, able to survive without U.S. military backing for at least several years, as decent people everywhere must hope it does, such a situation will indeed constitute "success." However, the fundamental question, again, is whether this was a reasonable hope, based on prudent, realistic planning, in early 2003. If "success" does occur, the question that will demand to be asked was whether all the death and destruction inflicted on Iraq, and was so obviously likely to be inflicted, justified the slim hope of success.

NOTES

1. Luke 14:31
2. Powell, quoted in William Hamilton, "Bush Began to Plan War Three Months After 9/11," April 17, 2004, *The Washington Post*, http://www.washingtonpost.com/ac2/wp-dyn/A17347-2004Apr16?language=printer (accessed October 12, 2007). According to the story, Powell made this statement, which he called "The Pottery Barn Rule," to Bush in 2002 during discussions of a possible war with Iraq. The statement was first recorded by reporter Bob Woodward in his 2004 book *Plan of Attack*.
3. Johnson, *War to Oust*, 38.
4. Bush, "The War Begins," 504.
5. Bush, "Iraq is Fully Capable," 557-59.
6. Bush, "The War Begins," 504.
7. If the President had defined "success" as "removing Saddam's regime," he would not have needed to make the other promises he made in the speech quoted above. Johnson, *War to Oust*, 65, makes the point strongly that success means achieving the aimed-for peace.
8. See maps at "WHKMLA Historical Atlas: History of Iraq," 2005, http://www

.zum.de/whkmla/histatlas/arabworld/haxiraq.html (accessed October 12, 2007), as well as "L'Empire ottoman en 1878," http://www.atlas-historique.net/1815-1914/cartes/Empire Ottoman1878.html (accessed October 12, 2007). An Internet search for "History of Kuwait" will lead to a string of articles claiming that Kuwait was essentially independent, and only "nominally governed by the Ottomans," until the British established a protectorate over Kuwait at the end of the nineteenth century. Modern Kuwaitis would like to believe this. In fact, Kuwait was at the fringe of a fading empire at that point, which gave it a great deal of autonomy (like other poor parts of that empire), but that does not establish its independence. Kuwait played off the British against the Ottomans, but even the British did not want either (a) to support a truly independent Kuwait or (b) to remove it formally from the Ottomans and make it part of their own empire. The argument for centuries of Kuwaiti independence often appears backed by modern oil money.

9. Hiro, "The Post-Saddam Problem," 560.

10. Even Pollack, in *Threatening Storm*, 390-92, warns of the possible dangers of a takeover of Iraq, such as a civil war. However, Pollack sees it as the likely result of the "Pragmatic Approach," i.e., replacing Saddam with a group of local leaders, even if one of them turns into a dictator. What Pollack never really explains is how his own recommendation, the "Reconstruction Approach," would avoid this danger. He never really shows *how* the U.S. government could have "help[ed] create a new pluralist, inclusive political system that might not be a Western-style democracy but might be the first Arab-style democracy." The details, other than huge numbers of troops and vast expenditures, are all missing. (On "Arab-style democracy," there were several others in 2002 that already fit the bill.)

11. Bush, "Iraq is Fully Capable," 557.

12. Bush, "Iraq is Fully Capable," 558.

13. Concerning "presumptuous," it is fair to point out that the Muslims of Iraq and the world never chose the President of the United States as their spokesman either. As for "insulting," this looks like a political pose, a stance chosen by the President and the others who used this line of argument for political advantage within the United States more than anything else. If they were motivated by a passionate love and concern for Arabs and Muslims, where are the other signs of their great interest in Arab and Muslim culture? The critics generally did not in fact say "Arabs/Muslims are inferior people who cannot be democratic," but "this is not the way to achieve democracy, especially given the reality on the ground."

14. Many writers who warned of the dangers that could arise in Iraq after a U.S. invasion could be cited. Here is just one, CIA analyst Pollack in *Threatening Storm*, 390. Pollack (arguing for a U.S.-led invasion!) notes the dangers of ethnic cleansing and the danger that each group would use whatever federal government arose (absent firm U.S. guidance!) to safeguard group interests only. On p. 391 he warns that Sunnis would resist a new power-sharing setup (but does not say how a U.S. invasion could avoid this outcome). On p. 392 Pollack writes that a new Sunni general attempting to become dictator would provoke a civil war, with the neighbors drawn in as in Lebanon and Afghanistan. (Since he already said the Sunnis would resist losing power, that means a civil war was simply likely if any new system was to be put in place.) On p. 402 he warns it is "vital we have a clear idea of post-war Iraq," but sadly his own descriptions (p. 396-410) avoid the vital details needed for a "clear idea." On p. 403 Pollack writes we "must prevent all revenge killings," but in Kosovo NATO forces failed to prevent massive ethnic cleansing after taking over, and Pollack does not explain how the same problem could be avoided in Iraq. On p. 409 Pollack writes: "Whenever we have taken the easy way out, the result has been civil war, chaos, and dictatorship . . . All signs indicate that the same would hold

true in Iraq." In contrast, he offers Germany, Japan, and South Korea. Germany and Japan are discussed elsewhere in this book. The key fact to note about South Korea is that there was not an independent, self-governing Korea that was then invaded by the United States, making this a vague and approximate comparison at best.

15. Weigel, *Against the Grain*, 254-55.
16. Bush, "Iraq is Fully Capable," 558.
17. Ricks, *Fiasco*, 127.
18. Ricks, *Fiasco*, 139.
19. Ricks, *Fiasco*, 139-40.
20. Jay Garner, identified in Ricks, *Fiasco*, xii, as "chief of the Office of Reconstruction and Humanitarian Assistance, first senior U.S. civilian official in Iraq."
21. Paul Bremer, identified in Ricks, *Fiasco*, xii, as "chief, Coalition Provisional Authority; replaced Garner."
22. L. Paul Bremer and Malcolm McConnell, *My Year in Iraq: the Struggle to Build a Future of Hope*, (New York: Simon & Schuster, 2006), 89.

Chapter Eleven

Replies to Neoconservative Objections

Armed with such realism, the student of Augustine has no illusions about the utopia of the world state. He is prudent, cautious, and restrained. . . . he is braced for the interminable conflicts of world politics, for pressure, tension, and power politics are inherent in the nature of things human, and no panacea of human construction can eliminate these realities.

— John East, "The Political Relevance of St. Augustine"[1]

The bedrock Catholic conviction [is] that *stuff counts*. . . . Whenever and how-ever it appears, though, gnosticism teaches the same seductive and devastating message: stuff *doesn't* count . . . what counts is the *gnosis*, the arcane know-ledge, that lifts the elect, the elite, out of the grubbiness of the quotidian.

—George Weigel, *Letters to a Young Catholic*[2]

Introduction:

Having set out in preceding chapters an analysis of how well the war met each of the six classic just war criteria, it is now appropriate to consider one set of objections as a group. In the run-up to the war, some of the most prominent voices proclaiming how just war theory should be applied to the war belonged to a small group that, on this issue at least, seemed strongly identified with the American neo-conservatives: Weigel, Neuhaus, and Johnson. While they used the six criteria used here,[3] they clearly showed themselves, despite occasional diffidence, to be part of the pro-war camp.

These writers claim for themselves the just war theory mantles of Thomas Aquinas, Augustine, and Cicero. Classic just war theory, they wrote before and after the war began, was a far different thing from what many anti-war writers were assuming or stating. However, many of the claims they made concerning others who spoke and wrote on the subject seem based on distortions of classic theory carefully considered. Five major themes of these writers, and one major omission, bear critiquing.

213

The "Presumption Against War"

The Problem As Some Neoconservatives See It

There is a struggle within the ranks of just war theorists over how to frame the theory. Certain writers have made heavy weather of the statement by the Catholic bishops of the United States, and others, that just war theory begins with "a presumption against war," or sometimes "a presumption against force." Johnson, for example, writes,

> *The Challenge of Peace* [by the Catholic bishops in 1983] described Catholic just war doctrine as beginning with a general "presumption against war" and represented the jus ad bellum criteria as guidance for determining whether this presumption should be overruled in particular cases or not. The classical tradition, by contrast, had thought of the use of force as morally neutral, good when a war was determined to be just (*justum bellum*), a use of force by the sovereign authority of a political community for a just cause, rather narrowly defined, and with a right intention, defined negatively as the avoidance of a number of wrong motives, including self-aggrandizement, theft, bullying, and action out of hatred of the other simply for being the other, and defined positively as intended to establish or restore peace. To cast the just war idea as beginning with a general presumption against war was to make it into something different from what the classic idea had been.[4]

For Johnson, this different beginning turns the whole of just war theory into a different thing. He poses the question "whether the just war proponents here did not give up too much [by adopting the 'presumption'], making the idea of just war over into a position effectively pacifist in practice. But the deeper question is whether the result was faithful to the classic idea of just war at all."[5]

The "presumption," besides being wrong, also leads in the wrong direction. A little later Johnson remarks,

> I have often wondered why the aim of peace was left out of the just war jus ad bellum as stated by *The Challenge of Peace*; I think it is because once one has begun by describing war as something always negative, it is conceptually impossible to represent it as a way to peace. This is profoundly different from the sensibility expressed in classic just war thought, where armed force is a tool that may be used for good or ill and where the assumption was not "against war" but against the evil and injustice that unfortunately abound in the affairs of men and nations, which armed force may be required to remedy. Augustine explained the end of peace in these terms: "We do not seek peace in order to be at war, but we go to war that we may have peace." This is an idea wholly lacking in *The Challenge of Peace*, which frames peace wholly in terms of the absence of war, despite the threats to peace that may remain.[6]

Thus, for Johnson, this starting point is so badly mistaken that if you begin just war theory here, you are already wrong, and you are almost sure to go further wrong. Besides the prevailing fear of nuclear war, Johnson blames the adoption of the "presumption against war" among the Catholic bishops on a desire to share as much ground as possible with pacifists within the Church, as well as to accommodate a general pacifist sentiment: "The presumption against war idea provided a middle ground on which those who favored a just war approach and the pacifists could come together: both shared that presumption."[7]

Johnson is far from alone in this critique. Weigel made much the same point in 1987 in his book *Tranquillitas Ordinis: The Present Failure and Future Promise of American Catholic Thought on War and Peace*. According to Peter Dula, the book alleges "that liberal Catholic theologians and ethicists, under the influence of 'an anti-anti-Communist' ideology and a naïve pacifism, abandoned a proper understanding of the just-war tradition."[8] In the buildup to and during the Iraq war, Weigel returned to these themes in a series of articles in the magazine *First Things*. Many of Weigel and Johnson's writings on just war in recent years include long, detailed rebuttals of those who believe in "starting" just war thinking with a "presumption against war."

After Johnson covered this ground in an essay[9] in *First Things* in January 2005, to its credit, *First Things* went on to publish an "exchange"[10] in April of that year between Paul Griffiths and George Weigel on the "presumption." Griffiths argued that as a matter of logic alone, for any action that is permitted in some circumstances but not permitted in others, there is a presumption against that action. He argued that the various conditions on granting drivers' licenses in his state (the age restriction and the requirements to pass vision and driving tests, etc.) amounted to a rebuttable presumption against granting licenses. Griffiths wrote that Johnson's argument against the "presumption" in his January 2005 essay "amount[ed] to nothing more than the blowing of thick clouds of smoke." Weigel replied, beginning with a humorous parable about a father who, after numerous warnings, finally spanks a child who is playing with matches and trying to set a pile of leaves by the garage on fire, a story meant to demonstrate that there is not "a presumption against spanking." He went on to list numerous minor, straightforward conditions for getting a driver's license, rhetorically asking, "Does any of this reasonably constitute 'a presumption against licensing drivers' which the state can 'override' when certain other conditions are met?" Just because there are conditions to be met before some activity is permitted, in other words, that does not constitute a presumption against that activity.

Just War Theory Is Not Pacifism in Disguise

Before embarking on a critique of Weigel and Johnson and the "anti-presumptionists," it should be stated that they are correct in their assertion that some writers have defined just war theory in such terms that it is either much weaker than the teaching of Aquinas, or even verges on pacifism. Griffiths himself, in an earlier "exchange"[11] in *First Things* with Weigel, claimed that accurate knowledge of whether there is a just cause for a proposed war is impossible for citizens to get, therefore they may not, according to just war theory, consider any war to be just. While Griffiths' seems right that getting accurate information on a proposed war is quite difficult, his response effectively turns just war theory into a road that leads to no destination but pacifism. If the theory has any validity, it must be valid despite such difficulties, which have always been with us. Despite such difficulties, Augustine seemed to believe that just wars had been fought. There are likely enough many other ways in which a tendency toward pacifism has crept into contemporary just war theory, Catholic and otherwise. The frustration Weigel and Johnson show over such attempts to use just war theory to prove the impossibility of a just war is understandable.

Cautionary Note: Distinguishing among "Goods" and "Evils"

"The presumption against war has smuggled into just war thinking a pacifist premise—armed force is wicked—that classic just war thinking rejects," wrote Weigel in his debate with Anglican Archbishop Rowan Williams.[12] Johnson writes "Just war tradition has to do with the possible good use of force, not finding exceptional cases when it is possible to use something inherently evil (force) for the purposes of good."[13] Here it is useful to recall the way thinkers like Aquinas used these terms. For Aquinas, sin is an "evil," and sickness is an "evil" (with sin being a greater evil). Existence itself is a "good," so that a wicked person is "good," at least to the extent that he exists (and if he has strength, intelligence, and charisma, those are also "goods" in themselves). In this sense, to the extent that war deprives human beings of life and limb, it involves "evil" and is not in itself "good." On the other hand, a war may be "good" in the sense that it is justly begun and waged in defense of the innocent. Yet to the extent that war deprives some persons of life, health, sanity, or liberty, it can be said to involve "evil," since these things are good and generally humans are endowed with them. These meanings should not be confused. In these particular quotations from Weigel and Johnson, that confusion appears to exist. Those who approvingly use the phrase "the presumption against war" are often not saying it is always morally evil to go to war or use force (pacifists say that), but they are indeed implying (or stating) that war and force always involve the "evils" of depriving human beings of life or liberty. Just war theory is precisely about how to determine when it is morally good to use something that involves evil (the destruction of things that are in themselves good) in order that a greater good may come. If there were no "evil" involved in war, there would be no need for just war theory. (There is no "just eating theory" or "just walking theory.")

The Ordinary Meaning of a "Presumption Against" an Activity

Weigel and Johnson appear to be wrong about this phrase, for many reasons. First, in ordinary usage, and as the Catholic bishops and many others use it, the phrase "presumption against war" simply means that a government should not begin a war without very good reasons. A presumption against an activity simply means that it is not to be considered normal, natural, and freely permitted: it is instead permitted only under certain conditions, and those wishing to undertake them must justify them. Many activities are normal and everyday and need no particular justification; others are not, and must be carefully justified—concerning these latter, we can say there is a presumption against them. Take a few trivial examples: cracking one's knuckles is in the former category. There is no particular need to justify this act. The fact that it is not an appropriate thing to do when everyone else is silent during a church service or corporate meeting does not constitute a "presumption against" knuckle-cracking—it does not rise to that level. Slapping a stranger hard on the back, or grabbing him from behind and squeezing hard, are in the latter category. If the person is choking, one of these may be exactly the right thing to do. It is not that they should never be done, just that they should be done rarely, and with very good reasons, and never without such reasons.

Another, weightier example: there is a presumption against carrying concealed weapons in public in the laws of the United States. Permits may be obtained for this activity, with varying requirements. There is certainly a presumption against using such weapons against others: such use must be carefully justified, in terms of self-defense or defense of others. The culture and law of the United States do not say that backslapping strangers, or carrying concealed weapons, or use of concealed weapons by civilians, are evil in and of themselves. Not at all. Nonetheless, unlike knuckle-cracking and running hands through one's hair, they carry serious consequences, and must be justified. It is reasonable and natural to say that there is "a presumption against" them. The Catholic bishops and others appear in general to be simply saying that war is in this latter category. The "presumption against war" means simply that a government planning to go to war needs to have compelling reasons (although in a clear case of self-defense, the justice of repelling an attack under way is self-evident). It must share these reasons with its citizens and the world. This thought is not just fully compatible with classic just war theory, one might almost say that it is the essence of that theory.

Structure of the Theory in Accord with Presumption Against War

Contrary to Johnson's claim, it is actually rather clear that the very structure of just war theory that Johnson and Weigel outline presupposes a presumption against war, understood in the normal sense of those words outlined above. If there were not a presumption against war, if making war were actually considered as normal as issuing drivers' licenses, to take Griffiths' example, then the whole theory would be set up the other way around. Just war theory sets up, in every case, restrictions on war: just cause, right intention, competent authority, reasonable chance of success, proportionality of ends, and last resort delineate circles within the conjunction of which war may justly be waged. Outside the area of overlap where all the conditions obtain, war is not permitted, it becomes sinful, unjust, or as Aquinas wrote, "unlawful." If there were no presumption, then just war theory would instead point out the narrow circumstances in which war would be wrong: unjust cause, wrong intention, lack of competent authority, and so forth. Outside those circumstances, the theory would say, make war at will. It would be like knuckle-cracking, permitted except in a narrowly defined set of circumstances.

Weigel notes that Aquinas places his discussion of just war within the treatise on charity ("caritas," divine love) in the *Summa*.[14] Weigel's fundamental point seems to be that for Aquinas, a just war is an act of love by the ruler, in that he is defending his people from harm even at risk to himself (something that may be questionable for modern rulers). Nonetheless, it is inescapable that Aquinas, in that discussion of war, is carving out a very narrow set of circumstances within which war can be just, and outside which war is indeed sinful. As Williams put it in his exchange with Weigel, "Formally, this is a consideration of those conditions under which what would otherwise be gravely sinful would not be so."[15] The only just wars, for Aquinas, are those that fall where all three of his conditions hold, that is, where the restrictive circles in fact overlap.

This point is more clear when we look at the way Aquinas actually frames his argument on just war. The first "question" is "whether it is always sinful to wage war?" The question itself, given the restrictions that follow, strongly implies that it is often sinful to wage war. It is followed by four objections, which state the points of view that Aquinas intends to refute. All these "objections" are framed in absolute terms: "it would seem that it is "always sinful to wage war," "war is always sinful," "war is always a sin," and "war is a sin in itself." Each objection presents a biblical or logical reason for this conclusion. When Aquinas rejects these positions and states his own, in his "On the contrary," he quotes Augustine to the effect that "If the Christian religion forbade war altogether" then John the Baptist would have counseled soldiers to give up soldiering—but he did not. In other words, the objectors claim war is always sinful, and Aquinas replies, in effect, "no, not always—it is not altogether forbidden." This is hardly a ringing endorsement of war.

Not only that, but consider again Weigel's point that Aquinas places his discussion of war within his treatise on charity. Weigel believes this is to show "that rightly constituted authority is under a strict moral obligation to defend the security of those for whom it has assumed responsibility."[16] But a look at the whole treatise on Charity in the *Summa* gives a different impression. First comes a discussion of charity itself, and then of the "acts" of charity, all very positive. Then comes a list of the vices opposed to charity: the "questions" in this section begin with the following titles: "hatred, sloth, envy." Next is a series of "vices opposed to peace" (as peace is the effect of charity): "discord, contention, schism, war, strife, sedition, scandal."[17] The first article for each of these questions asks whether it is a sin, or a mortal sin, or a special sin, or always a sin, and the answer is always "yes." "War" is the exception, in that the question is whether it is "always sinful," and the answer is, in effect, "no, not always." (Under sedition, Aquinas casually calls war a "sin." "I answer that: sedition is a special sin, having something in common with war and strife, and differing somewhat from them. It has something in common with them, in so far as it implies a certain antagonism, and it differs from them in two points." War in general for Aquinas is here just one more sin, unless it meets the exceptional requirements of a just war.) There is no evidence here for Weigel's contention about why "war" falls under "charity." In fact, war is generally caused by a lack of charity, just like the other vices in the list. That is why it is listed here, in line with Aquinas' usual practice throughout the *Summa*, listing and considering under a major heading not only the subsidiary virtues under the larger virtue, but the vices that are contrary to that virtue. Archbishop Williams is vindicated by the table of contents alone, as well as the details: war in general is "gravely sinful:" it is only when it meets the exceptional requirements of just war theory that it is just.

Aquinas' full answer ("I answer that . . .") begins with restrictive conditions: "In order for a war to be just, three things are necessary." Clearly all three conditions must be met, according to Aquinas, and so any war that fails to meet even one of the three is unjust. (He explicitly states that a war may meet the first two requirements and be "rendered unlawful" through a "wicked intention," violating the third.) Anyone who had read Weigel and Johnson before reading Aquinas might have expected a long preamble on the obligation of the sovereign to promote justice outside his borders, and the main question to be "whether it is ever sinful to wage war." Instead, a careful reading of Aquinas shows that he seems to live in much the same moral universe as the Catholic bishops.

Force, Sometimes Necessary, Violates Human Dignity

The reason the use of force in general on human beings is problematic, and that it may be used only when positively necessary and then carefully justified, is that freedom is the natural state of human beings. Use of lethal force is even more of a violation of human freedom and dignity, and has often irreversible consequences. Where is the dignity of human life if governments may casually take it, for weak reasons and with little or no explanation? As Williams wrote in his response to Weigel's essay "Moral Clarity in a Time of War," for Aquinas:

> Violence is an external force compelling certain kinds of action; as such it is bound to appear as against nature or against justice. . . . The ruler who administers the law may use coercion for the sake of the common good in domestic policing and in international affairs. But such coercion will always need publicly available justification in terms of the common good, since otherwise it will appear as an arbitrary infringement of natural justice.[18]

To reinforce that point, in another context Christopher West wrote "persons—precisely because they are persons—are meant to be their own masters. Their dignity demands it. [Pope] John Paul [II] stresses that the person 'surpasses all measures of appropriation and domination, of possession and gratification.'"[19] Simone Weil, in a work published in 1939 on the eve of war, "defines force as 'that x that turns anybody who is subjected to it into a *thing*,' either literally as a corpse or figuratively as a defeated foe begging for mercy or a slave."[20] It is a terrible act to turn a person into a thing, unless absolutely necessary. If compulsion of one human being by another (as in prison, for example) must be rare, and requires careful justification, how much more the taking of human life.

Usually, Justice Can Be Promoted without Force

It is important, in the context of the Weigel/Johnson thesis, to stress that most of the time, in fact, justice is promoted without force. Anyone who has lived in a reasonably happy family or a decent small town, or has studied or

worked in a well-run school, knows that authorities are most often able to defend
the peace of right order through implicit acceptance of their authority by those
under it, an acceptance that is strengthened by parental instruction to children,
peer pressure, civic rituals, exhortation, the work of individual consciences, and,
most especially, the perception that their authority is in fact in the service of
justice. The more this is so, the less is force necessary. Authority figures may
have force available to them, but if things are going well, they can deal with
problems without needing to resort to using it. (Even tyrannical authorities typically try to use these same factors, minus conscience and plus fear, rather than
endless force, to gain obedience.) Force is available, under the right conditions,
as a last resort. It is a last resort in part, of course, because (what Weigel and
Johnson rarely if ever seem to mention) even the best governments can be carried away by power. "Power tends to corrupt," as Lord Acton noted, and once
we make the use of force into something expected and without the need to be
explained, the use of force by government itself is more and more likely to be
employed for unjust ends.

"Morally Neutral" Is False Language for the Use of Force

A key consideration here is Johnson's claim that "The classical tradition, by
contrast, had thought of the use of force as morally neutral, good when . . . determined to be just." Is this accurate? Consider a range of actions: going for a
walk, taking a meal to a sick neighbor, sexual intercourse, cutting off someone's
leg without anesthesia, and killing one's neighbor. Going for a walk is not generally considered to be on a high level of moral importance. Although it can be
abused (someone might do it habitually to avoid responsibilities), walking is
generally healthy but otherwise morally neutral. Taking a meal to a sick neighbor is almost always a good idea, although you could spoil it if your main purpose was to gloat over her sickness, or, in a bizarre but not inconceivable case,
to figure out how to rob her later. There are greater consequences here, for good
or evil, than in taking a walk. Sexual intercourse is a much more serious matter.
For everyone with a system of morality, it is a morally important act with serious
consequences, and serious restrictions (including at the least that it must always
take place without coercion). It can be either a great good, or a great evil, depending on the circumstances, but it would be quite strange for anyone (at least
from the Christian or any classic tradition) to call sexual intercourse in general
"morally neutral."

Cutting off someone's leg without anesthesia can be precisely the right,
lawful thing to do, if you are with a group of soldiers under siege, with no hope
of short-term rescue, the leg is gangrenous, and you have no anesthetics. It might
be the right thing to do, and take a great deal of courage, but it would be agoniz-
ing to do, and the loss of a leg is always, in itself, a cause for sadness. In almost
any other circumstance, cutting off a leg is a hideously evil act. Killing one's
neighbor may result from legitimate self-defense, or defense of another, if he
attempts rape or murder, but there will never be joy involved. It could be called

"good," but only in a rather technical sense: not good in itself, but good only as preventing a great evil.

The range of acts listed above runs from morally neutral to deeply morally consequential. War clearly falls at the latter end of this range, a long way from the category of taking a walk (neutral), or helping one's neighbor (usually good, but not deeply consequential in itself). War is sometimes permitted, and can be the right thing to do, but only rarely, and only under highly restricted circumstances, and it is never something that objectively should cause rejoicing. Loss of human life (much more than loss of one leg) is always, in itself, a cause for sadness (even a vicious killer has the potential, by grace, to become a good person), and the certain loss of many lives, much more so. If we found someone arguing that sexual intercourse should be seen as "morally neutral," or that cutting off legs, or killing one's neighbor, needed to be seen as "good when . . . determined to be just" we would find that very argument a use of confusing and misleading language.

Support for this approach can be found in the *Summa*. Question 18 of the "First Part of the Second Part," entitled "The good and evil of human acts in general" (*Summa*, I-II, 18, 2-4), makes it clear that for Aquinas, the good and evil of human actions is determined by their objects, and affected by circumstances as well. For a specific example, consider what Aquinas wrote about sexual intercourse: "The conjugal act and adultery, as compared to reason, differ specifically and have effects specifically different; because the one deserves praise and reward, the other, blame and punishment" (*Summa*, I-II, 18, 5, reply to objection 3). Consider Thomas' description of an action which is "indifferent in its species" (i.e., of good or evil): "it may happen that the object of an action does not include something pertaining to the order of reason; for instance, to pick up a straw from the ground, to walk in the fields, and the like: and such actions are indifferent according to their species." (*Summa*, I-II, 18, 8, "I answer that"). Taking a walk or picking up a straw may be called "morally neutral;" but the use of force is either good or evil, depending on the aim and the circumstances.[21]

Classic Just War Writers Used Strong, Negative Language for War

Not only is this language of "moral neutrality" unfitting, it is emphatically not the language used by the classic just war thinkers. A few quotations from Augustine and Aquinas (especially significant due to the constant appeals to these two giants of the "classic tradition" in Weigel and Johnson's works) will make this clear. Begin with Augustine, whom Aquinas quotes continually in his article on war in the *Summa*. First, nowhere in those quotations does Augustine state that war itself, even just war, is or even can be "good." Johnson, in *The War to Oust Saddam Hussein*, quotes Augustine numerous times, and again nowhere in those quotations does Augustine say the use of armed force, or war, can be "good"—nor, in fact, that it is "morally neutral." It would be odd if he did, since in *The City of God*, Book 19, Chapter 5, Augustine writes "On all hands

we experience these slights, suspicions, quarrels, war, all of which are undoubted evils." In Chapter 7, he laments,

> but how many great wars, how much slaughter and bloodshed, have provided
> this unity [of the Roman Empire]! And though these are past, the end of these
> miseries has not yet come . . . But, say they, the wise man will wage just wars.
> As if he would not all the rather lament the necessity of just wars, if he re-
> members that he is a man; for if they were not just he would not wage them,
> and would therefore be delivered from all wars. . . . Let everyone, then, who
> thinks with pain on all these great evils, so horrible, so ruthless, acknowledge
> that this is misery. And if anyone either endures or thinks of them without men-
> tal pain, this is a more miserable plight still, for he thinks himself happy be-
> cause he has lost human feeling.[22]

All wars, then, for Augustine are "undoubted evils" and even just wars are
"miseries" and "great evils" that no one with "human feeling" should think of
"without mental pain." Much later, in Aquinas' article on war, when war meets
the three, restricti ve conditions he sets, he describes it not as "good" but as "lawful." Later still, Alphonsus de Liguori offered what is surely common sense wisdom when he wrote: "There is no doubt that since war generally brings in its
train so many evils and so much harm to religion, to innocent people, to the hon-
or of women, etc., in practice it is hardly ever just if declared on probable reasons of justice alone and not certain reasons."[23]

From an author often acknowledged as one of the great neo-Scholastics,
Suarez: "*Jus belli est odiosum, et poena ejus gravissima; ergo restringenda est
quod fieri potest.*" "The right of war is hateful, and its punishment is most grave;
therefore it is to be restricted as far as can be."[24] To cite an analogous concept
from Islam: within Islam divorce is permitted, but it is explicitly called "*akrah
al-masmoohat*," "the most hated of the permitted things." In Islamic thinking, in
other words, God himself hates divorce, but permits it. The concept illustrates
how even just war seems to be viewed in the actual writings of classic just war
thought—while unjust war is, of course, viewed with complete horror in this
tradition. These kinds of frank acknowledgments of the certain miseries of
war—slaughter, bloodshed, misery, harm, dishonor—are, doubtless, a part of the
"distinctive moral texture"[25] of warfare in classic just war theory, even if they
are generally quite hard to find in the writings of Weigel and Johnson.

Up to this point, the positive argument has been made that the phrase "presumption against war" can be and most naturally should be understood as well
within the bounds of classic just war theory. There are more specific logical errors in the Weigel/Johnson campaign against "the presumption," and the overall
negative consequences that result from their push in the opposite direction.

Lost Distinction: "Presumption Against" vs. "Prohibition Of"

It seems Weigel and Johnson have muddied the distinction between "presumption against" and "prohibition of." Possibly as a result of this, important
errors have crept into their own statements about presumptions. This appears to

begin with Johnson's statement above that "The presumption against war idea provided a middle ground [for Catholics] on which those who favored a just war approach and the pacifists could come together: both shared that presumption." Not so: pacifists believe in a prohibition of war rather than a "presumption against" it. The "presumptions" against force, violence, and war are not shared with pacifists. It is true that strict just war theorists and pacifists may end up in practice in a similar position: opposing some wars. It is this that is the middle ground, not "the presumption" (and there is nothing inherently wrong with seeking and finding such a political middle ground: real politics is packed with such alliances). Another example of this muddying is found in Johnson's quotation above where he writes that "in classic just war thought . . . the assumption was not 'against war' but against the evil and injustice that unfortunately abound in the affairs of men and nations, which armed force may be required to remedy." (Johnson means moral evil here, for armed force rarely helps against the evils of poverty and sickness.) This is confusion: war in just war theory is a grave undertaking, with important moral consequences, that is permitted under conditions. "Evil and injustice," on the other hand, are never permitted under any circumstances. There is neither an "assumption" nor a "presumption" against evil and injustice, but an absolute prohibition against taking part in them. The parallel is false, as is that of Weigel when he writes, in "Just War: An Exchange,"[26] that "[j]ust war thinking starts with 'a presumption for justice,' not a 'presumption against violence.'" There is a proper time for a government to use force, but there is never a proper time to commit injustice. And, as noted above, there is no need to set the pursuit of justice against the avoidance of violence, because in most cases justice can and should be pursued without the use of force. Governments should always seek justice, wherever possible without the use of force.

Red Herring: A "Priority" without Consequences

In his "exchange" in *First Things* with Williams, Weigel never directly addressed the Archbishop's point concerning Aquinas' article on war that: "Formally, this is a consideration of those conditions under which what would otherwise be gravely sinful would not be so."[27] Weigel asks, "Why can a sovereign ruler override what Dr. Williams calls Aquinas' 'prima facie case against war,'" thus quietly allowing that Aquinas makes such a case (if not, it would be meaningless for Weigel to say it can be overridden). Weigel insists, though, as if the point contradicts that "prima facie case," that rulers have "a prior moral obligation, a responsibility to defend the peace of right order. That prior obligation is the beginning of all morally serious thinking about the use of armed force for morally serious ends."

The "priority" of the obligation should be analyzed. In looking at the work of government from any non-anarchist and non-libertarian theoretical standpoint, it is necessary at some point to posit the duty of the government to establish a just and peaceful order, at least within the borders the government controls. In a consideration of the work of government, this duty is likely enough to come prior to considering the issue of war. However, just war theorists (as opposed, generally, to pacifists and anarchists) believe in a government that is authorized to use force at least some of the time. That is true even of openly "presumption against war" just war theorists. Therefore, the issue Weigel is so concerned about here is simply a given for the majority of Weigel's non-pacifist opponents. The reason they do not hammer away at the issue is not that they do not believe it; rather, it is because it is so fundamental to their beliefs that it does not cross their minds to raise it.

But does prior acknowledgment of this moral obligation actually makes a difference? Let someone begin by positing that a government has an obligation to establish "the peace of order," using force when necessary, at least within its own borders. It seems certain that Williams agrees with such a statement—the Church of England does not pick anarchists to be Archbishops of Canterbury. Next, the question arises: when may the same sovereign make war *outside* his borders? We have now "begun" in the right place, according to Weigel, we have got our priorities right, yet—the question is just as difficult as if we had not done so. Why? Because there is almost always another government there, with rights and responsibilities, one would think, within *its* borders. When is it right, there-fore, for a government to use force beyond its own borders to promote peace (however defined) against the will of another government, especially if the first government's country is not under any visible or demonstrable attack? How are all the conflicting claims of sovereign authorities to be reconciled? Weigel gives no direct answer to these questions in his answer to Williams. It seems that using Weigel's prescribed starting point simply doesn't help at all in resolving the nit-ty-gritty question of when a war is actually just or unjust.

Consider a parallel case, the presumption of innocence in court. The pre-sumption of innocence in law is in practice a presumption against a jury's be-lieving the prosecution (i.e. the government), until it proves guilt beyond reason-able doubt. This presumption may be looked at both in terms of where it falls in a theory of criminal justice, and in terms of whether it prevents or discourages prosecutions. There would be little point in debating where thinking about crim-inal justice ought to begin, as somewhere in the theory government is said to be in the business of enforcing the laws. Somewhere else along the way, at least in the Anglo-Saxon tradition, juries are said to be under a duty to assume the inno-cence of the accused until their guilt is demonstrated beyond reasonable doubt. Although the duty of government may be logically prior to the presumption of innocence, the presumption of innocence already assumes that government is at work enforcing the laws. What difference does it make whether this assumption about the government enforcing its laws is made explicit or not? In practical terms, hundreds of years of the presumption of innocence in Anglo-Saxon law have not prevented governments from prosecuting criminals, nor from winning convictions against them (including, sometimes, the innocent—it is worth not forgetting that). It seems clear that the order of considering these two facts with-in the theory makes no practical difference, and beginning with the presumption of innocence would in practice make no difference in the fact of prosecutions and convictions. (Perhaps, though, if there were an effort to try to drown out talk of the presumption of innocence due to a perceived "conflict" between that and the obligation of governments to enforce the laws, it might erode the presumption of innocence—not to the benefit of citizens, since that presumption is vital precisely because governments too can be immoral, and power corrupts.)

And what is the effect of this presumption against believing the government, when a prosecution is successful and the jury finds against the defendant? In fact, because of the existence of this presumption, citizens are more sure the jury did rightly—it did not lightly decide to deprive the defendant of money, liberty, or life, but only after it overcame the presumption of the defendant's innocence. This negative presumption actually strengthens our confidence in the rightness of the action the government wished to take, without in any way making convictions impossible.[28] There is no reason for a "presumption against war" not to have the same effect.

Not Seeing That Standards Cut Both Ways

Weigel wrote against Williams, a few sentences after his remarks on the "prior obligation" of the sovereign, that the "presumption against war" has not reinforced the "obvious" truth that "public authority has to make a moral case that the use of armed force in defending the peace of right order is the only reasonable option in this instance, because other nonmilitary means have failed or have been reasonably judged to be unavailing, given the threat and the aggressor." On the contrary, surely by its nature it reinforces that very truth, to the extent that people think about it, and many did before the Iraq war. The government "has to make" the moral case for war, precisely because other "public authorities" have a presumptive right not to be attacked, and because, as Williams notes, war is "gravely sinful" if fought for the wrong reasons: war is "presumed to be unjust" until convincingly demonstrated to be otherwise (and ugly, as Augustine notes, even when it is the right thing to do). That is precisely why Aquinas wrote that war is only just when it meets certain conditions, and why governments strive to show that they have met those conditions. Weigel appears to ignore the possibility that some of those opposing the war did so not out of pacifism but precisely because they did not believe the public authority had convincingly made "a moral case that the use of armed force . . . is the only reasonable option in this instance, because other nonmilitary means have failed or have been reasonably judged to be unavailing," and because they judged the evidence about "the threat and the aggressor" insufficient. It appears that Weigel nowhere in that essay accounted for this possibility, but in fact, many opponents of the war were obviously not pacifists. Many opponents of the war, whether pacifists or not, in fact made many of their arguments against the war in precisely these terms: they argued, with evidence, that "public authority" had failed to "make a moral case" in favor of the war. Like Johnson at times, Weigel appears in this passage unable to see that a standard, by its very nature, can cut both ways. In this case, if a standard shows when a war is just, it can also, by definition, show that a war is unjust.

False Analogies and a Missed One: JWT and Force in General

Looking carefully at Weigel's spanking example at the beginning of this chapter, and his use of Griffiths' driving license example, one finds serious problems, as well as a missed chance to broaden the application of the theory. There is not a presumption against spanking—but that is because the word "spanking" itself already includes the idea of a controlled and proper use of force (rather like "just war"). There is, of course, a presumption against the use of force against children, which is nicely parallel to just war theory: the use of force against children should not be a normal, unrestricted activity. It should be used only for a right cause, with the right intention (for the child's good, not to satisfy parental fury), it should be practiced by the competent authority (the parent, or a designated guardian, or, in an emergency, a competent adult), it should be proportionate to the disobedient act, and it should be a last resort, not used if a lesser sanction, such as a stern warning, will be sufficient. (Reasonable chance of success is more or less a given, or perhaps this is why sixteen-year old boys are rarely spanked.) In this analogy, the pacifist would be the "never spank" parent, and the "war is normal" theorist the casually violent parent who smacks or cuffs a child without warning and for any reason. The word "war" is properly parallel to "force," not "spanking." (To make parallel concepts of war and spanking is an ugly idea, in part because a proper spanking almost never causes lasting physical damage at least, whereas even the best-justified war involves death, chaos that allows ugly violence free rein, and destruction.) Weigel's humorous little spanking parable actually reinforces Griffith's point.

While Weigel is right that Griffiths' example of licensing drivers is a strange use of language, that is because issuing driving licenses is a natural, everyday activity, with very minor restrictions. There is a range of human activities—as noted above, some (like knuckle-cracking or taking a walk) come with a very few, very minor restrictions or none, while others come with heavy, serious restrictions. To use "presumption against" language when there are few, minor restrictions is an odd use of language, because we usually restrict such language to activities with serious possible consequences. But when Weigel accepts Griffiths' licensing analogy while denying that there is a "presumption against" issuing licenses, he implicitly accepts a parallel between making war and issuing drivers' licenses, with a presumption against neither. That parallel would make war an everyday, normal occurrence—an activity that every "sovereign authority" should practice as often as his heart desires, a tool of statecraft as unexceptional as sending ambassadors or organizing cultural exchanges. To make war equivalent to issuing licenses in explicit terms would be horrifying, but that is the direction in which Weigel's language pushes him. The whole parallel expresses an overreaction in theory that, in rhetoric at least, has lost touch with the underlying reality.

Weigel misses a much better analogy than that of spanking and war. First, one can one in fact say there is a healthy presumption (understood in the normal, natural sense) against the use of force against any human being, whether by the forces of order or by other citizens—force should only be used under certain highly restrictive conditions. It is not normal to use force against human beings, but at times it may or should be done. However, if we ask when it is permissible to use force, just war theory offers an excellent analogy to other situations. One more example: the police. When do we as citizens want to see the police use force? Well, for a just cause, with a right intention, when they have the proper authority under law (just because they are the police does not prove they are enforcing the law in a particular instance), when the ends are proportionate to the means, when there is a reasonable chance of success, and as a last resort. The parallel with just war theory is excellent. Perhaps Weigel missed it because he has come to think of war as normal and unexceptional, something quite alien to the thought of Aquinas.

Confusion on Private Use of Force

Weigel also claims that the "presumption against violence" "collapses *bellum* into *duellum*," or "conflates the ideas of violence and war." For Weigel, "*duellum*" signifies "the use of armed force for private ends by private individuals:"

> If the just war tradition is a theory of statecraft, to reduce it to a casuistry of means-tests that begins with a "presumption against war" is to begin at the wrong place. The just war tradition begins somewhere else. It begins by defining the moral responsibilities of governments, continues with the definition of morally appropriate political ends, and only then takes up the question of means. By reversing the analysis of means and ends, the "presumption against war" starting point collapses *bellum* into *duellum* and ends up conflating the ideas of "violence" and "war." The net result is that warfare is stripped of its distinctive moral texture. Indeed, among many American religious leaders today, the very notion of warfare as having a "moral texture" seems to have been forgotten.[29]

In fact, Weigel appears to collapse the private use of force into violence, and to have the wrong idea of what makes the use of force moral. Say a stranger rushes at my wife in the street, red-faced and shouting. I interpose myself, and, when the man tries to shove me out of the way, I wrestle him to the ground. This is private use of force, with no sanction by the state at all, and for a private end—the defense of my wife. Yet, is it immoral? Surely not. Surely it would be fully justified and moral. It is not, as Weigel appears to imply, that government use of force is good and private use is not—that is simply confusion. Instead, there are moral and immoral uses of force, both for individuals and for governments. In both cases, there is a "presumption against violence." If the same stranger, instead of rushing at my wife, shouted at her from across the street, "I hate you! Watch out, you're going to get it," would I be justified in crossing the street and pummeling him, with fists or some weapon, or shooting him if I had a pistol with me? No, but not primarily because it would be a private use of force, rather because the presumption against violence rules it out. While the words are hostile, there appears to be no imminent danger. The ideas of "last resort" and "proportionality" interpose themselves as well, just as they should for a government in an analogous situation. It is not the private use of force that is ruled out, but the use of force that is not in accord with justice and prudence.

It is true that in Augustinian and Thomist thought, a soldier is justified, during a just war, in seeking to kill enemy soldiers because of the command of a right authority, whereas the private person, for Aquinas, is justified in killing even in self-defense only by "double-effect" reasoning—he aims to defend himself, rather than to kill, even if the proportionate defensive action he takes does in fact kill his attacker. Nonetheless, even this permission to aim to kill in warfare does not grant blanket permission to kill enemy soldiers. For example, a slaughter of enemy soldiers who have laid down their arms and surrendered is most definitely not a moral act according to just war theory, whatever the orders of superiors may be. There is no blanket permission in just war theory to use force in warfare, even in a just war, any more than in private life. For the state and for the individual, the use of force must be justified.

When Weigel refers to "the distinctive moral texture of warfare" in this context, perhaps he is unconsciously guilty of government-worship. Warfare has the same "moral texture" (in one sense of the term) as any human activity: if in accord with prudence and justice, it is moral; if not, it is immoral. Warfare is different from the private use of force not because one is moral and the other immoral, but because warfare is a corporate activity, subject to different rules from those that govern private action, even if those rules are based on the same underlying principles. But what is truly distinctive about the moral texture of warfare, as opposed to other corporate activities, it is precisely its hatefulness even when right, an idea strongly supported by the writings of Augustine, Alphonsus de Liguori, and Suarez, as well as the list in which Aquinas places "war."

Getting the Practical Consequences of "the Presumption" Wrong

A counterexample to Weigel and Johnson's claims the phrase "the presumption against war," or the concept as an introduction to just war theory, leads by some powerful inner logic to pacifist conclusions is found in the Bishops' letter "The Challenge of Peace" itself, the very document that seems to Johnson to lead in the wrong direction. In the first instance where the phrase is used in that document, the full paragraph (70) runs thus:

> As we have already noted, however, the protection of human rights and the preservation of peace are tasks to be accomplished in a world marked by sin and conflict of various kinds. The Church's teaching on war and peace establishes a strong presumption against war which is binding on all; it then examines when this presumption may be overridden, precisely in the name of preserving the kind of peace which protects human dignity and human rights.[30]

First, the bishops state that the over-riding concern is the "protection of human rights and the preservation of peace." Peace is defined in a variety of ways over the preceding sixty-nine paragraphs, but is expressly stated not to be merely "the absence of war" (see paragraph 68). The bishops then state that there is a presumption against war, and immediately that it may indeed be overridden (in other words, to be crystal clear, the bishops are stating here when wars may rightly be begun), precisely to preserve a peace that is not just the absence of war, as Johnson wrongly complained of their description, but a peace "which protects human dignity and human rights."

In fact, it appears quite inaccurate to say, as Johnson does, that "*The Challenge of Peace* described Catholic just war doctrine as beginning with a general 'presumption against war.'" It would be more accurate to say that "The Challenge of Peace" begins its discussion of war with a long, multi-faceted discussion of peace, including the idea of justice, and then moves on to just war theory only after that context has been established. In fact, the sixty-nine paragraphs that precede that mention of a "presumption against war" are largely about the deeper meaning of "peace," in all its complexities, including the requirement of right order, or justice. In one of the first attempts to define "peace" in biblical terms the document states, "true peace implied a restoration of the right order not just among peoples, but within all of creation" (paragraph 32). Soon after, it states: "The lament of Isaiah 48:18 makes clear the connection between justice, fidelity to God's law, and peace" (paragraph 35). And, in paragraph 68 (with slight repetition):

> Peace is not merely the absence of war. Nor can it be reduced solely to the maintenance of a balance of power between enemies. Nor is it brought about by dictatorship. Instead, it is richly and appropriately called "an enterprise of justice" (Is. 32:17). Peace results from that harmony built into human society by its divine founder and actualized by men as they thirst after ever greater justice.

It is indeed possible to move directly from a "presumption against war" to a discussion of how and when to go to war in response to grave injustice, and that is explicitly stated by the very document Johnson and Weigel single out as exemplifying the trend toward pacifism. Note that, despite Johnson's dark suspicions about "why the aim of peace was left out of the just war jus ad bellum as stated by *The Challenge of Peace*," Weigel himself left that aim out of his own short list of jus ad bellum criteria in "Moral Clarity in a Time of War."[31] The likeliest explanation in both cases is simply that the "aim of peace" falls rather naturally under "right intention," as Johnson himself notes in his January 2005 essay, as well as in his book *The War to Oust Saddam Hussein*—and Aquinas discusses the aim of peace under right intention as well.[32]

Conclusion on "the Presumption"

"The presumption against war has smuggled into just war thinking a pacifist premise—armed force is wicked—that classic just war thinking rejects," writes Weigel contra Williams. Not at all—the "presumption against war" is simply a restatement in new terms of the classic position. Classic just war theory allows war under limited conditions, but shows a strong and well-justified distaste for war, which is gravely sinful if it does not meet the conditions. Classic just war theory does not "begin" with a broad, general obligation of all rulers to stop evil everywhere (see section below on "The Sovereign's 'Obligation'") because such an obligation would not solve precisely the problem that (except in a purely and clearly defensive war) needs solving: when is the lack of rightly-ordered peace in the other state so great that war is justified? "The presumption" does not presume that "armed force is wicked," as Weigel claims, but rather that the use of armed force conflicts with what is normally good—liberty, and that its full-blown use kills humans—which is tragic. Weigel's logical fallacy here is the "excluded middle." Either you believe force is inherently "wicked," or you regard it as completely normal and "neutral." The truth is in the middle—war is often wicked, and when it is lawful, it is still regrettable. If pacifism has been smuggled into the classic just war tradition (and regrettably, that is often true), there is no reason to blame it on "the presumption."

On the one hand, the attempt to show that just war theory has been weighted toward pacifism is a perfectly legitimate one—the case can easily be made. However, the overreaction by Weigel and Johnson in their long fight against "the presumption against war" basically tips the just war theory boat over on the other side, toward a "presumption in favor of war." It does this first in the very denial of the concept of a presumption against war, because if there is no presumption against some activity, that activity has to be considered normal, natural, and always acceptable, like issuing a driving license, picking a straw off the ground, or taking a walk. It is doubtful that classic just war theory ever described war in such terms. Secondly, it harms just war theory by an overwhelming use of positive language about war, with only token remarks about its negative certainties.

Weigel even writes in one essay, "Thus, in the just war tradition, war is not an abandonment of the moral realm; war *is* a moral category—war is the use of proportionate and discriminate armed force by the legitimate public authority in order to secure certain worthy public goods. Anything else is brigandage, in one form or another."[33] Yet if it were true that "war" in the just war tradition is "the use of proportionate and discriminate armed force by the legitimate public authority in order to secure certain worthy public goods," there would have been no need for Augustine and Aquinas to write of "just" and "unjust" wars, nor for Aquinas to put "war" in the middle of his list of uncharitable acts. In Weigel's definition here, all wars are just, and only "brigandage" is unjust.

In a similar vein, Johnson writes "Just war tradition has to do with the possible good use of force, not finding exceptional cases when it is possible to use something inherently evil (force) for the purposes of good."[34] While this is partially correct, it is also sharply misleading, like saying the building code "has to do with defining when a building is safe," or that the speed limit "has to do with the possible good uses of speed." Just war theory is not a guide for praising rulers who start wars any more than it is a grab-bag of all-purpose condemnations of the use of force. It is a set of standards: it consists of criteria. According to one on-line definition, a criterion is "a standard of judgment or criticism; a rule or principle for evaluating or testing something." It comes from a Greek root meaning to separate, or decide.[35] Moral criteria, by definition, do not exist for the purpose of showing merely what is good and acceptable. By their existence, such criteria unavoidably show also what is evil or unacceptable.

In conclusion, it is not only possible to make a "just war" case for war after starting at the "presumption against war," it is a perfectly good place to start, because war is simply not an everyday activity, nor is it desirable except in carefully delimited circumstances. This is both explicitly and implicitly acknowledged by Augustine, Aquinas, and others in the classic tradition, and is clear enough in the very framework, the six classic criteria, that Weigel and Johnson use. Unless it is abused in some way, the neutral, descriptive phrase "the presumption against war" falls well within classic just war theory. Creeping pacifism should be fought on other grounds.

Prudence, the Morality of Human Action, and Aquinas

Downgrading the Prudential Criteria

Johnson expresses some reservations about the three "prudential" criteria (although he follows up immediately with the statement that the prudential criteria "are clearly important concerns"):

> I have also criticized the priority given in some recent just war thinking to three moral criteria not found in classic statements of the just war idea. My concern with these is not simply that they are new, but that they are at best supportive concerns having to do with the wise practice of government, not primary concerns having to do with establishing and protecting the goods of politics themselves. To treat them as if they are of the same character as the requirements found in classic just war thought, or even as more important, warps just war reasoning. The traditional just war criteria—sovereign authority, just cause, and right intention, including the end of peace—are deontological in character; they impose duties on the person or people having ultimate moral responsibility for the good of the political community and for good relations among political communities. The newly added criteria . . . are consequentialist in nature, requiring an estimate of outcomes and a weighing of the wisdom of resorting to force in a given case.[36]

Johnson restates this caution against treating the prudential criteria as equal to the others in a number of places. Weigel goes further in his downgrading: after denouncing what he perceives as too much emphasis on the prudential criteria, he drops them almost completely from the discussion in his April 2005 article, despite its sweeping title, "Iraq: Then & Now."

While Johnson's division between deontological and prudential criteria is an acceptable one, it appears that Johnson and Weigel make far too much of it. Note, first, what appears to be an ambiguity in Johnson's formulation. When he writes that "The traditional just war criteria . . . are deontological in character; they impose duties" on political leaders, it is not clear from reading Johnson that sometimes the duty imposed is that of *not* going to war. A binding obligation generally binds both ways: the wedding vow commits a husband both positively, to love his wife, and negatively, not to have affairs with other women. The criterion "just cause," for example, binds a nation to seek justice for its citizens and, to some extent, those of other nations (sometimes, but not often, through war).

Considered by itself, this criterion cannot possibly bind a nation to go to war, otherwise the remaining criteria would be superfluous. But this criterion, by itself, clearly binds a nation not to go to war without a just cause. It is not clear that Johnson has demonstrated that there is a duty to go to war even when all six criteria have been met—might there not be a case in which some of the prudential criteria, while judged to be met, were not overwhelmingly met? If the proportionality of ends criterion, for example, had led only to a weak judgment that the damage from a war was likely to be less than the evil to be halted, or if the chance of achieving success were judged likely but not extremely likely, has Johnson clearly shown the duty of country A to wage war on the behalf of the people of country B?

Secondly, just as the prudential criteria require "an estimate of outcomes" and a "weighing of wisdom," so the deontological criteria require "estimates" and "weighings" of justice, intentions, and legality. No one, statesmen included, (they are, after all, politicians) perceives the force of the law, justice, and the rightness of his own and his nation's intentions with the simplicity of someone perceiving the color of a leaf or measuring the length of a two-by-four. There are difficulties in perception here as much as in the prudential criteria, and motives intrude just as much. Aquinas himself makes this clear (see below).

Later in *The War to Oust Saddam Hussein*, Johnson criticizes a Jimmy Carter editorial[37] for (among other things) getting the criteria out of order, and for putting a prudential criterion, last resort, first. In his critique of Carter's editorial, Johnson says these criteria "have to do with the wisdom of doing what has already been determined to be justified. That is, they are about whether it is worth the risk to do what we know is right. This is a question that should be asked, but it is not the first or most important question to ask."

The first problem with Johnson's analysis here is that in effect he completely divorces the deontological from the prudential criteria, assigning all the moral weight to the first set, and going further to say the prudential criteria provide a mere risk calculation. Johnson's recommended sequence of considering the criteria appears to be one of the most logical ones, but even if we follow it we have not established the right and wrong of the matter until we are done with all the criteria. For example, the present or future rulers of China might, perhaps, be shown to be as despotic and as guilty of crimes against their "own people" as Saddam ever was, and a calculation made of whether the United States should "oust" them. The questions of sovereign authority, just cause, and right intention, including the U.S. purpose of "restoring peace," might be settled. Perhaps a future U.S. administration could show that it could neutralize China's nuclear arsenal, probably with preemptive nuclear strikes (to reach hardened underground missile silos). Would that establish the rightness of a war with the Chinese leadership? Wouldn't some other questions need to be examined before the plan was pronounced "right?" For example: the questions of how many millions of Chinese civilians (as well as soldiers) might die in the conflict, how those millions of deaths compared to the damage done by the leadership, what practical hope of a better government after such a nuclear strike and subsequent war existed, and whether any other means of producing positive change were possible? Johnson's assigning of the entire moral weight to the first group of criteria and none to the second seems impossible to defend. The evaluation of the second prudential group of criteria in every case forms an integral part of the total justice or lack thereof of a decision to go to war.

Prudential Criteria Form a Useful Shortcut to Evaluation

But that suggests another consideration: the fact that the prudential criteria must be met in order for a war to be just provides a useful short cut. If it is quite clear that one or more of the prudential criteria is in a given situation impossible to meet, why waste time considering the justice of a proposed war in the abstract, except as an intellectual exercise? The example of China above illustrates very well the value of this short cut: no sensible writer would bother to discuss the justice of such a war, because it is clear the costs would be so horrific, and the outcome so uncertain, that the overall justice of the idea is not even worth considering. On a smaller scale, the same is true of North Korea: even without nuclear weapons, the devastation the North, with its well-buried artillery, could wreak on the South is so huge that only a clearly imminent and devastating planned attack by the North could make a first strike (even a non-nuclear one) on the North just, despite the truly odious character of the North's regime. There appear to be no serious calls by anyone for waging preemptive or preventive war on North Korea, presumably because of this rather simple calculation.

For Aquinas, Justice without Prudence Is Inconceivable

In this connection, note also the classical listing of the "cardinal virtues," which include both justice and prudence. Plato lists them,[38] and the Biblical book of Wisdom (which remains part of Catholic bibles) does also: "virtues . . . temperance and prudence, justice and fortitude" (Wisdom 8:7, New Jerusalem Bible). Justice is not first in that list. When Aquinas lists the moral virtues, he rearranges them, putting not justice but prudence in the first place.[39] In an earlier article, Aquinas indicates why he does so:

> Gregory says . . . "the other virtues, unless we do prudently what we desire to do, cannot be real virtues." . . . Moral virtue cannot be without prudence, because it is a habit of choosing, i.e. making us choose well. Now in order that a choice be good, two things are required. First, that the intention be directed to a due end. . . . Secondly, that a man take rightly those things which have reference to the end: and this he cannot do unless his reason counsel, judge, and command aright, which is the function of prudence and the virtues annexed to it.[40]

It seems rather clear from these statements that Aquinas would regard justice without prudence not as something incomplete, but as something impossible. For Aquinas, without prudence it is impossible to "choose well," even in the seeking of justice. This reinforces the earlier point that justice must be weighed and argued rather than directly perceived, and that rulers and moralists are just as liable to error in this endeavor as in the "estimation of outcomes" involved in applying the prudential criteria. Aquinas' and Gregory's point in this paragraph could be rephrased in terms of war: the justice a nation seeks to achieve in war can be neither chosen nor achieved without prudence.

But there is more to be said about Aquinas' views on justice and prudence. Aquinas' brief article on war is an integral part of his vast *Summa*, and the context in which he placed this one small piece of his work offers rich insights. The article on war comes in the third main division of the *Summa*. In the second part of that work, Aquinas has a great deal to say about right and wrong and human actions. Question 18, "the good and evil of human acts, in general," is key here. In the early parts of that "question," Aquinas asserts, contrary to what might be expected, that the goodness of a moral action is not a mere question of abstract definition, but is related to the object of the action: "the primary goodness of a moral action is derived from its suitable object . . . an action is said to be good from the fact that it can produce a good effect. Consequently the very proportion of an action to its effect is the measure of its goodness."[41] Aquinas then goes further, and ascribes a key role to the circumstances around an act: "On the contrary, the Philosopher [Aristotle] says (Ethic. ii, 3) that a virtuous man acts as he should, and when he should, and so on in respect of the other circumstances. . . . Therefore human actions are good or evil according to circumstances."[42] This leads to a summation in the fourth article of this "Question:"

> Accordingly a fourfold goodness may be considered in a human action. First, that which, as an action, it derives from its genus; because as much as it has of action and being so much has it of goodness, as stated above (Article 1). Secondly, it has goodness according to its species; which is derived from its suitable object. Thirdly, it has goodness from its circumstances, in respect, as it were, of its accidents. Fourthly, it has goodness from its end, to which it is compared as to the cause of its goodness.[43]

How does a good or just war fit in here? The first kind of goodness is the elementary goodness of being a complete action—the goodness of existence, not really what our era would call a part of moral goodness. The second derives from the object, and here we deal with "just cause." The third kind of goodness derives from circumstances, and here "prudence" is vital, along with the prudential criteria. Perhaps sovereign authority, or questions of legality, come under this heading as well. The fourth kind of goodness is from its end, or object, and this is most closely associated with right intention, or the aim of peace.

Later in this second main division of the *Summa*, Aquinas deals with prudence as one of the intellectual virtues. He asserts that prudence, the virtue of knowing how to achieve good aims,

> is most necessary for human life. For a good life consists in good deeds. Now in order to do good deeds, it matters not only what a man does, but also how he does it; to wit that he do it from right choice, and not merely from an impulse or passion. And since choice is about things in reference to the end, rectitude of choice requires two things; namely, the due end, and something suitably ordained to that end [i.e. the means].[44]

Looking at these remarks, which all precede the article on war, it is clear that for Aquinas no action can be good unless it meets prudential criteria as well as deontological ones, to use Johnson's terms. For Aquinas, the right choice necessary to do any good deed, including choosing and embarking on a just war, requires suitable means, chosen through reason so that they actually lead to the aimed-for result in a given situation.

As discussed in Chapter 7, the concept of "right intention" for Aquinas is firmly tied to the idea of an "end," and this again links the prudential criteria to the others. Aquinas does not use the term "right intention" in a feel-good, fuzzy way, such that anyone who claimed it got credit. While Aquinas' article on war deals entirely with the core question of right and wrong, without mentioning any prudential considerations, it is nonetheless situated in the middle of the *Summa.* Given that context, it is inconceivable that Aquinas would have believed that a decision to go to war could be morally right without satisfying prudential requirements.

A Thomist Case for Each Prudential Criterion

Going further, a strong case can be made for each of the prudential criteria from specific statements by Aquinas in other contexts. First, proportionality, perhaps the clearest. Consider Aquinas' view of a similar subject to war, the overthrow of a tyrant, expressed in his article "Sedition."[45] He wrote: "There is no sedition in disturbing a [tyrannical] government . . . unless indeed the tyrant's rule be disturbed so inordinately, that his subjects suffer greater harm from the consequent disturbance than from the tyrant's government." The point is reinforced in the article on killing in self-defense: "And yet, though proceeding from a good intention, an act may be rendered unlawful, if it be out of proportion to the end."[46]

Next, last resort. In Aquinas' discussion of killing in self-defense, he offers a limited defense of such killing, on the basis that the intention is self-preservation, and with the strict qualification that the violence is necessary for self-defense:

> Accordingly the act of self-defense may have two effects, one is the saving of one's life, the other is the slaying of the aggressor. Therefore this act, since one's intention is to save one's own life, is not unlawful, seeing that it is natural to everything to keep itself in "being," as far as possible. And yet, though proceeding from a good intention, an act may be rendered unlawful, if it be out of proportion to the end. Wherefore if a man, in self-defense, uses more than necessary violence, it will be unlawful: whereas if he repel force with moderation his defense will be lawful.[47]

Here we see a condemnation of "more than necessary" violence on the individual level. The "end" or aim is self-defense: staying alive. In that context, an act that leads to the death of the assailant is only justifiable as "necessary violence." It makes good sense to extrapolate from this discussion, on the individual level, to the level of the state. If the just aim of a state can be achieved without violence, that is, without war, it is not lawful to use war, which involves olence, to achieve it. "Last resort" as a criterion for a just war is strongly implied here.

Finally, reasonable chance of success. As noted above, the only justification for an act of self-defense which involves taking the life of a human being is that the intention of the one acting is "to save one's own life." Therefore, an act ostensibly in self-defense, but which in reality cannot possibly save one's own life, would be ruled out. In the realm of violence in self-defense on an individual level, it would seem that a reasonable possibility of achieving the aim (saving one's life) is necessary to justify a resort to violence. Extrapolating to the corporate level, how could a war not in immediate self-defense be justified if it had no chance of righting the wrong that was the cause of the war?

Moving away from Aquinas himself, the downgrading of prudential considerations to a risk calculation afterthought that Johnson has suggested here is in stark contrast to an important stream of Catholic philosophy, including that which is most appreciative of Aquinas' thought. As Josef Pieper writes:

> Prudence is the cause of the other virtues' being virtues at all. . . . Virtue is a "perfected ability" of man as a spiritual person; and justice, fortitude, and temperance, as "abilities" of the whole man, achieve their "perfection" only when they are founded upon prudence, that is to say upon the perfected ability to make right decisions. . . . Prudence is the "measure" of justice . . . The free activity of man is good by its correspondence with the pattern of prudence. What is prudent and what is good are substantially one and the same; they differ only in their place in the logical succession of realization. For whatever is good must first have been prudent.[48]

"The Community of Nations"

Johnson argues that Aquinas, in constructing his overall theory, "builds down from his overall conception of the sovereign's responsibility for the good of the political community," and says Aquinas sees "punishment of evil" as a specific justification "within this larger conception of the public good." However, this is a sweeping reading of Aquinas' words, especially if Johnson means by "the political community" the community of nations, as his context appears to indicate.[49] Weigel writes again and again of the defense of "order" among nations as a reason for war in classic just war theory.[50] Both writers appear to glide imperceptibly, as if by sleight of hand, from classic statements about a government's duty to defend order within its borders and its citizens against attack to new and unlimited statements about a generalized duty to defend order everywhere.

These broad statements do not appear to be supported by a careful reading of the classical writers. In Aquinas' core statement under the "sovereign authority" section, he says that just as it is lawful for those in authority to have recourse to the sword in defending that common weal against internal disturbances, when they punish evil-doers, according to the words of the Apostle (Rom. 13:4): "He beareth not the sword in vain: for he is God's minister, an avenger to execute wrath upon him that doth evil"; so too, it is their business to have recourse to the sword of war in defending the common weal against external enemies."

The question here is the good of the citizens who are the direct responsibility of the authority, not of those outside his rule.

Next, here is Aquinas' entire paragraph on just cause:

Secondly, a just cause is required, namely that those who are attacked, should be attacked because they deserve it on account of some fault. Wherefore Augustine says . . . "A just war is wont to be described as one that avenges wrongs, when a nation or state has to be punished, for refusing to make amends for the wrongs inflicted by its subjects, or to restore what it has seized unjustly."

Here too, the focus is on specific wrongs, not "evil" in general, and in the quotation from Augustine, the specific wrongs appear to have been committed against the nation avenging them. The very word "avenges" (except in the case of God, as in "vengeance is mine, saith the Lord,") strongly implies action taken by the victim of the original wrong, or at least someone closely related.

Finally, in this same short section, Aquinas' first sentence under "right intention" lists "the advancement of good, or the avoidance of evil." In none of the three sections is there any specific reference to the community of nations (a concept Aquinas could have easily conveyed, living as he did in an avowedly Christian Europe ruled by a variety of sovereign princes who fought each other rather often). Where there is any focus on specified threats or evil actions, they are, either explicitly or implicitly, against those specific persons for whom those in authority are responsible. In other words, it appears to be generally assumed by Aquinas that an authority that declares war on another nation will do so in response to specific threats or evil done to its own citizens. While the "right intention" paragraph also speaks of "securing peace, of punishing evil-doers, and of uplifting the good," it seems most natural to read these "right intentions" in light of the previously mentioned limited causes, rather than as conveying a broad responsibility to a "sovereign" to "defend the common good" outside his borders. Any attempt to find a defense of an expansive "international order" in these words of Aquinas requires rather loose reading of his words.

It would strengthen Johnson's and Weigel's position if they were to quote an explicit reference in either Aquinas or Augustine that advised or countenanced the punishment or removal of Government A by Government B for either the wrongs Government A had committed against its own citizens or against Nation C. A right, in extraordinary circumstances, to interfere in another country in such a case, may be derived from the positions of Augustine and Aquinas,[51] but it is not clearly stated there, and that is not the focus of their teaching. Perhaps other writers in the classic just war tradition have clearly stated that the defense of "order" among nations is a legitimate cause for war. As writers who are extremely skeptical of the competence of the United Nations to settle disputes, or even to act with authority, Weigel and Johnson are left to build on the right of individual nations to create or "restore" "world order," a difficult concept in itself.

The Sovereign's "Obligation"

Is There an Obligation beyond a Government's Borders?

Weigel and Johnson claim that the place to "begin thinking about" just war is the obligation of the sovereign authority to defend "the peace of order." As Weigel writes, "Why can a sovereign override what Dr. Williams calls Aquinas' 'prima facie case against war'? Because, I suggest, the ruler is under a prior moral obligation, a responsibility to defend the peace of right order. That prior obligation is the beginning of all morally serious thinking about the use of armed force for morally serious ends." Johnson at one point claims that just war theory is an "obligation-based moral logic."[52] Yet there is barely a hint of any obligation at all in Aquinas' article "On War." Throughout the article, Aquinas frames his argument in terms of justice and lawfulness, never "obligation." That is true even when he compares the defense of the "common weal against internal disturbances" with the defense of the realm "against external enemies." (Perhaps Aquinas saw rulers as eager enough to start wars without an "obligation" to start them.) The classic on-line Catholic Encyclopedia[53] begins its article on war with "the right of war," not "the duty of war." The classic just war theorist Suarez writes: "*Jus belli est odiosum, et poena ejus gravissima; ergo restringenda est quod fieri potest.*" "The right of war is hateful, and its punishment is most grave; therefore it is to be restricted as far as can be." Even the name of the branch of just war theory with which this whole book is concerned, *jus ad bellum*, indicates that it concerns the *right* in connection with going to war, not the responsibility to do so.

According to the Catholic Encyclopedia on war, there is indeed an obligation in connection with war:

> The right of war is the right of a sovereign state to wage a contention at arms against another, and is in its analysis an instance of the general moral power of coercion, i.e., to make use of physical force to conserve its rights inviolable. Every perfect right, i.e., every right involving in others an obligation in justice a deference thereto, to be efficacious, and consequently a real and not an illusory power, carries with it at the last appeal the subsidiary right of coercion. A perfect right, then, implies the right of physical force to defend itself against infringement, to recover the subject-matter of right unjustly withheld or to exact its equivalent, and to inflict damage in the exercise of this coercion wherever, as is almost universally the case, coercion cannot be exercised effectively without such damage.

However, it is clear here that the "obligation" does not mean an obligation of the sovereign to defend the peace of order, rather it is the obligation of the unjust party to the conflict to render justice in some way, a very different idea. The aggrieved party has the *right* to go to war in order to enforce the other party to live up to its obligations, not an *obligation* to go to war to do so. Classic just war theory does not appear to impose any general obligation on a ruler to "defend the peace of order" outside his country.

The obligation of a government to defend peace within its borders is widely acknowledged (except by hard-core libertarians or anarchists), so that is hardly a live issue for most. When the subject is starting a war that is not clearly defensive, however, the question usually concerns the use of force beyond the nation's borders. As noted above, there is almost always another government across the border, with its own rights and responsibilities. Does a government ever have an obligation to leave its own borders to establish order?

If There Is an Obligation, What Are Its Limits?

In a number of places, Weigel writes as if there are no limits on the region in which "the peace of right order" is to be defended, implying that in the classic tradition every ruler, everywhere, should end evil in every part of the world, even if most cannot (although the U.S. government, he implies, can and should). In "Moral Clarity in a Time of War,"[54] he wrote first "that rightly constituted public authority is under a strict moral obligation to defend the security of those for whom it has assumed responsibility." This is certainly the clearly discernible view of Augustine and Aquinas (although "assumed responsibility" is debatable). But shortly thereafter in the same essay he refers to "the moral obligation of government to pursue national security and world order, both of which were directly threatened by the terrorist networks."[55] "World order" has crept in here as an equivalent responsibility to the protection of a government's citizens. This view is missing from Aquinas' writing, as noted above. But even if one can "tease out"[56] such an obligation, through extrapolation and analogy, surely an obligation to defend "world order" could hardly be unlimited. Would New Zealand have an unlimited responsibility, for example, to contribute troops in the defense of world order? What about U.S. responsibility toward the Chechens, or the Tibetans, or the long-suffering people of Zimbabwe? As the leading military power in the world, would the United States have an unlimited obligation to end injustice everywhere?

This creation, intentional or not, of an unlimited responsibility to create justice everywhere, appears completely unworkable. Weigel thinks highly of Augustine. Yet the Augustinian conception of a flawed world implies, at the very least, that not every wrong can be righted by a human ruler, who will always be flawed himself. Even a just ruler cannot put absolute justice into effect in the realm of his own responsibility, much less everywhere. A broader "Augustinian" awareness would suggest that those attempting to right wrongs have to be aware that they too are susceptible to the temptation to commit injustice, sure to act imperfectly, and likely to fall seriously in some way—and wars often lead to vast unintended consequences.

Surely it makes much more sense to speak of a limited right to defend world order, rather than an unlimited obligation to do so. The limits on that right, of course, are those in just war theory.

Who Should Apply Just War Theory?

Weigel and others have several times called to task theologians who take it upon themselves to apply the criteria and decide whether they have been met in a particular case. Weigel wrote in January 2003:

> If the just war tradition is indeed a tradition of statecraft, then the proper role of religious leaders and public intellectuals is to do everything possible to clarify the moral issues at stake in a time of war, while recognizing that what we might call the virtue or moral habit [originally "charism"] of responsibility lies elsewhere—with duly constituted public authorities, who are more fully informed about the relevant facts and who must bear the weight of responsible decision-making and governance.[57]

In May 2003, in "The Sounds of Religion in a Time of War," Neuhaus, after writing that "[t]he cause must be just, and in this case the just cause is the disarmament of Iraq," continued:

> How best to vindicate the just cause, I insisted, is a matter of practical wisdom, of what is called prudential judgment. In just war doctrine, the Church's competence and responsibility is to set forth the pertinent moral principles. As No. 2309 of the Catechism of the Catholic Church makes clear, the application of those principles to specific cases is the responsibility of political leaders. It is true that religious leaders can claim that the principles are being ignored or misapplied, but in the latter case they do so at the considerable risk of exceeding their competence and undermining their credibility.[58]

While Neuhaus is surely right that churches are generally wise not to issue pronouncements on whether the just war criteria have been met in particular cases, both Neuhaus and Weigel went further than that, sharply criticizing "religious leaders and public intellectuals," a category that surely includes trained theologians who speak in public and write books, people like Neuhaus and Weigel, simply for publicly analyzing whether just war criteria had been met. Neuhaus stated his principle broadly: "the application of those principles to specific cases is the responsibility of political leaders." It is ambiguous language: the narrow interpretation of this statement would be that the political leaders are the ones who must make the decisions applying the principles. But Neuhaus clearly was criticizing his fellow intellectuals and religious leaders, not for trying to usurp the decision-making power of political leaders, but for the "application of those principles" in their analyses. Johnson wrote in his book on the war, "One may reasonably wonder what special wisdom the president of the U.S. Catholic

Conference brings to making a prudential judgment on the effects of a military action against the Saddam Hussein regime. This kind of judgment belongs properly to those entrusted with the office of government, and moral analysis oversteps its role when it tries to usurp that judgment for itself."[59]

As noted, Weigel writes, "the proper role of religious leaders and public intellectuals is to do everything possible to clarify the moral issues at stake in a time of war," implying that they should then be silent on whether a given war is actually just or unjust. He then turned around and advanced his own guess at the reason for Pope John Paul II's lack of use of the word "unjust" to describe the war in Iraq.[60] But if Weigel is right that churches should be silent on precisely this question, then there is simply no legitimate inference to be made from that silence. (Weigel's guess about the Pope's opinion was that "perhaps in part" he refused to call the war unjust because "Catholic Church leaders in Iraq had thanked U.S. diplomatic representatives for liberating their country." In the context of the Pope's strenuous arguments against the war, as well as the well-known courtly manners practiced in Arab culture, that is a remarkable leap.)

In weighing these arguments, it is useful to begin with the sentence in the Catechism to which Neuhaus was referring: "The evaluation of these conditions for moral legitimacy belongs to the prudential judgment of those who have responsibility for the common good." First, although the Catechism uses different language for just war theory, it is quite clear from the entire section (No. 2309) that "these conditions" that need to be evaluated are not only the prudential ones, but the question of just cause itself. One of the conditions stated is "the damage inflicted by the aggressor on the nation or community of nations [here is the 'just cause' concept] must be lasting, grave, and certain." Therefore, if Neuhaus believed that theologians, either as "religious leaders" or as part of the "Church," should limit themselves to "set[ting] forth the pertinent moral principles," he has already broken his own rule in the preceding paragraph by writing that "the just cause in this case is the disarmament of Iraq." He cannot have it both ways: if theologians should not "evaluate the conditions" by pronouncing that some criteria of the theory (including "just cause") are not met, neither should theologians state that they are met. To paraphrase Neuhaus' own words, "It is true that religious leaders can claim that the principles are being correctly applied, but they do so at the considerable risk of exceeding their competence and undermining their credibility."

Weigel's articles before the Iraq war and for some time after it began followed the Weigel/Neuhaus rule: theologians should clarify the issues, but not pronounce whether criteria were met. Later, however, he simply broke it. In his April 2006 article "Iraq: Then & Now"[61] as well as his April 2007 article in *First Things*, "Just War and Iraq Wars,"[62] Weigel engages in multiple evaluations of whether just war criteria were met by the Bush administration. The same is true of much of "Internationalisms, etc.," an extended rumination by Neuhaus in *First Things* in December 2004.[63]

The argument against theologians making pronouncements on whether criteria are met is largely based on their perceived lack of expertise in dealing with strategic and geopolitical issues. It is interesting in that context to note that Neuhaus, a priest and theologian, believed himself qualified to critique, and dismiss as "crackpot realism,"[64] an article on war and strategy by Andrew Bacevich, a West Point-trained colonel with a PhD in international affairs. Neuhaus' belief in the limits of theologians' expertise had its decided limits in this case. While in the application of just war principles he demanded that others exercise deference to government officials, Neuhaus was willing to go far beyond the boundaries of his own training.

Neuhaus appears to follow Johnson in assuming that the deontological criteria are simply clear and obvious (especially to moral theologians, perhaps?), while the prudential criteria require the calculations of experts. "The cause must be just, and in this case the just cause is the disarmament of Iraq. . . . How best to vindicate the just cause, I insisted, is a matter of practical wisdom, of what is called prudential judgment." Yet, as an example of how easy it is for a moral theologian to be mistaken on the facts bearing on "just cause," consider one statement in Neuhaus' article "The Sounds of Religion in a Time of War." Near the end of his five-sentence evaluation of the just cause, Neuhaus writes, "none of these facts were in dispute." Two of the "facts" he cited were "[Saddam] possessed and was bent upon further developing more horrible weapons," and "his refusal to disarm." These were not facts, but conjectures, and they were most certainly in dispute, no matter how many U.S. officials had asserted them over the years. In article after article, evidence had been marshaled against these supposed "facts." The most powerful consideration, of course, was that UN inspectors, guided by U.S., British, and Israeli intelligence, had scoured the country for years without finding a single piece of evidence that these "facts" were true. The UN, it should be noted, did not assert them. When Neuhaus writes that the "just cause," the "disarmament of Iraq," was "affirmed by multiple resolutions of the UN Security Council," he leaves the impression that these multiple resolutions stated that Iraq was not disarmed. Yet Resolution 1441 of November 2002 stated no such thing: concerning WMD it "deplored" the lack of full disclosure of records of the programs, and the lack of unrestricted access for the UNSCOM and UNMOVIC (and IAEA) inspectors. The resolution did not even imply UN knowledge, or even a UN opinion, that Saddam possessed such weapons: UN weapons inspectors had had years in which to find them, but had never managed to do so. Neuhaus' apparent intellectual isolation on this subject is a striking demonstration of how wrong is the assumption that the deontological criteria are easy for theologians to judge, while the prudential criteria can only be dealt with by government officials.

Weigel states that public authorities "are more fully informed about the relevant facts," presumably a reference to intelligence not available to laymen. First, there is an oversimplification of the intelligence process in that remark. Intelligence is rarely the gathering of undisputed "facts." Rather, intelligence is about gathering statements and documents that might be false or counterfeit rather than true, as well as photographs and other kinds of evidence that also require verification or interpretation. There is a flood of such "evidence," and because much of it has no validity, it absolutely must be sifted, verified, and interpreted. This can only be done by fallible human beings, and as noted in

Chapter 4, Objection 4, there is strong evidence that the process can be subject to intense political pressure. Second, to give only the most spectacular example, U.S. public authorities flatly stated that Saddam's Iraq had WMD, only to backtrack completely a year a year and a half after the invasion. Weigel was writing before the Duelfer report was published, but he could have found plenty of earlier examples of public authorities being wildly wrong on the facts, despite firm statements about intelligence findings.

Neuhaus writes: "As No. 2309 of the Catechism of the Catholic Church makes clear, the application of those principles to specific cases is the responsibility of political leaders." It is important to note that the Catechism does not say "political leaders" in this context, but "those who have responsibility for the public good." While clearly government decisions must be made by elected officials, in accordance with the Constitution and the laws, it is also the case that all thoughtful adults have some "responsibility for the public good," a responsibility acknowledged by the theory of democracy as well as the entire theory of the "image of God." (And, as this is a Catholic argument by Neuhaus, a Catholic response is appropriate: isn't God's implicit answer to Cain's sarcastic question of whether he was his brother's keeper "yes, to some extent"?) This is not an exotic idea in Catholic theology: in the well-known Vatican II document *Gaudium et Spes*, it is written concerning "men, families and the various groups which make up the civil community" that "each one makes his specific contribution every day toward an ever broader realization of the common good."[65] In the context of the Catechism's teaching about the value of political freedom, surely the statement "The evaluation of these conditions for moral legitimacy belongs to the prudential judgment of those who have responsibility for the common good" means simply that leaders of each society are meant to use just war theory criteria to make decisions about war and peace in accordance with the legal structure of each society. In no way does it even imply that citizens have nothing to say about the matter, or should be silent and not critique their political leaders.

In addition, surely it is only the public critiques that politicians receive that make them even attempt, in many cases, to defend their policies in moral terms. It is in part the lack of such a public critique that makes despotism, whether Saddamist, communist, or other, so bad. Note that *First Things* itself includes, issue after issue, critiques of decisions by government officials. Clearly the authors of such articles are not suggesting that the editors of *First Things*, rather than judges, should decide the issues before the Supreme Court, for example, yet they critique those decisions nonetheless, suggesting a belief that it is not in fact impossible for well-informed persons to equal or even surpass political leaders in expertise on the application of moral principles.

Who will analyze prospective wars for us in a just war framework? First, the "experts" in government are not going to put the issues into a just war framework unless and until just war theory becomes a common and accepted way of examining whether, why, and how to go to war. The American people are not there yet, despite Weigel's "confidence that the debate will continue to be morally informed here in America."[66]

Even if just war theory became the prevalent framework of analysis, would it be wise to hope that U.S. military experts would apply just war theory in some useful way? Weigel is right that the U.S. military grapples with *jus in bello* questions, but it is clear that military officers of all ranks, even the highest, consciously avoid the *jus ad bellum* issues, except, at times, to support the rightness of a given war. That is largely because according to U.S. theory (as well as practice) politicians make these decisions, not soldiers. Of course, Caspar Weinberger, as a civilian Secretary of Defense, and later, Colin Powell, made attempts to bring just war thinking into U.S. government strategic decision-making.[67] However, in the end Powell, even as Secretary of State, had almost nothing negative to say in public about the launching of war against Iraq, despite the fact that his rules for thinking about conflict were clearly not being followed. Generals not yet retired made only veiled comments, and one active duty general, Eric Shinseki, was publicly humiliated and forced into early retirement for his deviation, under questioning before the Congress, from the administration's policy. In general, active-duty U.S. military officers rarely offer any input whatsoever to the public discussion of whether or not to go to war (although they are brought out as expert witnesses if and only if they agree with the administration in power). U.S. military officers cannot be depended on to provide the needed, impartial analysis.

Will civilian experts in government employ do better? We must remember first that such experts work for and are evaluated by bureaucrats who report to other bureaucrats, who report to political figures appointed by an administration. Even if such civilian experts use just war theory, it is their presumed job to do so while defending the current administration's policy. (Overall policy is always set by an administration, never by officials within the bureaucracy.) As a result, we can always expect government officials, even if they use a just war framework, to present the best possible just war case for any war desired by the current administration. That is acceptable in itself, but only if we understand it. Because of this built-in bias, we must not expect an objective evaluation from such officials. And the politicians who direct the experts will pitch their discourse to the existing public debate, which is only somewhat influenced in the United States by just war theory.

Finally, the freedom of priests, writers, and others to speak openly about the actions and policies of their government is one that Weigel himself justly celebrates when discussing (in his *Letters to a Young Catholic*) the revolution in Eastern Europe. Once again, you cannot legitimately "eat your cake and have it too." What is permitted and often praiseworthy under communism (critiques by citizens, including members of religious bodies) is surely, in principle at least, permitted and praiseworthy in a democracy.

While we all hope war decisions are made by elected leaders in accordance with our existing laws and with sound principles such as those enunciated by just war theory, as citizens of democratic states we all have a significant role to play in applying just war theory to proposed and actual wars. As voters we have opinions about all the important acts of our leaders, otherwise our votes for or against them when they run for reelection would be meaningless. Our areas of experience and expertise are limited: all the more reason for a public conversation before a war that includes contributions from all sides.

Omission: Systematic Application of the Six Criteria

It is striking that writers who called public attention to the six classic criteria of just war theory as the war began have not systematically applied them to the decision to go to war in Iraq. They did not apply the criteria, one by one, in detail, to the facts at hand, considering other renderings and interpretations of those facts, and arguments made by those who disagree with them.

Johnson

Johnson's 2005 book *The War to Oust Saddam Hussein* comes closest to providing the necessary full application of the six criteria. It is described inside the dust jacket as "the first and only book to provide a moral analysis of the war in Iraq." The jacket also calls Johnson "our foremost historian of the just war tradition" (quoting Jean Bethke Elshtain) and "our wisest guide through the thickets of the just war tradition" (quoting Weigel). Rather than devoting a chapter to each criterion, Johnson covers all six *jus ad bellum* criteria in his short (twenty-three pages) third chapter, with the subtitle "Was the Use of Force Justified?" Johnson uses a great deal of that limited space critiquing the critiques of others. The chapter title itself is "The Debate over Using Force Against the Saddam Hussein Regime." It appears that even here Johnson did not intend to offer what the dust jacket promises, "a moral analysis of the war in Iraq," but perhaps instead a moral analysis of the *debate* over going to war in Iraq. While the chapter contains analyses of all six criteria, they are scattered, with no organized progression from one to the next. It is difficult to find clear and unequivocal judgments as to whether the criteria were met, and even if Johnson hints strongly that some of them were and some were not, he does not state the implications of these implied findings. Although he judges the critics, he provides no clear judgments of the government's action in going to war.

Johnson explains his diffidence about actually providing a moral analysis of government action in several statements concerning the role of the moralist. One statement confines itself to prudential judgment: "prudential judgment . . . belongs properly to those entrusted with the office of government, and moral analysis oversteps its role when it tries to usurp that judgment for itself."[68] But a bit later Johnson makes the point more broadly, and in connection with preemption, a key part of the "just cause" argument of the administration (and therefore situated in one of the deontological rather than prudential criteria, in Johnson's own terms):

> a moralist working within the just war tradition may make clear that there must be justification, but it is going beyond this role to pass judgment on the facts of the case so that preemption is presented as morally impossible. The role of making such a judgment does not belong to the moralist but is among the obligations of those holding the office of government . . . people not in that position

of authority may give their opinions, and they may participate in holding their political leaders to account for their decisions and actions, but they do not have the right to decide whether preemption is justified on their own.[69]

Near the end of the chapter, he returns to this thought:

> We moralists do not bear political responsibility, and in our reflection and in our advice, whether solicited or unsolicited, we need to take care that we do not act as if we do. The Land letter got this right, leaving the decision to use force with the political authority. But all citizens of a democratic society, including moralists, may rightly hold to account those who do bear the office of political responsibility to act according to that responsibility.[70]

To sum up, Johnson insists that moralists may not rightly "pass judgment on the facts of the case," neither concerning (by implication) the deontological nor especially (and explicitly) the prudential criteria.

In the last quotation above, however, he praises the "Land letter,"[71] a public letter from a group of prominent Protestant theologians that carefully went through a set of criteria and pronounced each one met. Although this letter violated Johnson's rule that only those holding political office may "pass judgment on the facts of the case," Johnson does not call any attention to this fact, and praises the letter because it left "the decision to use force with the political authority." However, it did not even do that: it stated explicitly that "any further delay in forcing the regime's compliance would be reckless irresponsibility in the face of grave and growing danger." Anti-war critics said it would be wrong to invade Iraq; the Land letter said it would be wrong not to invade. The Land letter did the very thing Johnson condemned: it told the authorities what the right decision was. That is just what Johnson is so reluctant to do openly and clearly himself.

Occasionally, Johnson also breaks his rule directly. In the same chapter of *The War to Oust Saddam Hussein* he writes, partway into a paragraph on his regret over the lack of attention to the requirement for an "aim of peace" before the war:

> My position has been that the use of force to remove the Saddam Hussein regime was justified. I came to this position by a route that included the same two lines of reasoning that President Bush laid out in his second and third justifying arguments; indeed, I have thought the use of force to unseat Saddam Hussein and his regime justified since the aggression against Kuwait in 1990. The crimes of subsequent years only strengthened the case.[72]

Despite their casual air of a statement of personal belief, these sentences are certainly an example of "pass[ing] judgment on the facts of the case." But instead of making such a judgment the conclusion of an argument, Johnson drops this thought parenthetically into a paragraph on another subject. It appears that Johnson, by not making systematic pronouncements on the facts of the case, is trying to be consistent with his theory of what moralists should do. He seems, though, to fail to see that stating a judgment that government met the criteria is also "pass[ing] judgment on the facts of the case."

Not only does Johnson fail to achieve consistency, but the point of his over-all stance is not clear. Granted that in a government, office-holders rather than moralists or other citizens make the decisions. But very few deny that almost painfully obvious fact. Would Johnson rebuke those who write about Supreme Court decisions because, in our system, justices decide these cases? Especially in light of Johnson's sentence admitting the right of all citizens to "hold to account" our political leaders, why should not Johnson, or indeed the conference of Catholic bishops, render judgments, the one as a well-informed citizen and the other as an institution with its own sense of responsibility? While Johnson is right that "we moralists do not bear political responsibility," the moral responsibility of those who are silent or who speak out for or against a proposed war exists, whether or not they make the actual decisions—and the more they know or should know, and the more they are listened to, the heavier that moral responsibility.

A further problem with Johnson's approach is that it effectively makes all criticism of (sovereign) rulers who go to war illegitimate. Consider: for the core criteria, any amount of evil appears to amount to just cause (Johnson never attempts to define, in *The War to Oust Saddam Hussein*, a minimal threshold of evil that justifies war, yet every regime or ruler does some evil); and Johnson does not state in the same book that the failure in Iraq to meet the core, "deontological" criterion of "right intention," a failure he hints at strongly, made the war unjust. For the prudential criteria, no one in Johnson's view may legitimately advise rulers on whether they meet them. Whether Johnson intends to come to this conclusion or not, the effective result of his various restrictions on criticism is to put all five criteria besides "sovereign authority" outside the permitted realm of judgment by anyone but the ruler involved, and perhaps God. On the other hand, Johnson has praised writings by non-rulers in which rulers are urged to go to war. He does not explain this paradox.

A closely related paradox is contained in Johnson's pronouncement on sovereignty: "According to the older, moral understanding of sovereignty, though, [Saddam] forfeited the right to sovereign immunity and, indeed, the right to govern Iraq with his tyrannical exercise of government."[73] Yet Johnson does not seem to define the level of tyranny which removes sovereign immunity, making it hard to see how this guidance can be applied. Have all non-democratic rulers forfeited their right to govern? Why is Johnson an authority on this subject, when others are rebuked for "passing judgment on the facts"? He does not say.

It is a shame Johnson makes pronouncements of his conclusions only in a casual and parenthetical way, first because it deprives us of a systematic analysis from Johnson. Second, Johnson's authority behind his pronouncements about the statements of others is not clear—if in Johnson's view moralists have no right to pronounce on the actions of governments, what gives Johnson the right to pronounce on the statements of moralists? And finally, Johnson's argument about the right to pronounce becomes, in effect, a red herring: a reason for discussing at great length whether this or that figure has the right to pronounce this or that conclusion, rather than discussing how the criteria apply to the facts.

Weigel

Consider Weigel's first extensive article applying just war theory to the decision to go to war in Iraq, "Iraq: Then & Now," first published in *First Things* in April 2006, and reprinted in 2008 as Chapter 10 of his book *Against the Grain*.[74] In Weigel's original essay, he wrote "let me offer a just war defense of the moral probity of the decision to remove Saddam by armed force, with specific focus on the classic *ius ad bellum* criteria that are the intellectual and moral core of the just war tradition."[75] That article contains some serious discussion of "just cause," "sovereign authority," and "last resort." "Right intention" is mentioned, but without any analysis. "Proportionality of ends" and "reasonable chance of success" appear to be entirely missing. In the revised version in the book, Weigel changed his description of his purpose in the essay to, "Three just war criteria were prominent in the pre-invasion debate . . . Each of these criteria belonged to the *ius ad bellum*, or war-decision law: competent authority, just cause, and last resort. An examination of each is essential in making a comprehensive just war case for the war against Saddam Hussein."[76] Essential, yet not sufficient—and this limited aim (which drops right intention) comes under the header with the bold claim "The Just War Case for the War." Right intention is mentioned half-way through a paragraph, under the subhead "Extending the Just War Tradition" (odd, since right intention is part of the core of the tradition going back to Augustine)[77] but without any apparent assertion that the intention displayed by the administration was in fact right, nor any argument backing such a claim. The closest to anything resembling a judgment on whether the Bush administration demonstrated a right intention is this: "Given the new realities of the post-9/11 world disorder, I believe there was no responsible alternative to setting sail on those uncharted waters."[78] Clearly that is not phrased as a conclusion on the right intention criterion, but it is the closest thing in the essay to such a conclusion.

It appears surprising that Weigel, after years of writing that there are six classic just war criteria, should "offer a just war defense" that contains no application of three of the six, including one of the "core" criteria identified by Aquinas. Weigel republished the essay without addressing in any substantive way the missing criteria.

A year later, in April 2007, Weigel published his next extensive look at the subject, "Just War and Iraq Wars,"[79] also in *First Things*. (Again, a lightly revised version is available in *Against the Grain*, as Chapter 11.) Weigel begins with an extensive discussion of whether a new branch of just war theory, "*ius post bellum*," "right after war," is needed. Weigel notes that he "is inclined to Johnson's position" that the ius post bellum idea is already contained in "right intention."[80] Weigel next introduces the idea that there have actually been four wars in Iraq, the first of which consisted purely of the military overthrow of Saddam's regime[81] (see Chapter 10, Objection 1).

Weigel then very briefly discusses "just cause," ending with this sweeping assertion:

> Regime change in Iraq was a necessity: It was necessary for the people of Iraq; it was necessary for peace in the Middle East; it was necessary to vindicate the fragile steps toward world order that had been taken since [the end of World War II]; and it was necessary in order to challenge Arab self-delusion [original version: "an Arab political culture warped by irresponsibility, authoritarian brutality, rage, and self-delusion"], out of which had emerged, among other things, contemporary jihadism.[82]

Ironically, on the page before Weigel had stated that various "academic guilds . . . seem, in the main, to have concluded that the invasion of March 2003 did not satisfy the *ad bellum* criteria of a just war. Yet that conclusion is more often asserted than argued." Not only does Weigel apparently not see that his one-sentence justification of the war is simply assertion without argument, he also misses the point that the burden of proof, at least before a war, is always on those claiming that a war is just. (This quick dismissal of those who believe the war unjust seems to assume the opposite, that those against war must prove their case.) The article goes on to analyze Bush administration "mistakes" for a number of pages, and then turns to the present and the future. To sum up, Weigel presents an analysis of "right intention" that leaves out the culpability of those who fail to demonstrate it, and goes on to a quick, bare assertion of just cause. That is it, in this article, for the six "*jus ad bellum*" criteria.

Neuhaus

As noted, Neuhaus break his rule that "the application of those principles to specific cases is the responsibility of political leaders" (his paraphrase of the *Catechism*) by "applying the principles" to Iraq himself. He also gave a very skimpy evaluation (in five sentences) of the just cause as he saw it. It is true that Neuhaus stated at the beginning of the quoted essay that he was a giving "a précis of the arguments I've been making." Nonetheless, the very section of the *Catechism* that he quoted, No. 2309, also states that "rigorous consideration" of "the strict conditions for legitimate defense by military force" is necessary. Neuhaus, as Editor-in-Chief of *First Things*, a magazine that published numerous articles about just war theory, including applications of the theory to the Iraq war, could easily have requested an article, or even a series of articles, that systematically applied the six criteria to the war, but never did.

Inadequate Conclusions Concerning Unmet Criteria

The pro-war just war analyses of the Iraq war that have been published, including those of Johnson and Weigel discussed above, often leave conclusions unstated, or suggest that we need to learn a lesson for the future from this or that "mistake." But the question demands to be asked: did the war, considered at the time of decision, meet this criterion, and that one, and the next? As Johnson rightly notes in another context, "The debate was about the prospect, and that is where moral decision making has to take place."[83] For each criterion, if the proposed war failed to meet it, based on careful consideration of knowledge available at the time, what conclusion follows? Aquinas was blunt: "In order for a war to be just, three things are necessary." Weigel and Johnson, scholars who claim to follow in the footsteps of Aquinas, are here avoiding his key statement on what makes a war just. A statement that a criterion was not met is, for Aquinas, not merely a subject for thoughtful ruminations on the need to get things better next time—it is equivalent to a statement that the war in question was unjust. One quotation from Johnson on the deficiencies of the pre-war debate on the "aim of peace" may stand in the place of far too many similar ones: "we should have known better . . . we need to learn from that and try to do better in the future."[84] Aquinas wrote, after all, that failure to meet one of the criteria could render a war "unlawful," not "imperfect and full of mistakes."

To conclude: the in-depth case that the decision to go to war in Iraq was just in terms of just war theory has simply not been made by these writers, nor did they demonstrate in consistent terms why moralists should not attempt to do so.

NOTES

1. John East, "The Political Relevance of St. Augustine," *Modern Age*, spring 1972, 174 (Quoted in Schall, *Another Sort of Learning*, 181).
2. Weigel, *Letters to a Young Catholic* (New York: Basic Books, 2004) 86-87.
3. In fact, it was these writers who led me to the criteria.
4. Johnson, *War to Oust*, 27.
5. Johnson, *War to Oust*, 28.
6. Johnson, *War to Oust*, 29.
7. Johnson, *War to Oust*, 28.
8. Peter Dula, "The war in Iraq: how Catholic conservatives got it wrong," *Commonweal*, December 3, 2004, http://findarticles.com/p/articles/mi_m1252/is_21_131/ai_n13787465?tag=content;col1 (accessed October 18, 2007).
9. Johnson, "Just War, as It Was and Is."
10. Paul J. Griffiths and George Weigel, "Who Wants War? An Exchange," *First Things*, no. 152 (April 2005): 10-12.
11. Paul J. Griffiths and George Weigel, "Just War: An Exchange," *First Things*, no. 122 (April 2002): 31-36.
12. Rowan Williams and George Weigel, "War and Statecraft: An Exchange," *First Things*, no. 141 (March 2004): 19.
13. Johnson, *War to Oust*, 36.
14. Weigel, *Against the Grain*, 209. Johnson makes the same point in "Just War, As it Was, and Is," 17. Weigel calls Aquinas' article "his discussion of *bellum iustum*," but this is not accurate: it is not a discussion of "just war," but a discussion which distinguishes just from unjust wars.
15. Williams and Weigel, "War and Statecraft," 15.
16. Weigel, *Against the Grain*, 209. Note that while this reading justifies defensive war, "public authority" is only responsible according to Aquinas for the people within the borders it administers, so this remark does not help his case for a U.S. war thousands of miles from American shores unless the country attacked has previously attacked the United States.

17. *Summa*, NewAdvent.org, http://www.newadvent.org/summa/3.htm.

18. Williams and Weigel, "War and Statecraft," 15.

19. Christopher West, *Theology of the Body Explained: A Commentary on John Paul II's "Gospel of the Body"* (Boston: Pauline Books and Media, 2003) 403. Weigel wrote the forward of this important book.

20. Quoted in "Achilles in Iraq: The Poem of Force," *The Goat Rope*, August 3, 2003, http://goatrope.blogspot.com/2006_07_30_archive.html (accessed March 13, 2009). I first discovered the Weil quotation in Joe Sobran, "The Reluctant Anarchist," *Sobran's*, December 2002, http://www.sobran.com/reluctant.shtml (accessed March 13, 2009).

21. As with several insights in this book, I am indebted to one of the tutors at Thomas Aquinas College for directing me to this section of the *Summa*.

22. Augustine, *The City of God*, Christian Classics Ethereal Library, http://www.ccel.org/ccel/schaff/npnf102.iv.XIX.5.html (Chapter 5), and http://www.ccel.org/ccel/schaff/npnf102.iv.XIX.7.html (accessed December 4, 2007).

23. *De Quinto Praecepto Decalogi*, quoted in *Neo-CONNED*, 226. I take "certain" here to mean "reasonably certain," not "absolutely certain" for de Liguori. However, it here to mean "reasonably certain," but it must mean at least "beyond reasonable doubt." Fr. Franziskus Stratmann (quoted in *Neo-CONNED*, 398) says Suarez recognized a just cause if "after careful examination of the cause of dispute, the prince or ruler considers that there is more to be said on one side than on the other." But, Stratmann writes, "A lively protest was raised against this weakening of the teaching of St. Augustine and the Thomists."

24. Francisco Suarez, S. J., *De Caritate*, XIII, 7, 4 (quoted in *"Neo-CONNED,"* page preceding dedication).

25. Weigel, *Against the Grain*, 209.

26. Griffiths and Weigel, "Just War: An Exchange," *First Things*, no. 122 (April 2002): 34.

27. Williams and Weigel, "War and Statecraft," 15.

28. I am (again) indebted to my friend, Thomas Aquinas College tutor John Nieto, for this observation.

29. Weigel, *Against the Grain*, 209.

30. *The Challenge of Peace*, paragraph 70.

31. Weigel, *Against the Grain*, 210.

32. Johnson, "Just War, as It Was and Is," 20.

33. Weigel, *Against the Grain*, 232-33. Unfortunately, this statement is not taken out of context. There is nothing in the immediate surrounding text about the possibility of an unjust war. It is true that Weigel elsewhere discusses unjust wars, but to write statements like the one quoted appears to demonstrate a serious loss of balance. Coupled with his assertion that Aquinas article is on "iustum bellum," rather than "bellum," it strongly implies a presumption in favor of the justice of war in Weigel's thinking. Aquinas' writings carry no such presumption.

34. Johnson, *War to Oust*, 36.

35. "Criterion," *Dictionary.com*, http://dictionary.reference.com/browse/criterion (accessed December 4, 2007).

36. Johnson, *War to Oust*, 36.

37. Johnson, *War to Oust*, 59.

38. Quoted in *A Summa of the Summa: The Essential Philosophical Passages of St. Thomas Aquinas' Summa Theologica Edited and Explained for Beginners*, (San Francisco: Ignatius Press, 1990), 451.

39. Aquinas, *Summa*, I-II, 61, 2. It is true that Aquinas sees justice as "foremost among all the moral virtues," *Summa*, I-II. 58, 12, and the importance of justice among the virtues for Aquinas can hardly be overstated, but this does not indicate that it can stand alone.

40. Aquinas, *Summa*, I-II, 58, 4.

41. Aquinas, *Summa*, I-II, 18, 2.

42. Aquinas, *Summa*, I-II, 18, 3.

43. Aquinas, *Summa*, I-II, 18, 4.

44. Aquinas, *Summa*, I-II, 57, 5.

45. Aquinas, *Summa*, II-II, 42, 2.

46. Aquinas, *Summa*, II-II, 64, 7.

47. Aquinas, *Summa*, II-II, 64, 7.

48. Josef Pieper, *The Four Cardinal Virtues*, Richard and Clara Winston, Trs., Lawrence E. Lynch, Tr., Daniel F. Coogan, Tr. (Notre Dame: The University of Notre Dame Press, 1966). Quoted in *MAGNIFICAT*, August 2007, 40.

49. Johnson, "Just War, As It Was and Is," 17.

50. Weigel, *Against the Grain*, 221, and elsewhere.

51. "War," *Catholic Encyclopedia*, http://www.newadvent.org/cathen/15546c.htm (accessed October 18, 2007).

52. Johnson, *War to Oust*, 49.

53. See "War," *Catholic Encyclopedia*.

54. Weigel, *Against the Grain*, 209.

55. Weigel, *Against the Grain*, 210.

56. Weigel, *Against the Grain*, 231.

57. Weigel, *Against the Grain*, 222.

58. Neuhaus, "The Sounds of Religion," 76.

59. Johnson, *War to Oust*, 49.

60. Weigel, *Against the Grain*, 230.

61. Weigel, *Against the Grain*, 224-49.

62. Weigel, *Against the Grain*, 250-69.

63. Neuhaus, "Internationalisms, etc.," *First Things* no. 148 (December 2004): 64-68.

64. Neuhaus, "Interests, Ideals, and World War IV," *First Things* no. 152 (April 2005): 59.

65. "Gaudium et Spes," *New Advent*, http://www.newadvent.org/library/docs_ec21gs.htm (accessed February 28, 2009), paragraph 74.

66. Williams and Weigel, "War & Statecraft," 21. The fact that the U.S. government has, without generating significant protest, named a tank after General Sherman, who deliberately used artillery on civilians in Georgia, and the main State Department building after Harry Truman, who ordered the intentional bombing of civilians at Hiroshima and Nagasaki, suggests that U.S. emotional attachment to just war theory may be rather weak.

67. Andrew Bacevich wrote in *The New American Militarism: How Americans Are Seduced by War*, (New York: Oxford University Press, 2005) 47-49, that young U.S. military officers who saw in Vietnam a failure by politicians to examine the political dimensions of their military moves were determined to raise their voices if future wars followed the same patterns. Powell was part of this determination.

68. Johnson, *War to Oust*, 49.

69. Johnson, *War to Oust*, 52.

70. Johnson, *War to Oust*, 67.

71. "The So-Called Land Letter," The Ethics and Religious Liberty Commission of

the Southern Baptist Convention, 2002, http://erlc.com/article/the-so-called-land-letter (accessed November 19, 2007). This letter reported the judgment of some evangelical Christian leaders that "your stated policies concerning Saddam Hussein and his headlong pursuit and development of biochemical and nuclear weapons of mass destruction are prudent and fall well within the time-honored criteria of just war theory."

72. Johnson, *War to Oust*, 66.
73. Johnson, *War to Oust*, 63.
74. Weigel, *Against the Grain*, 234-49.
75. Weigel, "Iraq: Then & Now," *First Things* no. 162 (April 2006): 36.
76. Weigel, *Against the Grain*, 232.
77. Weigel, *Against the Grain*, 245.
78. Weigel, *Against the Grain*, 246.
79. Weigel, "Just War and Iraq Wars," *First Things* no. 172 (April 2007): 14-20.
80. Weigel, *Against the Grain*, 253.
81. Weigel, *Against the Grain*, 254.
82. Weigel, *Against the Grain*, 256.
83. Johnson, *War to Oust*, 51.
84. Johnson, *War to Oust*, 67.

Part III

CONCLUSION

Whereas a man has it in his power to be just, if he have but the will to be so, and therefore injustice is thought the most dishonorable, because it is the least excusable.

—Plutarch (*Plutarch's Lives, Volume II* [New York: The Modern Library, 2001], 299.)

The groups we will describe are utopian . . . They believe that an ideal social order can be created in which man's potentialities can flower freely. They are "coercive" because in their zeal for attaining an ideal order they seek to impose their blueprints in ways that go beyond legitimate persuasion.

—Rael Jean Isaac and Eric Isaac (*The Coercive Utopians: America's Power Players* [Chicago: Regnery-Gateway, 1983], 2, quoted in Schall, *Another Sort of Learning*, 127.)

The significant thing was the ready acceptance of fantasy as reality; even a predilection in favour of fantasy, and a corresponding abhorrence of reality. Why?

—Malcolm Muggeridge (*Chronicles of Wasted Time: The Infernal Grove, vol. 2* [New York: Morrow, 1974], 16, quoted in Schall, *Another Sort of Learning*, 73.)

Chapter Twelve

Was It Just?
Evaluation and Consequences

"War is an act of force," Clausewitz writes, ". . . which theoretically can have no limits." . . . That is why it is so awful (though Clausewitz does not tell us this) to set the process going: the aggressor is responsible for all the consequences of the fighting he begins. . . . they are always potentially terrible.

—Michael Waltzer, *Just and Unjust Wars*[1]

It's not enough to say "I take responsibility," the ubiquitous catchall for *not* taking real responsibility in our society. We have to take the consequences that go along with the responsibility.

—Weigel, *Letters to a Young Catholic*[2]

Introduction

After considering each criterion in light of facts available at the time, an overall conclusion is required. The implications of that conclusion must be considered for the United States, whose lawful government launched the war in accord with internally accepted constitutional standards for government action.

Just or Unjust?

In conclusion, after considering each of the classic just war criteria in the light of a great deal of evidence readily available at the time, and in light of the additional principles (based on widely accepted moral reasoning) advanced in Chapter 2: the contemplated war clearly failed to satisfy five of the six criteria. A failure to meet even one of the core, deontological criteria, according to Aquinas, renders a war unjust. The *Catholic Catechism*, in line with a long tradition of just war argumentation, extends the requirement of meeting all the criteria to the prudential criteria as well. However, as argued in Chapter 2, authorities such as these merely buttress, for those who accept them, what is evident to careful reasoning: each of the criteria is necessary for a just war, and a war that fails to meet one of the criteria is unjust. A decision to go to war that failed five of the six criteria was an unjust decision, which led to an unjust war.

Note that the conclusions reached in this book are not a result of starting out with pacifist presumptions. They are not the result of an animus against George

W. Bush, nor of an animus against the Republican Party. They are not the result of any kind of partisanship whatsoever. The conclusions flowed from a careful examination of the realities of Iraq and the Bush administration decision to invade, illuminated by the completely neutral criteria of classic just war theory, as sketched out by leading conservative thinkers such as Johnson, as well as others.

Some Final Objections Considered

An Art, Not a Science?

A variety of objections may be raised to this conclusion. First, that just war theory is not a science, but an art. In the post-invasion words of Michael Novak in *First Things*, "Just-war decisions are not geometry but practical wisdom—prudence. In the case of Iraq, there were strong reasons against and strong reasons for, and the issue was well argued for some months before the decision was finally made."[3] (It is fair to point out, as Novak does not do here, that his position has changed sharply. He argued at the Vatican just before the war that it was "morally obligatory."[4]) Novak appears to imply, in these words of July 2007, that "this is a broad set of principles that are guidelines only. One practitioner will apply them one way, and another in another way. There is no single way of doing it, and no real way to see if someone has done it rightly or wrongly." However, Novak's interpretation here would make meaningless the requirement in the *Catholic Catechism* of "rigorous consideration" of "strict criteria," as well as the obvious implication that if a case for war does not hold up under such rigorous consideration, it is an inadequate case. It is true that during rigorous consideration of the criteria, differences may arise. Any analysis of a broad range of facts (not just those favorable to one's own case), applying the criteria to them in a rigorous fashion and addressing adequately the arguments of the other side, is almost surely legitimate. However, Novak's position here simply dismisses arguments that it was clear at the time the war was unjust, as if those arguments had been addressed and answered. Certainly Novak himself did not provide a rigorous analysis of anti-war arguments in his statements at the Vatican. Rather than face the implications of his past arguments, his 2007 comment denigrates argumentation itself, as well as just war theory, which relies on such argumentation.

Others Have Analyzed, and Come to a Different Conclusion?

Second: others, in a variation on Novak's response, may content themselves with the thought that those who have contended that the war was just have made one case, and this book has made another, and so there is disagreement on the conclusion. The preceding chapter not only points out errors by Weigel, Johnson, and Neuhaus in applying the theory, it also addresses the lack of any systematic analysis by them that applied the six classic criteria to the facts. Anyone wishing to rely on the contention that "a strong pro-war case based on classic just war theory exists," should point to such a systematic analysis and the specific arguments it makes that counter the arguments here.

Questioning Each Part of an Argument Is Not Enough?

Third: A good argument might be that applying extreme rigor to each criterion in turn ignores the holistic effect of the total case that was made for the war. By separating each criterion from the others, the cumulative effect of adding the arguments for each one together was lost—and in the real world, we must often rely on such holistic arguments.

First, such an argument makes most sense when each part of the whole is closely related to the others, such that the likelihood of one piece being true reinforces the likelihood of others also being true. If there were some thread connecting the administration's case for the last four criteria, for example, and that thread had some connection to the key parts of the administration's case for a just cause, then this kind of argument would make some sense. Instead, a careful consideration of the last four criteria shows that there simply was no realistic planning based on the existing reality. The administration's "just cause" argument consists of a number of elements put together with a very weak connection, namely that a future possibility based on those elements created a deadly danger with no other rational response but war. The stated connection between the parts of the argument was simply, "since each of these is true, there is a high degree of danger." Showing that each assertion lacked convincing evidence that it was true demonstrated that the danger could not reasonably be said to be anywhere near the level claimed. In fact, this larger argument can be turned back on the one making it: it is those who objected to the war who took a holistic approach. They saw (intuitively in some cases) that the lack of realistic planning for the post-war situation destroyed the possibility of meeting four out of the six criteria.

Secondly, the argument that "the holistic effect of the sum of the pieces is essential" is most useful in a situation where we believe we must choose between existing "givens:" whether to belong to this church or that, or to vote for this politician or the other, to be an atheist or follow some religion; in other words, in a situation where absolute proof is unlikely to be achieved but we feel an inner compulsion to make a choice, based on some inner standard. Where the question is instead "does the case for X meet an objective standard," there is no necessity to choose between options. A jury does not need to choose the most likely murderer, nor is it asked to agonize over the danger of freeing a murderer. Instead, it simply must ask whether a convincing, "beyond reasonable doubt" case has been made that Smith did it. If a convincing case has been made, Smith should be punished; but if the case is not convincing, Smith should be set free. Many possible but unconvincing assertions about Smith do not amount to a compelling case of guilt. If there were significant, unresolved doubts about each part of the administration's case, as clearly demonstrated in preceding chapters, then the case did not add up to a "beyond reasonable doubt" case.

Implications of an Unjust War

Costs and Benefits of the War

Consider a few of the costs of this war. In terms of deaths of U.S. soldiers, a count at the end of January 2009 showed over 4,200 had died in Iraq.[5] The wounded appear more difficult to count. According to another account, at the end of January 2009 over 30,000 U.S. Army wounded and needing evacuation from Iraq since the beginning of combat in March 2003.[6] But that grisly count is a tiny fraction of the number of dead and wounded. There are several estimates of Iraqi civilian deaths due to violence since the U.S.-led invasion. The "Iraq Body Count" organization noted in January 2009 that "documented civilian deaths from violence" between the invasion in March 2003 and that date were between 90,554 and 98,846.[7] The actual number of deaths is likely far higher than the number documented, as documentation during a war is notoriously poor. A high estimate, computed using standard methodology for estimating deaths in "conflict zones" was over 600,000 through the end of June 2006. The study which produced this estimate was published by the respected British medical journal The Lancet, and some British officials have stated that its methods were based on sound scientific methods for estimating deaths in conflict zones where precise measurement is impossible.[8] It is certain that many more deaths have occurred since June 2006, so if the methodology was correct, the death toll now is far higher. A British survey of Iraqis suggested in September 2007 that over a million Iraqis had died due to strife since the conflict began.[9] Such estimates, even if scientifically based, are impossible to verify at this time, and a better estimate of "excess deaths" due to the conflict may have to wait, but the possibility of such high numbers should be borne in mind. Even the lower figure of close to 100,000 verified deaths is immense. The numbers of wounded are usually far higher than the numbers of dead.

In December 2008, the United Nations High Commissioner for Refugees (UNHCR) had this to say about Iraqis who had fled their homes since the conflict began:

> Iraqi refugees throughout the region have become increasingly desperate. Despite a decline in violence in the second half of 2007, only a small number have gone home, often because their resources are exhausted. Of those who returned to Iraq, many found their property occupied and suffered secondary displacement.

> UNHCR estimates more than 4.7 million Iraqis have left their homes, many in dire need of humanitarian care. Of these, more than 2.7 million Iraqis are displaced internally, while more than 2 million have fled to neighbouring states, particularly Syria and Jordan. Many were displaced prior to 2003, but the largest number has fled since. In 2006, Iraqis became the leading nationality seeking asylum in Europe.[10]

Both in terms of deaths and in terms of lives interrupted or ruined, these are immense human costs, whatever the exact numbers, which will never be known. Almost all refugees have tragic stories of property loss and disrupted lives. Many can also tell of dead and wounded relatives, and the experience of rape, or of raped wives, mothers, sisters, and daughters.

No one knows if reconciliation between ethnic and religious groups in Iraq will take place, or how long it might take. No one is certain if the existing Iraqi government, or any reasonably stable Iraqi government, will last for a year after the withdrawal of U.S. troops.

No attempt has been made here to detail the economic cost of the war, but it is clearly colossal. The total direct financial cost to date in early 2009 was widely reckoned to be close to a half a trillion dollars, a figure that does not include such items as future medical care for wounded veterans or higher costs for oil in the years after the invasion.[11] Nor does it include the damage to Iraqi property, public and private.

Were there benefits? Certainly Saddam's loss of power is a good thing, considered in isolation. His particular brand of tyranny is gone for the time being, and that is a benefit to Iraq and the world. Is there democracy in Iraq, or stability, or peace in the Middle East? There have been some elections, but can we now say democracy is in place? Will there be a democracy in Iraq two years from now? If there is, will it respect the rights of minorities? All decent people hope so, but there are no guarantees. The history of governments that are put together with the military backing of a foreign power suggests that many do not last long after that foreign power departs. Often, the departure of occupying forces unleashes a struggle for power, and the government left behind struggles to prove it is not a puppet of the invaders. If that happens in Iraq, stability will lie farther down the road. As of mid-2009, internal stability appeared fragile at best, and stability without the presence of foreign troops had not arrived, over six years after the U.S. invasion.

Concerning peace in the wider Middle East, in the sense of accepted solutions to ongoing problems, certainly such solutions did not seem to exist at the end of Bush's mandate, and there was no proof that the war had brought them any closer than they were in March 2003.

Concerning terrorism, the very fact that the Bush administration so often called Iraq "the central front in the war on terror" in the years after the invasion shows a tremendous step backwards on that front, as that was an impossible description of Iraq in February 2003. In his UN speech in February 2003, Powell made no such assertion. Instead, he made a cautious yet dubious case for a "nexus between Iraq and the al Qaeda terrorist network headed by Abu Musab Al Zarqawi." The best he could do to link them was to claim that Al Zarqawi's camp was located "in northeastern Iraq," in territory over which Saddam had no control,[12] that Saddam "has an agent in the most senior levels" of the organization, and that various Al Qaeda agents moved "freely" in and out of Baghdad.

The overall balance between the staggering costs and the tenuous benefits of this war, many of which may melt away in the near future, is the responsibility of those who began this war, and, to some extent, of those who cheered them on.

Implications for the U.S. Moral Stance

Unfortunately for the United States, starting a non-defensive, unjust war is equivalent to aggression. This is in fact an extremely grave crime, both in international law and in terms of morality. It is one of the ugliest acts that can lie on a nation's conscience. Two quotations may serve to drive home this point:

> The 1945 Nuremberg Charter [written by the United States and its allies] . . . is clear: "To initiate a war of aggression . . . is not only an international crime, it is the supreme international crime in that it contains within itself the accumulated evil of the whole." At the Nuremberg trial of the Nazi leadership, counts one and two [were] "Conspiracy to wage aggressive war" and "waging aggressive war."[13]

> In his 1939 letter to Adolph Hitler, President Roosevelt wrote: "Nothing can persuade the peoples of the earth that any governing power has any right or any need to inflict the consequences of war on its own or any other people save in the cause of self-evident home defense."[14]

One often forgotten point should be emphasized: if aggression is waged against a country (you may substitute the phrase "unjust war" for "aggression" above), then the soldiers in the invading army are committing an objectively immoral act when they kill even enemy soldiers, who have by definition the right to defend their country against an unjust attack. Now, this would not make every soldier in the coalition automatically guilty of war crimes. Most soldiers presumably believed the war to be just when they began their part in it, and most soldiers lack the time and the background to make good assessments themselves of such questions. For such soldiers, killing enemy soldiers would be objectively wrong, but would not make them personally guilty.[15] This is not the case for the leaders who sent the soldiers into the war, however. The blood not only of Iraqi civilians but even of Iraqi soldiers who died defending their country against a U.S. invasion is on the hands of the United States in some sense, due to the launching and waging of an unjust war.

In addition, the United States voluntarily signed the United Nations Charter, which thus has the force of a treaty freely entered into. Both in moral or ethical terms and in terms of international law, agreements freely undertaken are considered binding. (Unlike Saddam Hussein agreeing to resolutions after his war of aggression against Kuwait, the United States was under no armed pressure to sign the UN Charter. In fact, the U.S. government was heavily involved in drafting it.)

Not only that, but the U.S. Constitution stipulates, in Article VI, the following:

> This Constitution, and the Laws of the United States which shall be made in Pursuance thereof; and all Treaties made, or which shall be made, under the Authority of the United States, shall be the supreme Law of the Land; and the

Judges in every State shall be bound thereby, any Thing in the Constitution or Laws of any State to the Contrary notwithstanding.[16]

Those who claim to respect the authority of the Constitution need to face the fact that under that document, formally accepted treaty obligations become "the supreme Law of the land." The UN Charter is a treaty among the nations who signed it, and it was duly ratified by the United States according to the Constitution. The Charter stipulates (in Article 2, numbers 3 and 4):

All Members shall settle their international disputes by peaceful means in such a manner that international peace and security, and justice, are not endangered.

All Members shall refrain in their international relations from the threat or use of force against the territorial integrity or political independence of any state, or in any other manner inconsistent with the Purposes of the United Nations.

A cursory look, then, would seem to indicate no room at all for UN member states to use force to settle disputes. However, Chapter V of the Charter introduces the Security Council. Article 24, numbers 1 and 2, lays out the Council's "Functions and Powers":

In order to ensure prompt and effective action by the United Nations, its Members confer on the Security Council primary responsibility for the maintenance of international peace and security, and agree that in carrying out its duties under this responsibility the Security Council acts on their behalf.

In discharging these duties the Security Council shall act in accordance with the Purposes and Principles of the United Nations. The specific powers granted to the Security Council for the discharge of these duties are laid down in Chapters VI, VII, VIII, and XII.

Chapter VII, the chapter under which the Council authorized "all means necessary" (i.e., force) against Iraq to expel it from Kuwait, lays out the rules for the use of force under direction of the Council: thus, this is one exception to the prohibition in the Charter on the use of force: if it is authorized by the Security Council. There is one more clear exception in Chapter VII to the prohibition of force by member states, namely Article 51, which states:

Nothing in the present Charter shall impair the inherent right of individual or collective self-defence if an armed attack occurs against a Member of the United Nations, until the Security Council has taken measures necessary to maintain international peace and security. Measures taken by Members in the exercise of this right of self-defence shall be immediately reported to the Security Council and shall not in any way affect the authority and responsibility of the Security Council under the present Charter to take at any time such action as it deems necessary in order to maintain or restore international peace and security.[17]

In terms of the Charter, there was clearly no authorization from the Security Council to use force in 2003 (nor earlier, via covert methods). Just as clearly, there was no aggression under way against the United States by Saddam (much less the "armed attack" the Charter speaks of),[18] and so the war against him was simply not a defensive war. Thus, not only has the United States "waged aggressive war," it has also broken a treaty obligation freely entered into, the UN Charter (which is also, according to the U.S. Constitution, a part of "the supreme Law of the Land"). If the U.S. government expects other nations to obey UN resolutions (and declares its right to make war to enforce them!), what does it say when a U.S. administration flouts the more fundamental rule of the Charter itself?

The aggression of the United States in March and April of 2003 is not the same as the aggression of a Genghis Khan or a Napoleon or a Hitler. Nonetheless, the moral ugliness of aggression as an act, regardless of the extent of it, must be emphasized. Those who take justice seriously, and those who are convinced that just war theory is a convincing framework for judging the rightness or wrongness of a war, must wrestle with this fact.

Next Step: Detoxifying the Fruit of the Poisoned Tree?

In the words of Ricks, "the U.S. position . . . suffers from the strategic problem of the fruit of the poisoned tree—that is, when a nation goes to war for faulty reasons, it undercuts all the actions that follow, especially when it won't concede those errors."[19] These "errors" had a moral dimension. It was clear enough, based on knowledge available at the time, that the case for war could not withstand rigorous consideration. The jury that approves a weak case for executing a man may later plead groupthink or excitement or any number of excuses, but there is a moral responsibility to overcome just such obstacles to clear judgment, especially in gravely important matters. Failure to do so is a moral failure, and such failures carry guilt—of varying degrees, depending on the level of responsibility and what each person said and did. In such a trial, to the extent that they have the ability to see the case's weakness, the courtroom crowd that cheers the prosecution, and even those who are silent, all bear some measure of responsibility. In the United States, this sharing of responsibility and guilt, in varying measures, applies from the head of government down to aware citizens.

What is the first response to a mistake that involved a moral failure? As C.S. Lewis writes, "Evil can be undone, but it cannot 'develop' into good. Time does not heal it. The spell must be unwound, bit by bit, 'with backward mutterings of dissevering power'—or else not."[20] In a less poetic form, when you have done something wrong against someone else, if you cannot begin by saying you are sorry, you have no reason to hope you can "fix" the situation. And the kind of apology needed is not "I am sorry, I made a mistake," nor "I'm sorry you feel that way about our action," nor is it a "sorry" mixed with any excuses whatsoever. The only kind of apology that has a hope of restoring relationships between friends, or parents and children, or husbands and wives, runs something like: "I did something wrong. I knew or should have known it was wrong. I'm sorry."

By analogy, this is necessary between nations, from the government of the United States to the government and people of Iraq.

What is the next step in Iraq after such an apology? Of course, between friends or spouses or even strangers, the next step is an offer to help put matters right. (At times, the response to such an offer will be, "get out.") How to do that is beyond the scope of this book. There is no way to predict in what situation the United States will find itself in the months and years to come. One thought suggests itself, however, for the present or the future. If, in the midst of an unjust war, citizens of the nation that launched it decide that it is unjust, they must ask not only "what will happen if we leave?" That question, asked alone, cuts off an entire avenue of possible responses, because it stops us from asking another, very important question: "what will happen if we stay?"

In the midst of an unjust war citizens of the country that launched it may decide that one reason there was no reasonable chance of success is that the war plan included elements that produced resistance. The war plan may have called for an indefinite presence of occupying forces, and yet the presence of those forces may deprive any new national government of legitimacy—as they will be seen as cooperating with an occupying army, like Quisling in Nazi-occupied Norway, or the forces of Vichy France. In such a situation, the longer the occupying army stays, the more anger and resentment it produces and the less likely success becomes. This is especially true when there is a cultural gulf as wide as that between U.S. forces and the average Iraqi, a gulf that separates the two in terms of culture, language, religion, and history.[21]

Michael Waltzer has suggested that "an unjust war (*ad bellum* and/or *in bello*) that nonetheless produces a just peace" is harder to imagine than a just war of which the aftermath is botched.[22] There does not appear to be much in the literature about how to mitigate the damage caused an unjust war, nor how a nation ought to proceed when it discovers it has begun such a war, and is still in the midst of it. Those who take just war theory seriously as an analytical tool will ask how the criteria might be useful even in this situation. One beginning in such a situation would be a rigorous application of the six just war criteria to the possible *continued* use of force, while removing as far as possible any emotional stakes in the conflict, whether for or against. In such a situation, we should bear in mind that there will almost surely be mixed feelings among the people of the unjustly invaded country. Some will have benefitted from the invasion, while others have lost power. Many may have seen suffering in their families and groups due to the war. There may be deep divisions among them, as there appear to be in Iraq.

Next, before even beginning to think about just cause or right intention for staying in a war and continuing to use force, a detailed definition of "success" is necessary. Absent that, a game is being played with a moving set of goalposts—but it is not a game, it is war, with the death and destruction that always entails. If a definition of success is provided, there is a foundation for looking at "right intention." At that point, it is time to ask the questions in the three prudential criteria, as well as whether there are detailed plans to achieve that success.

It seems unlikely that one nation can heal another. How much more is that true if the would-be healer began with an unjust war against the nation supposed to be helped, and cannot even apologize for that wrong. Yet, if the leaders in particular of the United States were to acknowledge the guilt of the U.S. government in this matter (which is unequally distributed), along with that of the pundits and opinion leaders (and even citizens capable of research) who cheered an immoral course of action, and if the United States were then to apply just war theory to the possible continuation of that course of action, good could still be done, in spite of everything. It would not bring back the dead, or restore sight to the blind or walking ability to paraplegics, or sanity to those who have lost it in this war. Nonetheless, it would surely produce a better outcome than the one likely to be produced by an insistence, contrary to the facts, that "the war was justified, it is only that mistakes were somehow made along the way." It might also lead to greater wisdom concerning what the United States as a nation can and should try to accomplish in the world.

NOTES

1. Walzer, *Just and Unjust Wars*, 23.
2. Weigel, *Letters to a Young Catholic*, 114.
3. Michael Novak, "Reply," "Letters to the Editor," *First Things*, no. 174 (June/July 2007): 7.
4. Novak, "'Asymmetrical Warfare' and Just War: A Moral Obligation," *National Review Online*, February 10, 2003, http://www.nationalreview.com/novak/novak021003 .asp (accessed February 12, 2008). In January 2003, speaking at the Vatican, Novak gave no indication whatsoever that he saw "strong reasons against" a war against Iraq. If he thought then that there were such reasons, surely justice called for him to mention them then. If he learned later that there had been strong reasons against the war, perhaps he owes an account, given his role of advocate for the war, of what those reasons were and when he learned them.
5. "Iraq Coalition Casualty Count," *icasualties.org*, http://icasualties.org/Iraq/index .aspx (accessed January 31, 2009).
6. "U.S. Casualties in Iraq," *GlobalSecurity.org*, http://www.globalsecurity.org/ military/ops/iraq_casualties.htm (accessed January 31, 2009).
7. " Iraq Body Count: Documented Civilian Deaths from Violence," *Iraq Body Count*, http://www.iraqbodycount.org/ (accessed January 31, 2009).
8. Jill Lawless, "British backtrack on Iraq death toll," *Independent* (UK), March 27, 2007, http://news.independent.co.uk/world/middle_east/article2396031.ece (accessed October 12, 2007). The article notes: "British government officials have backed the methods used by scientists who concluded that more than 600,000 Iraqis have been killed since the invasion, the BBC reported yesterday. The Government publicly rejected the findings, published in The Lancet in October. But the BBC said documents obtained under freedom of information legislation showed advisers concluded that the much-criticised study had used sound methods. The study, conducted by researchers from Johns Hopkins University in Baltimore and the Al Mustansiriya University in Baghdad, estimated that 655,000 more Iraqis had died since March 2003 than one would expect without the war. The study estimated that 601,027 of those deaths were from violence. The researchers, reflecting the inherent uncertainties in such extrapolations, said they were 95 per cent certain that the real number of deaths lay somewhere between 392,979 and 942,636 . . .

the chief scientific adviser to the Ministry of Defence, Roy Anderson, described the methods used in the study as 'robust' and 'close to best practice.' Another official said it was 'a tried and tested way of measuring mortality in conflict zones.'" See Gilbert Burnham, Riyadh Lafta, Shannon Doocy, and Les Roberts, "Mortality after the 2003 invasion of Iraq: a cross-sectional cluster sample survey," BrusselsTribunal.org, http://brusselstribunal.org/pdf/lancet111006.pdf (accessed January 31, 2009).

9. Tina Sussman, "Poll: Civilian Toll in Iraq may top 1 million," *Los Angeles Times*, September 14, 2007, http://www.latimes.com/news/printedition/asection/la-fg-iraq14sep 14,1,1207545.story (accessed December 21, 2008).

10. "The Iraq Situation," *UNHCR.org*, http://www.unhcr.org/iraq.html (accessed December 21, 2008).

11. See for example Lawrence B. Lindsey, "What Iraq will cost the U.S.," *Fortune*, http://money.cnn.com/2008/01/10/news/economy/costofwar.fortune/ (accessed February 12, 2008). Lindsey is a former White House economist who left the White House after his public estimate that the war might cost up to $200 billion displeased his bosses. On January 31, 2009, the estimate of direct costs of the war by the "National Priorities Project," showed a total cost to date in excess of $593 billion. "Cost of War," *National Priorities Project*, http://www.nationalpriorities.org/costofwar_home (accessed January 31, 2009).

12. Powell, "Presentation to the U.N.," 475.

13. John Pilger, "The Epic Crime That Dares Not Speak Its Name," *LewRockwell .com*, October 31, 2005, http://www.lewrockwell.com/pilger/pilger34.html (accessed December 21, 2008). Pilger's quotation from the Nuremberg Tribunal may be found directly at "International Military Trials/Nuremberg" under "Index," section "1. Judgement," bullet three "The Common Plan of Conspiracy and Aggressive War," at http://www.derechos.org/nizkor/nuremberg/judgment/cap4.html (accessed October 26, 2007). Note that Article 6 of the "Charter of the International Military Tribunal" listed in first place under the "acts" that are "crimes coming within the jurisdiction of the Tribunal for which there shall be individual responsibility" the following: "(a) Crimes against Peace: namely, planning, preparation, initiation or waging of a war of aggression, or a war in violation of international treaties, agreements or assurances, or participation in a Common Plan or Conspiracy for the accomplishment of any of the foregoing." See "Nuremberg Trial Proceedings, Volume 1/Charter of the International Military Tribunal," *The Avalon Project at Yale Law School*, http://www.yale.edu/lawweb/avalon/imt/proc/imtconst .htm#sec1 (accessed October 26, 2007).

14. Michael Rozeff, "Success in Iraq?" *LewRockwell.com*, November 24, 2005, http://www.lewrockwell.com/rozeff/rozeff45.html (accessed December 21, 2008).

15. Jeff McMahan points out that although international law treats soldiers on both sides of any conflict as morally equivalent, and bound only by the laws of *jus in bello* (i.e., soldiers are never held liable for killing soldiers, even if those killing are part of an unjust war), there is still a "moral asymmetry" between soldiers on the two sides, since one group is aiding an unjust cause. See Jeff McMahan "The Morality of War and the Law of War," http://philosophy.rutgers.edu/FACSTAFF/BIOS/PAPERS/MCMAHAN/ The_Morality_of_War_and_the_Law_of_War.pdf (accessed December 22, 2008).

16. *Constitution of the United States*, Article VI.

17. Johnson's long discussion in *War to Oust*, 127, of how for the U.S. and British governments "the common-law tradition influences the interpretation of what actually is the content of international law, including the status of the United Nations as an organization and the black-letter provisions of the Charter" is discussed in Chapter 5.

18. Weigel demonstrated the desperation needed to find continuing aggression in Saddam's Iraq with this sentence in April 2006: "By its international and domestic beha-

vior, its weapons capabilities and ambitions, and its stated intentions, the Iraq regime of Saddam Hussein had shown that it constituted, de facto, an 'aggression under way.'" (*Against the Grain*, 240.) All this does is make the word "aggression" capable of meaning anything. A regime does not "constitute" aggression, not if the word has its normal meaning. Aggression consists of actions, or behavior. If Weigel believed the Iraqi regime was guilty of aggression in 2003, he needed to point to concrete acts that constituted aggression.

19. Ricks, *Fiasco*, 431.

20. Lewis, *The Great Divorce*, vi.

21. I believe the civilizational boundaries suggested by Samuel Huntington's *Clash of Civilizations* would be very useful for citizens of any nation considering the possibility of doing good in some situation through the use of military force. The greater the cultural divide, the less likely that outside military forces will be seen as friendly or even neutral, especially under the stress of an occupation following a forceful entry into a country.

22. Weigel, *Against the Grain*, 253.

Appendix A

Thomas Aquinas on War

(Note: this is the full text of Aquinas' article on war in the *Summa*. It is found in the Second Part of the Second Part, Question 40, Article 1, entitled "Whether it is always sinful to wage war." The other three, much less quoted articles in the question are: "(2) Whether it is lawful for clerics and bishops to fight? (3) Whether it is lawful to lay ambushes in war?" and "(4) Whether it is lawful to fight on holy days?")

Question 40. War

Article 1. Whether it is always sinful to wage war?
Objection 1. It would seem that it is always sinful to wage war. Because punishment is not inflicted except for sin. Now those who wage war are threatened by Our Lord with punishment, according to Matthew 26:52: "All that take the sword shall perish with the sword." Therefore all wars are unlawful.

Objection 2. Further, whatever is contrary to a Divine precept is a sin. But war is contrary to a Divine precept, for it is written (Matthew 5:39): "But I say to you not to resist evil"; and (Romans 12:19): "Not revenging yourselves, my dearly beloved, but give place unto wrath." Therefore war is always sinful.

Objection 3. Further, nothing, except sin, is contrary to an act of virtue.

But war is contrary to peace. Therefore war is always a sin.

Objection 4. Further, the exercise of a lawful thing is itself lawful, as is evident in scientific exercises. But warlike exercises which take place in tournaments are forbidden by the Church, since those who are slain in these trials are deprived of ecclesiastical burial. Therefore it seems that war is a sin in itself.

On the contrary, Augustine says in a sermon on the son of the centurion [Ep. ad Marcel. cxxxviii]: "If the Christian Religion forbade war altogether, those who sought salutary advice in the Gospel would rather have been counselled to cast aside their arms, and to give up soldiering altogether. On the contrary, they were told: 'Do violence to no man . . . and be content with your pay' (Luke 3:14). If he commanded them to be content with their pay, he did not forbid soldiering."

I answer that, In order for a war to be just, three things are necessary. First, the authority of the sovereign by whose command the war is to be waged. For it is not the business of a private individual to declare war, because he can seek for redress of his rights from the tribunal of his superior. Moreover it is not the business of a private individual to summon together the people, which has to be done in wartime. And as the care of the common weal is committed to those who are in authority, it is their business to watch over the common weal of the city, kingdom or province subject to them. And just as it is lawful for them to have recourse to the sword in defending that common weal against internal disturbances, when they punish evil-doers, according to the words of the Apostle (Romans 13:4): "He beareth not the sword in vain: for he is God's minister, an avenger to execute wrath upon him that doth evil"; so too, it is their business to have recourse to the sword of war in defending the common weal against external enemies. Hence it is said to those who are in authority (Psalm 81:4): "Rescue the poor: and deliver the needy out of the hand of the sinner"; and for this reason Augustine says (Contra Faust. xxii, 75): "The natural order conducive to peace among mortals demands that the power to declare and counsel war should be in the hands of those who hold the supreme authority."

Secondly, a just cause is required, namely that those who are attacked, should be attacked because they deserve it on account of some fault. Wherefore Augustine says . . . : "A just war is wont to be described as one that avenges wrongs, when a nation or state has to be punished, for refusing to make amends for the wrongs inflicted by its subjects, or to restore what it has seized unjustly."

Thirdly, it is necessary that the belligerents should have a rightful intention, so that they intend the advancement of good, or the avoidance of evil. Hence Augustine says (De Verb. Dom. [The words quoted are to be found not in Augustine's works, but Can. Apud. Caus. xxiii, qu. 1]): "True religion looks upon as peaceful those wars that are waged not for motives of aggrandizement, or cruelty, but with the object of securing peace, of punishing evil-doers, and of uplifting the good." For it may happen that the war is declared by the legitimate authority, and for a just cause, and yet be rendered unlawful through a wicked intention. Hence Augustine says (Contra Faust. xxii, 74): "The passion for inflicting harm, the cruel thirst for vengeance, an unpacific and relentless spirit, the fever of revolt, the lust of power, and such like things, all these are rightly condemned in war."

Reply to Objection 1. As Augustine says (Contra Faust. xxii, 70): "To take the sword is to arm oneself in order to take the life of anyone, without the command or permission of superior or lawful authority." On the other hand, to have recourse to the sword (as a private person) by the authority of the sovereign or judge, or (as a public person) through zeal for justice, and by the authority, so to speak, of God, is not to "take the sword," but to use it as commissioned by another, wherefore it does not deserve punishment. And yet even those who make sinful use of the sword are not always slain with the sword, yet they always perish with their own sword, because, unless they repent, they are punished eternally for their sinful use of the sword.

Reply to Objection 2. Such like precepts, as Augustine observes (De Serm. Dom. in Monte i, 19), should always be borne in readiness of mind, so that we be ready to obey them, and, if necessary, to refrain from resistance or self-defense. Nevertheless it is necessary sometimes for a man to act otherwise for the common good, or for the good of those with whom he is fighting. Hence Augustine says (Ep. ad Marcellin. cxxxviii): "Those whom we have to punish with a kindly severity, it is necessary to handle in many ways against their will. For when we are stripping a man of the lawlessness of sin, it is good for him to be vanquished, since nothing is more hopeless than the happiness of sinners, whence arises a guilty impunity, and an evil will, like an internal enemy."

Reply to Objection 3. Those who wage war justly aim at peace, and so they are not opposed to peace, except to the evil peace, which Our Lord "came not to send upon earth" (Matthew 10:34). Hence Augustine says (Ep. ad Bonif. clxxxix): "We do not seek peace in order to be at war, but we go to war that we may have peace. Be peaceful, therefore, in warring, so that you may vanquish those whom you war against, and bring them to the prosperity of peace."

Reply to Objection 4. Manly exercises in warlike feats of arms are not all forbidden, but those which are inordinate and perilous, and end in slaying or plundering. On olden times warlike exercises presented no such danger, and hence they were called "exercises of arms" or "bloodless wars," as Jerome states in an epistle.

Appendix B

Quotations from the Duelfer Report

Except for the first quotation below, all material in this appendix was taken from the "Comprehensive Report of the Special Advisor to the DCI on Iraq's WMD (September 30, 2004)," also known as "the Duelfer Report," found at the CIA website (www.cia.gov). Duelfer led the "Iraq Survey Group" (ISG).

Announcing the formation of the ISG, U.S. Undersecretary of Defense for Intelligence Stephen Cambone described, on May 30, 2003, the enormous effort and resources that would go into the group:

> Now, the Iraq Survey Group [ISG] represents a significant expansion of effort in the hunt for weapons of mass destruction, as we build on the efforts that are ongoing. The ISG will mean more people applied to the task, to be sure. But this is not the most important point. Rather, the ISG will consolidate the efforts of the various intelligence collection operations currently in Iraq under one national-level headquarters. Moreover, the ISG will have a powerful intelligence analytical element forward-deployed in the region, with virtual connectivity to an interagency intelligence community fusion center here in the D.C. area. The ISG also has a pretty potent WMD [weapons of mass destruction] disablement and elimination capability assigned.
> So, what's the ISG going to do? Well, the first priority, of course, is the search for and elimination of weapons of mass destruction. But in addition to WMD, the ISG will collect and exploit documents and media related to terrorism, war crimes, POW [prisoner of war] and MIA [missing in action] issues, and other things relating to the former Iraqi regime. It will interrogate and debrief individuals, both hostile and friendly, and it will exploit captured materiel. The goal is to put all the pieces together in what is appearing to be a very complex jigsaw puzzle.
> Now, how are we going to do this? The ISG, as currently planned, will be manned by between 1,300 and 1,400 people from the United States government interagency, from the United Kingdom and Australia. The main effort is going to be in Iraq, with the headquarters in Baghdad. This collection operation will include a joint interrogation debriefing center, a joint materiel exploitation center, chemical and biological intelligence support teams and the ISG operation center. The main analytic effort will be co-located with CENTCOM forward, as will the combined media processing center. Furthermore, the ISG is going to have liaison elements with CJTF-7 in Kuwait and with other U.S. government agencies inside Iraq. And finally, the intelligence fusion center will be here in Washington, D.C. And all are going to be linked electronically.[1]

The report that resulted from this massive effort is found on the CIA website by clicking "library," "reports," and then "general reports."[2] In late 2007 through early 2009, it was the first report listed under "general reports." Within that website, the specific web addresses for the sections quoted are placed in the notes. The report highlights its finding that Saddam wished to restart his WMD programs if possible, at a future date when sanctions were lifted. There is no need to dispute that conclusion. However, it should be emphasized that Saddam's keeping open the possibility of a future WMD program did not contravene Resolution 687 in and of itself, nor even that it would have been practical, or possible, to forbid the regime to have capabilities that could be used in a future program. (The resolution did not demand, for example, that Saddam expel or exile from Iraq all scientists whose expertise could be useful in a future WMD program.) From a moral standpoint, intent even without action may be as serious as an action itself, but from a legal standpoint, it is irrelevant in this case: the resolutions did not specify an acceptable intention, they specified actions. The main action specified under the WMD heading was the destruction of the weapons themselves and the ending of the programs that produced them. The findings concerning the existence or non-existence of WMD themselves and WMD programs in 2003, and the dates they were destroyed, were the key elements much of the world wanted to hear from the Duelfer Report, and that has guided the selection process here.

I. Nuclear Weapons/Weapons Programs: Selected Quotations from Chapter 1, "Regime Strategic Intent":

> Iraq began a nuclear program shortly after the Ba'thists took power in 1968. The program expanded considerably in 1976 when Saddam purchased the Osirak reactor from France, which was destroyed by an Israeli air strike in 1981. Saddam became very concerned about Iran's nuclear weapons program late in the Iran-Iraq war and accelerated Iraq's nuclear weapons research in response, according to Vice President Ramadan. Massive funds were allocated to develop infrastructure, equipment, scientific talent, and research. By January 1991, Iraq was within a few years of producing a nuclear weapon.

> Coalition bombing during Desert Storm, however, significantly damaged Iraq's nuclear facilities and the imposition of UN sanctions and inspections teams after the war further hobbled the program. It appears Saddam shifted tactics to preserve what he could of his program (scientific talent, dual-use equipment, and designs) while simultaneously attempting to rid Iraq of sanctions.[3]

II. Nuclear Weapons/Weapons Programs: Selected Quotations from Chapter 4, "Nuclear":

> Key Findings

> Iraq Survey Group (ISG) discovered further evidence of the maturity and significance of the pre-1991 Iraqi Nuclear Program but found that Iraq's ability to reconstitute a nuclear weapons program progressively decayed after that date.

Saddam Husayn ended the nuclear program in 1991 following the Gulf war. ISG found no evidence to suggest concerted efforts to restart the program.

Although Saddam clearly assigned a high value to the nuclear progress and talent that had been developed up to the 1991 war, the program ended and the intellectual capital decayed in the succeeding years.

Nevertheless, after 1991, Saddam did express his intent to retain the intellectual capital developed during the Iraqi Nuclear Program. Senior Iraqis—several of them from the Regime's inner circle—told ISG they assumed Saddam would restart a nuclear program once UN sanctions ended.

Saddam indicated that he would develop the weapons necessary to counter any Iranian threat.

Initially, Saddam chose to conceal his nuclear program in its entirety, as he did with Iraq's BW program. Aggressive UN inspections after Desert Storm forced Saddam to admit [in 1992] the existence of the program and destroy or surrender components of the program.

In the wake of Desert Storm, Iraq took steps to conceal key elements of its program and to preserve what it could of the professional capabilities of its nuclear scientific community.[4]

III. Biological Weapons/Weapons Programs: Selected Quotations from Chapter 1, "Regime Strategic Intent":

The Coalition destroyed all of Iraq's known BW facilities and bombed some of the suspect BW sites during the 1991 Gulf war. After the Desert Storm, the Regime fabricated an elaborate cover story to hide the function of its premiere BW production facility at Al Hakam, while at the same time it continued to develop the sites potential. The UN suspected but could not confirm any major BW agent production sites until Iraq partially declared its BW program prior to the departure of Husayn Kamil in 1995. Iraq eventually owned up to its offensive BW program later that year and destroyed the remaining facilities in 1996 under UN supervision. From 1994 until their departure at the end of 1998, and from late 2002 until the start of Operation Iraqi Freedom, UN inspectors monitored nearly 200 sites deemed to have some potential use in a BW program. Iraq's actions in the period up to 1996 suggest that the former Regime intended to preserve its BW capability and return to steady, methodical progress toward a mature BW program when and if the opportunity arose. After 1996, limited evidence suggests that Iraq abandoned its existing BW program and that one Iraqi official considered BW personnel to be second rate, heading an expensive program that had not delivered on its potential (see the BW chapter for additional information).[5]

IV. Biological Weapons/Weapons Programs: Selected Quotations from Chapter 4, "Biological Warfare"

With an eye to the future and aiming to preserve some measure of its BW capability, Baghdad in the years immediately after Desert Storm sought to save what it could of its BW infrastructure and covertly continue BW research, hide evidence of that and earlier efforts, and dispose of its existing weapons stocks.

From 1992 to 1994, Iraq greatly expanded the capability of its Al Hakam facility. Indigenously produced 5 cubic meter fermentors were installed, electrical and water utilities were expanded, and massive new construction to house its desired 50 cubic meter fermentors were completed.

With the economy at rock bottom in late 1995, ISG judges that Baghdad abandoned its existing BW program in the belief that it constituted a potential embarrassment, whose discovery would undercut Baghdad's ability to reach its overarching goal of obtaining relief from UN sanctions.

In practical terms, with the destruction of the Al Hakam facility, Iraq abandoned its ambition to obtain advanced BW weapons quickly. ISG found no direct evidence that Iraq, after 1996, had plans for a new BW program or was conducting BW-specific work for military purposes. Indeed, from the mid-1990s, despite evidence of continuing interest in nuclear and chemical weapons, there appears to be a complete absence of discussion or even interest in BW at the Presidential level...

ISG judges that in 1991 and 1992, Iraq appears to have destroyed its undeclared stocks of BW weapons and probably destroyed remaining holdings of bulk BW agent. However ISG lacks evidence to document complete destruction. Iraq retained some BW-related seed stocks until their discovery after Operation Iraqi Freedom (OIF).[6]

V. Chemical Weapons/Weapons Programs: Selected Quotations from Chapter 5, "Iraq's Chemical Warfare Program"

Key Findings

Saddam never abandoned his intentions to resume a CW effort when sanctions were lifted and conditions were judged favorable:

Saddam and many Iraqis regarded CW as a proven weapon against an enemy's superior numerical strength, a weapon that had saved the nation at least once already—during the Iran-Iraq war—and contributed to deterring the Coalition in 1991 from advancing to Baghdad.

While a small number of old, abandoned chemical munitions have been discovered, ISG judges that Iraq unilaterally destroyed its undeclared chemical weapons stockpile in 1991. There are no credible indications that Baghdad resumed production of chemical munitions thereafter, a policy ISG attributes to Baghdad's desire to see sanctions lifted, or rendered ineffectual, or its fear of force against it should WMD be discovered.[7]

VI. General: Selected Quotations from Chapter 1, "Regime Strategic Intent:"

Key Findings

Saddam's primary goal from 1991 to 2003 was to have UN sanctions lifted, while maintaining the security of the Regime. He sought to balance the need to cooperate with UN inspections—to gain support for lifting sanctions—with his intention to preserve Iraq's intellectual capital for WMD with a minimum of foreign intrusiveness and loss of face. Indeed, this remained the goal to the end of the Regime, as the starting of any WMD program, conspicuous or otherwise, risked undoing the progress achieved in eroding sanctions and jeopardizing a political end to the embargo and international monitoring.

Saddam wanted to recreate Iraq's WMD capability—which was essentially destroyed in 1991—after sanctions were removed and Iraq's economy stabilized, but probably with a different mix of capabilities to that which previously existed. Saddam aspired to develop a nuclear capability—in an incremental fashion, irrespective of international pressure and the resulting economic risks—but he intended to focus on ballistic missile and tactical chemical warfare (CW) capabilities.

Iran was the pre-eminent motivator of this policy. All senior level Iraqi officials considered Iran to be Iraq's principal enemy in the region. The wish to balance Israel and acquire status and influence in the Arab world were also considerations, but secondary.[8]

NOTES

1. http://www.defenselink.mil/transcripts/transcript.aspx?transcriptid=2685, (accessed December 4, 2007)
2. https://www.cia.gov/library/reports/general-reports-1/iraq_wmd_2004/index.html (accessed October 4, 2007).
3. https://www.cia.gov/library/reports/general-reports-1/iraq_wmd_2004/chap1.html (accessed October 4, 2007).
4. https://www.cia.gov/library/reports/general-reports-1/iraq_wmd_2004/chap4.html (accessed October 4, 2007).
5. https://www.cia.gov/library/reports/general-reports-1/iraq_wmd_2004/chap1.html (accessed October 4, 2007).
6. https://www.cia.gov/library/reports/general-reports-1/iraq_wmd_2004/chap6.html (accessed October 4, 2007).
7. https://www.cia.gov/library/reports/general-reports-1/iraq_wmd_2004/chap5.html (accessed October 4, 2007).
8. https://www.cia.gov/library/reports/general-reports-1/iraq_wmd_2004/chap1.html (accessed October 4, 2007).

Appendix C

About the Author

Craig M. White lived in the Middle East for almost a decade before going to work for the U.S. State Department in 1991. Living in the Persian Gulf in the 1980s, working and socializing with Arabs (many but not all of whom were Muslims), as well as Indians, Europeans, and others, he had to think about his government's support for the state of Israel, his government's considerable support for the physically closer state of Iraq in its long war with Iran (which went on for most of the 1980s), and the long history of the Middle East. He discussed these with friends and co-workers—often speaking in Arabic with the Arabs. Since 1991, as a U.S. diplomat, he has practiced foreign relations at the working level. In U.S. embassies abroad, including several in the Middle East, he has analyzed and reported on political, economic, and social developments, and has done his best to help diplomats and citizens of other countries see the United States and U.S. policies and actions in the best possible light.

In this book, he stepped out of that official role, as the disclaimer at the beginning of the book notes, writing this book in his free time and as a citizen, not as an official of a particular administration. He believes love of country should include not only the normal sense of feeling affection for it, but also Aquinas' sense when he wrote, quoting Aristotle, "to love a person is to wish that person good."[1] He endorses a favorite statement of Father Richard John Neuhaus (RIP), priest, writer, and editor: "On balance and considering the alternatives, America has been and is an influence for good in the world."[2] But those who love are occasionally compelled to call the one loved back to her best, as spouses and siblings, parents and even children usually know—and the same may go for one's country.

He strongly agrees with George Weigel that "stuff counts" (Chapter 11). If any theory is to be useful, it must be applied to the dense texture of the existing world.

NOTES

1. Aquinas, *Summa*, I, 20, 1, reply objection 3.
2. Neuhaus, "Internationalisms," 66.

Bibliography

Ajami, Fouad. "Iraq and the Arabs' Future." *Foreign Affairs* 82, No. 1 (January/February 2003): 2-18.

Albright, Madeleine. "Madeleine Albright – 60 Minutes." *Youtube.com.* May 12, 1996. http://www.youtube.com/watch?v=FbIX1CP9qr4&feature=related (accessed January 31, 2009).

Alighieri, Dante. *The Divine Comedy 3: Paradise.* London: Penguin Books, 1962.

Amnesty International: Report 2003. New York: Amnesty International Publications, 2003.

Aquinas, Thomas. *Summa Theologica.* NewAdvent.org. http://www.newadvent.org/summa/index.html (accessed December 6, 2007).

Aristotle. *Nichomachean Ethics.* New York: Penguin Classics, 2003.

———. *Politics.* "The Internet Classics Archive," http://classics.mit.edu/Aristotle/politics.html (accessed November 18, 2008).

———. *Rhetorica ad Alexandrum,* quoted in Mohammad Taghi Karoubi, *Just or Unjust War?* Aldershot: Ashgate Publishing Limited, 2004.

"The Atomic Bombings of Hiroshima and Nagasaki." *Atomicarchive.com.* http://www.atomicarchive.com/Docs/MED/med_chp10.shtml (accessed April 18, 2008).

Augustine. *The City of God.* "Christian Classics Ethereal Library," http://www.ccel.org/ccel/schaff/npnf102.iv.XIX.5.html.

"Authorization for Use of Military Force against Iraq Resolution of 2002 (H.J.Res.114)." Pp. 378-83 in *The Iraq War Reader: History, Documents, Opinions,* edited by Micah L. Sifry and Christopher Cerf. New York: Touchstone, 2003.

Bacevich, Andrew. *The New American Militarism: How Americans Are Seduced by War.* New York: Oxford University Press, 2005.

———. "The Real World War IV." *Syracuse University.* http://faculty.maxwell.syr.edu/merupert/BACEVICH%20The%20Real%20World%20War%20IV.pdf (accessed January 23, 2008).

Bamford, James. *A Pretext for War: 9/11, Iraq, and the Abuse of America's Intelligence Agencies.* New York: Random House, 2004.

Blix, Hans. "Hans Blix's briefing to the security council." *The Guardian.* February 14, 2003. http://www.guardian.co.uk/Iraq/Story/0,2763,895882,00.html (accessed October 4, 2007).

Bovard, James. "The Farcical Definition at the Heart of the War on Terrorism." *LewRockwell.com.* January 31, 2006. http://www.lewrockwell.com/bovard/bovard20.html (accessed October 10, 2007).

281

"Briefing Maps: Official maps of the theatre of operations." UK Ministry of Defense. http://www.mod.uk/DefenceInternet/DefenceNews/InDepth/UkMilitaryOperationsIn Iraq.htm (accessed December 4, 2007).

Buchanan, Pat. "The Democracy Worshipper." *LewRockwell.com.* June 20, 2007. http:// www.lewrockwell.com/buchanan/buchanan60.html (accessed October 10, 2007).

———. "First and Last War of the Bush Doctrine?" *The American Cause.* March 12, 2003. http://www.theamericancause.org/patfirstandlastwar.htm (accessed October 17, 2003).

Burnham, Gilbert, Riyadh Lafta, Shannon Doocy, and Les Roberts. "Mortality after the 2003 invasion of Iraq: a cross-sectional cluster sample survey." *BrusselsTribunal.org.* http://brusselstribunal.org/pdf/lancet111006.pdf (accessed January 31, 2009).

Bush, George H. W., and Brent Scowcroft. "Why We Didn't Go to Baghdad." Pp. 101-2 in *The Iraq War Reader: History, Documents, Opinions,* edited by Micah L. Sifry and Christopher Cerf. New York: Touchstone, 2003.

Bush, George W. "A Grave and Gathering Danger." Pp. 313-18 in *The Iraq War Reader: History, Documents, Opinions,* edited by Micah L. Sifry and Christopher Cerf. New York: Touchstone, 2003.

———. "Iraq is Fully Capable of Living in Freedom." February 26, 2003. Pp. 557-59 in *The Iraq War Reader: History, Documents, Opinions,* edited by Micah L. Sifry and Christopher Cerf. New York: Touchstone, 2003.

———. "Remarks at West Point: 'New Threats Require New Thinking.'" June 1, 2002. Pp. 268-71 in *The Iraq War Reader: History, Documents, Opinions,* edited by Micah L. Sifry and Christopher Cerf. New York: Touchstone, 2003.

———. "The War Begins: 'The Tyrant Will Soon Be Gone.'" Pp. 503-4 in *The Iraq War Reader: History, Documents, Opinions,* edited by Micah L. Sifry and Christopher Cerf. New York: Touchstone, 2003.

"Bush On Al Qaeda Not Existing In Iraq Before Invasion: 'So What?'" *Think Progress.* 2008. http://thinkprogress.org/2008/12/15/bush-so-what/ (accessed December 26, 2008).

Byrd, Robert. "No Place for Kings in America." Pp. 375-77 in *The Iraq War Reader: History, Documents, Opinions,* edited by Micah L. Sifry and Christopher Cerf. New York: Touchstone, 2003.

———. "Sleepwalking through History." February 12, 2003. Pp. 482-85 in *The Iraq War Reader: History, Documents, Opinions,* edited by Micah L. Sifry and Christopher Cerf. New York: Touchstone, 2003.

Carter, Jimmy. "Just War – or a Just War? Op-ed by Jimmy Carter 9 Mar 2003." *The Carter Center.* http://www.cartercenter.org/news/documents/doc1249.html (accessed October 10, 2007).

Catechism of the Catholic Church, Second Edition. Washington, D.C.: United States Catholic Conference, Inc.—Libreria Editrice Vaticana, 1997.

Charles, J. Daryl. *Between Pacifism and Jihad: Just War and Christian Tradition.* Downer's Grove: InterVarsity Press, 2005.

Charter of the United Nations. http://www.un.org/aboutun/charter/ (accessed November 22, 2008).

Cheney, Dick. "The risks of inaction are far greater than the risk of action." Pp. 298-300 in *The Iraq War Reader: History, Documents, Opinions*, edited by Micah L. Sifry and Christopher Cerf. New York: Touchstone, 2003.

Cicero, Marcus Tullius. *De Officiis*. http://www.stoics.com/cicero_book.html (accessed November 18, 2008).

———. *Treatise on the Commonwealth. The Online Library of Liberty.* http://oll .libertyfund.org/?option=com_staticxt&staticfile=show.php%3Ftitle=546&chapter= 83302&layout=html&Itemid=27 (accessed November 16, 2008).

Cockburn, Andrew, and Patrick Cockburn. "We Have Saddam Hussein Still Here." Pp. 91-100 in *The Iraq War Reader: History, Documents, Opinions*, edited by Micah L. Sifry and Christopher Cerf. New York: Touchstone, 2003.

The Constitution of the United States. "United States Constitution." *Legal Information Institute, Cornell University Law School.* http://www.law.cornell.edu/constitution/ constitution.articlevi.html (accessed November 22, 2008).

"Cost of War." *National Priorities Project.* http://www.nationalpriorities.org/costofwar_ home (accessed January 31, 2009).

Crane, Conrad C., and Andrew Terrill. "Reconstructing Iraq: Insights, Challenges, and Missions for Military Forces in a Post-Conflict Scenario." *Strategic Studies Institute: United States Army War College.* February 2003. http://www.strategic studiesinstitute.army.mil/pdffiles/PUB182.pdf (accessed July 14, 2007).

"Did Saddam Hussein and his regime pose an immediate threat?" *US - Iraq ProCon.org.* 2008. http://usiraq.procon.org/viewanswers.asp?questionID=891 (accessed January 24, 2009).

Dula, Peter. "The war in Iraq: how Catholic conservatives got it wrong." *Commonweal.* December 3, 2004. http://findarticles.com/p/articles/mi_m1252/is_21_131/ai_n1378 7465?tag=content;col1 (accessed October 18, 2007).

"L'Empire ottoman en 1878." http://www.atlas-historique.net/1815-1914/cartes/Empire Ottoman1878.html (accessed October 12, 2007).

Elshtain, Jean Bethke. *Just War Against Terror: The Burden of American Power in a Violent World.* New York: Basic Books, 2003.

"Fact Sheet." *Bureau of International Security and Nonproliferation (ISN), U.S. Department of State.* April 20, 2006. http://www.state.gov/t/isn/rls/fs/64874.htm (accessed October 3, 2007).

Fallows, James. "The Fifty-First State?" Pp. 535-59 in *The Iraq War Reader: History, Documents, Opinions*, edited by Micah L. Sifry and Christopher Cerf. New York: Touchstone, 2003.

Fiala, Andrew. *The Just War Myth: The Moral Illusions of War.* Lanham: Rowman & Littlefield, 2008.

Fleming, Thomas. "The Historian Who Sold Out." *George Mason University's History News Network*, 6-09-03. http://hnn.us/articles/1489.html (accessed October 16, 2007).

"Frontline: Beyond Baghdad: Map: Iraq's People and Politics." *PBS.org.* http://www.pbs .org/wgbh/pages/frontline/shows/beyond/etc/map.html (accessed January 24, 2009).

"The Future of Iraq Project." *The National Security Archive*. September 1, 2006. http://www.gwu.edu/~nsarchiv/NSAEBB/NSAEBB198/index.htm (accessed October 11, 2007).

Graham-Brown, Sarah. "No-Fly Zones: Rhetoric and Real Intentions." *Middle East Report*. February 20, 2001. http://www.merip.org/mero/mero022001.html (accessed October 11, 2007).

Greenwood, Christopher. "International law and the pre – emptive use of force: Afghanistan, Al-Qaida, and Iraq." *San Diego International Law Journal* Vol. 4: 7, 2003.

Griffiths, Paul J., and George Weigel. "Just War: An Exchange." *First Things*, no. 122 (April 2002): 31-36.

———. "Who Wants War? An Exchange." *First Things*. no. 152 (April 2005): 10-12.

Hauerwas, Stanley. *Against the Nations: War and Survival in a Liberal Society*. Notre Dame: University of Notre Dame Press, 1992.

Hamza, Khidhir, with Jeff Stein. "Behind the Scenes with the Iraqi Nuclear Bomb." Pp. 191-95 in *The Iraq War Reader: History, Documents, Opinions*, edited by Micah L. Sifry and Christopher Cerf. New York: Touchstone, 2003.

Hiltermann, Joost R. "The Man Who Helped the Man Who Gassed His Own People." Pp. 41-44 in *The Iraq War Reader: History, Documents, Opinions*, edited by Micah L. Sifry and Christopher Cerf. New York: Touchstone, 2003.

Hiro, Dilip. "The Post-Saddam Problem." Pp. 560-64 in *The Iraq War Reader: History, Documents, Opinions*, edited by Micah L. Sifry and Christopher Cerf. New York: Touchstone, 2003.

Hersh, Seymour. "Did Iraq Try to Assassinate Ex-President Bush in 1993? A Case Not Closed." Pp. 140-61 in *The Iraq War Reader: History, Documents, Opinions*, edited by Micah L. Sifry and Christopher Cerf. New York: Touchstone, 2003.

Hornberger, Jacob. "They Lied About the Reasons for Going to War." *LewRockwell.com*. October 24, 2006. http://www.lewrockwell.com/hornberger/hornberger106.html (accessed October 10, 2007).

Hussein, Saddam. "Iraq Has No Interest in War." P. 464 in *The Iraq War Reader: History, Documents, Opinions*, edited by Micah L. Sifry and Christopher Cerf. New York: Touchstone, 2003.

"Iraq Body Count: Documented Civilian Deaths from Violence." *Iraq Body Count*. http://www.iraqbodycount.org/ (accessed January 31, 2009).

"Iraq Coalition Casualty Count." *icasualties.org*. http://icasualties.org/Iraq/index.aspx (accessed January 31, 2009).

"The Iraq Liberation Act of 1998." October 31, 1998. *www.findlaw.com*. 1998. http://fl1.findlaw.com/news.findlaw.com/hdocs/docs/iraq/libact103198.pdf (accessed October 11, 2007).

"IRAQ No-Fly Zone Violations." *Defend America*. http://www.defendamerica.mil/iraq/Iraq_nofly.html (accessed October 11, 2007).

"Iraq: Oil and Economy." *About.com: U.S. Government Info*. http://usgovinfo.about.com/library/weekly/aairaqioil.htm (accessed October 11, 2007).

"The Iraq Situation." *UNHCR.org*. http://www.unhcr.org/iraq.html (accessed December 21, 2008).

Johnson, James T. "Just War, as it Was and Is." *First Things*, no. 149 (January 2005): 14-24.

————. *The War to Oust Saddam Hussein.* Maryland: Rowman & Littlefield, Inc., 2002.

Keegan, John. *The Iraq War.* New York: Alfred A. Knopf, 2004.

Kinzer, Stephen. *Overthrow.* New York: Times Books, 2006.

Lashmar, Paul, and Raymond Whitaker. "MI6 and CIA: The New Enemy Within." Pp. 479-81 in *The Iraq War Reader: History, Documents, Opinions*, edited by Micah L. Sifry and Christopher Cerf. New York: Touchstone, 2003.

Lewis, Bernard. "The Regional Implications of Pursuing 'Regime Change' in Iraq (Part I)." *The Washington Institute for the Middle East, Weinberg Founders Conference.* October 2002. http://www.washingtoninstitute.org/templateC07.php?CID=114 (accessed October 22, 2007).

Lewis, C. S. *The Great Divorce.* New York: MacMillan Publishing Co., Inc., 1946.

MacArthur, John R. "Remember Nayirah, Witness for Kuwait?" Pp. 135-7 in *The Iraq War Reader: History, Documents, Opinions*, edited by Micah L. Sifry and Christopher Cerf. New York: Touchstone, 2003.

McMahan, Jeff. "The Morality of War and the Law of War." http://philosophy.rutgers.edu/FACSTAFF/BIOS/PAPERS/MCMAHAN/The_Morality_of_War_and_the_Law_of_War.pdf (accessed December 22, 2008).

Mearsheimer, John, and Stephen Walt. "An Unnecessary War." Pp. 414-24 in *The Iraq War Reader: History, Documents, Opinions*, edited by Micah L. Sifry and Christopher Cerf. New York: Touchstone, 2003.

"Military: Iran-Iraq War (1980-1988)." *GlobalSecurity.org.* http://www.globalsecurity.org/military/world/war/iran-iraq.htm (accessed October 2, 2007).

Nagy, Thomas. "The Secret Behind the Sanctions: How the U.S. Intentionally Destroyed Iraq's Water Supply." *CommonDreams.org.* 2001. http://www.commondreams.org/views01/0808-07.htm (accessed October 11, 2007).

Negroponte, John. "Negroponte Urges Prompt Adoption of New Iraq Resolution." *GlobalSecurity.org.* 24 February 2003. http://www.globalsecurity.org/wmd/library/news/iraq/2003/iraq-030224-usia10.htm (accessed December 22, 2007).

Neuhaus, Richard John. "Internationalisms, etc." *First Things*, no. 148 (December 2004): 64-68.

————. "The Sounds of Religion in a Time of War." *First Things*, no. 133 (May 2003): 76-82.

Novak, Michael. "'Asymmetrical Warfare' and Just War: A Moral Obligation." *National Review Online.* February 10, 2003. http://www.nationalreview.com/novak/novak021003.asp (accessed February 12, 2008).

————. "Reply." "Letters to the Editor." *First Things.* June/July 2007. http://www.firstthings.com/article/2007/05/junejuly-letters-19 (accessed October 16, 2007).

Novak, Robert. "No Meeting in Prague." Pp. 266-67 in *The Iraq War Reader: History, Documents, Opinions*, edited by Micah L. Sifry and Christopher Cerf. New York: Touchstone, 2003.

"Nuremberg Trial Proceedings, Volume 1/Charter of the International Military Tribunal." *The Avalon Project at Yale Law School.* http://www.yale.edu/lawweb/avalon/imt/proc/imtconst.htm#sec1 (accessed October 26, 2007).

O'Huallachain, D. Liam and J. Forrest Sharpe, eds. *Neo-Conned!: Just War Principles: A Condemnation of War in Iraq.* Norfolk, VA: IHS Press, 2006.

"OPCW Member States." *Organization for the Prohibition of Chemical Weapons.* http://www.opcw.org/nc/about-opcw/member-states/?tx_opcwmemberstate_pi1%5B sortField%5D=0&tx_opcwmemberstate_pi1%5BsortReverse%5D=0&tx_opcwmem berstate_pi1%5Bpointer%5D=3 (accessed January 19, 2009).

Paul, Ron. "Questions That Won't Be Asked About Iraq." Pp. 304-06 in *The Iraq War Reader: History, Documents, Opinions,* edited by Micah L. Sifry and Christopher Cerf. New York: Touchstone, 2003.

Pilger, John. "The Epic Crime That Dares Not Speak Its Name." *LewRockwell.com.* October 31, 2005. http://www.lewrockwell.com/pilger/pilger34.html (accessed December 21, 2008).

Plato. *The Republic.* London: Penguin Books Ltd, 1987.

Pollack, Kenneth M. "Can We Really Deter a Nuclear-Armed Iraq?" Pp. 403-11 in *The Iraq War Reader: History, Documents, Opinions,* edited by Micah L. Sifry and Christopher Cerf. New York: Touchstone, 2003.

———. *The Threatening Storm: The Case for Invading Iraq.* New York: Random House, 2002.

Powell, Colin. "Presentation to the U.N. Security Council: a Threat to International Peace and Security." Pp. 465-78 in *The Iraq War Reader: History, Documents, Opinions,* edited by Micah L. Sifry and Christopher Cerf. New York: Touchstone, 2003.

"Presidential Medal of Freedom Recipient L. Paul Bremer III." *The Official Site of the Presidential Medal of Freedom.* 2004. http://www.medaloffreedom.com/Paul Bremer.htm (accessed December 19, 2008).

"Protocol for the Prohibition of the Use in War of Asphyxiating, Poisonous or Other Gases, and of Bacteriological Methods of Warfare (Geneva Protocol)." *U.S. Department of State.* http://www.state.gov/t/ac/trt/4784.htm (accessed September 30, 2007).

Rangwala, Glen, Nathaniel Hurd, and Alistair Millar. "A Case for Concern, Not a Cause for War." Pp. 457-63 in *The Iraq War Reader: History, Documents, Opinions,* edited by Micah L. Sifry and Christopher Cerf. New York: Touchstone, 2003.

"Report: Global terrorism up more than 25 percent." *CNN.com.* April 30, 2007. http://www.cnn.com/2007/US/04/30/terror.report/index.html (accessed January 24, 2009).

Ricks, Thomas. *Fiasco: The American Military Adventure in Iraq.* New York: The Penguin Press, 2006.

Ritter, Scott. *Iraq Confidential: The Untold Story of the Intelligence Conspiracy to Undermine the UN and Overthrow Saddam Hussein.* New York: Nation Books, 2005.

Riverbend. "Baghdad Burning." *Riverbendblog.* August 24, 2003. http://riverbendblog.blogspot.com/2003_08_01_riverbendblog_archive.html (accessed October 11, 2007).

Rozeff, Michael. "Success in Iraq?" *LewRockwell.com.* November 24, 2005. http://www.lewrockwell.com/rozeff/rozeff45.html (accessed December 21, 2008).

Schall, James V. *Another Sort of Learning: Selected Contrary Essays on How Finally to Acquire an Education While Still in College or Anywhere Else: Containing Some Belated Advice about How to Employ Your Leisure Time When Ultimate Questions Remain Perplexing in Spite of Your Highest Earned Academic Degree, Together with Sundry Book Lists Nowhere Else in Captivity to Be Found.* San Francisco: Ignatius Press, 1988.

Schell, Jonathan. "Pre-emptive Defeat, or How Not to Fight Proliferation." Pp. 506-26 in *The Iraq War Reader: History, Documents, Opinions,* edited by Micah L. Sifry and Christopher Cerf. New York: Touchstone, 2003.

Schneider, William. "Marketing Iraq: Why Now?" *CNN.com: InsidePolitics.* September 12, 2002. http://archives.cnn.com/2002/ALLPOLITICS/09/12/schneider.iraq/index.html (accessed October 10, 2007).

Scowcroft, Brent. "Don't Attack Saddam." Pp. 295-97 in *The Iraq War Reader: History, Documents, Opinions,* edited by Micah L. Sifry and Christopher Cerf. New York: Touchstone, 2003.

"Security Council Resolutions – 1990." *UN.org.* http://www.un.org/Docs/scres/1990/scres90.htm (accessed August 27, 2007).

Sifry, Micah L., and Christopher Cerf, eds. *The Iraq War Reader: History, Documents, Opinions.* New York: Touchstone, 2003.

"The So-Called Land Letter." The Ethics and Religious Liberty Commission of the Southern Baptist Convention. 2002. http://erlc.com/article/the-so-called-land-letter (accessed November 19, 2007).

Solzhenitsyn, Aleksandr. *The Gulag Archipelago.* New York: Harper and Row, Publishers, 1985.

"Status of Nuclear Weapons States and their Nuclear Capabilities." *Federation of American Scientists.* http://www.fas.org/nuke/guide/summary.htm (accessed April 18, 2008).

Taft, William H. IV, and Todd F. Buchwald. "Pre-emption, Iraq and International Law." *American Journal of International Law* Vol. 97: 3, 2003.

"Terrorism: A Navy Department Library Research Guide." *U.S. Navy Department Library.* http://www.history.navy.mil/library/guides/terrorism.htm (accessed December 4, 2007).

The United States Chemical Convention Website. http://www.cwc.gov (accessed September 30, 2007).

"UNSCOM: Chronology of Main Events." *United Nations Special Commission: UNSCOM.* http://www.un.org/Depts/unscom/Chronology/resolution949.htm (accessed October 11, 2007).

"UN Security Council Resolution 242." November 22, 1967. http://www.un.org/documents/sc/res/1967/scres67.htm (accessed October 19, 2007).

"U.S. Casualties in Iraq." GlobalSecurity.org. http://www.globalsecurity.org/military/ops/iraq_casualties.htm (accessed January 31, 2009).

U.S. Conference of Catholic Bishops. *The Challenge of Peace.* 1983. http://www.usccb.org/sdwp/international/TheChallengeofPeace.pdf (accessed February 15, 2008).

Walzer, Michael. *Just and Unjust Wars: A Moral Argument with Historical Illustrations.* New York: Basic Books, 1977.

Wasserstrom, Richard A., ed. *War and Morality.* Belmont: Wadsworth Publishing Company, 1970.

"Weapons of Mass Destruction: Nuclear Non-Proliferation Treaty [NPT]." *Federation of American Scientists*. http://www.fas.org/nuke/control/npt (accessed October 2, 2007).

Weigel, George. *Against the Grain: Christianity and Democracy, War and Peace*. New York: The Crossroad Publishing Company, 2008.

———. "Iraq: Then & Now." *First Things*, no. 162 (April 2006): 34-42.

———. "Just War and Iraq Wars," *First Things*, no. 172 (April 2007): 14-20.

———. "Moral Clarity in a Time of War," *First Things*, January 2003. http://www.first things.com/article/2008/01/001-moral-clarity-in-a-time-of-war-30 (accessed February 15, 2008).

———. *Letters to a Young Catholic*. New York: Basic Books, 2004.

West, Christopher. *Theology of the Body Explained: A Commentary on John Paul II's "Gospel of the Body."* Boston: Pauline Books and Media, 2003.

"WHKMLA Historical Atlas: History of Iraq." 2005. http://www.zum.de/whkmla/hist atlas/arabworld/haxiraq.html (accessed October 12, 2007)

Williams, Rowan, and George Weigel. "War and Statecraft: An Exchange." *First Things*, no. 141 (March 2004): 14-22.

Wright, Susan. "The Hijacking of UNSCOM." Pp. 186-90 in *The Iraq War Reader: History, Documents, Opinions*, edited by Micah L. Sifry and Christopher Cerf. New York: Touchstone, 2003.

Index

Made in the USA
San Bernardino, CA
27 August 2013